Media, Culture, and the
Modern African American Freedom Struggle

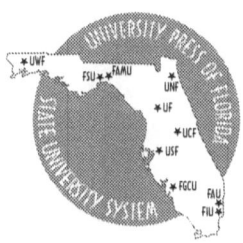

Florida A&M University, Tallahassee
Florida Atlantic University, Boca Raton
Florida Gulf Coast University, Ft. Myers
Florida International University, Miami
Florida State University, Tallahassee
University of Central Florida, Orlando
University of Florida, Gainesville
University of North Florida, Jacksonville
University of South Florida, Tampa
University of West Florida, Pensacola

Media, Culture, and the Modern African American Freedom Struggle

Edited by Brian Ward

University Press of Florida

Gainesville · Tallahassee · Tampa · Boca Raton

Pensacola · Orlando · Miami · Jacksonville · Ft. Myers

First cloth printing, 2001
First paperback printing, 2003

Library of Congress Cataloging-in-Publication Data
Media, culture, and the modern African American freedom struggle / edited by Brian Ward.
     p. cm.
Includes bibliographical references and index.
ISBN 0-8130-2074-3 (cloth : alk. paper), ISBN 0-8130-2744-6 (pbk.)
1. African Americans and mass media. 2. African Americans—Civil rights. 3. Mass media—
United States. 4. United States—Ethnic relations. I. Ward, Brian, 1961–
P94.5.A372 U56 2001
302.23'089'96073—DC21   2001027082

The University Press of Florida is the scholarly publishing agency for the State University
System of Florida, comprising Florida A&M University, Florida Atlantic University, Florida
Gulf Coast University, Florida International University, Florida State University, University
of Central Florida, University of Florida, University of North Florida, University of South
Florida, and University of West Florida.

University Press of Florida
15 Northwest 15th Street
Gainesville, FL 32611–2079
http://www.upf.com

Contents

Acknowledgments

Most of the essays in this collection derived from papers presented at the second Martin Luther King Jr. Memorial Conference on Civil Rights and Race Relations, held at the University of Newcastle upon Tyne in May 1998. Like its predecessor in 1993, the 1998 conference comprised more than just an academic gathering; it also featured a brace of public lectures and an art exhibition designed to present some of the issues raised in this volume to a more diverse audience. The conference was also the occasion for the University to award an honorary doctorate to the great African American artist, entertainer, and humanitarian Harry Belafonte. Thirty-one years previously it had bestowed the same honor on Belafonte's friend and colleague Martin Luther King Jr. Few can speak with more authority than Belafonte about either King or the role of the media and culture in shaping and commemorating the postwar struggle for African American respect, freedom, and opportunity—a relationship that forms the main thematic concern of this book.

As both director of the conference and editor of this volume my list of thank-yous is necessarily a lengthy one. Andy Nicol was lured by the promise of riches beyond his wildest dreams—and the actuality of an all-you-can-eat Chinese buffet—into serving most ecumenically as conference secretary. Melanie Reed, seasoned by the experiences of 1993, was again a good friend to me and to the conference, taking personal responsibility for much of the publicity and program production. Wendy Love similarly shouldered a good deal of the burden for organizing the public lectures, while Sharon O'Donnell and John Dersley helped to secure important funding. The website and various other technical shenanigans were in the very capable—and remarkably steady—hands of Damon Querry, who also revealed himself to be a very resourceful bibliographer. Once more Vice-Chancellor James Wright, Registrar Derek Nicholson, and Jerry Paterson—who occupies far too many valuable roles in the University to bother listing them—were important supporters of the whole endeavor; so, too, was Bernard Porter, as head of the Department of History.

My undergraduate Martin Luther King Special Subject class of 1997–98 offered all kinds of useful help both before and during the conference.

My particular thanks go to Dave Foster, Megan Mackeson-Sandbach, and Rob Orr—and to Leighton Birtchnell, who wasn't actually taking that class, but drank and pitched in as if he were. I am also very grateful to graduate students Paul Metcalfe, Will Naylor, and James Waite, who helped to host the conference and look after our visitors. Special mention is due to Jenny Walker—another veteran from the 1993 conference, who gave invaluable administrative assistance, contributed a chapter, and helped with copyediting—as well as to Zoe Greer, who did a good job with many of the initial editorial chores associated with the manuscript. As ever, Janice Cummin and Eleanor Cunningham of the Department of History looked after me and worked beyond the call of duty whenever the need arose.

The academic side of the conference was enriched by papers from Peter Ling, Waldo Martin, Danielle Ramsay, and Jill Terry, and I am also grateful to those who chaired sessions and public lectures: Tony Badger, Scot French, Marybeth Hamilton, Judie Newman, John White, and especially Celeste Marie-Bernier, who stood in at short notice when George Lewis was left cruelly indisposed by a rogue shrimp. I am also very appreciative of the helpful reports on the entire manuscript provided by the University Press of Florida's two anonymous readers, and of the efforts of Meredith Morris-Babb, whose qualities as an editor are matched only by her kindness and beguiling way with cheese grits.

Finally, in listing the many organizations and institutions that generously offered financial assistance for the conference and its attendant projects, I should like to offer particular thanks to Tony Badger, Rob Rutter, Paul Williams, and Caroline Wintersgill for their personal commitment. Thanks are due also to the British Association for American Studies; Catherine Cookson Foundation; Imperial Swallow Hotels; Paul Mellon Fund, University of Cambridge; Merrill Lynch; Rolls Royce; Taylor and Francis; and, within the University of Newcastle upon Tyne, the Department of English Literary and Linguistic Studies, the Department of History, and the Public Lectures Fund.

BW
Gainesville, Florida

Abbreviations

AACM Association for the Advancement of Creative Musicians

AP Associated Press

BADA Black Anti-Defamation Association

BARTS Black Arts Repertory Theater/School

CAP Congress of African Peoples

CFUN Committee For Unified Newark

FBI Federal Bureau of Investigation

FCC Federal Communications Commission

KKK Ku Klux Klan

MFDP Mississippi Freedom Democratic Party

MIA Montgomery Improvement Association

NAACP National Association for the Advancement of Colored People

NCCF National Committee to Combat Fascism

SCLC Southern Christian Leadership Conference

SNCC Student Nonviolent Coordinating Committee

SRC Southern Regional Council

UPI United Press International

Forgotten Wails and Master Narratives

Media, Culture, and Memories of the Modern African American Freedom Struggle

Brian Ward

Only the forgotten wails of a few black
   poets and artists
shall survive the then of then,
   the now of now.
   Conrad Kent Rivers, "In Defense of Black Poets"[1]

What is represented in the music, dance, painting, sculpture, literature, and architecture of a given group of people in a particular time, place, and circumstance is a conception of the essential nature and purpose of human existence itself. . . . It is a way of sizing up the world, and so, ultimately, and beyond all else, a mode and medium of survival.
   Albert Murray, *The Omni-Americans*[2]

No social movement of a protest nature . . . can be successful or have any positive meaning unless it is at one and the same time a *political, economic and cultural movement.*
   Harold Cruse, *The Crisis of the Negro Intellectual*[3]

In 1990, the distinguished African American historian-activist Vincent Harding noted that scholars of the civil rights and black power movements had been rather slow to address the cultural and artistic coordinates of the postwar black freedom struggle. Movement historians, Harding explained, tended to reduce their subject to a "manageable category called civil rights"—by which they usually meant conventionally understood political activities like courtroom battles against discriminatory practices, voter registration drives, mass direct action protests, struggles over legislative reform, and later the urban riots, paramilitary tactics, and new black electoral politics. Without denying the crucial importance of such sites and expressions of black activism and resistance, Harding pointed out that this perspective left little room for explorations of the "rich outpouring of

African-American music, literature, dance, cinema, and graphic arts that marked those movement years."[4]

At the start of the twenty-first century, Harding's criticisms still seem broadly justified. By and large, mainstream Movement historians have continued to pay relatively little attention to the various insights that scholars from elsewhere in the humanities—in film, media studies, cultural studies, literature, music, and fine art—might offer into a period whose changing race relations and protest politics they otherwise study so assiduously. This is not to suggest that the Movement historiography is, or ever has been, entirely bereft of a cultural perspective, or that it has been indifferent to the role of the mass media and culture industries in shaping and interpreting the postwar black freedom struggle. Nevertheless, in most overviews and many monographs on the subject, coverage of the Movement's cultural aspects typically consists of little more than a cursory mention of the freedom songs, or perhaps James Baldwin's jeremiad *The Fire Next Time,* or maybe Aretha Franklin's "Respect" and James Brown's "Say it Loud, I'm Black and I'm Proud," or possibly the Black Arts Movement of the later 1960s.

Traditionally, accounts of the "black power" phase of the postwar freedom struggle have paid somewhat more attention to black cultural developments than those which focus on the earlier "civil rights" era.[5] Yet, even here, the coverage is often quite perfunctory and there is a strong tendency to reduce important artistic movements and cultural innovations to little more than consolation prizes designed to make African Americans feel better when the "real" Movement for racial equality fractured and stalled in the second half of the 1960s. Clayborne Carson, for example, has suggested that since black power groups largely failed in their diverse efforts "to produce greater power for black people," the only really enduring achievements of the era were to be found in the realm of culture and ideas. "Lasting contributions," he argues, "were more significant in the intellectual and cultural rather than the political arena."[6] Irrespective of whether or not one agrees with Carson's analysis, he is representative of those Movement historians who, when they have considered black culture, art, and entertainment at all, portray them as somehow posterior, ancillary, or alternatives to the real political nitty and economic gritty of the postwar black freedom struggle.

In fact, as Vincent Harding and many Movement activists appreciated, African American art and culture did not just reflect, either directly or through artistic abstraction, putatively more important developments in the formal, organized, conventionally "political" freedom struggle; they also played an active role in creating that Movement, defining its goals and methods, and expressing them to both the black community and to a wider, whiter American public. More generally, the worlds of American media and culture comprised major arenas in which black and white racial identities, values, and ambitions were variously articulated, affirmed, attacked, and adjusted.

In the decade since Harding's critique, important works by the likes of William Van Deburg, Robin Kelley, Barbara Dianne Savage, Komozi Woodard and several others indicate that historians of the African American freedom struggle have begun to rise to his challenge.[7] Although the significance of their work has yet to register fully in the mainstream of Movement historiography, these writers have revealed much about the sources, nature, and legacy of the postwar black freedom struggle by exploring its cultural coordinates, artistic expressions, and representations in the mass media. In their very different ways, each of the essays in this volume continues that project. Collectively, they certainly introduce a range of themes, subjects, perspectives, and voices seldom brought together in more traditional Movement histories.

With an emphasis on music, film, literature, and the electronic and print media, the collection obviously makes no pretense to be comprehensive. As is perhaps inevitable with such volumes, different chapters will no doubt seem more innovative and informative, relevant and revelatory, to different readers, depending on the particular expertise and expectations they bring to their reading. Hopefully, however, the cumulative impact of the collection will be, first, to illustrate the kinds of insights into postwar American race relations, black and white racial consciousnesses, and the struggle for racial justice which can be afforded by closer attention to the interlocking worlds of media and culture, art and entertainment; second, to illustrate how the postwar freedom struggle has itself provided both context and content for some of the most significant developments in the modern American media and culture industries; and finally, to draw attention to the process by which a conventional "master narrative" of the freedom struggle of the 1950s and 1960s has come to dominate American social memory, largely as a consequence of contemporary depictions and retrospective portrayals of the Movement in American culture and the mass media.

Participants in the civil rights movement often described it as a singing movement, referring to the mighty freedom songs which kept up the spirits and articulated the goals of those engaged on the frontline of the southern struggle. Yet, while few were immune to the communalizing power, emotional uplift, and liberating messages of these songs, the main musical soundtrack to the civil rights and black power years for the majority of African Americans was not provided by freedom songs, but by the sounds of rhythm and blues, rock and roll, soul, funk, jazz, blues, and gospel. Consequently, several of the chapters in this volume focus on the relationship between African American popular music forms, race relations, and the freedom struggle.

Guido van Rijn recovers and analyzes a long-forgotten corpus of blues and gospel songs which dealt directly with civil rights issues between 1947 and 1968. In the process, he reveals a rich vein of black vernacular commentary on key events in the Movement and on its pantheon of black and white heroes and villains. At the same time, van Rijn suggests how the demands of the white-dominated recording and broadcasting industries, coupled with the legitimate concerns of black performers about their own physical and financial well-being, severely limited the recording and release of such overtly political material until the late 1960s.

Peter Townsend's essay focuses on another African American musical form: the New, or Free, Jazz of the 1950s and 1960s. Townsend explains how, against the backdrop of a burgeoning mass struggle, musicians like Ornette Coleman, John Coltrane, and Charles Mingus self-consciously rejected what had widely been perceived to be jazz's next logical progression as an evolving art form, which was toward some kind of rapprochement with classical music. Instead, these artists distanced themselves from western ideas of harmony—the cornerstone of the European classical tradition—and reinvigorated jazz's commitment to collective improvisation in what was a musical analogue to the early civil rights movement's quest for a "beloved community."

Townsend also describes how the black jazz community, frustrated by the exploitation and racism operating within the established entertainment industry, created musical counterparts to the sort of parallel political institutions pioneered by Bob Moses and the Student Nonviolent Coordinating Committee (SNCC) in Mississippi. The Jazz Artists Guild and the Association for the Advancement of Creative Musicians in Chicago represented attempts by African American artists to take control of the circumstances in which they made and marketed their music.

While van Rijn and Townsend concentrate on how black music functioned within an insurgent black community, David Chappell's essay on what he describes as a form of musical "racial cross-dressing" maps the influence of black artists and styles on mainstream American popular music during the decade or so before the rock and roll explosion of the

mid-1950s. Yet Chappell insists that this was very much a reciprocal process. He shows how on the eve of a mass movement hoping to secure
equality of black social, economic, and political opportunity in American
life, black and white musicians were engaged in a vibrant, essentially
democratic frenzy of musical borrowing, theft, homage, parody, and mutual instruction across racial lines. Moreover, he manages to tell this story
without reducing it to the usual hackneyed tales of unrelieved white exploitation and expropriation of black musical genius. That, Chappell argues, was but one dimension of a much more complicated and revealing
story.

Although it lies beyond the main brief of Chappell's chapter, it is interesting to consider whether such biracial musical tastes and exchanges
really did translate into more progressive racial attitudes among whites, or
in some other way prepared the ground for the civil rights movement of
the 1960s. Clearly, there has never been any necessary causal connection
between white admiration for black cultural forms and performative excellence—whether expressed in music, dance, literature, the visual arts,
sports, verbal dexterity, sartorial splendor, or any other creative idiom—
and more enlightened racial attitudes. Nevertheless, such white predilections for black culture could at least open up the *potential* for more
progressive racial views. Although precious little of that potential was
realized, Movement historians should not ignore a time when black musical infiltration of white consciousness, consciences, and pop charts was
considered a very important dimension of the broader attack on white
racism and its institutions. After all, even Black Panther Minister of Information Eldridge Cleaver could recall a time when the twist dance craze of
the early 1960s was greeted as "a guided missile, launched from the ghetto
into the very heart of suburbia. [It] succeeded, as politics, religion, and
law could never do, in writing in the heart and soul what the Supreme
Court could only write on the books."[8]

By the black power era, when Cleaver and the Black Panthers were in
their pomp, such faith in the efficacy of black cultural assaults on white
racism had all but evaporated. Many black activists, artists and critics
increasingly embraced variants on the "black aesthetic"—a much-vaunted,
if somewhat elusive, visceral and intellectual framework within which it
was suggested all genuine African American culture must be produced,
consumed, and interpreted.[9] The black aesthetic was, by definition, unavailable to whites. Indeed, as what had previously passed for a biracial
civil rights consensus unravelled in the face of rejuvenated white racial
conservatism and insurgent black nationalism, some black radicals de-

clared that cultural dialogue across racial lines was not only impossible, but even undesirable.

Highly publicized and important though such separatist impulses were, they did not constitute the whole story. Many black artists, performers, critics, and activists continued to resist attempts from both within and beyond the black community to circumscribe the legitimate thematic scope, technical range, audience appeal, and ultimate influence of African American art and culture. "We have to resist the tendency to 'program' our art, to set unnatural limitations upon it," warned writer-critic-activist Larry Neal. A leading black cultural nationalist who quickly rejected some of the more chauvinistic and parochial implications of that credo, Neal championed a black art which, "through the strength of all its ingredients—form, content, craft and technique—illuminates something specific about the living culture of the nation, and, by extension, reveals something fundamental about man on this planet."[10]

My own essay, along with those by William Van Deburg, Eithne Quinn, and Scot French, takes us back into the heart of this black power era, when various forms of cultural and identity politics helped to define a highly charged moment in the history of the Movement and American race relations. My chapter uses soul and jazz music to frame a reassessment of the fiery debates about the correct role and content of African American culture in the Struggle. In contrast to accounts which continue to draw overly simplistic distinctions between cultural nationalists like Imamu Amiri Baraka and Maulana Ron Karenga, and revolutionary nationalists like the Black Panther Party, the essay suggests that there was much more common ground than either faction recognized, or at least felt able to acknowledge. It also contains a cautionary tale: many of the most passionate black power arguments over the black aesthetic and the nature of a truly "authentic" black revolutionary culture took place far removed from the work-a-day concerns of ordinary African Americans, most of whom responded to the bitter scramble for ideological ascendancy within the Movement with eloquent indifference.

William Van Deburg argues in his essay that the intensity of white hostility to the black power movement of the late 1960s and early 1970s was only partly explicable in terms of its perceived threat to the established, white-dominated social, economic, and political order—a threat which, he notes, was in fact minimal and rather easily, if often brutally and cynically, contained. In Van Deburg's view, the sheer virulence of white opposition to black power can only be fully understood in the context of culturally constructed white perceptions of what "blackness" actually meant. By offering a wide-ranging historical analysis of how white Americans—and white westerners more generally—had come to associate blacks with evil and malevolence, Van Deburg explains how the specific fears unleashed by the black power movement connected to traditional white fears of black people, especially when linked to notions of power. In so doing, he also demonstrates the value of moving beyond a narrow focus on events in postwar America to adopt a much broader geographical and chronological perspective on the freedom struggle.

Near the heart of black power's cultural agenda, according to Van Deburg, was the celebration of real and fictitious black figures who were, according to mainstream values, villains, rogues, and bandits. These were the independent, evil, cunning, streetwise "Bad Niggers" whites dreaded, but who black power artists and activists embraced as revolutionary heroes. Whereas a preoccupation with respectability was a hallmark of the early civil rights movement, in the black power era these black badmen were to be applauded and even emulated for rejecting the values of a corrupt and racist mainstream culture which now seemed irredeemable.

In rather different ways, the essays by Eithne Quinn and Scot French are also concerned with the construction and symbolic function of such African American antiheroes. Quinn examines the place of the pimp figure in black popular culture and American consciousness. Carefully situating the intensification of interest in the black pimp within the political and social turmoil of the late 1960s and early 1970s, she explains that much of his appeal came—as with Van Deburg's black bandits—from his flaunting of conventional attitudes toward work, leisure, sex, style, and pleasure. Yet, Quinn also emphasizes that black pimps operated according to their own strict codes of conduct and style: they valued their capacity for a pleasure-laden brand of hard work; they set much store by education, albeit of a street-oriented, rather than bookish nature; and they saw themselves very much in the role of dynamic, upwardly mobile, black entrepreneurs. Thus, while pimps challenged traditional notions of class and status, virtue and morality, work and leisure, they substituted a distinctive and, in its own terms, coherent alternative. Although their gender politics were extremely retrogressive, they offered beguiling images of spectacular material success won strictly on black male terms.

Scot French's essay on the aborted attempts to film William Styron's controversial novel *The Confessions of Nat Turner* confirms the special place that slave rebel Nat Turner occupied in the pantheon of black badmen and revolutionary icons. French describes how in the late 1960s various black and white constituencies battled for control over the film project. In the process, he reveals how the movie industry itself became an important arena within which the struggle for control over the creation and dissemination of images relating to the black community and its history was fought.

Similar issues of black creative and economic power also loomed large in the recording industry—as the essays by van Rijn and Townsend reveal—and in the radio industry, which is the subject of Stephen Walsh's chapter. Despite its near-invisibility in most histories of the civil rights movement, Walsh argues that radio probably constituted the most important mass communications medium among southern African Americans in the 1950s and 1960s.[11] Because most black-oriented stations were white owned and managed, and were usually heavily dependent on white sponsorship and advertising revenue, there were very real restrictions on their capacity to contribute to, or sometimes even to report on, black political activities. Nevertheless, Walsh outlines how black-oriented programming could not only encourage a sense of black pride and solidarity by airing black cultural forms and news stories of particular interest to the black community, but constantly strove to aid the Movement in more practical ways.

Black cultural heroes and innovations, much like the story of the freedom struggle itself, have become important touchstones of contemporary American musical, literary, and visual, as well as political, culture. Certainly, the ways in which the Movement and its leaders—most conspicuously Martin Luther King and Malcolm X—have been pressed into symbolic service in film, music, and literature have helped to establish powerful popular notions, a "master narrative," of what the postwar black freedom struggle, in all its various phases and incarnations, was really about.[12]

The idea of a master narrative—perhaps best understood as a conventional, lay-person's sense of what the civil rights and black power movements were and meant—is, of course, a terribly reductive and brittle formulation. Nevertheless, there is little doubt that there now exists in mainstream American social memory a dominant—if hardly uncontested—set of conventional wisdoms about the postwar freedom struggle and its origins, nature, trajectory, achievements, and legacies. The key elements of this master narrative are to be found, not just in the pages of many popular high school and college surveys of postwar American history, but also in public celebrations, like those held for Martin Luther King's birthday, journalistic accounts, memoirs of activists, novels set in

Movement days, Hollywood feature films, popular songs, and television dramas and documentaries on the subject.

This popular understanding of the civil rights and black power movements is not unrelated to what Movement historians might refer to—with all due humility and philosophical disclaimers—as the "truth" about the modern black freedom struggle; yet it has little truck with the nuances and ambiguities of that story. Indeed, in many ways the master narrative tends to run counter to, almost in proud defiance of, the thrust of much of the specialist literature on the freedom struggle which has emerged during the past twenty years or so. While some of that writing remains in unhealthy and uncritical thrall to the celebratory perspectives generated by the Movement itself, historians have offered increasingly complex and penetrating analyses of the postwar Struggle, its ruptures and continuities, its achievements and failures, its shrewdness and naiveté, its pragmatism and moralism, its insights and blind-spots, its heroes and villains.

The point, however, is that beyond the academy all this scholarly endeavor has made relatively little impression on the master narrative sustained by more popular and public cultural means. At the heart of that story are simple parables of good and evil, unequivocal rights and incontrovertible wrongs, unimpeachable heroes and unspeakable villains. This narrative continues to define the chronology, achievements, and lessons of the African American freedom struggle almost exclusively in terms of the heroic King years—which is to say, the ones between Montgomery and Selma. By contrast, the black power era is usually portrayed as a tragic epilogue of unmitigated disaster, madness, and mayhem, which saw the betrayal of King's integrationist dreams and nonviolent methods.

One of the most powerful forces for the perpetuation of this master narrative is the national commemoration of King's birthday. With few exceptions, the American hero celebrated each January is safely frozen in his 1963 "I Have a Dream" incarnation, at the zenith of a nonviolent campaign for integration into the American polity. Despite efforts to complicate and deepen this simplistic, static vision of King, there is little space in the public celebrations for the post-Selma King: the democratic socialist who, like many of the black power radicals to whom he is often favorably contrasted, clearly saw the interconnectedness of racism, militarism, and economic exploitation, and at the time of his death had resolved to fight them all.

In a sense, what we see here is but one aspect of the battle to define the meaning and legacy of King and the modern black freedom struggle which has raged in America's media and culture ever since a viable mass civil rights movement emerged in the late 1950s and early 1960s. Directly and indirectly, the essays in this collection by Julian Bond, Jenny Walker, Allison Graham, Sharon Monteith, and Trudier Harris all address this theme, considering how a master narrative of the freedom struggle has been constructed, contested, and reconstructed in American media, culture, and memory over the past forty-five years.

Julian Bond and Jenny Walker both explore the role of the contemporary electronic and print media in that process. Bond fuses his personal experiences as SNCC's director of communications with an historical perspective in order to chronicle how sympathetic press coverage was vital to the emergence and initial successes of the early southern civil rights campaign. As he explains, it was thanks largely to an important corps of sympathetic white southern liberal journalists that the early Movement was able to represent itself to the nation-at-large as a legitimate struggle for quintessentially American goals waged by respectable and, above all, nonviolent means. Ultimately, the generally positive print and electronic news coverage of the early Movement helped to establish its moral authority, recruit activists, and persuade many whites to support black demands for basic civil and voting rights.

Jenny Walker argues that one of the ways in which national press sympathy for the goals and tactics of the early Movement manifested itself was in a widespread failure to report fully on the extent of the black violence which existed in the midst of a campaign which was presented to the nation as stoically nonviolent. Without denying that southern civil rights activists demonstrated a remarkable degree of nonviolent discipline in the face of tremendous white provocation, Walker argues that black violence—real and threatened, organized and spontaneous, individual and collective—was entirely commonplace in and around the southern Movement.

Ignored, downplayed, or simply misinterpreted in the contemporary media and all but a handful of subsequent historical studies, the story of southern black violence has clearly made little impact upon the master narrative of the civil rights era, with its reification of King and nonviolent direct action tactics. By contrast, the black power era is often conveniently distinguished from the early Movement by—among other factors—the allegedly new levels and intensity of black violence it witnessed. Once again, both Bond and Walker agree that the contemporary press has much to answer for in helping to characterize the black power era in this way.

While Bond and Walker demonstrate how both popular and scholarly conceptions of the civil rights and black power eras retain the imprint of contemporary media coverage, Allison Graham concentrates primarily on the ways in which television and film have also helped to shape those conceptions. Graham points out that television newscasts of the late 1950s and early 1960s were dominated by images of southern racial convulsions and, in particular, by images of the fearful violence directed against peaceful black protesters by southern law enforcement officers. Meanwhile, the southern-based feature films and television entertainments of the period vacillated between endorsing the notion that the South was indeed a place of brutish violence, and offering alternative, much more sympathetic, visions of the region's values, sensibilities, and, in the person of genial Andy Griffith, even its police officers.

As Graham stresses, both contemporary and retrospective television and film portrayals of the civil rights and black power movements have always had a decidedly mixed record with regard to both their historical accuracy and their ability to capture the Movement's enormous moral force. Nevertheless, good, bad, and indifferent, these media creations—from the much-criticized film *Mississippi Burning,* to the much-admired television documentary series *Eyes on The Prize*—clearly continue to affect popular (mis)understandings of the modern black freedom struggle, and of the region where it waged some of its most important battles.

Intellectual historian Richard King once recommended that "one of the best ways to establish a more immediate relation to the civil rights movement is to pay more attention to the fiction that has explicitly thematised the Movement. For, it is there that one gets something like a simulacrum of the experience of the movement or at least certain aspects of it." King appreciated that Movement historians often have difficulty gaining access to the emotional and visceral aspects of their subject, let alone finding the analytical tools, or even the expressive language, to do justice to these vital elements. For King, fiction provided one possible answer to this problem: "It has," he argued, "cognitive, as opposed simply to aesthetic, self-referential value . . . historical understanding may be enhanced—though never automatically—by a fictional working-through of historical phenomena. . . . At its best fiction can illuminate certain dimensions of the experience of politics that otherwise might have remained hidden."[13]

Of course, King's insights do not apply merely to written Movement fiction. Something similar might be said about the "working-through" of the material and psychological dimensions of the modern freedom struggle in many other cultural forms: an Elizabeth Catlett sculpture, a

John Coltrane solo, an Emory Douglas cartoon, a Nikki Giovanni poem, a Temptations dance routine, a Melvin Van Peebles film, even Angela Davis's Afro hairdo, or a Muhammad Ali feint and hook might all be said to communicate something of the feeling, "a simulacrum of the experience" of being part, if not always of the organized Movement, then of an energized black community fighting for self-respect and equality.

In the final two essays in the collection, Sharon Monteith and Trudier Harris examine how a number of white and black writers have "worked-through" the freedom struggle in their fiction, and thereby participated in the ongoing debate over its nature, meanings, and legacies. Monteith considers how southern white women fiction writers have depicted female interracial relationships in the wake of the civil rights movement. More specifically, she concentrates on how the white women in these fictions have tried to forge personal relationships with African American women, not only in the context of the practical changes in southern life wrought by the freedom struggle, but also with reference to the continuing symbolic resonances of the Movement and Martin Luther King. As Monteith notes, King—usually decked out here in his traditional ideological garb as apostle of peace and unconflicted champion of integration—works in these fictions as the embodiment of all that is good, virtuous, loving, and tolerant. Admired, if rather differently understood, by characters on both sides of the racial divide, it is the memory of King which encourages the white women in these novels to continue to work toward an idealized vision of southern racial harmony and community which has, in reality, proved extremely elusive.

Trudier Harris's essay switches the focus away from white fiction to consider how African American writers have incorporated Martin Luther King, his doctrine of nonviolence, and the meaning of his martyrdom into their work. Harris reminds us that during the last years of his life, King's reputation among many of the militant young writers associated with the black power movement was decidedly mixed. He was frequently accused of being too cautious and conciliatory, while some viewed his continued advocacy of nonviolence as a dangerous anachronism in an era of violent police repression, armed self-defense strategies, and urban riots. Harris suggests that it was only in death that King was able to fulfil his preacherly function of converting the black community to a common cause. Ironically, however, King's martyrdom united many African Americans, not in a shared commitment to nonviolence, but in a common sense of outrage and a powerful desire to wreak vengeance on white America. These widespread feelings found public expression, not only in the rioting which followed King's murder, but in a literature of ferocious anger and resentment as black writers transformed King's life, beliefs, and death into vehicles for their own excoriations of white racism and lurid imaginings of bloody revenge.

Perhaps appropriately, Harris concludes both her essay and this volume by discussing a very different work of black fiction—Charles Johnson's novel *Dreamer*. In this book, the despair and anger which characterized much black literature in the aftermath of King's death is replaced by an attempt to rekindle his visionary dream of a beloved community. Some have dismissed this as utopian fantasy or misplaced nostalgia for a Movement which, for all its many remarkable achievements, actually fell far short of securing genuine equality of opportunity for the mass of African Americans. Nevertheless, Johnson's novel testifies to King's continuing capacity to encourage people to harbor such dreams and work toward a more just and humane world. However much historians may rightly strive to complicate popular understandings of Martin Luther King, to place his achievements in proper context, and to extend their studies of the postwar Movement far beyond King into new methodological, interpretative, and empirical territories, this remains a magnificent legacy.

Notes

1. Conrad Kent Rivers, "In Defense of Black Poets" (1968), in *The Black Poets*, ed. Dudley Randell (New York: Bantam, 1971), 200–1.

2. Albert Murray, *The Omni-Americans: Some Alternatives to the Folklore of White Supremacy* (New York: Viking, 1983), 54–55.

3. Harold Cruse, *The Crisis of the Negro Intellectual* (New York: William Morrow, 1967), 86

4. Vincent Harding, *Hope and History: Why We Must Share the Story of the Movement* (New York: Orbis, 1990), 126–27.

5. Ironically, this emphasis on the cultural aspects of the black power era has been at the expense of the sort of detailed examinations of more "conventional" political activity in black communities that dominate civil rights–era studies. Although political scientists have done rather better than historians in this regard, the historiography on how black communities, especially in the South, sought to utilize the vote, effect meaningful school desegregation, participate in federal antipoverty programs, and practice other forms of "conventional" political activity during the late 1960s and early 1970s remains decidedly patchy in terms of both scope and quality.

6. Clayborne Carson, "Black Political Thought in the Post-Revolutionary Era," in *The Making of Martin Luther King and the Civil Rights Movement*, ed. Brian Ward and Tony Badger (New York: New York University Press, 1996), 122.

7. See, for example, William Barlow, *Voice Over: The Making of Black Radio* (Philadelphia: Temple University Press, 1998); Scott DeVeaux, *The Birth of Bebop: A Social and Musical History* (Berkeley: University of California Press, 1997); Robin D. G. Kelley, *Race Rebels: Culture, Politics and the Black Working Class* (New York: Free Press, 1996); Barbara Dianne Savage, *Broadcasting Freedom: Radio, War, and the Politics of Race, 1938–1948* (Chapel Hill: University of North Carolina Press, 1998); William L. Van Deburg, *New Day in Babylon: The Black Power Movement and American Culture, 1965–1975* (Chicago: University of Chicago Press, 1992), and *Black Camelot: African-American Culture Heroes in their Times, 1960–1980* (Chicago: University of Chicago Press, 1997); Melissa Walker, *Down From The Mountaintop: Black Women's Novels in the Wake of the Civil Rights Movement, 1966–1989* (New Haven: Yale University Press, 1991); Brian Ward, *Just My Soul Responding: Rhythm and Blues, Black Consciousness and Race Relations* (Berkeley: University of California Press, 1998); Komozi Woodard, *A Nation Within a Nation: Amiri Baraka (LeRoi Jones) & Black Power Politics* (Chapel Hill: University of North Carolina Press, 1999); Clyde Woods, *Development Arrested: Race, Power, and the Blues in the Mississippi Delta* (London: Verso, 1998). Although some of these works suffer from a fairly flimsy, or overly romantic, grasp of the nitty-historical-gritty of the postwar freedom struggle, they all offer useful interpretive insights and factual material for understanding what that Struggle actually was, where and how it was fought, and how it was felt by combatants and non-combatants alike.

8. Eldridge Cleaver, *Soul on Ice* (New York: Dell, 1967), 173–83. For a fuller discussion of the relationship between white admiration of African American music and white racial attitudes during the civil rights and black power eras, see Ward, *Just My Soul Responding*, especially 37–39, 225–52.

9. See Addison Gayle Jr., ed., *The Black Aesthetic* (Garden City, N.Y.: Doubleday, 1972).

10. Larry Neal, "The Black Writers Role II: Ellison's Zoot Suit," (1970), in Neal, *Visions of a Liberated Future: Black Arts Movement Writings* (New York: Thunder's Mouth, 1989), 44.

11. Two recent publications reflect a growing interest in the role of the radio in the modern freedom struggle. Barbara Dianne Savage's *Broadcasting Freedom* is an exemplary account of how radio programming featuring or relating to African Americans during World War II helped to place civil rights issues onto a national agenda. William Barlow's engaging overview of the entire history of black-oriented radio, *Voice Over*, is rather less historically assured and analytically sophisticated than Savage's book, but nonetheless includes fascinating sections on the medium and the freedom struggle.

12. I use the gendered term "master narrative" advisedly since, despite a recent spate of important scholarly and creative works highlighting the role of women in the civil rights and black power movements, their incorporation into the story of the postwar freedom struggle is still far from complete. For a useful introduction

to some of the most recent scholarly debates about women in the freedom struggle, and on gender issues in the Movement more generally, see Peter J. Ling and Sharon Monteith, eds., *Gender in the Civil Rights Movement* (New York: Garland, 1999).

13. Richard H. King, "Politics and Fictional Representation: The Case of the Civil Rights Movement," in *The Making of Martin Luther King*, ed. Ward and Badger, 162–63.

1

The Media and the Movement

Looking Back from the Southern Front

Julian Bond

The movement for civil rights from the mid-1950s through the 1960s was one of the great news stories of the modern era. Longer than almost any competing story—war, assassination, scandal—it consumed the interest of many Americans for years. What follows is a highly personal account of how the early southern Movement and the media intersected, how each served and used the other, and how they eventually grew apart. It is by no means comprehensive; there is much more to learn and understand about both. It is, however, based on the belief that until historians unravel the complex links between the southern freedom struggle and the mass media, their understanding of how the Movement functioned, why it succeeded, and when and where it failed, will be incomplete.

The story of how the black-oriented media responded to the challenges of the freedom struggle, often bringing African Americans news and information that the white media did not present, is an important and still largely untold one. However, my principal concern here is with the mainstream news media, by which I mean the national broadcasting networks (NBC, ABC, and CBS) and nationally prominent news publications such as *Time, Newsweek, Look, Life, Saturday Evening Post,* and the *New York Times.* These wholly white-owned, invariably white-staffed, and largely white-oriented media crucially shaped popular perceptions of the Movement throughout the nation. Of course, the southern-based white news media also warrant attention, since they too contributed to the telling—and, therefore, to the unfolding—of the story of the freedom struggle. Moreover, several southern journalists played an important role in reporting and legitimizing the activities of the early Movement to the nation at large.

The relationship between the mainstream news media and the struggle for African American civil rights can be crudely divided into two distinct periods. The first period, the one on which this essay concentrates, lasted roughly from the birth of mass black activism in the Montgomery bus boycott of 1955–56 to the Selma campaign of 1965 and corresponded with the zenith of southern civil rights protests. It was an era of mostly factual, objective reportage, when a great number of journalists and editors were generally sympathetic to the Movement's motives, techniques, goals, and personalities. For the early Movement, newspaper, radio, and television coverage brought the legitimate but previously unheard demands of southern blacks into the homes of Americans far removed from the petty indignities and large cruelties of southern segregation. These racial structures were indefensible; once challenged and exposed, they finally crumbled.

There is no neat terminal date for when this generally supportive phase of media coverage ended. Significant, largely negative, changes in the tone of Movement coverage coincided roughly with the emergence of the black power slogan during the 1966 Meredith March through Mississippi, and were intensified by the urban rioting that exploded in many of America's cities during the later 1960s. This new phase was characterized by much greater press suspicion of what appeared to be ever more radical black demands for the restructuring of America's economic, political, and social system. By the end of the decade, the Movement's means, motives, and leaders were subjected to intense critical scrutiny and, as Jenny Walker's essay in this volume describes in more detail, were frequently misrepresented by a hostile mainstream media.[1]

Back in the mid-1950s, the southern white press was in many ways the last place one might have expected to find enthusiasm or encouragement for the black struggle against segregation and disenfranchisement. In the decade after the Second World War, examples of racial liberalism among southern white journalists were relatively rare. True, editors like Harry Ashmore at the *Arkansas Gazette,* Jonathan Daniels at the *Raleigh News and Observer,* Ralph McGill at the *Atlanta Constitution,* Hodding Carter at the *Delta Democrat* in Greenville, Mississippi, and Hazel Brannon Smith at the same state's *Lexington Advertiser* encouraged moderation on racial issues, denounced the excesses of race-baiting demagogues, and generally argued for a better deal for southern blacks. Yet, even these men and women, the best of the bunch, were still a long way short of openly supporting desegregation. The white southern press generally paid little attention to blacks or their aspirations.[2]

In 1949, Southern Regional Council (SRC) president Marion A. Wright accurately summed up this situation when he wrote in *New South* that: "Local newspapers, with exceptions so small as to be negligible, are owned, published and edited by Southern whites. Their subscribers are white; their advertisers are white. Is it not going a little far to expect complete objectivity and candor of a white southern editor in discussing the duty of his subscribers and advertisers to members of a race that bring him no bread and butter?"[3]

Typically, southern newspapers of the period refused to give blacks honorifics like "Mr." and "Mrs.," and routinely referred to them derisively in the lower-case as "negro" or "colored." In a clear reflection of the white preference for racial segregation in all areas of southern life, many papers relegated their smattering of news about blacks to a separate "black page"—a single page, tucked away in the back of a paper, featuring non-threatening black news, usually relating to social functions, churches, sports, or other entertainments.

With papers like the *New Orleans Times-Picayune* even taking the trouble to airbrush black faces out of crowd photographs, it sometimes appeared as if criminal activity was the only way to ensure coverage of blacks in the southern white press.[4] One study of Deep South newspapers revealed that fully half of the stories printed about African Americans in the 1950s related to black crime. Revealingly, black-on-white crime was virtually guaranteed front-page exposure, but black-on-black crime was either ignored or relegated to the back pages.[5] Marion Wright appealed in vain to "the sense of fairness of southern editors and publishers," hoping to end the situation where, in crime stories, "the habitual use in headlines of 'negro' or 'black' and of no off-setting use of 'white' or 'caucasian' . . . built up in the public mind the impression of disproportionate criminality of the former—an impression to no degree warranted by the facts." By the early 1950s the ubiquity of such negative portrayals prompted Wright and the SRC to label the southern newspaper "the greatest single force in perpetuating the popular stereotype of the Negro."[6] The presence of these pejorative black images in the southern press reminds us that the Movement's concern for accurate coverage of its protest activities was linked to a much broader effort to secure more respectful treatment and more positive portrayals of African Americans in all sections of the media.[7]

Aside from the racial prejudices of many newspaper journalists, editors, owners, advertisers, and readers, there was one other consistent impediment to positive press coverage of African Americans and their civil rights activities, not just in the South, but throughout the nation: the Federal Bureau of Investigation (FBI). Thanks to scholars like David Garrow and Kenneth O'Reilly, the FBI's long and ignoble record of harassment, disinformation, disruption, and bureaucratic obstructionism aimed at the Movement is now well-known.[8] An important part of that story was the Bureau's use of the press to discredit the targets of Director J. Edgar Hoover's racial, sexual, and political paranoias. Although these efforts intensified along with the growth of a mass movement in the 1950s and 1960s, Hoover had actually been courting the press for decades. He and his staff put a good deal of effort into forging and preserving close personal relationships with individual journalists, editors, and publishers, in an attempt to secure favorable coverage for the Bureau's work and a sympathetic hearing for strategically leaked information about Hoover's opponents. In the racial arena, this meant that large numbers of American media outlets were fed a steady stream of "secret" FBI-generated material on black activism, designed specifically to denigrate civil rights workers' motives and character, or to link them with international communism. Such reports undoubtedly helped to stir suspicions about the legitimacy of the gathering challenge to segregation and disenfranchisement—particularly among southern newspapers more than willing to believe that any insurgency on the part of the region's blacks was inspired by outside agitators.

Sometimes the links between the FBI and specific papers were especially close. The Bureau's relationship to the main white Atlanta newspapers is instructive in this regard. During the 1930s, Hoover wrote fairly regularly to Clark Howell Sr., editor-president of the *Atlanta Constitution,* usually thanking the newspaperman for favorable published comments about the Bureau. When Clark Howell Jr. succeeded his father in early 1937, he too was regularly commended by the FBI's director for his continuing support. On a personal level, Hoover's efforts to maintain a close relationship with this influential paper clearly bore fruit. A typically laudatory article on Hoover was titled: "America's He-Man No. 1 Confesses to Yolande Gwin: 'I Always Get My Man—Someone Else Gets The Girl'"— perhaps with greater significance than the *Constitution*'s society editor intended, given the director's alleged secret fondness for cross-dressing.

But there was more to the relationship between paper, publisher, and police bureaucrat than simple exchanges of pleasantries. Cooperation eventually extended to the point where the newspaper even permitted the Bureau to censor and edit articles about its activities.[9] This cozy relationship continued for years, even under the editorship of the liberal Ralph McGill. Despite McGill's flirtation with suspiciously leftward-leaning groups like the Southern Conference for Human Welfare and the SRC, Hoover considered him a staunch anti-communist, and liked to think of him as a "close friend."[10] Even as, in the wake of *Brown v. Board of Education* and the emergence of the mass struggle, McGill eventually came to support desegregation, his newspapers still served as outlets for the slander against Movement-makers emanating from the House Un-American Activities Committee. FBI agents continued to serve as informants on civil rights activists to the *Constitution,* sometimes covertly meeting reporters at the Georgia Institute of Technology athletic field to avoid creating a paper trail. As late as the mid-1960s, Hoover was still trying to persuade his friend McGill to expose the Movement as a communist-inspired sham and Martin Luther King as an immoral charlatan. When McGill planned a dinner to honor King's receipt of the Nobel Peace Prize, the FBI immediately offered him evidence purportedly chronicling King's marital infidelities and other information designed to undermine McGill's respect for the leader.[11] Eugene Patterson, Ralph McGill's right-hand man at the *Constitution* in the 1960s, was also regularly approached by FBI agents and urged to publish defamatory stories about King. On one occasion he was offered "the name of the Florida airport and the time of day . . . when Dr. King was supposedly leaving for a tryst with some girlfriend."[12]

The FBI-*Atlanta Constitution* connection was all part of a much broader strategy whereby Hoover sought fertile media ground in which to sow stories favorable to the Bureau and harmful to the Movement. McGill was certainly not the only editor to be fed the results of the FBI's surveillance of King. As part of what constituted the "single most extensive program on an individual in the Bureau's history," numerous newspapers and magazines were supplied with information on the communist backgrounds of some of Dr. King's advisers, notably Stanley Levison, Bayard Rustin, and Jack O'Dell. Benjamin Bradlee, then *Newsweek* Washington bureau chief, and Jim Bishop of the Hearst newspaper chain were among the many supplied with wiretap transcripts, purporting to reveal King's extramarital affairs.[13]

The FBI eventually recruited more than three hundred newspaper reporters, radio commentators, and television personalities hoping to discredit the liberal press and the bleeding hearts who threatened Hoover's America. It targeted entire chains of newspapers, publications as varied as *Jet, Ebony,* the *Washington Post,* the *Washington Star,* the *Chicago Tribune,*

Reader's Digest, the *New York Daily News,* the *New York Herald Tribune,* and influential individuals like Walter Winchell and Fulton Lewis. The Bureau sometimes benefited directly from its cultivation of the media, as when press credentials allegedly provided by NBC enabled FBI agents to spy on the Mississippi Freedom Democratic Party (MFDP) at the 1964 Democratic Party Convention.

In the final analysis, the FBI's systematic efforts to prejudice press coverage of the civil rights struggle probably had a chilling, but not a catastrophic, effect on the way the mainstream media dealt with the Movement. The progressive *Atlanta Constitution,* for example, firmly rejected the FBI's scurrilous material, but then so too did the southern papers that supported segregation. Eugene Patterson recalled a phone call from Roy Harris, editor of the prosegregation *Augusta Chronicle,* after the FBI had provided Harris with information on Dr. King's extracurricular activities. "You'da thought they'da gone right into print with this information," Patterson explained, but Harris said, "'Hell, I wouldn't print that stuff. That's beyond the pale.'. . . It's a tribute to the press in the South, the *segregationist* press of that period, that not one word of this ever came into print until after the death of Dr. King. There were certain fences beyond which the press would not go in vilifying and damaging a man, and we didn't do it to Dr. King."[14] Similarly, while the archly conservative *U.S. News and World Report* lapped up much of Hoover's propaganda and sometimes painted King, and the wider Movement he came to symbolize, as manifestations of dangerous radicalism, it ignored the personal material. Meanwhile, *Time* and *Newsweek* took a more skeptical approach to all of the FBI's revelations. Richard Lentz has shown that these two mainstream journals of opinion often took issue with King over individual statements and tactical decisions but were generally supportive of his goals and methods until the later 1960s.[15]

Certainly, despite the FBI's best efforts, there were always local, regional, and national newspapers that reported the early southern Movement fairly from the outset; reporters who covered it objectively; and editors who crusaded on its behalf. And whereas many in the South responded to the emerging Movement with incredulity, indifference, contempt, or open hostility, there was a corps of southern white editors and journalists who sought to reconcile regional and racial loyalties with a growing recognition that the Movement represented justice and the future. By the early 1960s, even some of the older gradualists had come across to the Movement's side. Among these were McGill and Hazel Bran-

non Smith, whose transition from staunch Dixiecrat in 1948 to bold supporter of the Freedom Riders and direct action in 1961 was proof of what
the Movement could achieve.[16]

Some of the basic characteristics of the press coverage of the early
Movement began to appear with the year-long Montgomery bus boycott,
which began in December 1955 when Mrs. Rosa Parks refused to give up
her bus seat to a white passenger as instructed by the driver. If it is too
simplistic to say that the Movement "began" in Montgomery, it was nevertheless a seminal campaign that eventually attracted widespread public
attention. Montgomery showed how the Movement, with the careful cultivation of sympathetic—or at least acquiescent—forces within the media,
managed to project the first of its many faces to the American public.

One of the earliest newspaper stories about the Montgomery bus boycott was written by Joe Azbell, city editor of the local *Montgomery Advertiser,* in the immediate aftermath of Parks's arrest. In straightforward fashion, the story announced that "Negro groups" were arranging a secret
meeting to plan a boycott of the city's buses. Rev. Wilson, the pastor of the
church where the secret meeting was to be held, declined to divulge
names of others who would attend.[17]

While there is limited value in such counterfactual history, it is nevertheless intriguing to speculate how, with the same facts at hand, Azbell
might have approached this story had he been overtly hostile to the protest, or simply writing in a later, more cynical era. He might well have
downplayed the widespread unity in support of the boycott by reporting on
the smoldering factionalism within black Montgomery and emphasizing
the pockets of opposition to the proposed protest. He might have changed
Rev. Wilson's answer that he would not divulge the leaders' names "under
any circumstances" to the tougher, more critical, "Rev. Wilson *refused* to
divulge" the names. He might have searched police and other records for
details of Rosa Parks's background, unearthing her experiences with the
National Association for the Advancement of Colored People and the
Highlander Folk School—both of which were perceived as communist-
inspired organizations by many white southerners. Just as later civil rights
leaders would be routinely grilled about their attitudes toward the most
radical and incendiary black figures of the day—be they Malcolm X,
Stokely Carmichael, or Louis Farrakhan—Azbell surely would have asked
Rev. Wilson what he thought about Dr. W. E. B. Du Bois, another conspicuous black—and "red"—figure in the demonology of the white South.

In later stories, the *Advertiser's* reporters, guided by more sensationalist
imperatives, might have inquired into the drinking and sexual habits of the

young Dr. King. It is hard to imagine that the story of one boycott leader's celebrated race down a Montgomery main street inches ahead of an irate, hatchet-wielding, jealous husband would not have been repeated end-lessly as the boycott's fortunes ebbed and flowed, either to titillate readers or to undermine the Movement's credibility and effectiveness.

The fact is, however, that these lines of questioning were not taken; none of these potentially damaging storylines were pursued in the Mont-gomery press—or in the national media, which began to pick up on the story in early 1956. Partly this was a consequence of the fact that journal-istic ethics in the mid-1950s seemed to preclude such prurient peeks into the private lives of public figures. Yet, it also indicated some sympathy for the boycott and its goals and tactics by journalists and editors. Even more crucially, it reflected the remarkable skill with which the Montgomery protesters presented themselves to the press, and through the press to the nation, as models of patriotic virtue and moral respectability. With its church-based leadership, its much-vaunted adherence to nonviolence in the face of enormous white provocation, and its repeated appeals to American constitutional rights and democratic values, the Montgomery Movement had seized the moral high ground from the segregationists.[18]

When, in the wake of the mass indictment of nearly one hundred Montgomery Improvement Association (MIA) leaders, most of them cler-ics, the protest finally made it onto the front pages of the *New York Times* and the *New York Herald Tribune* on February 22, 1956, even the television networks began to feature regular boycott stories. So, too, did other important journals of opinion, like *Newsweek, Time,* and *U.S. News and World Report*. With varying degrees of alacrity and enthusiasm, all of these news media ultimately endorsed this carefully orchestrated confrontation between the forces of justice, respectability, decency, and progress and those of bigotry, violence, lawlessness, and ignorance.

There was much empirical truth in this depiction of the Montgomery protest, and even more moral force. Nonetheless, in some ways the Move-ment and the press conspired to simplify the Montgomery story and make it the subject of a convenient, potent, and enduring media myth. In this myth, a largely unlettered and unorganized population, which had previ-ously meekly succumbed to racial oppression, suddenly rallied to the non-violent leadership of Martin Luther King Jr.—an erudite and charismatic young minister steeped in Gandhian philosophies of social change, and blessed with Christ-like forbearance—and abandoned public transporta-tion for more than a year rather than submit themselves to the indignities of segregation any longer. With minor nuances, this myth still survives in popular memory of the Movement's origins, although within the historiography of the postwar freedom struggle the scholarship of David Garrow, Aldon Morris, and others began to expose its shortcomings in the 1980s. This scholarship, coupled with the reminiscences of key players in the boycott like Rosa Parks and Jo Ann Robinson, has revealed a pre-history of black activism in the city long before King arrived; it has questioned King's nonviolent credentials in the opening phase of the protest; and it has confirmed the festering factionalism and class cleavages within Montgomery's black community that did sometimes threaten the unity of the boycott.[19] In the late 1950s and early 1960s, however, it was the media myth of Montgomery and King, not the more complex historical reality, that became the standard against which other civil rights campaigns would be measured for both moral authority and practical effectiveness.

Like news reporting in any era, the news media's coverage of the civil rights movement of the late 1950s and early 1960s reflected the personal biases and economic agendas of the people who reported, edited, and bankrolled it. The reporters, in particular, were an interesting, impressive, and influential group. At a 1987 University of Mississippi symposium of journalists who had covered civil rights in the South, including eleven Pulitzer Prize winners and three Emmy awardees, not a few asserted that they had made the Movement. But it could be argued as surely that the Movement made many of them. Frank McGee, for example, was anchorman at WBAF, an NBC affiliate and one of two television stations in Montgomery, before his coverage of the bus boycott won him a job at the network. He was the first of many journalists whose careers soared with the rise of the southern Movement.

Others in this first wave of journalists who helped turn civil rights into a regular media beat included Rex Thomas, Associated Press's (AP) bureau chief in Montgomery from 1944 to 1979, and Mississippi-born Jack Nelson, who covered race-related stories for the *Atlanta Constitution* from 1952 to 1956, before becoming a major presence at the *Los Angeles Times*. Robert E. L. Baker reported for the *Washington Post* in the 1950s and 1960s, while Haynes Johnson did the same for the *Washington Star*. Herb Kaplow began covering racial issues on May 17, 1954, when the Supreme Court outlawed school segregation in the historic *Brown* decision. John Chancellor began covering civil rights for NBC at Little Rock in 1956. Paul Duke was a lynchpin of the AP's coverage of the Movement from 1954 to 1957, while Karl Fleming emerged as *Newsweek*'s key man in the South in the early 1960s. David Halberstam cut his teeth on civil rights issues covering the local sit-in movement for the *Nashville Tennessean* before taking his concern for racial justice to the *New York Times,* where he worked from 1960 to 1967. John Herbers was the Jackson, Mississippi, United Press International (UPI) bureau chief from 1953 to 1963, before joining Halberstam and several other reporters with good civil rights pedigrees, like Roy Reed and Gene Roberts, at the *Times.*[20]

Arguably the most important of all the journalists during this early phase of the Movement, however, was Claude Sitton. Sitton covered the South for the International News Service from 1949 to 1951 and for UPI from 1951 to 1955. Then he joined the *New York Times,* effectively replacing John Popham, who since 1947 had been the sole reporter for a national newspaper who was based permanently in the South. During the momentous years of struggle from 1957 to 1964, Sitton was the *Times*'s chief southern correspondent. He set the standard and led the pack. Stories—probably apocryphal—were told that New York-based television editors would buy the early edition of the *Times* the night before its official publication date, so they would know where to send their reporters the next day: wherever Claude Sitton's by-line said he was turned out to be where the news would be made.

It was this first corps of reporters who helped to bring news of the burgeoning Movement to the nation and the world. All were white, most were men, and, perhaps crucially, many were southerners who had reportorial experience in the region before 1955. These were men who, unlike many of the journalists who followed them onto the southern civil rights beat in the later 1960s, knew the region, its politics, and its racial conventions well. They also knew the principal actors on both sides of the unfolding story of racial change in the South. Most were of a more liberal persuasion than their predecessors and, although sensitive to the dilemmas of a region in crisis, were generally convinced of the righteousness of the black challenge to the racial status quo. Moreover, they were eager to support the Struggle through their reporting, and the Movement quickly recognized the need to cultivate such sympathies. As John Lewis recalled, at the start of the 1960 Nashville sit-ins, David Halberstam "had been the only one covering us. . . . We knew we needed the press to get our message out, and early on this tall, skinny guy with his big brown eyeglasses *was* the press. . . . If he had any problem with being objective, it might have been that he was sympathetic to us, and it showed."[21]

The print media remained important throughout the southern civil rights revolution, but by the mid-1950s television had become a potent and ubiquitous presence in American—especially white American—lives. Consequently, the great news stories of the day were also played out on the small screen. The man most responsible for bringing television to the civil rights movement was Laurens Pierce. In 1955, Pierce was selling cameras and film equipment in Montgomery. He filmed the mass meetings of the MIA and begged the news-film distribution companies and the networks to buy his film. "He thought something important was happening," his sound man Leroy Rollins said. After a wire service report on Montgomery broke news of the boycott outside the region, Rollins said, "CBS called Pierce and said, 'Do you have film?' Pierce said, 'I've got it in my hand.'"[22]

Laurens Pierce died in 1982 after working for CBS for nearly thirty years. He had filmed the Movement from Montgomery onwards. He was in St. Augustine, Selma, and Bogalusa—everywhere the Movement was, Laurens Pierce was too. By the mid-1960s, he had even taken to carrying a gun to protect himself from the violence frequently directed at television crews trying to capture white racial repression in action. This was probably prudent, since Pierce had an uncanny knack for being close to moments of political violence: he was in Dallas when President John F. Kennedy was killed, in Memphis when Dr. King was killed, and close to segregationist icon George Wallace when Wallace was shot on the presidential campaign trail in 1972; he won an Emmy for his coverage of the attempted assassination.

Wire service reports—like the dispatch from Montgomery—and mainstream media coverage helped to spread news of southern civil rights activities to an audience far beyond the immediate locales where protests were taking place. This in turn helped to stimulate further activism, encouraging the growth of a genuine southern-wide mass movement, rather than a series of isolated local campaigns. More generally, the media kept the grim, incontrovertible, fact of southern racial oppression in the public eye.

My own experiences are testimony to the importance of this process. At various crucial moments, the media helped to raise my own appreciation of the sheer savagery of southern racism, heightened my understanding that there were those—not too different from myself—who were actively challenging racial injustice, and even provided the catalyst for my own entry into the Movement ranks. In retrospect, press coverage of the murder of Emmett Till in 1955, the Little Rock school desegregation crisis of 1957, and the Greensboro sit-ins of 1960 provided stepping stones leading inexorably toward my involvement in the freedom struggle.

Like a whole generation of young blacks, I was given an unforgettable insight into the cruelties of southern-style racism and moved along the path to later activism by the graphic pictures that appeared in *Jet* magazine of Emmett Till's swollen and misshapen body. Seeing the corpse of this young, innocent boy, tortured and savagely beaten almost beyond recognition before being killed—all on account of some minor perceived transgression of southern racial etiquette—we all thought: it could easily have been me.

Before Till's mother agreed to let photographs of the open-casket funeral appear, her son's murder had attracted little mainstream press interest. Thanks largely to the pictures, however, all three television networks and between fifty and seventy reporters were on hand to cover the trial of the two men accused of his murder in Sumner, Mississippi. "I think the picture in *Jet* magazine showing Emmett Till's mutilation was probably the greatest media product in the last forty or fifty years," claimed Michigan Congressman Charles Diggs in a 1987 interview. "That picture stimulated a lot of interest and anger on the part of blacks all over the country."[23] The coverage of the killing—and of the farcical exhibition of southern justice in Sumner, where the murderers were summarily acquitted—also nibbled at the consciences of many whites, who began to see the South's racial practices in a troubling new light.

Almost exactly two years later, the media brought news of the events and personalities in the clash between the federal and state authorities in Little Rock, Arkansas. Again, it was the black press that reached me first, but this time the story secured instant and widespread national coverage. Before Little Rock, I had been a happy-go-lucky teenager, seventeen years old, whose chief worries were whether girls liked me as much as I liked them. My role models—although we did not call them that then—were white teenagers, mostly Italian American youngsters who danced five afternoons a week on ABC's *American Bandstand*. I was a rural, small-town kid, who had not gone to a school with indoor plumbing until I entered high school. These youngsters were big-city sophisticates to me, and I aped their clothes and their style. I even knew their names—Carmen and Bob and Justine.

But suddenly the nine brave young people of Little Rock's Central High School—the Little Rock Nine—replaced my former idols. My new models didn't seem to wear the proper hip clothes, but they possessed something the *Bandstand* dancers did not—grace and courage under great pressure. Day after day, amid the most horrendous verbal and physical abuse, they sought to exercise their court-ordered right to attend classes, just as white segregationists used a mixture of legal machinations, intimidation, and violence to try to drive them away.

I learned all their names too. I knew of Ernie Green, at seventeen the most like me: a senior, who seemed to me to represent everything a college-bound young man should be. Minnie Jean Brown, a "bad" girl; not that her morals were suspect, but "bad" in the sense that Minnie Jean took nothing from nobody—she would never take a blow.

Most memorable was Elizabeth Eckford. On the first day of the school year, the nine black students were advised to wait for a police escort before attempting to enter the school. Governor Orval Faubus had already ordered the National Guard to prevent the students' entry and a large segregationist mob had gathered outside Central High, equally committed to the same goal. Elizabeth did not have a telephone and never got the message to wait for the police. She took a bus and faced the snarling white mob alone. I recall that she wore dark glasses because she had light-sensitive eyes. I remember her holding her books before her, stepping off a city bus into a mob of screaming harpies. You could not always tell what they were shouting at her, but you knew from their distorted, hateful faces that they were things you would not want anyone to say to you. When Elizabeth Eckford came home from school the next day, her mother said her dress was so wet with spit that she could wring it out.

The coverage of the Little Rock crisis, which culminated in the federalizing of the National Guard and the deployment of paratroopers by President Dwight Eisenhower to ensure the safety of the black students, profoundly affected me, and those of my generation who could identify so closely with the youngsters involved. African American audiences were thrilled and inspired by the heroism of the black students. We were also generally encouraged by Eisenhower's eventual use of federal force to uphold black rights—even if we knew it was tardy and grudging, and carefully noted that the intervention had been a consequence of civil disorder, not of a moral or even legal commitment to doing what was right.

The story also had a major impact beyond black America. CBS correspondent Robert Schanke summed up the wider significance of the television coverage of the crisis: "Little Rock was the first case where people really got their impression of an event from television. It was the event that nationalized a news story that would have remained a local story if it had just been a print story."[24] Indeed, it was Little Rock—even more than Montgomery—that established the key conventions for successful Movement coverage during the southern campaign. The Little Rock crisis was made for television. It had drama, tension, and the ever-present whiff of real and threatened violence, all concentrated into a manageable geographic area and relatively brief time frame. The other classic set-piece confrontations of the southern Movement—Ole Miss, Birmingham, Tuscaloosa, and Selma—would all follow much the same pattern.

Generally speaking, Robert Schanke's positive assessment of the impact of Little Rock on popular white perceptions of the black struggle for civil rights seems persuasive. Yet, Allison Graham is surely also right to note that the press coverage of the crisis played differently for different white audiences.[25] When *Time*'s September 23 cover story depicted Arkansas's obstructionist Governor Orval Faubus as a "slightly sophisticated hillbilly" with "milk dribbling down his chin" and a habit of greeting his guests with a hearty belch, the governor was instantly placed within a venerable tradition of stereotypically ignorant and reactionary southern rednecks: here, non-southern whites were assured, was the root cause of the South's "race problem."[26] The Movement needed the press to create such unalloyed white demons just as much as it needed it to promote blemishless black heroes. Later, other segregationist politicians and lawmen like George Wallace, Eugene "Bull" Connor, and Jim Clark would join Faubus as the objects of national media ridicule and condemnation. These men were similarly held up as personifications of the brutish ignorance and superstition that underpinned southern racism and had precipitated the region's racial crisis.[27]

If there was more than a shred of truth in this version of events, it was still a simplistic vision of the white South that reduced the spectrum of opinion on how to confront the racial question to one-dimensional images of unconstitutional, often violent, last-ditch resistance. Ultimately, these relentlessly hostile and stereotypical press depictions may even have helped generate sterner southern opposition to desegregation. Dick Sanders, a television reporter who worked in Mississippi in the late 1950s, recognized this paradox: "After Little Rock, there was a great deal said about how the TV coverage . . . opened the eyes of the United States to the plight of the Negro. What it did in Mississippi to a large extent was galvanize the white opposition."[28] As Allison Graham has suggested, far from recognizing themselves in the pictures and stories emanating from Little Rock, ordinary southerners felt insulted and victimized by these crude stereotypes. Feeling embattled, misunderstood, and stigmatized by the rest of the nation, many abandoned any pretense of moderation on the race issue and rallied to the only figures in the region who appeared unapologetic about their race and southerness: the die-hard segregationists.[29]

On February 3 or 4, 1960, I was sitting in Yates and Milton's Drugstore in Atlanta, an off-campus hangout for students from the six schools of the

Atlanta University Center. I was approached by Lonnie King, a fellow Morehouse student who showed me a copy of that day's *Atlanta Daily World*. The black-owned paper carried a UPI account of the continuing sit-in demonstration at a Woolworth's in Greensboro, North Carolina, that had begun on February 1. The story was a virtual "how-to" manual for potential sit-inners; it described the tactics and organization of the Greensboro students, even what they wore, and how they comported themselves.

King asked if I had seen the story. Thinking he was asking if I had read a newspaper, I answered, "Yes." He persisted. "What do you think?" he asked. "I think it's great," I answered. "It's about time something like that happened." "Don't you think it ought to happen here?" he asked. "I'm sure it will happen here. Someone will make it happen here." "Don't you think *we* ought to make it happen here?" he insisted. "What do you mean we?" I weakly responded, but his force could not be resisted. He had recruited me, we recruited others, and in a few days, with that newspaper account as a guide, the Atlanta sit-ins began.

Perhaps surprisingly, the only detailed analysis of press coverage of the sit-ins has revealed that southern papers tended to report the demonstrations more fully, and with a greater diversity of black and white sources, than the northern press—with the exception of the *New York Times*, which devoted more column inches to the protests than any other paper.[30] Of course, not all of this coverage was positive. There was no shortage of southern editorials railing against the protesters' disregard for local Jim Crow laws and property rights, or charging sinister allegiances with outside agitators. Indeed, notwithstanding David Halberstam's sympathetic reports of the Nashville campaign for the *Tennessean*, the southern white press was generally at best suspicious and at worst openly hostile to the sit-ins and direct action protests.

Nevertheless, the southern press did produce at least one example of an unlikely—if temporary and inadvertent—Movement ally in the form of a widely reprinted column by James J. Kilpatrick, the segregationist editor of the *Richmond News Leader*. He contrasted the dignified black students "in coats, white shirts, ties" to their rowdy white attackers—"a ragtail rabble, slack jawed, black jacketed, grinning fit to kill and some of them . . . waving the proud and honored flag of the Southern states in the last war fought by gentlemen. Eheu!"[31] Such coverage, even in the "enemy" press, again confirmed the wisdom of deploying respectable, nonviolent direct action tactics in the pursuit of white support. Such tactics made it much easier for those sympathetic to the black cause to portray it as a clear-cut battle between heroes and villains, right and wrong.

From Montgomery and the sit-ins, through the freedom rides to the campaigns in Birmingham, St. Augustine, and Selma, mainstream press coverage of the Movement increased steadily. An analysis of major newspapers in Atlanta, Boston, Chicago, and New York has revealed that the space devoted to African Americans rose from barely one percent in the 1950s, to between two and four percent in the 1960s, more than seventy percent of which was on Movement matters.[32] This coverage in turn helped to expand support among the general population for federal action to correct the most blatant forms of racial discrimination in southern life. A study of congressional voting by John Kingdom later confirmed what contemporary strategists within the Movement knew only too well: that well-publicized campaigns could create irresistible pressure on the federal government to support civil rights legislation. "Printed and broadcast media are capable of the kind of continuous and prominent coverage of a story which makes it virtually impossible for a Congressman to ignore," Kingdom wrote. "The mass media may be powerful agenda-setters" with a "substantial impact on the determination of which issues will be seriously considered [by Congress] and which will not."[33]

Yet, within this broad pattern of steadily expanding media coverage of civil rights issues there were definite periods of reduced press interest in the Movement. A comparison of the space devoted to civil rights in the *New York Times* over twenty-five years showed a three-fold increase between 1954 and 1956, the year of the Montgomery bus boycott. Following an upsurge with Little Rock, civil rights coverage shrank by nearly half in 1958 and 1959, but then increased in 1960 with the sit-ins, and slightly again in 1961 when the Freedom Rides occurred. In 1963, when the Birmingham campaign, Governor George Wallace's infamous "Schoolhouse Door" stand in an effort to prevent the desegregation of the University of Alabama, and the March On Washington were part of an unprecedented number of protests that year, coverage of the Movement doubled. In 1964, the year of the Mississippi Summer Project, it doubled again and remained at that level through 1965, the year of Selma, the Voting Rights Act, and, perhaps more portentous for the future of the Movement, the Watts riots in Los Angeles. The same study revealed that civil rights coverage in the largest circulation magazines of the 1950s and 1960s—*Reader's Digest, Ladies Home Journal, Life,* and the *Saturday Evening Post*—had registered enormous increases in 1956 and 1957, as did coverage in *Time, Newsweek,*

the *New Republic,* and the *New York Times Magazine.* Civil rights coverage in all the magazines except *Reader's Digest* jumped to record levels
from 1960 through 1965 when both the survey and the high tide of southern mass activism ended.[34]

What these statistics confirm is that the level of the media's coverage of
the black struggle for civil and voting rights ultimately depended on the
Movement's capacity to generate newsworthy stories, dramatic confrontations, and charismatic personalities. The mainstream press may have been
broadly sympathetic to the fundamental moral and constitutional issues at
stake in the early southern Struggle, but it could only put out so many
earnest statements of principle and editorials on the subject before losing
the interest of readers, viewers, and listeners. What the media craved was
a steady diet of bold mass action campaigns in the streets, ideally faced by
violent white resistance, which would dramatize the issues at stake and
make good print or electronic copy.

Such realities crucially shaped the way in which the Movement worked
and where it focused its energies. In perhaps the most obvious examples,
Martin Luther King and the Southern Christian Leadership Conference
chose to join indigenous movements in Birmingham and Selma, in part
because they knew Commissioner of Public Safety Bull Connor and Sheriff Jim Clark could both easily be provoked. They would provide the kind
of graphic violence which would attract media attention, stimulate public
outrage, and thus create pressure on the federal government to respond.
King knew that the earlier Albany movement in Georgia in 1961 had largely
failed because Police Chief Laurie Pritchett knew how to "meet nonviolence with nonviolence," and to hide any police brutality from the media.[35]
In the absence of the "right" sort of pictures, the media—especially the
electronic media—quickly lost interest in the Albany campaign.

In Mississippi, where the slow, painstaking work of voter registration
was more common than mass direct action protests, the heroic story of the
struggle to end black disenfranchisement was initially harder to present to
the nation in a media-friendly way. Deep poverty, rigid segregation, and
fearsome barriers to black political participation were endemic in Mississippi, the most intransigent of all the southern states. Violence against
and intimidation of civil rights workers and potential black voters were
commonplace too. Yet economic intimidation and veiled threats were hard
to capture on film, and physical violence invariably took place in jails and
on back roads, far away from the media spotlight. As leaders of the Council of Federated Organizations—the umbrella organization that coordi-

nated voter registration work in Mississippi—appreciated, the key to getting adequate press coverage of the Mississippi movement was to make sure that whites—preferably well-to-do whites—as well as blacks were exposed to this grim pattern of abuse and harassment.

In 1964, Freedom Summer brought the white sons and daughters of privilege to live and work and share danger with the poorest people in America. This eventually produced an explosion of media coverage. In my capacity as the Student Nonviolent Coordinating Committee's (SNCC) Communications Director, I helped coordinate much of that coverage. At the Oxford, Ohio, training site for summer volunteers, I directed a propaganda apparatus that photographed each student, front and profile, and recorded the name of his or her local newspapers and radio stations in anticipation of the person's expected arrest or beating in Mississippi. SNCC's publicity office tape-recorded field reports that we edited into "actualities" and fed to radio networks or hometown stations each day. Press releases were written and dispatched on a regular basis. But it was the murders of James Chaney, Andrew Goodman, and Mickey Schwerner that ensured a flood of coverage our best efforts could not have created. Their deaths made real our predictions of violence, which had been dismissed as paranoia; the presence of Goodman and Schwerner, both white, ensured America's interest in the Mississippi campaign as Chaney's death alone could not have done.

As print, radio, and television reporters, cameramen, and photographers flocked to the state and became immersed in the environment of relentless oppression, they carried back news, not just of the murders and the hunt for the killers, but also of the reasons why the Movement had come to Mississippi in the first place. As John Lewis has recalled, while they:

> tried to remain objective . . . the reporters covering Mississippi Summer became very sympathetic. They couldn't help it. Day in and day out, going into those backwoods communities as well as to the more visible towns and cities of that state, watching people singing and praying from the bottom of their souls, seeing the sorts of conditions these people were living in, with nothing for a front step but an old metal bucket turned upside down, with front porches that were nothing but a couple of planks nailed over dirt and mud with no plumbing or electricity or decent clothes for their children or themselves, just pure and utter poverty—these reporters *had* to be moved.[36]

By the time the MFDP arrived in Atlantic City to challenge the regular, whites-only, delegation at the Democratic Party's national convention that fall, this coverage meant that much of America knew what was at stake in Mississippi. For those who did not, Mrs. Fannie Lou Hamer's televised testimony to the Credentials Committee of the Convention bore unforgettable personal witness to the injustice that festered in the state and spoke eloquently of the need for change. Although the 1964 bid to unseat the regular delegation ended in failure, the widespread coverage of the Freedom Summer, of the Atlantic City challenge, and of the following year's bloody Selma campaign combined to change the climate of public opinion about the need for federal protection of black voting rights. The result was the 1965 Voting Rights Act.[37]

In this essay, I have suggested that for much of the decade after Montgomery an endlessly resourceful Movement, aided by the intemperate efforts of die-hard segregationists, furnished the media with a cavalcade of vivid confrontations, tragic setbacks, stirring victories, charismatic heroes, and demonic villains. This was just what was needed to keep the civil rights struggle at the forefront of public consciousness. Selma in 1965, however, marked the last great interracial nonviolent campaign seeking goals generally agreed upon by most Americans. Many whites believed that the passage of the Civil Rights and Voting Rights Acts rendered further black demands and protests little more than wanton troublemaking. By contrast, elements within an increasingly frustrated and fragmented Movement had begun to challenge liberal assumptions about how to correct the systemic racial inequalities that those legislative victories left untouched.

After Selma, amid calls for black power and scenes of urban rioting, white media sympathy and public support for further action on behalf of African Americans steadily evaporated. By the end of his life, even Martin Luther King was regularly castigated in the mainstream media, whether for his "unpatriotic" opposition to the war in Vietnam, or his increasingly radical critique of American capitalism and attempts to forge a class-based alliance of poor people.[38] Civil rights had stopped being a newsworthy story, although violent racial conflict and internal factionalism within the Movement could still generate headlines.

In 1964, journalist Nicholas Von Hoffman had noted that "the political position of the freedom movement is such that Negroes only win public sympathy when they are the beaten, not the beating, party."[39] Emmett Till, the Montgomery bus boycotters, the Little Rock Nine, the sit-inners, the freedom riders, the Freedom Summer volunteers, and those who marched in Birmingham and Selma were all victims: they were the wronged, the beaten, the abused, the murdered. In the late 1960s and early 1970s, press reports of black rioters and armed self-defense groups like the Black Panther Party helped to transform African Americans into the beaters. These reports varied widely in objectivity and accuracy, but the end result was that in the eyes of many whites former victims had become oppressors. Peaceful protesters were replaced by malignant looters; petitioners for a piece of the American dream were supplanted by terrorists demanding the dismantling of the state; organized nonviolent protest became armed rebellion. Even the police were sometimes now recast as noble guardians of law and order, and protectors of decent whites—the new victims—against black vengeance, rather than as instruments of racial oppression.

These new attitudes affected the media's handling of all racial matters. In February 1968, three student protesters at South Carolina State College in Orangeburg died after being shot in the back by state troopers. It was precisely the sort of outrage that had rallied much of the nation to the black cause a few years earlier. But this was a very different moment. The Orangeburg incident was very under-reported compared with earlier racial atrocities, or with the later tragedy involving the shooting of four white antiwar demonstrators by Ohio National Guardsmen at Kent State University in May 1970. Moreover, most of the limited mainstream media coverage of Orangeburg echoed the official line that the state troopers had merely responded to a lethal threat from armed black radicals. Even when overwhelming evidence emerged that a police massacre of unarmed demonstrators had actually taken place, few papers bothered to make any correction or comment, with the notable exception of the *Charlotte Observer* and the *Los Angeles Times*, where veteran Movement reporters Jack Bass and Jack Nelson, respectively, investigated the story.[40]

Bass and Nelson were part of the generation who had presented the initial story of southern black protest to a national audience as a heroic drama, a morality play that pitted black saints against southern white sinners. By contrast, their successors tended to portray the black struggle as a clash between opposing forces equally deserving of suspicion. It is worth noting that this new perspective was not restricted to civil rights and racial issues, but reflected broader shifts within American political journalism. Disillusionment with the government's conduct of the Vietnam War, the debacle of Watergate, and even the Chappaquiddick incident helped to sour the press's and the public's perceptions of American politics and its leaders. As old patterns of deference and respect for public figures and their professed ideals disintegrated, intense commercial competition and new social values encouraged increasingly sensationalist reporting of American political life and its murkier private backwaters. Consequently, whereas the profession had always attracted its share of skeptics and cynics, news coverage became discernibly more skeptical and cynical—some might say more realistic and honest—during the later 1960s and early 1970s.[41]

Paul Good had covered the Movement in the 1960s as a network bureau chief and correspondent, and as a freelancer. In his memoir, *The Trouble I've Seen,* he quotes from a UPI story sent to thousands of newspapers and hundreds of television stations during the Meredith March in the summer of 1966. It perfectly captures the cynicism and ironic detachment of a new generation of press reporters working the southern civil rights beat:

> This march has become part movement, part circus. Among the 350-odd marchers . . . are about fifty white youths who wear t-shirts and denims, sandals and weird cowboy hats adorned with Freedom buttons. One is an avowed Marxist. Another is a one-legged red-head who forsook the United States and lives in exile in Mexico.
>
> There is one marcher who starts each day at the head of the column, then drops out when the news cameras are turned off.
>
> Another white man approached a reporter to talk about the coming sexual revolution, which he said would be centered around homosexuality.
>
> This is a great assembly of kooks, said a Mississippi highway patrolman. Most newsmen agreed.[42]

Good himself felt very differently about the March and mourned his colleagues' lack of sensitivity to, or interest in, the real issues it raised. Perhaps significantly, however, his own piece appeared in the SRC's *New South,* not in the mainstream press. Nevertheless, his comments serve as a fitting epitaph for the kind of sympathetic coverage that the Movement had once been able to secure, and that had in turn helped that Movement to re-make America:

> Perhaps most newsmen in the truck rented by the wire services and TV networks that rolled at the head of the march did agree with UPI's expert appraiser of human behavior. I once saw them shoot from the truck like flushed quail when two marchers almost came to blows. Dissension was a sought-after theme. But mile after uneventful mile they sat there in the truck looking out at the shacks where the essence of the march was made flesh in the lives of Negroes

whose median income was $600 a year, whose atrophied political instincts were still held in check despite the Voting Rights Act by threat of dispossession from the land, firing from jobs or other retaliations. And those who marched in their behalf, according to this great news gathering agency, were kooks?

The astigmatic press could overlook fieldhand trucks loaded with Negro choppers heading for the $3 day-in-the sun, serfs in a cotton industry receiving a billion a year in federal subsidies. It would not bother to investigate the poverty program. Most of the press could see dissension and miss needs, point up confusion and stare straight ahead through realities of a deep South that was changing grudgingly and only when pressure grew too great to bear.[43]

Notes

1. See Jenny Walker, "A Media-Made Movement? Black Violence and Nonviolence in the Historiography of the Civil Rights Movement," in this volume.

2. For more on the postwar dilemmas and contributions of the liberal southern press, see Tony Badger, "Fatalism Not Gradualism: Race and the Crisis of Southern Liberalism, 1945–1965," in *The Making of Martin Luther King and the Civil Rights Movement*, ed. Brian Ward and Tony Badger (New York: New York University Press, 1996), 67–71.

3. Marion A. Wright, "Outside Interference in Civil Rights," *New South* 4, no. 4 (March 1949): 8.

4. Carolyn Martindale and Lillian Rae Dunlap, "The African Americans," in *U.S. News Coverage of Racial Minorities: A Sourcebook, 1934–1996*, ed. Beverly Ann Deepe Keever, Carolyn Martindale, and Mary Ann Weston (Westport, Conn.: Greenwood, 1997), 82. Martindale and Dunlap's article provides an excellent introduction to media coverage of African Americans and has greatly informed the discussion that follows.

5. Helen Louise Tatro, "Local News Coverage of Blacks in Five Deep South Newspapers, 1950 to 1970," *Journalism Abstracts* 10 (1972): 336.

6. Marion A. Wright, "Southerners for Civil Rights," Speech, April 17, 1953, Series 4, Folder 430, Box 23, Marion A. Wright Papers, Southern Historical Collection, Wilson Library, University of North Carolina, Chapel Hill; Martindale and Dunlap, "African Americans," 82.

7. For the role of respectability as both vehicle and goal of the southern civil rights movement, see Marisa Chappell, Jenny Hutchinson, and Brian Ward, "'Dress Modestly, Neatly . . . as if you were Going to Church': Respectability, Class and Gender in the Montgomery Bus Boycott and the Early Civil Rights Move-

ment," in *Gender in the Civil Rights Movement,* ed. Peter Ling and Sharon Monteith (New York: Garland, 1999), 69–100.

8. Kenneth O'Reilly, *Racial Matters: The FBI's Secret File on Black America, 1960–1972* (New York: Free Press, 1989); David J. Garrow, *The FBI and Martin Luther King, Jr.* (New York: Penguin, 1983).

9. For example, when, in the spring of 1940, a *Constitution* writer asked the Atlanta FBI office to furnish material for a feature story on the Bureau, the Atlanta Special Agent in Charge told the reporter that the FBI reserved the right to read the article before publication and "review it in the interests of accuracy." Ten days later the Atlanta agent, R. G. Danner, wrote to Hoover, telling him that the reporter "assured me that prior to printing anything he will furnish a story to this office for transmission to the Bureau for purposes of censoring it, stating that he did not desire to print anything that did not have the full approval of the Bureau." The agent sent the story to Hoover; once approved, it appeared on March 3, 1940. Other articles in the series were similarly submitted by the *Constitution* to the Atlanta FBI office and forwarded to Washington for Hoover's perusal. The Atlanta agent was warned that "he should not give the impression that the changes came from Washington." See R. G. Danner, Special Agent in Charge, Atlanta FBI, letter to J. Edgar Hoover, January 11, 1940; R. G. Danner, Special Agent in Charge, Atlanta FBI, letter to J. Edgar Hoover, January 23, 1940; R. C. Herndon, memorandum to Clyde Tolson, March 2, 1940. All FBI materials in possession of the author after a Freedom of Information Act application.

10. Barbara Barksdale Clowse, *Ralph McGill: A Biography* (Macon, Ga.: Mercer University Press, 1998), 150, 155.

11. Ibid., 215.

12. Eugene Patterson, interview by Howell Raines, in *My Soul Is Rested: The Story of the Civil Rights Movement in the Deep South,* ed. Raines (New York: Penguin, 1983), 368–69

13. Garrow, *The FBI and King;* Richard Lentz, *Symbols, the News Magazines, and Martin Luther King* (Baton Rouge: Louisiana State University Press, 1990), 135–40.

14. Eugene Patterson, interview by Howell Raines, in *My Soul Is Rested,* ed. Raines, 370.

15. See Lentz, *Symbols,* 138–40.

16. Badger, "Fatalism Not Gradualism," 69.

17. For accounts of the Montgomery bus boycott, see Martin Luther King Jr., *Stride Toward Freedom: The Montgomery Bus Boycott Story* (New York: Harper, 1957); David Garrow, *Bearing the Cross: Martin Luther King, Jr., and the Southern Christian Leadership Conference* (New York: William Morrow, 1986), 11–82; Jo Ann Robinson, *The Montgomery Bus Boycott and the Women Who Started It* (Knoxville: University of Tennessee Press, 1987); Taylor Branch, *Parting The Waters: America in the King Years, 1954–1963* (New York: Simon and Schuster, 1988), 143–205.

18. See Chappell, Hutchinson, and Ward, "Dress Neatly," 83–96.

19. See Garrow, *Bearing the Cross*; Aldon Morris, *The Origins of the Civil Rights Movement* (New York: Free Press, 1980); Robinson, *The Montgomery Bus Boycott*; John White, "'Nixon Was The One': Edgar Daniel Nixon, The MIA and the Montgomery Bus Boycott," in *The Making of Martin Luther King*, ed. Ward and Badger, 45–66; Rosa Parks, *Rosa Parks: My Story* (New York: Dial, 1992).

20. Much of the material on reporters and the Movement comes from *Covering the South: A National Symposium*, University of Mississippi, 1987, videocassette. See also Paul L. Fisher and Ralph L. Lowenstein, eds., *Race and the News Media* (New York: Praeger, 1967); Carolyn Martindale, *The White Press and Black America* (Westport, Conn.: Greenwood, 1986).

21. John Lewis, *Walking with the Wind: A Memoir of the Movement* (New York: Simon and Schuster, 1998), 112.

22. Leroy Rollins, interview by author, March 22, 1990.

23. Charles Diggs, quoted in Juan Williams, ed., *Eyes on the Prize Reader: America's Civil Rights Years, 1954–1965* (New York: Viking, 1987). The impact of the Till murder on contemporary opinion and subsequent scholarship is sensibly reviewed in Anne Sarah Rubin, "Reflections on the Death of Emmett Till," *Southern Cultures* 2, no. 1 (Fall 1995): 45–66.

24. Robert Schanke, quoted in Rodger Streitmatter, *Mightier than the Sword: How the News Media Have Shaped American History* (Boulder, Col.: Westview, 1997), 173.

25. Allison Graham, "Remapping Dogpatch: Northern Media on the Southern Circuit," *Arkansas Historical Quarterly* 56, no. 3 (Autumn 1997): 334–40.

26. *Time*, September 23, 1957, 1/12–13; Graham, "Remapping Dogpatch," 338.

27. For more on how images of these "redneck" segregationists fitted into a broader tradition of cultural representations of southern lawmen, see Allison Graham, "Reclaiming the South: Civil Rights Films and the New Red Menace," in this volume.

28. Dick Sanders, in *Covering the South*.

29. Graham, "Remapping Dogpatch," 339–40.

30. Sharon Bramlett-Solomon, "Southern vs. Northern Newspaper Coverage of the Dime Store Demonstration Movement: A Study of News Play and News Source Diversity," *Mass Communications Review* 15 (1988): 24–30.

31. James Jackson Kilpatrick, Editorial, *Richmond News Leader*, February 22, 1960.

32. Martindale, *White Press and Black America*, 79–80.

33. John W. Kingdom, *Congressmen's Voting Decisions*, 3rd ed. (Ann Arbor: University of Michigan Press, 1989), 223, 284.

34. Gerald N. Rosenberg, *The Hollow Hope* (Chicago: University of Chicago Press, 1991), 111–16.

35. See Laurie Pritchett, interview by Howell Raines, *My Soul Is Rested*, ed. Raines, 361–66.

36. Lewis, *Walking with the Wind*, 267–68

37. For the Freedom Summer, see Doug McAdam, *Freedom Summer* (New York: Oxford University Press, 1988). For more on the role of SNCC's Communications Office in coordinating press coverage of events, see Mary King, *Freedom Song: A Personal Story of the 1960s Civil Rights Movement* (New York: William Morrow, 1987).

38. For increasingly hostile newsmagazine coverage of King's last years, see Lentz, *Symbols*, 236–80.

39. Nicholas Von Hoffman, *Mississippi Notebook* (New York: David White, 1964), 14.

40. See Jack Bass and Jack Nelson, *The Orangeburg Massacre* (Macon, Ga.: Mercer University Press, 1984).

41. In a 1990 study of presidential politics, Professor Thomas Patterson of the Maxwell School of Government said the tone and content of news coverage of politics had darkened dramatically over the previous thirty years. In the 1960 presidential campaign, he found that 60 percent of the coverage of the candidates in *Time* and *Newsweek* was favorable. In 1988, only 30 percent of the coverage was favorable. The same trend could be found among newspapers and television. "Increasingly, the thread running through it is, there is something wrong with the campaign, there is something wrong with the candidate," Professor Patterson said. Thomas Patterson, quoted in Michael Oreskes, "America's Politics Loses Its Way As Vision Changes World," *New York Times*, March 18, 1990.

42. Paul Good, *The Trouble I've Seen: White Journalist, Black Movement* (Washington, D.C.: Howard University Press, 1975), 256–57.

43. Ibid., 257.

2

A Media-Made Movement?

Black Violence and Nonviolence in the Historiography
of the Civil Rights Movement

Jenny Walker

On June 18, 1963, the *New York Times* carried a front page story about racial clashes that had erupted the previous night in Harlem. The trouble occurred when a policeman asked a black ice-cream seller to move on because he had no vendor's license. According to the *Times*, the ice-cream seller grew irate and refused to move. Within a few minutes, the altercation had attracted a large crowd that quickly became agitated and "set off a series of clashes between angry Negroes and the police [in which] . . . several persons were injured, including two policemen, and at least twenty-seven were arrested." The article continued, "stones shattered the windows of a jewelry store and a flying bottle struck a patrol car." As more police arrived, tensions mounted. Fires were started and "Two shots were reported fired. . . . The police estimated that one thousand persons were in the scattered crowds at their height. . . . It looked like an armed camp."[1]

In stark contrast to much of the reporting of urban unrest later in the 1960s, the treatment of this story by the *New York Times* was relatively even-handed, taking care to point out that although two shots were fired "police were unable to learn the source of the shooting." Later in the decade, newspapers would tell of "nests of snipers" waging guerrilla warfare on police with far less evidence to sustain their claims than here. Most significantly, the article did not refer to the event as a "riot," preferring to designate it less sensationally—and more accurately—as "a series of clashes."[2]

Some three years later, another "series of clashes," this time in Cambridge, Maryland, did not receive such objective reporting in the nation's press. On July 24, 1967, H. Rap Brown, the outspoken chairman of the

Student Nonviolent Coordinating Committee (SNCC), traveled to Cambridge. The Black Action Federation, a local black protest group, had invited Brown to the city in response to a wave of violent attacks on the black community by the Ku Klux Klan (KKK) and the States Rights Party. That evening, Brown addressed a crowd of several hundred young black citizens. He told them, "If America don't come around, we're going to burn it down. . . . We are going to burn it down if we don't get our share of it." Brown berated the crowd: "You got to own some of them stores. I don't care if you have to burn [the white man] down and run him out. . . . Don't love him to death . . . shoot him to death."[3]

The following day newspapers reported that, shortly after Brown's speech, Cambridge had exploded into violence and that Brown was now wanted by the Federal Bureau of Investigation (FBI) on charges of "inciting a riot." In discussing this "riot," the print media focused on gun battles that it claimed had taken place between blacks and police officers, and on a wave of arson attacks that had resulted in many buildings being burned to the ground. Thus it highlighted what were conventionally agreed to be the chief ingredients of a riot: mass violence against people and property along with a general breakdown of law and order.

The *New York Times,* for example, described a night of "wild shooting in the Negro district" and quoted from Brown's speech at some length. It further reported that Brown himself had been shot "in the left forehead by a single pellet from one of more than a dozen shotgun blasts on Pine Street in the Negro section of Cambridge about an hour after his fiery speech." Shortly afterward, the *Times* continued, "a white city policeman . . . riding through the Negro district was shot in the face and right hand."[4]

A day later, the *Times* was luridly referring to the Cambridge incident as "a night of gunfire and arson . . . a night of incendiarism and sniping." It described how, "fires, raging out of control for hours early this morning, destroyed nearly two blocks of the city's Negro section."[5] The *Washington Afro-American, Washington Post, Time* magazine, and the *New Republic,* among numerous other newspapers and magazines, agreed with the *New York Times* that a riot had indeed taken place in Cambridge.[6]

In contrast to these contemporary press reports, an analysis of the events in Cambridge by David Boesel and Louis Goldberg for the President's National Advisory Commission on Civil Disorders (also known as the Kerner Commission), which was never formally published as part of the Commission's findings, told a somewhat different story. Their investigation revealed that "what has come to be known as the Cambridge riot was in fact a low-level civil disturbance. . . . there were small scale disorders by Negro crowds, but nothing of the magnitude anticipated by local authorities or reported in the press."[7]

According to the Commission, the first violence in the Cambridge disturbance had taken place at 10:05 P.M. on the night of July 24, when Brown, followed by twenty-five to thirty people, was walking away from the meeting. "Without prior warning, a deputy sheriff stationed at Race Street discharge[d] a shotgun twice. Brown [was] slightly wounded by one of the pellets."[8] This explanation of how Brown came to be shot is certainly at odds with reports in the contemporary press that implied he was caught in the crossfire of bullets in the black neighborhood. The Commission was quite clear that Brown had been shot by a policeman, but the *New York Times* did not report this; instead, it pointedly stated that the shooting had involved "a total of about fifteen blasts over a period of more than an hour. . . . Newsmen and persons on the crowded street fell to the ground and took cover in the doorways as shots rang out."[9]

At 10:10 P.M., continued the Commission's report, a group of whites drove through the black neighborhood three times "either shooting or throwing firecrackers" at the local residents. Although, according to the media, a full-scale armed black uprising was already underway by this time, it was not actually until the third run through the black neighborhood, at 12:30 A.M., that some locals apparently armed themselves and returned fire. Moreover, while one police officer was shot that evening, the shooting occurred far away from the main unrest in the city and, according to the report, there were certainly no gun battles with police as the press had indicated.[10]

The media accounts of widespread arson attacks were also misleading. There were only three fires started that evening. One occurred when a group of black youths poured some gasoline on the road and lit it. A second fire was started in a store. Both fires were extinguished almost immediately. The only fire that caused any significant structural damage during the alleged "riot" was at a local black school—a school that even the city officials had admitted was a fire trap. According to the Commission, the school had become a symbol in the black community of "an intransigent school system" and consequently there had already been two or three previous attempts to burn it down.[11] The newspapers predictably neglected to mention this context and laid the blame squarely on H. Rap Brown's inflammatory speech.

In all, sixteen buildings were damaged by the school fire, which quickly engulfed two blocks of the black business district. This, however, was not, as the press had implied, an indication of widespread arson and violence in Cambridge. Rather it was evidence that one of the three fires set that night had got out of control. Indeed, although a group of blacks had gathered around the scene of the school conflagration, the Commission noted that they were "not violent [and] many of the members want[ed] to help put out the fire." Interviews with Cambridge black residents in the wake of the disturbance revealed that far from inciting people to riot and burn, "there [was] little evidence that Brown's speech stirred the crowd to action." Indeed, "the response to his exhortations was not universally favorable, some Negroes taking exception to his strident militancy. And immediately after the speech the crowd began to disperse." While Brown's speech may have added to the tense atmosphere within which the evening's disturbances took place, Boesel and Goldberg insisted that there was no hard evidence that Brown was responsible for starting the "riot," and that the press had relied on "the constant repetition of 'Brown—riot in Cambridge' . . . [to] help create th[at] impression."[12] Their report concluded that "if we accept widespread mass violence as one of the definitive characteristics of a riot, the term seems inappropriate to the events in Cambridge."[13]

Various other sources also cast doubts on the accuracy of contemporary press accounts of the Cambridge incident and, in particular, of Rap Brown's responsibility for the violence. Perhaps not surprisingly, Brown's own account of that evening does not suggest that he went to Cambridge intent on starting a riot; rather he argues that the police were the ones who started the trouble. In his autobiography, *Die Nigger Die!*, Brown recalled that his speech passed off without incident, although there was a strong police presence that agitated the crowd. After his speech, he agreed to walk a young woman home because she was afraid of the large number of police who were hanging around in the black neighborhood. Brown recalled, "I was walking down the street with her and I noticed that everybody was walking with us. . . . We got about halfway down the street and somebody opened fire from some bushes. . . . I got shot—I was shot in the head with some of the shotgun pellets. . . . The cops who were doing the shooting just kept shooting."[14]

Former Cambridge civil rights leader Gloria Richardson also believed that the police were more responsible for the violence in Cambridge than Rap Brown. She remembered that General Gelston of the National Guard had contacted her prior to Rap Brown's arrival in Cambridge asking to speak with him, to "set up something [with Brown] that would contain whatever Cambridge police might try to do." Brown refused to speak to him, but Richardson nevertheless tried to warn Rap Brown not to incite the crowd. But, she recalled, "he went on and did it anyhow. So, I guess the police were probably ready for him."[15]

In the end, in a manner that was repeated time and again in the fiery atmosphere of the late 1960s, there was more than an element of self-fulfilling prophecy about the trouble in Cambridge. Sensational stories of Rap Brown's impending arrival and the violence that would inevitably follow filled the pages of the local press and terrified Cambridge's local authorities, who promptly increased the police presence in the black neighborhood. For a black community, resentful and angry at a long record of police brutality, and bitter about its lack of real progress, such an increased police presence could only add to the sense of oppression. In such a tense and suspicious climate real violence was much more likely to occur. Brown clearly did not initiate the violence in Cambridge, but he was hardly a passive figure in the unfolding events. As Gloria Richardson suggested, Brown was only too aware that the police were just waiting for a signal that a riot was about to begin, and were primed to respond forcefully. Brown's speech provided that signal and, as such, was undoubtedly the catalyst for the violent outbreak.

Nevertheless, it is crucial to recognize the precise nature of Brown's influence on these events. As Boesel and Goldberg appreciated, "To the extent that Brown encouraged anybody to engage in precipitous or disorderly acts, the city officials are clearly the ones he influenced most. Indeed, the riot existed for the most part in the[ir] minds."[16] Essentially, Brown went ahead and gave a speech that he fully expected would provoke a violent response from law enforcement officers—but the point is that this was not substantially different from the actions of Martin Luther King and other nonviolent activists who frequently staged protests anticipating the sort of violent police responses on which they depended for favorable publicity. If there was a difference, it was that Brown was far more attuned than King to the very real possibility of black retaliation; yet King himself was often unpleasantly surprised when—as in the Southern Christian Leadership Conference's (SCLC) own 1963 campaign in Birmingham, Alabama—blacks refused to turn the other cheek against police brutality.

The lack of evidence to justify exaggerated press accounts of a full-scale "riot" in Cambridge raises the question of why that incident received sensational media coverage when events in Harlem in 1963 had not. Part of the answer is that, in 1963, the Harlem story was simply not considered as newsworthy, or perhaps even as significant in terms of America's wider racial situation, as similar incidents later in the decade. The major racial news stories of the early 1960s were not of riots, but rather of mass "nonviolent" protests in Birmingham and elsewhere in the South, led by "peaceful" men like Martin Luther King Jr. The Harlem incident, it would seem, was treated as a northern aberration in an otherwise largely southern-based, nonviolent movement for black civil rights.

By the time of the Cambridge incident, however, America had witnessed four successive summers of racial disturbances. With its shocking levels of destruction, violence, and fatalities, the Watts riot of August 1965 had represented something of a watershed in popular and press attitudes to urban strife. Watts announced the continued anger, frustration, and disaffection of many African Americans and deeply shocked those complacent whites who believed that America's racial problems had ended with the passage of the 1964 Civil Rights Act and the 1965 Voting Rights Act. Furthermore, on the very day in July 1967 when Brown was visiting Cambridge, newspapers were full of stories of what were—by almost any meaningful definition—riots in numerous cities including Englewood, New Jersey; Grand Rapids, Michigan; Phoenix and Tucson, Arizona; and, most seriously, Detroit. In this atmosphere the press seemed inclined to interpret almost any violent urban incident with racial overtones as a riot. An August 5, 1967, *New Republic* article titled "Blow-Up in the Cities" clearly demonstrated this tendency, noting that "We can now see that the mass protests of the early and middle 1960s and the response of the Congress were only dimly relevant to the lives of most Negroes." For this reason, "combat areas multiply as more and more Negroes pile into the cities, which more and more look like overcrowded prisons." The article then listed these so-called combat areas: "In 1965, Watts; in 1966, Chicago, Cicero, Harlem; in 1967, Newark, Detroit, Minneapolis, Plainfield, New Jersey; Hartford, Connecticut; Kansas City, Missouri; Waterloo, Iowa." The list concluded with "Cambridge, Maryland."[17]

There was clearly a vast chasm between the Detroit riot and the Cambridge disturbance in terms of the nature and extent of black violence in the two cities, but the mainstream press ignored such nuances and interpreted events in both places in much the same way. Even SNCC's newspaper, *The Movement,* followed this trend—although for entirely different reasons. By August 1967, the rapidly radicalizing organization was only too eager to encourage the idea that black America was in a state of rebellion. Editorializing that "America's poor are in revolt. In Watts, Harlem, Cambridge, Newark, the violent uprisings of black people were the last defense against physical and cultural extermination," *The Movement* joined the mainstream media in choosing to ignore the manifold differences between these disturbances and opted to dub them all "violent uprisings."[18]

Despite the lack of evidence for characterizing the Cambridge incident as a riot, histories of the freedom struggle during the black power era largely replicate contemporary press accounts. For example, Harvard Sitkoff's standard overview, *The Struggle for Black Equality*, has Cambridge exploding into violence and slavishly follows the press line by blaming Brown's speech.[19] Robert Weisbrot's *Freedom Bound* similarly repeats the story of how "blacks rioted in downtown Cambridge," and offers no analysis or commentary beyond those provided at the time by the press and the far-from-objective Maryland governor, Spiro Agnew, who "blamed H. Rap Brown as the root cause as well as catalyst of the Cambridge riot. Agnew hoped that authorities would jail the SNCC leader 'and throw away the key.'"[20] Clayborne Carson's *In Struggle* explains that "No violence occurred during Brown's speech, but about an hour afterwards gunshots were exchanged between black residents and police." There were no such exchanges in Cambridge; they existed only in the pages of the press. By early next morning, Carson casually notes, "seventeen buildings had been damaged or destroyed, and recently elected governor Spiro T. Agnew sent the National Guard to the city."[21] Like the press accounts, Carson offers no qualification for this statement and thus wrongly implies that there were many fires started that evening.

To be fair, other historians more fully immersed in the study of the black power era have been rather more aware of the distortive tendencies of the press and its proclivity for sensationalism and exaggeration. For instance, William Van Deburg notes in *New Day in Babylon* that "The historical context in which the militant operated magnified their every threat and made it appear that Armageddon was as near as they claimed."[22] And yet, all too often, less sensitive historians evoke a new breed of black power militants whose threat to society, while exaggerated in the press, was nevertheless predicated upon a very real—and a very new—repertoire of violent gestures, language, and action that would have been anathema in the nonviolent era. What, perhaps, is under-emphasized in the historiography is the degree to which this symbolic, rhetorical, and actual violence was not a new departure in the black freedom struggle at all, but an extension of some decidedly violent aspects of the supposedly "nonviolent" era. In other words, the historiography of the Movement still turns largely around a media-inspired, but historically flawed contrast between a southern, church-based nonviolent civil rights movement and a secular, violent black power era centered on the cities of the North. In fact, as this essay will suggest, there was a great degree of continuity in the character and extent of black violence between the two eras. Moreover, the failure of many historians to recognize this fact, or at least to incorporate it into what Brian Ward has dubbed the "master narrative" of the modern freedom struggle, is one legacy of the distinctly partisan treatment of the early Movement by important sections of the mass media.[23]

In their own way, national press reports of the civil rights movement in the late 1950s and early 1960s were just as culpable as those in the black power era for misrepresenting the extent and nature of black violence in the freedom struggle, thus helping to obscure the continuities between the two eras. During the earlier period, elements in the American press—black and white, conservative and liberal, northern and southern—often seemed inclined to ignore, downplay or de-politicize incidents of black violence and inflammatory rhetoric in civil rights protests—or at least they strove to disassociate such phenomena from the mainstream civil rights movement. In so doing, these press reports underrepresented the relatively high incidence of black violence—rhetorical and actual—that occurred around the edges, and occasionally in the midst, of the putatively nonviolent Movement.

This sort of willful media myopia has had a particularly distortive effect on histories of the early southern Movement, which are often heavily dependent on contemporary media accounts for their broad narrative framework and much of their finer interpretative detail. Whereas some of the scholarship on black power now betrays a healthy skepticism toward the press's sensationalist coverage of black violence, historians of the southern civil rights campaigns have tended to be far less sensitive to possible biases in the press's descriptions of stoically nonviolent black protests. This uncritical dependence on press coverage has often rendered black violence either invisible or, at best, a shadowy, barely apprehended—and badly comprehended—anomaly in most historical accounts of the early Movement. In fact, the black potential for, and sometimes recourse to, violence was a critical element in the southern freedom struggle, enjoying a symbiotic relationship with the nonviolent direct action wing of that insurgency.

The Montgomery bus boycott of 1955–56 provides an excellent example of the way in which an overreliance on press accounts has distracted historians' attentions from the latent potential for black violence during a remarkably, but by no means universally, nonviolent campaign. The moment when black violence most obviously became a distinct possibility was in the wake of the bombing of King's home on January 30, 1956, when an angry and armed crowd of black citizens gathered outside, intent on revenge. Journalists and historians in telling this story have focused on the fact that King persuaded the seething mob to return home peacefully. Thus, the departure from nonviolent discipline is reduced to a parable about King's unswerving commitment to that philosophy and the extent of his personal charisma—which he employs to revitalize the black community's own momentarily wavering passion for nonviolence.[24]

Yet viewed from another perspective, this same incident invites a rather different interpretation: that a willingness to take up arms to resist white aggression, sometimes spilling over into a desire for vengeance against an oppressive and sometimes brutal white community, lurked permanently beneath the respectable surface of the nonviolent boycott. There is certainly plenty of evidence of such attitudes in black Montgomery. In the early days of the protest, before becoming the figure most readily associated with nonviolence and redemptive love for one's enemies, Martin Luther King Jr. had angrily told a meeting of the Montgomery Improvement Association (MIA) that "What needs to be done is for a couple of those white men to lose some blood; then the Federal Government will step in."[25] The future apostle of nonviolence even had guns in his home and—unlike the Black Panthers a decade or so later—did not even have a permit for them. At an MIA executive board meeting, King announced, "I went to the sheriff to get a permit for those people who are guarding me. Couldn't get one."[26] There were guns everywhere in February 1956 when Bayard Rustin arrived in Montgomery to advise King on the principles and practicalities of Gandhian nonviolence; when he returned in March, Rustin noted that "[King's] house was still being protected by armed guards."[27]

Elsewhere in Montgomery, legitimate black anger sometimes fueled a desire to exact bloody revenge on racist whites, rather than to convert or redeem them through the black capacity to suffer. On July 22, 1956, a mass meeting was held in Montgomery. Glenn Smiley, the Fellowship of Reconciliation's emissary and a leading tactician of nonviolent direct action, was directing the proceedings. Earlier that day, two black girls had gone to a grocery store to buy some grapes. When the storekeeper's son charged the girls sixteen cents for the grapes the girls confessed that they only had fifteen cents and therefore they could not buy them. The shopkeeper's son told them that they must buy the grapes and the girls once again told him that they did not have enough money. After several minutes of this pointless exchange, the girls, now scared to death, ran away. The boy chased them out of the shop and beat them up. The mass meeting that evening had been called to decide whether or not the community should boycott the store. The boy's father, only too aware of the damage that such a boycott would do to his store, attended the meeting to apologize for his son's actions, but the assembled crowd would not listen. Instead, as Smiley recalled, "the majority of Negroes there were 'yelling for the man's blood.'"[28]

Five days later on July 27, the day after King had been arrested for operating a car pool in Montgomery, boycotters were overheard commenting on their attitudes toward the white community. Willie Mae Wallace stated, "I'm so mad I don't know what to do. Do you know those bastards put Rev. King in jail last night? . . . They think they bad cause they got guns, but I sho hope they know how to use 'em cause if they don't, I'll cut em wid this razor. . . . He'll be in pieces so fast he won't know what hit im. . . . I don't mind dying, but I'm sho taking a white bastard with me"; other boycotters claimed, "Dey best not come into our neighborhood by de self. . . . some of 'em gonna mess right round here and get killed."[29] Crucially, such stories did not make it into press accounts of Montgomery, where they would have complicated—and perhaps even compromised—the overwhelmingly positive portrayal of a campaign for legitimate civil rights pursued by righteous, civilized and, above all, peaceful means.[30]

The process by which civil rights stories came to appear or, just as importantly, not appear in the pages of the American press, and the manner in which they were treated in those pages, was a complex affair. It is beyond the scope of this essay to discuss those politics of production at any length but, as Brian Ward has pointed out, the style, scope, and substance of Movement coverage was invariably negotiated between editors, sponsors, and a large disparate group of "journalists, . . . publishers, advertising salesmen, lawyers, market researchers and accountants." The very appearance, not to mention the tone, content, and moral thrust, of any story was likely to emerge from the interplay of their "often competing, personal and professional agendas."[31] Broadly speaking, however, it seems that the relative neglect of southern black violence during the nonviolent era, in both the black and white press, derived mainly from two related concerns. The first was a desire not to undermine the effectiveness and appeal of nonviolent direct action; the second was a desire not to encourage more notionally "militant" forms of black activism and resistance.

These twin agendas can certainly be detected in the response of the press to Robert Williams and the activities of his armed self-defense group in Monroe, North Carolina. As Tim Tyson—one of the few Movement historians to grapple seriously with the tradition of violent black resistance in the modern freedom struggle—has recounted, in 1957 Williams and his followers met a KKK attack with gunfire, causing the Klan to flee.

In the wake of this incident, the city government passed an ordinance banning parades or caravans of more than three cars from entering the town without a police escort. This effectively put an end to the sixty-car convoys that had been terrorizing the black community. Black Monroe had been asking for such an ordinance for years, but it was only in the wake of Williams's violent resistance that it was secured.[32] Given the magnitude of this achievement—that armed black resistance had succeeded where nonviolent direct action had conspicuously failed—perhaps it should not surprise us that there was an almost complete news blackout of the event. Only three news publications carried the story: the *Norfolk Journal and Guide*, the *Baltimore Afro-American*, and *Jet* magazine. No white newspaper even so much as alluded to the incident.[33]

For the white press, especially conservative southern newspapers, black nonviolent direct action protests were enough of a threat to the racial status quo, without drawing attention to the fact that some blacks were angry enough to challenge segregation, disenfranchisement, and the tyranny of white power in more aggressive, even violent ways. Indeed, many southern newspapers were reluctant to carry stories about black protests—violent or otherwise—at all. As Birmingham's civil rights leader Fred Shuttlesworth recalled, "You got to remember the press did a lot to block out our program. For the first seven years, if I wanted to get a release out of Birmingham I would call Carl and Anne Braden in Louisville, and they would put out over the [National Newspaper Press Association]; and many times, things would be carried to New York . . . ."[34]

On the rare occasions when southern white papers did report on black violence in places where an organized movement was underway, they were usually very eager to disassociate it from any political motive, preferring to portray such violence as simple acts of black criminality. For instance, in December 1956, the *Birmingham News* carried a report about how six young black boys had shot at a bus during the bus boycott in that city. Although the boys had fired into the white section of the bus, the paper went to great lengths to stress that "the incident had nothing to do with Negro efforts to end segregation on buses here."[35] Similarly, when black violence broke out at a sit-in demonstration in Knoxville, Tennessee, where "Negro youths were . . . running in a gang and knocking white people off the sidewalks" the *Birmingham News* was equally careful to insist that "those arrested were not taking part in the sit-in demonstrations."[36]

Northern white newspapers, even those liberal publications that generally supported the early Movement, seemed equally concerned not to dwell on incidents of black violence. While they were usually happy to promote the nonviolent struggle associated with the respectable and responsible Martin Luther King Jr., they did not want to promote what they considered to be a more militant, potentially violent, leadership. Julian Mayfield, a black journalist who worked with Robert Williams as well as writing about him, encountered this agenda when he tried to file his reports. "I could not get any information out . . . there was a blackout . . . or should I say a whiteout or something?" he recalled. "I mean the *New York Times* would not print anything. Ted Poston had introduced me over the telephone to [the] . . . editor of the *New York Post* who'd asked me for a series of articles . . . but he sent back the articles saying he'd read them and he liked them, but he wasn't going to print them . . . because he didn't approve of Williams . . . and I think the last line of his letter said something like this, 'I'll manage Martin Luther King Jr. . . . I really can't support your guy.'"[37]

For black newspapers, coverage of a story like the one in Monroe was a potentially dangerous undertaking that could lead to economic and terrorist reprisals. Robert Johnson, managing editor of *Jet* magazine, recalled how fellow editor Emory Jackson, of the *Birmingham World*, had a gun pulled on him in an elevator by a policeman anxious to persuade him to stop chasing a controversial story. On another occasion, a policeman burned Jackson with a cigarette.[38] C. A. Scott, editor of the *Atlanta Daily World*, agreed that editors needed to be careful about which reports they chose to publish. Explaining how he selected stories, he stated, "we certainly don't want to make unnecessary enemies for our race. . . . Therefore we must be careful and we must properly evaluate news in its presentation to our readers, because . . . it wouldn't be wise for us to present the news to our readers in such a fashion that it will eventually result in ill will and resentment toward the white race. That wouldn't be wise."[39]

Robert Williams also recognized this basic caution and defensiveness on the part of black proprietors and editors, who were keen to avoid trouble and therefore tended to steer clear of anything too controversial. Talking about reactions to his group's decision to defend itself with weapons, he said, "Blacks were so afraid until they didn't want to have anything to do with it at all . . . the black papers were hostile . . . toward the people in Monroe and me. And they were afraid it would appear that they were condoning self defense, and so they were trying to give an image of being pacifist, and being great supporters of Rev. King."[40]

That the press of all hues practiced some kind of voluntary censorship regarding Williams and the attack on the KKK seems all the more plausible in the light of the events of January 18, 1958, in Maxton, North Carolina, when a large group of Lumbee Indians attacked Klansmen attending a cross-burning rally. The Klan had launched a campaign of terror against the Lumbees in the preceding weeks and the Indians had finally had enough. They descended on the rally with guns, knives, and war whoops; the Klansmen fled without putting up any kind of fight, even though most of them were carrying weapons of their own. Unlike the incident in Monroe, which saw defensive violence employed by black residents protecting their homes and families, this incident involved offensive violence on the part of the Lumbees directed against a group of people who had legally rented private land in order to hold their meeting. The local sheriff, Malcolm McLeod, admitted to Klan Grand Wizard James "Catfish" Cole that "You have leased the field and have a right to be here." However, this did not stop him from indicting Cole with "inciting a riot" and from praising the efforts of the Lumbees who, one could argue, had denied the Klan of their constitutional right to assemble.[41]

In real terms then, the Lumbee assault on the Klan was far more aggressive and—at best—ambiguous in its legality than the black action in Monroe. Consequently, one could be forgiven for assuming that the whole affair might have been even less acceptable to the American media and to the white South than the Williams affair. The Lumbees, however, were not black; nor were they engaged in a rapidly congealing mass movement against white power, and this made a vital difference.[42] As Williams's earliest biographer Robert Cohen has suggested, "While [the Lumbee story] had sentimental value, it posed no danger to the status quo. What the blacks had done in Monroe, on the other hand, appeared to impress them as a potential threat."[43] Virtually every newspaper carried the story of the Maxton rout, praising the efforts of the Lumbees who had taught the Klan a lesson. In editorials around the country the Klansmen were the target of ridicule. The *Charlotte News* referred to "a rag-tag assortment of Ku Klux Klansmen . . . bed sheeted buffoons"; the *Montgomery Advertiser,* under the headline "Klusters Last Stand," argued that "the Klan trash has been made to look more ridiculous in their flight from the Indians than by all else together"; and the *Baltimore Sun* claimed that "The picture of Klansmen running from a fusillade of airshots reduces Klan pretensions to the raucously comic."[44]

Ironically, while the belligerent Lumbees got the press coverage that Monroe's defensive blacks did not, some of the black newspapers that had failed to report on the Williams incident bemoaned the fact that southern blacks did not stand up to the Klan. The *Pittsburgh Courier* hoped that

"Robeson County's Negroes may have learned something from the measures one thousand enraged Indians took to break up a giant rally of the KKK."[45] The *Amsterdam News* similarly reported that Lumbee Mayor Oxendine "said he feels the way the Indians dealt with the Klansmen is the way the Negroes should deal with them. One young Lumbee Indian was quoted as saying, 'The Negroes should have done something about this.'" In an editorial, the paper asked, "Since Negroes are constantly persecuted by the Klan, the question naturally arises as to whether or not the Indian treatment of the Klan offers a solution to the Negro's problem .... For we have noted that whenever and wherever a group of determined men have banded together and let the KKK know that they are not frightened by their hooded sheets, the Klan has turned tail and fled. Unfortunately in past years it has been Negroes who have fled."[46]

Such editorials illustrate the ways in which the black news media felt obliged to pick its way through the controversies that always seemed on the verge of engulfing the Movement. The Maxton story was safe in a way that the Monroe story could never be—not least because the white news media had reported it, thereby in effect declaring it fit for coverage. The Lumbee incident gave black newspapers the opportunity to speculate about the possibility of a similar black aggression against the Klan, but it was still considered far too dangerous to refer directly to a real instance— as in Monroe—where this had actually happened. Indeed, the *Amsterdam News,* when it called for blacks to follow the Lumbees' lead, was careful to stress that "We don't condone violence in any form. . . . we don't approve of the shooting."[47]

Whatever the precise reasons, the press's underreporting or misrepresentation of black violence in North Carolina was clearly a widespread phenomenon in the late 1950s and early-to-mid 1960s. Less than a month after Williams's shoot-out with the Klan and a little more than two months before the Lumbee incident, a group of black residents in Prattsville, Alabama, similarly armed and defended themselves against the Klan. Once again, in stark contrast to coverage of the Lumbee attack, no national white newspapers carried the story. And just as with the Williams incident, only the *Norfolk Journal and Guide* and the *Baltimore Afro-American* from the black press reported it at all. The *Guide* stated that "Colored citizens of this small Alabama town remained in a state of fear this week after police reported they had no clues or leads in the recent six cross burnings here. But some of the people readied shotguns just in case the incidents are repeated. Observers said six crosses were burned in the area last Tuesday and that several shots were fired by Negroes as excitement reached a peak during the night."[48] The *Baltimore Afro-American* similarly noted that "Several shots were fired and reporters found residents armed with shotguns when they went into the area."[49]

In August 1961 an anonymous report from a SNCC worker (believed to be James Forman) in Nashville, Tennessee, began, "Last night I witnessed the first reprisals by Negroes on white hoodlums who were threatening the very life of the innocent picketers in the front of H. G. Hills grocery store on 16th and Grand." A nonviolent picket that was being attacked by a white mob attracted a large black crowd of around four hundred people. According to the report, "a group of [blacks] crossed the street and stood in front of the thugs. The picketers continued to march nonviolently." The black crowd was goaded by the white thugs, who called them "cowards . . . [who] had better get back where they belong." As the report told it, "One white youth jumped out [of] his car and dared the Negroes to attack. The fight was on and it's difficult to say who started it. But in three minutes there were three police wagons, five squad cars and two motorbikes." Local and national papers again failed to produce a single news story relating to this incident.[50]

In April 1963, SNCC members were working in Greenwood, Mississippi, on a voter registration campaign. On April 3, while on a march to the city hall, the nonviolent demonstrators were ordered to disband by police. Mrs. Laura McGhee, unhappy at the treatment they were receiving at the hands of the local police, attacked a policeman, snatched his nightstick and would have beaten him with it if comedian-activist Dick Gregory had not restrained her.[51] Press reports the following day simply failed to mention this incident; rather they focused on the violent and unreasonable behavior of the police who, despite appearing to be "on their best behavior because of the presence of a swarm of news reporters and FBI agents," still managed to arrest the "Rev. Robert M. Kinloch, associate pastor of the Baptist Chapel of the Free Spirit, New York . . . with such force that his clerical collar flew open."[52]

A similar incident happened in Selma, Alabama, in January 1965. Black protesters were waiting to register to vote, when Sheriff Jim Clark and his deputies arrived and tried to stop the proceedings. Mrs. Annie Lee Cooper, much like Mrs. McGhee, objected to the rough treatment Clark meted out to the peaceful registrants. As David Garrow notes, when Sheriff Clark approached, Mrs. Cooper "managed to send [him] reeling with a powerful punch to the head." Clark and two deputies retaliated to this attack and "in the flailing, kicking struggle that followed Sheriff Clark clubbed her." On this occasion, the press did include an account of the incident in their coverage of the Selma protest, but chose to present it in the most sympathetic way possible by downplaying Mrs. Cooper's initial assault and focusing instead on Clark's excessive use of force. Accompanying a front page photograph of Mrs. Cooper being pinned down by the deputies while Sheriff Clark wielded his nightstick, *New York Times* reporter John Herbers wrote, "She put up quite a battle as the officers seized her and threw her to the ground . . . . [Sheriff Clark] then brought the billy club down on her head with a whack that was heard throughout the crowd." A similar report appeared in the *Washington Post,* subtly casting doubts on Clark's claim that he was responding to an assault, not initiating one (*"he said* she struck him" (italics added); not "she struck him"), and hinting that any violence by Mrs. Cooper was a defensive response to a vicious police beating ("she bites and fights *back*"—italics added). Thus, the press worked hard to transform an unmistakable breakdown in nonviolent discipline into a story that preserved something of the moral high ground for Mrs. Cooper and the Movement.[53]

David Garrow's sensitivity to the partisan reporting of the Cooper incident is relatively unusual, if by no means unknown among historians of the early southern Movement. By and large, however, their overreliance on the press has resulted in a failure to appreciate both the sheer pervasiveness and the significance of the black violence that permeated the era of nonviolent protest. Indeed, when they have caught glimpses of black violence, historians have often described them, with an undisguised hint of surprise, as aberrations. Robert Weisbrot, in recalling the "occasional scuffles between black youths and white toughs" that "marred the remarkable decorum of the sit-ins in 1960" and the "rock throwing in Birmingham" during SCLC's campaign there, is fairly typical in describing these events as "rare departures." The point, however, is that such incidents were far from rare; they were commonplace and an inextricable part of the milieu in which the Movement developed.[54]

On July 11, 1962, during the joint SNCC/SCLC campaign in Albany, Georgia, blacks on several occasions threw rocks and bottles at police. On a nonviolent SNCC march in Cambridge, Maryland, SNCC member Judy Richardson kicked an Atlanta policeman in the groin because he was mistreating a black demonstrator. In her defense, she simply said, "it forced me to do something."[55] C. T. Vivian, a worker in SCLC's 1964 campaign in St. Augustine, Florida, recalled that many members of the black community in that historic town were armed and prepared to defend themselves. He remembered how white racists "used to ride through the Negro neighborhoods and shoot out windows. Then the Negroes would shoot back."[56]

Robert Hayling, the local movement leader, recalled that "armed guards watched over [Martin Luther] King [Jr.] every night that he spent in St. Augustine."[57] Hayling also noted that there had been "a dispersing of arms" in the black community, due to "the extreme activity of the Klan, the lack of police protection, and so forth."[58] SCLC's Hosea Williams, in recalling his experiences during the same campaign, added, "If I had known what I know now about this town, I doubt if I would have come here. . . . Man, these Negroes were really violent."[59]

The SCLC campaign in Selma, Alabama, also experienced black violence—illustrating that Annie Lee Cooper's lapse was no isolated incident; it was part of a broader pattern where black frustration and anger often boiled over into acts of retaliatory violence against oppressors who were terrorizing the southern black population, especially those in and around the Movement. On March 7, 1965—"Bloody Sunday"—nonviolent marchers were attacked on Pettus Bridge and chased by Sheriff Jim Clark's men back toward the black neighborhood. Director of Public Safety Wilson Baker remembered that, once in the black section, "People were coming out of those houses with shotguns and rifles and pistols. . . . people were beginning to throw bricks and bottles and . . . we knew things were really fixing to pop."[60]

Even when southern civil rights activities passed without overt black violence, angry words, threats of violence, guns, and organized armed self-defense—elements not readily associated with the nonviolent era and explicitly disavowed by proponents of nonviolent direct action tactics—were rarely far away from sites of formal protest. For instance, when Autherine Lucy and the National Association for the Advancement of Colored People tried to integrate the University of Alabama in 1956, she was protected from a potential mob attack by black men with guns.[61] Similarly, in Little Rock in the wake of the desegregation of Central High in September 1957, Daisy Bates's home was protected by an armed guard. In her memoirs she recalls, "it took many weeks for me to become accustomed to seeing revolvers lying on tables in my own home."[62] In the same year, Fred Shuttlesworth had been mercilessly beaten by a mob for attempting to desegregate a Birmingham high school with his own children. That night with his head bandaged and an arm in a sling, he led a mass meeting. According to historian Glenn Eskew, "During the service, a patrol car quickly drove past armed guards of the [Alabama Christian Movement for Human Rights] stationed outside the church."[63]

In 1961, after the Freedom Riders had been beaten by the Klansmen in Anniston, Alabama, and the local hospital had refused to treat them,

Shuttlesworth led a caravan of cars to collect them. As Freedom Rider Hank Thomas recalls, "every one of those cars had a shotgun in it. And Fred Shuttlesworth had got on the radio and said . . . 'I'm a nonviolent man, but I'm going to get my people.'"[64] In an interview in 1968, Shuttlesworth recalled that "men had to guard my house for four years." He instructed his men that "if you got to shoot, shoot a man in the foot, don't try to kill anybody."[65] If this was a less than lethal brief, it was a long way from conventional understandings of nonviolent practice. Shuttlesworth's instructions to his guards never found their way into the press, nor do they appear in accounts of the Birmingham movement, although the literature on Birmingham has dutifully noted the black violence that followed the bombing of the Gaston Motel and other acts of extreme white terrorism.

At least as significant as the widespread neglect of the extent of black violence in the early Movement is a misunderstanding of the way in which it interacted with nonviolent protest. When historians have spotted incidents of black violence, they have tended to interpret them almost exclusively in terms of a degeneration of nonviolence—which, of course, they sometimes were. Yet, they have seldom fully explored black violence as a phenomenon that, paradoxically, often helped to generate an environment within which the nonviolent Movement could work more effectively. At a very fundamental level, Lawrence Guyot, chair of the Mississippi Freedom Democratic Party, had no doubt that the rallies, marches, and voter registration drives that took place in Mississippi were a lot easier to organize while the likes of Hartman Turnbow and his trusty shotgun were close at hand. Commenting on the ever-present threat of white terrorist violence against civil rights activists working in the community, Guyot noted that "It does make a difference for us to know that . . . if people surround the house, some of them are going to die before they get to you, and my nonviolent advocate, who professes nonviolence, is probably going to shoot the shit out of them."[66]

Equally important, yet similarly neglected, is the way in which eruptions and threats of black violence could sometimes bring recalcitrant white authorities hurrying to the negotiating table to meet with representatives of the nonviolent Movement. For instance, in describing Hosea Williams's 1963 campaign in Savannah, Georgia, Adam Fairclough has written that "The protests constantly threatened to degenerate into violence as marchers confronted police and National Guardsmen in Savannah's downtown squares. . . . On July 11 the demonstrations reached a Birmingham-like climax, with the police and National Guard resorting to tear gas and fire hoses, and angry marchers responding by throwing stones, setting fires, and breaking windows. [James] Bevel and [Andrew] Young now suspended the demonstrations. The art of nonviolent protest lay not merely in promoting direct action, but also in ending it at the appropriate time."[67] All of this is undoubtedly true. Yet Fairclough never really considers the extent to which it was the constant threat and occasional outbreaks of black violence—rather than the nonviolent marches themselves—that actually convinced civic leaders to negotiate and ultimately yield to the demonstrators' demands.

Martin Luther King Jr. was certainly aware of the ways in which the potential for black violence could, in some cases, provide his nonviolent Movement with vital leverage. As in his earlier "Letter From Birmingham Jail," in "I Have a Dream," the most celebrated speech of the nonviolent era, King quite deliberately raised the specter of black violence to keep the pressure on the federal government to pass stringent civil rights legislation. With the image of Malcolm X and the Black Muslim's advocacy of armed self-defense looming ever larger in the nation's consciousness, King recalled the racial turmoil of 1963—not least the trouble in Savannah, but equally the black, as well as white, violence that surrounded his own campaign in Birmingham, Alabama—and warned that "This sweltering summer of the Negro's legitimate discontent will not pass until there is an invigorating autumn of freedom and equality. Nineteen sixty-three is not an end, but a beginning. And those who hope that the Negro needed to blow off steam and will now be content, will have a rude awakening if the nation returns to business as usual."[68]

It is, perhaps, indicative of the lack of attention and importance ascribed to the subjects of black violence and self-defense that these subjects seldom warrant an index entry in histories of the Movement—certainly none exist in any of the works cited in this essay. By contrast, nonviolence and nonviolent direct action protest are always indexed. Aldon Morris's emphasis is fairly typical: "The modern civil rights movement . . . was the first time in American history that blacks adopted nonviolent tactics as a mass technique for bringing about social change. . . . Through continuous nonviolent workshops and constant appeals to the nonviolent tradition rooted in the black church and in the life of Jesus, blacks were persuaded to accept nonviolence."[69] Historian Sudarshan Kapur concurs: "Building on the struggles of earlier generations, the modern African American freedom movement (1955–1968), in the short span of slightly more than a decade, forced an otherwise unready and unwilling nation to move toward becoming a free and open society. The leap forward was a direct outcome of countless nonviolent initiatives of thousands of committed and courageous African Americans."[70]

And, of course, it is important never to lose sight of the brilliance and courage with which nonviolence was deployed in the South; just as it is important to acknowledge that there are some historians of the southern Struggle—like Timothy B. Tyson, David Garrow, Adam Fairclough on Louisiana, John Dittmer and Charles Payne on Mississippi, David Colburn on St. Augustine and Glenn Eskew in his study of Birmingham—who note and seek to analyze the presence of black violence in their studies of particular localities or individuals. What is striking, however, is what little effect this particularist scholarship has had on the "master narrative" of the nonviolent southern Movement. It is as if the local departures from nonviolence that these authors have uncovered are still seen as *sui generis*: unique, aberrant lapses that somehow cannot be accommodated within the broader story of the southern Struggle. In most historical surveys of the modern freedom struggle, black violence barely even exists in the South of the early 1960s—and certainly has nothing to do with the mass Movement which challenged segregation and disenfranchisement. Historiographically, we still live in a world where Richard Lentz—a commentator with a good sense of how the media operated—can remark of events in 1964 that "While white mobs ran unchecked through St. Augustine, blacks were rioting in the North," without any mention of the fact that black mobs in St. Augustine were armed and fighting back.[71] Similarly, in popular memory, the early civil rights success story continues to turn almost exclusively upon the southern black acceptance of nonviolence, just as the Movement's subsequent disintegration is conventionally linked to its rejection, principally in the North.

Violent rhetoric and posturing as well as actual instances of violence in the southern civil rights campaigns of the late 1950s and early 1960s molded and defined the early Movement to a far greater extent than the contemporary press and subsequent historians have allowed. Whatever the huge tactical and sometimes moral appeal of nonviolent direct action for black southerners, there was always a strong, competing impulse toward defensive violence, as well as toward revenge and retribution against the system and its white beneficiaries and guardians. By ignoring this, historians risk taking some of the passion and heart out of the nonviolent Movement; they portray one-dimensional characters with a natural predilection for nonviolent ideas, rather than a people rightly angry and bitter about their treatment and using what they believed to be the best weapon to fight injustice and white power. If historians do not fully acknowledge the reality of black violence, then they fail to capture what a remarkable achievement any significant display of nonviolent discipline was. Moreover, without the hovering specter of imminent black, as well as white, violence, a nonviolent direct action movement would have been meaningless. Nonviolence depended on a culture of violence against which to posit and define itself, or else it could not exist; its power and moral resonance—so crucial for winning white liberal support for the Movement—flowed from the very real presence of bloodier alternatives.

There is more at stake in this rehabilitation of black violence into the civil rights story than simply refining our understanding of how the early Movement functioned. If it is accepted that an undercurrent of black violence did pervade and in part shape the "nonviolent" civil rights era, then it is possible to really begin to see how the real and imagined violence of the black power era represented a far less radical departure than most historians have assumed. That is not to suggest, however, that the black violence of the two eras was identical; rather historians need to try to identify more clearly what was truly different between the two phases of the freedom struggle. One difference was that in the early southern civil rights movement most activists, even if they carried or condoned the use of guns for defensive purposes, still accepted a strategy of nonviolent protest. So, too, did the majority of those who supported the Movement from beyond its official ranks. This acceptance stemmed from the fact that the strategy, however imperfect, appeared to be successful in achieving its goals of dismantling statutory segregation and disenfranchisement. Conversely, in the black power era, some of the most conspicuous black leaders explicitly rejected nonviolent tactics as ineffectual in securing their diverse aims, and embraced a theory, rhetoric, and posture of armed self-defense. Whereas the teachings of Gandhi and Christ had provided the key moral, intellectual, and practical touchstones for the civil rights movement, in the black power era their place was taken by the likes of Malcolm X, Frantz Fanon, Fidel Castro, and Mao Tse Tung, with their various endorsements of violence as both a psychological and practical necessity for the liberation of oppressed people.

Yet even here, any neat categorical division between the two eras is problematic, since there were always those in the nonviolent era who conspicuously rejected, rather than simply lapsed from, nonviolence. Robert Williams clearly stood outside the nonviolent consensus, arguing in obvious opposition to the church-based leadership of the mainstream southern Movement of the early 1960s that "I believe if we are going to pray, we ought to pass the ammunition while we pray."[72]

When Black Panthers Huey Newton and Eldridge Cleaver called for blacks to "off the pigs," or when H. Rap Brown called for blacks to burn down white Cambridge in 1967, they were in part articulating variations on the same anger that most southern "nonviolent" protesters had felt, and some had vividly expressed, earlier in the decade. Another major difference in terms of black violence between the two eras, however, was that this anger, the inflammatory rhetoric and actual violence in and around the earlier civil rights movement, was rarely reported in the press and therefore has remained largely invisible in the historiography.

By contrast, in the black power era, all such signs of violence or expressions of anger, however slight, were seized upon by a mainstream press— a press spooked by fears of an impending race war and heavily implicated in a virulent white backlash against continuing black demands for genuine equality of opportunity. The mainstream black press, while less given than its white counterparts to the most crass exaggeration, also remained essentially conservative and largely hostile to perceived militants. It offered relatively little to counterbalance the sensationalist white reporting, and therefore provides equally problematic evidence for historians hoping to understand the role that violence of various types played within the black power era.

Ultimately, the natural tendency of the media to simplify and sensationalize, coupled with its shifting political agendas and priorities, dooms it to being an extremely unstable factual or interpretative foundation for Movement historiography. Yet, it is not just the hysterical reportage of the "riot-torn" late 1960s that needs to be treated with care: easy acceptance of the press's often partisan coverage of the early Movement is potentially just as damaging to our understanding of the freedom struggle.

Notes

1. *New York Times,* June 18, 1963, 1, 22.
2. Ibid.
3. H. Rap Brown, quoted in Clayborne Carson, *In Struggle: SNCC and the Black Awakening of the* 1960s (Cambridge: Harvard University Press, 1995), 25, and Robert Weisbrot, *Freedom Bound: A History of America's Civil Rights Movement* (New York: Norton, 1990), 264.
4. *New York Times,* July 25, 1967, 20.

5. Ibid., July 26, 1967, 19.

6. *Washington Afro-American*, July 29, 1967, 2; *Washington Post*, July 26, 1967; *Time*, August 4, 1967; *New Republic*, August 5, 1967, 5–6.

7. David Boesel and Louis Goldberg, "Crisis in Cambridge," in *Cities Under Siege: An Anatomy of the Ghetto Riots, 1964–1968*, ed. David Boesel and Peter H. Rossi (New York: Basic Books, 1971), 110–29.

8. Boesel and Goldberg, "Crisis in Cambridge," 111.

9. *New York Times*, July 25, 1967, 20.

10. Boesel and Goldberg, "Crisis in Cambridge," 111.

11. Ibid., 119

12. Ibid., 122.

13. Ibid., 114.

14. H. Rap Brown, *Die Nigger Die!* (New York: Dial Press, 1969), 100.

15. Peter S. Szabo, "An Interview with Gloria Richardson Dandridge," *Maryland Historical Magazine* 89, no. 3 (Fall 1994): 357–58; Gloria Richardson, interview by author, March 11, 1996, University of Newcastle upon Tyne Oral History Collection (hereafter cited as UNOHC).

16. Boesel and Goldberg, "Crisis in Cambridge," 127–28.

17. "Blow-Up in the Cities," *New Republic*, August 5, 1967, 5.

18. *The Movement*, August 1967, 1, reprinted in *The Movement, 1964–1970*, ed. Clayborne Carson et al. (Westport, Conn.: Greenwood Press, 1993), 268.

19. Harvard Sitkoff, *The Struggle for Black Equality, 1954–1992*, rev. ed. (New York: Hill and Wang, 1993), 203–4.

20. Weisbrot, *Freedom Bound*, 264.

21. Carson, *In Struggle*, 255–56.

22. William L. Van Deburg, *New Day in Babylon: The Black Power Movement and American Culture, 1965–1975* (Chicago: University of Chicago Press, 1992), 167.

23. Brian Ward has used the term the "master narrative" to describe "a conventional, lay person's sense of what the civil rights and black power movements really were and meant." These conventional wisdoms, he argues, "are to be found, not just in the pages of many popular high school and college surveys of postwar American history, but also in public celebrations, like those held for Martin Luther King's birthday, journalistic accounts, memoirs of activists, novels set in Movement days, Hollywood feature films, popular songs, and television dramas and documentaries on the subject." See Brian Ward, "Forgotten Wails and Master Narratives: Media, Culture, and Memories of the Modern African American Freedom Struggle," page 8 in this volume.

24. See, for example, Adam Fairclough, *Martin Luther King, Jr.* (Athens: University of Georgia Press, 1995), 24–25; Sitkoff, *Struggle for Black Equality*, 48; Taylor Branch, *Parting the Waters: America in the King Years, 1954–1963* (New York: Simon and Schuster, 1988), 164–66.

25. Interview with Martin Luther King Jr., File: Montgomery interviews: Mr.

Donald Ferron, Montgomery Bus Boycott Box, Preston Valien Papers, Amistad Research Center, Tulane University, New Orleans (Hereafter cited as MBB-PV).

26. Executive Board Meeting, February 2, 1956, MBB-PV.

27. Bayard Rustin, interview by Howell Raines, in *My Soul Is Rested: Movement Days in the Deep South Remembered*, ed. Raines (Harmondsworth, England: Penguin, 1983), 53.

28. Fellowship of Reconciliation Workshop—reporter Anne Holden, July 22, 1956, File: Montgomery interviews: Anne Holden, MBB-PV.

29. Interview with Willie Mae Wallace. Transcript. File: Montgomery interviews: Miss W. M. Lee, MBB-PV.

30. The best account of the Montgomery bus boycott, which does include some of the hostile feelings of the boycotters, is in Fairclough's *Martin Luther King*. I am grateful to Adam Fairclough for alerting me to records of the Montgomery movement held in the Preston Valien Papers at the Amistad Research Center.

31. Brian Ward, "Dissecting the Dream: Civil Rights and Race Relations in the United States," *The Historical Journal* 35, no. 4 (1992): 991.

32. Timothy B. Tyson, *Radio Free Dixie: Robert F. Williams and the Roots of Black Power* (Chapel Hill: University of North Carolina Press, 1999). See also Timothy B. Tyson "Robert Williams, 'Black Power,' and the Roots of the African American Freedom Struggle," *Journal of American History* 85, no. 2 (September 1998): 540–70. For more on Robert Williams, see Robert Carl Cohen, *Black Crusader: A Biography of Robert Franklin Williams* (Secaucus, N.J.: Lyle Stuart, 1972) and Robert F. Williams, *Negroes with Guns* (New York: Marzani and Munsell, 1962).

33. *Baltimore Afro-American*, October 19, 1957, 1, 2; *Jet*, October 31, 1957, 10–14; *Norfolk Journal and Guide*, October 12, 1957, 1.

34. Fred Shuttlesworth, interview by James Mosby, September 1968, Ralph J. Bunche Oral History Collection, Moorland-Spingarn Research Center, Howard University, Washington, D.C. (hereafter cited as RJB-OH).

35. *Birmingham News*, December 31, 1956.

36. *Birmingham News*, July 2, 1960.

37. Julian Mayfield, interview by Malaika Lumumba, May 13, 1970, RJB-OH.

38. Robert E. Johnson, interview by John Britton, September 6, 1967, RJB-OH.

39. C. A. Scott, interview by John Britton, January 25, 1968, RJB-OH.

40. Robert Williams, interview by James Mosby, July 22, 1970, RJB-OH.

41. McLeod, quoted in *Chicago Defender*, January 25, 1958, 1. For more on this incident, see Tyson, *Radio Free Dixie*, 137–40, and George Lewis, "Not So Well Red: Native Americans in the Southern Civil Rights Movement Reconsidered," *Borderlines: Studies in American Culture* 3, no. 4 (1996): 362–63.

42. Exactly who the Lumbee were is a vexed question. Their ethnic origins have long been debated. For more on the Lumbees see Lewis, "Not So Well Red," 362–75.

43. Cohen, *Black Crusader*, 108.

44. These editorial comments are taken from an editorial roundup: "Daily Press Views Indian-Klan Clash," *Baltimore Afro-American,* February 1, 1958, 5.

45. *Pittsburgh Courier,* January 25, 1958, 3.

46. *Amsterdam News,* January 25, 1958, 1, 7, 8.

47. Ibid.

48. *Norfolk Journal and Guide,* November 2, 1957, 1.

49. *Baltimore Afro-American,* November 2, 1957, 6.

50. "Anonymous report on Nashville, Tennessee, August 10, 1961," Reel 40, Student Nonviolent Coordinating Papers, Microfilm Collection, Alderman Library, University of Virginia, Charlottesville.

51. John Dittmer, *Local People: The Struggle for Civil Rights in Mississippi* (Urbana: University of Illinois Press, 1994), 155.

52. *New York Times,* April 4, 1963, 22.

53. David Garrow, *Protest at Selma: Martin Luther King, Jr., and the Voting Rights Act of 1965* (New Haven: Yale University Press, 1978), 45.

54. Weisbrot, *Freedom Bound,* 186.

55. Judy Richardson, quoted in Paula Giddings, *When and Where I Enter: The Impact of Black Women on Race and Sex in America* (New York: Bantam, 1985), 292.

56. C. T. Vivian, interview by Vincent J. Browne, February 20, 1968, RJB-OH.

57. David Garrow, *Bearing the Cross: Martin Luther King, Jr., and the Southern Christian Leadership Conference* (New York: Vintage, 1986), 330.

58. Robert Hayling, interview by John H. Britton, August 16, 1967, RJB-OH.

59. *Jet,* June 25, 1964, 18.

60. Wilson Baker, interview by Howell Raines, in *My Soul Is Rested,* ed. Raines, 202–3.

61. E. Culpepper Clark, *The Schoolhouse Door: Segregation's Last Stand at the University of Alabama* (New York: Oxford University Press, 1993), 78, 80.

62. Daisy Bates, *The Long Shadow of Little Rock: A Memoir* (New York: David McKay, 1962), 111.

63. Glenn Eskew, *But For Birmingham: The Local and National Movements in the Civil Rights Struggle* (Chapel Hill: University of North Carolina Press, 1997), 141.

64. Hank Thomas, interview by Howell Raines, in *My Soul Is Rested,* ed. Raines, 115. Freedom rider Thomas recalled, "Man, they came there and they were a welcome sight. And each one of 'em got out with their guns and everything. . . . They had rifles and shotguns. And that's how we got back to Birmingham."

65. Shuttlesworth interview, RJB-OH.

66. Lawrence Guyot, interview by Brian Ward and Jenny Walker, December 16, 1995, UNOHC.

67. Adam Fairclough, *To Redeem the Soul of America: The Southern Christian Leadership Conference and Martin Luther King, Jr.* (Athens: University of Georgia Press, 1987), 143–44.

68. Martin Luther King Jr., "I Have a Dream," in *A Testament of Hope: The*

Essential Writings and Teachings of Martin Luther King, Jr., ed. James M. Washington (New York: HarperCollins, 1991), 218.

69. Aldon D. Morris, *The Origins of the Civil Rights Movement: Black Communities Organizing for Change* (New York: Free Press, 1984), xi.

70. Sudarshan Kapur, *Raising Up a Prophet: The African-American Encounter with Gandhi* (Boston: Beacon, 1992), 1.

71. Richard Lentz, *Symbols, the News Magazines, and Martin Luther King* (Baton Rouge: Louisiana State University Press, 1990), 129.

72. Robert F. Williams, "Can Negroes Afford to be Pacifists?" *Liberation*, September 1959, 6.

3

Black-Oriented Radio and the Civil Rights Movement

Stephen Walsh

In August 1945, the National Association for the Advancement of Colored People's (NAACP) publicity director Consuelo Young wrote to New York broadcaster Morris Novik asking for a list of local contacts in the radio industry. In explaining the request, Young mentioned that "more and more occasions are arising for which the NAACP should have access to radio coverage on important current issues and problems." Writing the day before the second atomic bomb destroyed the city of Nagasaki, Young recognized not only the way in which the fight for equality would figure with increasing prominence in the postwar era, but also the important contribution that radio could make in informing the American people of the Association's work.[1]

In 1945, any evaluation of radio's value to the black cause was based on its status as the most popular general-appeal mass medium of the day. However, as the decade progressed, organizations such as the NAACP were increasingly faced with the opportunities and challenges of working with a new phenomenon—that of black-oriented radio.

Although radio programming directed toward an African American audience had existed since Jack Cooper pioneered the concept on WSBC-Chicago in 1929, it was not until the end of the Second World War that black radio flourished. Beginning in 1947, stations such as WDIA-Memphis and WOOK-Washington, D.C., pioneered the move toward the adoption of a completely black-oriented format. By 1956, there were forty-three such stations, mostly located in the South, of a total of more than seven hundred with some measure of black-appeal programming. By 1968, there were 108 completely black-oriented radio stations around the country.[2]

The rapid increase in the number of stations was just one index of the influence that black radio enjoyed in the African American community. A large number of studies confirmed the enthusiasm with which black listeners responded to radio programming aimed specifically at them. For example, Thomas Allen's 1968 study of mass media usage by black residents in Pittsburgh found that the average household listened to radio for five and a half hours a day. In 1972, a major survey commissioned by *Ebony* magazine sought to compare the attitudes of African Americans toward the different forms of mass media. Presumably to the dismay of the study's commissioners, it was not print journalism but black radio that ranked highest in such categories as empathy, honesty, objectivity, and entertainment. Two years later, J. Walter Thompson found 90 percent of African Americans to be regular consumers of black-oriented radio.[3]

Given the popularity of this medium, the fact that historians of the black freedom struggle have largely neglected black-oriented radio is particularly surprising. We have ample testimony to the importance of the media in general to the Movement, particularly in the case of television, but little appreciation of the role played by the medium that was most important to most African Americans.

Perhaps this can be explained by the fact that the vast majority of those academics who have studied black radio—usually historians of popular culture, sociologists, and media analysts—have been overwhelmingly critical in their assessments. One of the earliest commentators, Fred Ferretti, concluded his 1970 report with a damning indictment of the medium: "it reminds one of nothing so much as Newton Minow's historic description of American commercial television—'a vast wasteland.'" Ferretti's report was characteristic of several studies published in the early 1970s that condemned black-oriented stations for their dearth of public service programming and abstention from civil rights activity. Such works have set the tone for the generally negative treatment afforded to black radio by most authorities ever since.[4] Admittedly, recent commentators have identified more positive aspects. In particular, they have focused on the medium's celebration of black culture as a means of promoting racial pride and identity. However, they have mostly continued to suggest that direct support for the freedom struggle remained at best sporadic, or else have simply assumed and asserted that such support must have happened without presenting any real evidence.[5]

The assumption underlying such negative evaluations is that at the heart of black radio's problems lay, as Ferretti put it, "the white captivity" of the medium.[6] As late as 1970, only sixteen radio stations throughout the country were actually black-owned. Thus, the argument runs that white station owners, adhering to a strictly economic agenda and fearful of alienating potential advertisers, consistently eschewed such controversial topics as race relations. Consequently, according to most of the medium's detractors, increased black ownership was a vital prerequisite if radio were ever going to play a truly positive role in the African American community. As one insisted in 1976, "African Americans *must* own and operate radio stations if they are to shape the destiny of their people."[7]

However, while the call for increased black control was entirely justified, the preoccupation with the issue of ownership has sometimes obscured the genuine, positive contribution that many black-oriented radio stations did make to the African American freedom struggle. Focusing primarily on the 1960s, this essay outlines ways in which black radio did assist the cause, and seeks to evaluate the effectiveness of the service it rendered. While not denying the genuine limitations on how radio stations could contribute to the freedom struggle, it suggests that the debate concerning the role of the media in the Movement needs to be widened beyond television and print journalism, where the majority of work has thus far been done, in order to give much greater attention to black radio.

Black radio's relationship with the freedom struggle assumed many forms, but essentially fell into the categories of what can usefully be termed either "supportive" or "active" participation. By far the most common mode of involvement was supportive: stations rarely instigated or led the fight against racism and discrimination, yet by providing news coverage and airtime to civil rights activists, they frequently placed their facilities at the disposal of those who did.

At a local level, this can be demonstrated by the fact that an increasing number of individual protest campaigns and organizations drew on the facilities of the black-oriented stations in their region, either ad hoc, or on a more regular basis. WYLD-New Orleans, for example, was involved in publicizing the membership drives of the local chapter of the Urban League from at least as early as 1961. Two years later, WSOK in Savannah, Georgia, provided both the local NAACP and the Chatham County Crusade for Voters with a means of addressing the local black population through their own half-hour weekly shows. Movements in Cambridge, Maryland, and Danville, Virginia—where, according to the Student Nonviolent Coordinating Committee's (SNCC) Mary King, "we used the black radio stations all the time for voter registration activities"—benefited directly from the publicity afforded to them by black-oriented radio.[8] The extent to which radio was receptive to overtures from civil rights organizations was underlined by the results of a 1964 NAACP survey that revealed that, of all of the Association's branches that sought air time on their local station, 95 percent were accommodated.[9]

Certainly, in 1965, the National Urban League found no shortage of black-oriented stations willing to carry its two new weekly programs. Both *The Leaders Speak*, which offered a platform to different civil rights spokespersons, and *Civil Rights Roundup*, which provided a weekly digest of the Movement's activities, were aired on more than seventy black-oriented stations around the country, including such outlets in the heart of the South as WOKJ-Jackson, WENN-Birmingham, WRMA-Montgomery, WVOL-Nashville, and WAUG-Augusta. Noting the Urban League's example, the Southern Christian Leadership Conference (SCLC) also sought to harness black radio's popularity for its own ends by syndicating the speeches of Dr. King. "'Soul' stations are an excellent means of publicizing our work," enthused the SCLC's Tom Offenburger; "[a]lmost all 'Soul' stations are always interested in news from the Movement."[10]

Such an arrangement was advantageous to both broadcasters and activists. It spared a station the time and cost of producing the show, while still providing an invaluable medium for civil rights groups to educate listeners about their activities, appeal for funds and new members, and urge the importance of voter registration. Equally significant, in the provision of airtime as a public service to external organizations, broadcasters were able to maintain a fine balance between legitimately catering to the interests of their target audience while still maintaining at least a veneer of objectivity.

In this way, many stations certainly helped to inform, even inspire, their listeners, but they rarely instigated civil rights protests of their own. White ownership at all but a few black-oriented stations, heavy dependency on white sponsors and advertisers, and periodic acts of white segregationist terrorism against black-oriented stations deemed too involved in politics combined to retard the level of direct involvement of such radio stations in the Movement. Nevertheless, some stations were able and willing to become more overtly identified with the battle against Jim Crow.

Probably the most common form of such "active" participation was the airing of favorable editorials. Indeed, several stations went so far as to employ civil rights activists to prepare their editorials. As early as 1950, Jesse Blayton's WERD-Atlanta—the first black-owned station in the country—pioneered this trend, employing Dr. William Boyd of the Georgia State branch of the NAACP as the station's news analyst. For six years, Boyd used his tri-weekly appearances to denounce racism and urge black Atlantans to register to vote.[11] In 1954, WERD's status as the only completely black-oriented station in Atlanta was challenged when WAOK signed on air. Despite being under the white ownership of Zenas Sears and

Stan Raymond, the station made a genuine, and successful, attempt to integrate itself into Atlanta's African American community. Employees who worked for both stations, as well as civil rights activists, testify to the fact that WAOK's civil rights coverage was at least as comprehensive and sympathetic as that provided by its black-owned competitor.[12] In 1962, the station strengthened its ties with the Movement by hiring Jim Wood, then director of public relations at the SCLC, to direct its news operation and prepare its editorials.

Following Egmont Sonderling's takeover in 1965, WOL in Washington, D.C., also followed this trend by hiring the National Urban League's assistant director of public relations, Sherwood Ross, to be the station's director of public affairs. Ross editorialized regularly on the latest civil rights activity, agitated for Home Rule for the capital, and waged a vigorous campaign against the city's slumlords.[13]

Few stations were in a position to hire a Bill Boyd, Jim Wood, or Sherwood Ross, but a substantial number undertook their own attempts at editorializing. By 1966, *Broadcasting* magazine discovered that 55 percent of black radio stations did so on a regular basis, and 89 percent of these dealt specifically with issues of race.[14]

Less frequent were those occasions when a station actually assumed a key role in organizing a community for participation in civil rights activity. The most dramatic illustration of this particular element of black radio's relationship with the freedom struggle was provided during the Birmingham, Alabama, campaign of 1963. When the decision was taken by SCLC leaders to employ Birmingham's schoolchildren in nonviolent demonstrations, the local black-oriented station, WENN, was an ideal vehicle for getting word of the protests to the city's youth. Disc jockeys Shelley "The Playboy" Stewart and "Tall" Paul White repeatedly broadcast coded announcements concerning a "big party" to be held in the city's Kelly Ingram Park. Their exhortations played a key role in helping to publicize the protests; according to Taylor Branch "Nearly every Negro kid in Birmingham knew what he [White] meant."[15] Certainly, Larry Russell, a sixteen-year-old high school student in 1963, was no exception: "[w]e knew about the mass meetings from Shelley Stewart and Paul White. Paul White used to call the meetings 'a party'. We good old Baptists knew there wasn't going to be any dance."[16]

The episode offered a vivid testimony to the way in which black disc jockeys, in particular, could use their influence in the local community to the advantage of the freedom struggle. In Philadelphia, it was Georgie "The man with the Goods" Woods of WDAS who fulfilled a similar role.

Whether by paying for nine coachloads of Philadelphians to attend the March on Washington, or setting a personal example by participating in the Selma demonstrations of 1965, Woods ably demonstrated the extent to which a socially conscious deejay could use his position to great effect. As one listener recalled simply, "I wanted to go on the March on Washington—because of him."[17]

On occasion, black-oriented radio's role in the Movement extended beyond the contents of its broadcasts. In the case of WUST in Washington, D.C., the station's contribution was most notable for its provision, at no cost, of a venue for assemblies and meetings. Over the years, speakers at the WUST Radio Music Hall covered a broad spectrum of black activists, including Martin Luther King Jr., Malcolm X, and Stokely Carmichael.[18]

The willingness of WUST's management to donate the use of the Hall so freely also made it an ideal choice for the staging of civil rights activities such as voter registration drives. Most notably of all, in the weeks before the March on Washington in August 1963, the Hall served as the headquarters for the Washington branch of the planning operation—providing a vital administrative base during the hectic prelude to the March.[19]

As significant as such incidents of active community mobilization were on an individual basis, they were hardly typical of black radio's relationship with the civil rights movement. Thus, any overall assessment of the medium's performance is necessarily based primarily upon those activities that were most characteristic of the greatest number of stations.

In providing a vehicle for the dissemination of news, information, and editorial opinion concerning the freedom struggle, black-oriented radio was, of course, by no means unique among the mass media. However, there were several salient features that particularly characterized black radio's contribution and set it apart from the other media.

Without doubt, television played a crucial role in the freedom struggle. In many ways, the very genius of the Movement lay in its ability to generate the kinds of images from Birmingham and Selma that, beamed into homes throughout the land, helped to prick the conscience of a nation. But although television extensively covered the most dramatic moments of the southern freedom struggle and subsequently the urban riots, on a day-to-day basis it was not yet such an integral part of the black community.

Black radio, on the other hand, often served as a veritable bulletin board of community affairs, and was able to devote significantly greater attention to the local meetings and voter registration campaigns that, if somewhat more mundane, were equally vital for the Movement's overall prospects of success. Certainly, Ben Hooks—NAACP official, aide to Martin Luther King Jr. in Memphis, and subsequently the first African American to serve on the Federal Communications Commission (FCC)— appreciated that radio was less fickle in its attention to the black community than television, which quickly lost interest when the dramatic images were not forthcoming: "the black-oriented stations always covered. If I'd go into town with Dr. King, if there was nothing dramatic going on, after the press conference there'd be no coverage, but the black-oriented stations would always be there. . . . the fact of the matter is that they did a tremendous job."[20]

Obviously, television images of civil rights protests reached, and moved, a black as well as a white audience. However, as commentators such as Martin Luther King and the Kerner Commission on civil disorders both acknowledged, television in the 1960s continued to present the world through white eyes. Without even one African American newsman on a major network until the appointment of Mal Goode by ABC in 1962, television could speak to and about the black community, but rarely as part of it. As King put it in 1967, "television speaks not to [black] needs, but to upper-middle-class America."[21]

As a specifically black-oriented source of news, radio possessed both advantages and disadvantages when compared to black newspapers. Unlike the print press, radio's primary concern with entertainment usually resulted in the relegation of news reporting to a subsidiary role. Even at the most well-respected black stations, news occupied only a small fraction of the total airtime—in the early 1960s amounting to only 7 percent of the weekly schedule at WAOK-Atlanta, 4 percent at WDAS-Philadelphia, and less than 4 percent at WENN-Birmingham. Certainly, a typical news roundup, amounting to only a few minutes every hour, was rarely able to match the depth of coverage and level of analysis offered by a newspaper.[22]

However, it was precisely because of radio's preeminence as an entertainment medium that news and civil rights coverage found their targets and proved particularly effective. As the SCLC's Walter Fauntroy explained: "[p]eople tune in to listen to the music and they hear these . . . cultural amenities. They are listening and interested, then they hear about employment and slums and action. This is of tremendous value."[23]

Black-oriented radio also offered a far more effective outlet for addressing the mass of African Americans than the print press. As an example, *Martin Luther King Speaks* reached a weekly audience of over two million, including an estimated 100,000 Washingtonians and 175,000 Memphians;

at the same time the circulation of the *Washington Afro-American* and the *Memphis Tri-State Defender* stood at little over eight thousand and fifteen thousand respectively.[24]

Certainly, numerous civil rights activists recognized the benefits of black radio's greater reach. According to Martin Luther King Jr., "[t]he masses of Americans who have been denied and deprived educational and economic opportunity are almost totally dependent on radio as their means of relating to the society at large. They do not read newspapers, though they may occasionally thumb through *Jet*."[25]

Julian Bond, SNCC's communications director, reiterated this point, suggesting that, when he and his assistant Mary King wanted to reach the black middle classes, they used the print media, but if they wanted to reach the masses, they turned to radio: "[i]f you wanted to get to the large mass of people, you had to go to radio. Radio was what they listened to and radio was where they got their information."[26]

Black radio's value as a disseminator of information concerning the Movement was further enhanced by its immediacy. Radio was able to keep its audience continuously updated with the latest news as it happened, unlike the majority of black newspapers, which, with the important exceptions of the *Atlanta World* and the *Chicago Defender*, were usually only weekly publications. For Julian Bond, this was perhaps black radio's greatest significance: "almost all the black press is weekly, so you've got to wait until Friday or Thursday to see the results of anything you've done. But with the radio, you're right there, right today—five minutes from now, you're on the air."[27]

Finally, the significance of the news service offered by black radio stations transcended its educational function, and it assumed an important motivational role. Civil rights campaigners battling Jim Crow drew great support from the news of the struggles and successes of like-minded groups, and the continuous news updates provided by radio were an important means through which this could be accomplished. Mary King evaluated black-oriented radio's particular contribution along these lines: "[a]s far as the local black stations were concerned, it was an ongoing verbal 'pep' rally of letting them know that there were people who were active. . . . The whole thing just built solidarity, and built a conviction that there was something much bigger than any one town or city."[28]

Comments such as these offer an image of black radio that contrasts sharply with the impression of a purely exploitative medium sometimes advanced by its critics. They also cast doubt on the notion that white ownership alone was an automatic bar to black radio's involvement in the civil rights movement—a simplistic assumption that dominated the diverse campaign for increased black radio ownership in the late 1960s and early 1970s and has continued to color the literature on the subject ever since. This is not to suggest that most white owners of black-oriented stations were crusading civil rights supporters—although some, such as Harry Novik at WLIB-New York, Zenas Sears at WAOK, and Dolly Banks at WHAT-Philadelphia expressed an interest in the Movement that was more than perfunctory. The point, as at least Mark Newman and Brian Ward have acknowledged, is that virtually all station owners—regardless of race—were first and foremost entrepreneurs whose primary motivations were economic; issues of racial justice invariably were lower in priority, if they were considered at all.[29] Egmont Sonderling, who first ventured into black radio in 1950 when he changed the format of WOPA, his classical music station, was a typical example: "I used to have a station that I enjoyed listening to but it was going broke. Now I have six stations I can't listen to, but I make a lot of money."[30]

In truth, civil rights and other black interest groups secured coverage of their activities on black-oriented radio in spite of, rather than because of, the political agenda of individual owners. For example, even the Nation of Islam, an organization with a notoriously hostile stance toward white America, was accommodated by numerous white-owned stations, including, by 1963, WAUG-Augusta, WSID-Baltimore, WNOO-Chattanooga, WWRL-New York, and KSAN-San Francisco.[31]

Similarly, in New York, WLIB regularly offered airtime to Malcolm X and even boasted of its own role in his rise to prominence, while simultaneously distancing itself from his views. The station editorial at the time of his assassination was particularly revealing: "WLIB can lay undisputed claim to having afforded the late Malcolm X his initial springboard in New York. We were presenting him . . . when no other communications medium seemed interested. And we are happy that we did. . . . [but] As likeable as Malcolm X could be as an individual, as a Black Muslim and Nationalist he was a bitter, uncompromising fanatic about race."[32]

The real impetus for black radio's involvement in the freedom struggle stemmed less from the owners than from the African American community itself. At the level of individual stations this happened through various "tricks of the trade" employed by station personnel. A civil rights message could be incorporated without management even realizing, especially in the era of personality radio when many black deejays developed spontaneous "raps" on air. "We couldn't editorialize," recalled Chicago deejay Lucky Cordell, "but I would slip in little comments about certain meetings." Certainly, on those occasions when black-oriented radio actively engaged in community mobilization—as in Birmingham and Philadelphia—the driving force came more from individual deejays utilizing the force of their own personality than from deliberate station policy.[33]

Similarly, even though news staff often had to work within serious restrictions of time and resources, they still had an important role in presenting a favorable image of civil rights activities to listeners. In Memphis, NAACP stalwart Maxine Smith recalled with particular affection the approach favored by WDIA newsman Ford Nelson: "Ford would just ask a question—an open-end question—and let you say everything you want!"[34]

On a more general level, the relationship between black-oriented radio and the civil rights movement was essentially symbiotic. The medium not only helped to shape, but was itself shaped by, the African American fight for equality. The marches, sit-ins, boycotts, demonstrations, and voter registration campaigns that characterized the fight for civil rights had a profound impact on the content of black radio broadcasts.

First, the protests effectively "legitimized" the issue of civil rights in the eyes of many American citizens, making it a respectable, indeed fashionable cause in which to become involved. In such a climate, stations were more at liberty to address the issue of civil rights overtly, which they did increasingly from the mid-1960s.

Second, the Movement succeeded in heightening the political awareness of many African Americans. Either through direct participation, or through the mass media, increasing numbers of African Americans were exposed to the messages of civil rights activists. Consequently, any radio station that seriously purported to act as the mouthpiece of the black community could scarcely afford to ignore the freedom struggle if its credibility—and therefore, crucially, its profits—were to survive intact. Around the country, from KDIA-Oakland to WHIH-Portsmouth, Virginia, and from WAMM-Flint, Michigan, to WSRC-Durham, North Carolina, station managers and owners readily confessed it was the civil rights movement itself that provided the crucial catalyst for greater coverage of racial issues.[35]

For all its popularity and genuine degree of public service, black-oriented radio was certainly never without its faults. In the late 1960s and early 1970s, those faults were increasingly exposed by a diverse coalition of interest groups. The major civil rights organizations united with more specialist groups such as the Office of Communications of the United Church of Christ, Citizens Communications Center, Black Efforts for Soul in Television, the National Association of Television and Radio Announcers, and the National Black Media Coalition in a mounting chorus of discontentment, aimed at stations that were deemed to be failing to meet their responsibilities to the black community.

The spark that actually ignited a protest at any given station usually centered on issues of either employment or programming content. One particularly revealing example concerns the downfall of WOOK in Washington, D.C., which came at the hands of the Washington Community Broadcasting Company. Under the aegis of newspaper columnist Drew Pearson, the Company included several prominent civil rights figures, including Sterling Tucker, director of the Washington Urban League, and Carl H. Moultrie, president of the Washington NAACP. In June 1969, the Company alleged to the FCC that WOOK's Sunday programming featured a number of dishonest preachers who used their airtime to broadcast gambling tips—disguised as three digit biblical references—to those members of their congregations who sought salvation in the numbers game. The FCC, evincing a markedly greater determination to deal with transgressions concerning fraudulence and illegal gambling than those solely concerning race, promptly ordered an inquiry into the accusations. After protracted hearings, the station's license was finally revoked in 1978.[36]

Yet the real issue underlying the upsurge in community action against black-oriented stations—once again—was that of ownership. The protests were very much a product of their times—times that saw the rise of black power ideologies at the partial expense of the integrationist aims of the early civil rights movement. For all its conflicting agendas, black power did consistently focus attention on the need for increased black control of the institutions that shaped black life. Precisely because of black radio's integral role in the daily lives of millions of African Americans, the medium was a particularly high-profile symbol of continued white economic exploitation of the black community.

Even those white-owned, black-oriented stations that had made a significant contribution to the Movement were not immune to attack. In 1967 one-time ally WAOK-Atlanta became a target. Angered by the station's appointment of a white program director, Jay Dunn, both the SCLC and SNCC formally protested the overlooking of suitable African American candidates for the position. In May, the conflict intensified with a SNCC-led picket of the station. Announcing the boycott, SNCC'c description of the situation was couched in classic black power phraseology, "Zenas Sears and Stan Raymond . . . have seriously underestimated the mood of the Black community, which now demands that Black people control their communities and all enterprises which benefit from and make profit off of our people. . . . The issue is one of white bossism, not only here in Atlanta's WAOK, but in white owned, Black-oriented radio stations across the country."[37]

It was in this climate that the first wave of academic research into black radio was undertaken. At a time of community boycotts and petitions to the FCC, it is hardly surprising that commentators accentuated the medium's negative aspects. However, historians of the freedom struggle need to approach the subject with a better sense of perspective. The changes that occurred in the latter half of the 1960s had less to do with a deterioration in the quality of service and commitment offered by black-oriented stations to their primary audience than with how those stations were perceived in the African American community. The ideologies of black power established new criteria and exposed genuine shortcomings—especially in the realms of employment and ownership—at many stations. Yet, this upsurge in criticism did not mean that black radio had suddenly abandoned all attempts at public service; nor should it blind historians to black-oriented radio's efforts to render a meaningful contribution to the Movement in previous years. Certainly, if historians are truly to appreciate the role of the media in the Movement, and the ways in which civil rights activists utilized the mass media to disseminate their message, they cannot afford to neglect black-oriented radio. The limitations on what it could contribute are clearly visible, but had the medium never existed the fight for equality, and the life of the African American community as a whole, would have been much the poorer.

Notes

1. Consuelo C. Young to Morris Novik, August 8, 1945, II-A-158, National Association for the Advancement of Colored People Papers, Manuscript Division, Library of Congress, Washington, D.C. (hereafter cited as NAACP Papers).

2. "Negro Radio," *Sponsor*, July 9, 1956, section 2, 192; *New York Times*, November 11, 1968, Clippings File: "Radio," Schomburg Center for Research in Black Culture, New York.

3. Thomas H. Allen, "Mass Media Use Patterns in a Negro Ghetto," *Journalism Quarterly* 45 (Spring 1968): 525–27; Daniel Yankelovich, Inc., *An Insight into the Black Community: A Study Prepared for Ebony Magazine* (Chicago: Johnson, 1972), 28–32; J. Walter Thompson, *Advertising and Black America, Media Report*, cited in R. Dwight Bachman, *Dynamics of Black Radio: A Research Report* (Washington, D.C.: Creative Universal Products, 1977), 51.

4. Fred Ferretti, "The White Captivity of Black Radio," *Columbia Journalism Review* (Summer 1970), reprinted in *Our Troubled Press: Ten Years of the Columbia Journalism Review*, ed. Alfred Balk and James Boylan (New York: Little, Brown, 1971), 88. See also Anthony J. Meyer, *Black Voices and Format Regulations: A Case Study in Black-Oriented Radio* (Stanford: Eric Clearinghouse, 1971); Douglas O'Connor and Gayla Cook, "Black Radio: The 'Soul' Sellout," *The Progressive* (August 1973), reprinted in *Issues and Trends in Afro-American Journalism*, ed. James S. Tinney and Justine R. Rector (Lanham, Md.: University Press of America, 1980), 233–46; Stuart Surlin, "Black-Oriented Radio: Programming to a Perceived Audience," *Journal of Broadcasting* 16 (Summer 1972): 289–98, "Black-Oriented Radio's Service to the Community," *Journalism Quarterly* 50 (Autumn 1973): 556–60; Stuart Surlin, "Broadcasters' Misperceptions of Black Community Needs," *Journal of Black Studies* 4, no. 2 (December 1973): 185–93; G. K. Osei, *The Story of the Black Man in Radio* (London: The Afrikan Publication Society, 1976).

5. See, for example, William Barlow, *Voice Over: The Making of Black Radio* (Philadelphia: Temple University Press, 1998); Nelson George, *The Death of Rhythm and Blues* (New York: Pantheon, 1988); Mark Newman, *Entrepreneurs of Profit and Pride: From Black Appeal to Soul Radio* (New York: Praeger, 1988); Louis Cantor, *Wheelin' On Beale: How WDIA-Memphis Became the Nation's First All-Black Radio Station and Created the Sound that Changed America* (New York: Pharos, 1992); Brian Ward and Jenny Walker, "'Bringing the Races Closer'?: Black-Oriented Radio in the South and the Civil Rights Movement," in *Dixie Debates: Perspectives on Southern Cultures*, ed. Richard H. King and Helen Taylor (London: Pluto, 1996), 130–49.

6. Ferretti, "White Captivity," 87.

7. Osei, *The Story of the Black Man in Radio*, 15.

8. *Sponsor*, October 9, 1961, Part 2, 12; WSOK Application for Renewal of Broadcast Station License, December 13, 1963, Exhibit 7, 8, Box 309, FCC License Renewal Files, National Archives, Suitland, Maryland (hereafter cited as FCC License Renewal Files). On Danville, see Mary King interview by author, April 17, 1995, University of Newcastle upon Tyne Oral History Collection (hereafter cited as UNOHC). On Cambridge, see Gloria Richardson, interview by Jenny Walker, March 11, 1996, UNOHC.

9. "Publicity Handbook," n.d., 3-A-311, NAACP Papers.

10. Sherwood Ross, Memorandum to Regional Directors and Local League Executive Directors, June 30, 1965, 2-5-15, National Urban League Papers, Manuscript Division, Library of Congress, Washington, D.C.; Tom Offenburger, Memorandum to Steering Committee, Executive Staff Committee, Field Staff, February 2, 1968, B-IV-3, Southern Christian Leadership Conference Papers, Martin Luther King Center for Nonviolent Social Change, Atlanta, Georgia.

11. Paul E. X. Brown, interview by author, March 16, 1995, UNOHC.

12. Brown interview; Julian Bond, interview by author, August 17, 1995, UNOHC.

13. For examples of Ross's editorials, see Federal Communications Commission Docketed Case Files, #16533, Part VI, Exhibit 11, National Archives II, College Park, Maryland; Carl Bernstein, "Washington's Soul Radio," *Washington Post*, May 7, 1967, Potomac Magazine, 28.

14. "Radio a Leading Force in Negro Progress," *Broadcasting*, November 7, 1966, 72.

15. Taylor Branch, *Parting the Waters: America in the King Years, 1954–1963* (New York: Simon and Schuster, 1988), 755.

16. Larry Russell, quoted in Ellen Levine, *Freedom's Children: Young Civil Rights Activists Tell Their Own Story* (New York: Avon, 1993), 101.

17. Merv Caruth, quoted in James G. Spady, *Georgie Woods: I'm Only a Man: The Life Story of a Mass Communicator, Promoter, Civil Rights Activist* (Philadelphia: Snack-Pac, 1992), 173.

18. "Radio Music Hall Days," *Washington City Paper*, March 13–19, 1987; Cal Hackett, interview by author, February 8, 1995, UNOHC.

19. Hackett interview.; Colin Cromwell, Memorandum to Gloster Current, August 12, 1963, and Colin Cromwell, Memorandum to Dr. Morsell and Gloster Current, August 13, 1963, both III-A-228, NAACP Papers; Patrick Ellis, interview by author, February 8, 1995, UNOHC.

20. Ben Hooks, interview by author, August 3, 1995, UNOHC.

21. Martin Luther King Jr., "Transforming a Neighborhood into a Brotherhood" (address to the National Association of Television and Radio Announcers Convention, Atlanta, August 11, 1967), in *Jack The Rapper* (January 1989): 1; *Report of the National Advisory Commission on Civil Disorders* (New York: Bantam, 1968), 376.

22. See Section IV, Question 2 (a), of the following: WAOK Application for Renewal, December 29, 1963, WDAS Application for Renewal, April 16, 1963, WHAT Application for Renewal of Broadcast Station License, April 29, 1963—all Box 202, FCC License Renewal Files; WAAF Application for Renewal of Broadcast Station License, August 21, 1961, Box 199, FCC License Renewal Files; WENN Application for Renewal, December 11, 1963, Box 180, FCC License Renewal Files. Obviously, radio's historical emphasis on entertainment is equally true of general-market, as well as black-oriented, outlets.

23. Walter Fauntroy, quoted in Bernstein, "Washington's Soul Radio," 26–27.

24. Statistics on *Martin Luther King Speaks* taken from Offenburger Memorandum to Steering Committee et al.; newspaper statistics taken from *Ayer's Directory of Newspapers and Periodicals 1968* (Philadelphia: N. W. Ayer and Sons, 1968).

25. King, "Transforming a Neighborhood into a Brotherhood."

26. Bond interview.

27. Ibid.

28. King interview.

29. See Newman, *Entrepreneurs of Profit and Pride*; Brian Ward, *Just My Soul Responding: Rhythm and Blues, Black Consciousness and Race Relations* (Berkeley: University of California Press, 1998), 430–36.

30. Egmont Sonderling, quoted in Bernstein, "Washington's Soul Radio," 25.

31. *Muhammad Speaks*, December 30, 1962, 2, and February 4, 1963, 23.

32. "A Contorted Personality," WLIB Editorial, February 27, 1965, WLIB Application for Renewal of Broadcast Station License, February 28, 1966, Exhibit 4, Box 248, FCC License Renewal Files.

33. Lucky Cordell, quoted in Norman Spaulding, "History of Black-Oriented Radio in Chicago" (Ph.D. dissertation, University of Illinois at Urbana-Champaign, 1981), 90.

34. Hooks interview; Maxine Smith, interview by author, August 3, 1995, UNOHC.

35. "Stations Identify with Their Audience," *Broadcasting*, November 7, 1966, 84–89.

Although the Movement was a major factor in increasing black radio's sensitivity to race in the early 1960s, it was not the only one. On a more general level, the changing commercial environment of the radio industry in the 1960s had a significant impact. As many general market stations cornered the white youth market by adopting a Top Forty chart-oriented format in the wake of the 1960 payola scandals, black-oriented stations were therefore free—or forced—to pursue a more conspicuously "black" approach. For the increased segregation of black-white musical tastes and radio formatting by the mid-1960s, see Ward, *Just My Soul Responding*, 281–88.

36. *Washington Post*, September 1, 1966, and June 24, 1969; *Washington Star*, September 12, 1975, and January 23, 1978, all in Clippings File: "WOOK" Washingtoniana Division, Martin Luther King Jr. Public Library, Washington, D.C.

37. SNCC news release, May 24, 1967, C-I-143, Student Nonviolent Coordinating Committee Papers, Manuscript Division, Library of Congress, Washington, D.C.

4

Reclaiming the South

Civil Rights Films and the New Red Menace

Allison Graham

In 1996, film producer Fred Zollo pondered the strange historical connections between his two "civil rights" films, *Mississippi Burning* (1988) and *Ghosts of Mississippi* (1996). "Oddly enough," he noted, "when some of the critics said we rewrote history with *Mississippi Burning*, we *did*—in the bigger sense. The movie was essential to the retrial and successful reprosecution of Byron De La Beckwith."[1] As Zollo saw it, the path leading from the making of a film widely condemned as historically execrable to the sentencing of the murderer of Mississippi NAACP leader Medgar Evers began with an almost laughable lawsuit. In 1989, former Neshoba County Sheriff Lawrence Rainey filed an $8 million libel suit against Zollo and Orion Pictures, claiming he had been "portrayed unfavorably" in their fictionalized retelling of the 1964 Philadelphia, Mississippi, civil rights murders. "They have sure done some terrible harm," Rainey said. "Everybody all over the South knows the one they have playing the sheriff in that movie is referring to me."[2] While researching his defense, Zollo's Mississippi attorney Jack Ables came across John Birch Society member William McIlhany's book on Delmar Dennis, the Federal Bureau of Investigation (FBI) informant who helped break the Philadelphia case. The book, titled *Klandestine*, would resurface in legal circles several years later when Hinds County Deputy District Attorney Bobby DeLaughter was stalled in his attempt to reopen the Beckwith case, and would provide crucial evidence of Beckwith's public acknowledgment of the murder of Evers. DeLaughter, according to Zollo, however, would not have reopened the thirty-year-old Beckwith case in the first place had it not been for the investigative articles of Jackson newspaperman Jerry Mitchell, who claimed to have been "charged up" by *Mississippi Burning*. Within *Missis-*

sippi Burning, in other words, lay the key that would unlock the rusted chains of southern injustice: "No movie, no Jerry Mitchell, no Jack Ables, no *Klandestine,* no Delmar Dennis," producer Zollo reasoned. "And Beckwith is still living up in Tennessee a free man."[3]

For all of its self-serving convolutions, the line of succession posited by the Hollywood producer—in which reality begets fiction begets reality—describes fairly accurately the tangled contemporary relationship between history and historical reenactment. As Mississippi writer Willie Morris has noted in his journal of the making of *Ghosts of Mississippi,* the "uncanny blending of the 'real' and the re-created 'unreal,' between the authentic fact and the filmed fact, between the shadow and the act" created "layer upon layer of ironies . . . surreal to me in their unfolding."[4] Most surreal to Morris was the re-creation of Byron De La Beckwith. Under pounds of latex and paint, actor James Woods seemed literally to *become* the Klan killer—mimicking the voice and mannerisms of both the young and the old Beckwith with a dramatic flair that would earn him an Oscar nomination for Best Supporting Actor. Oddly, Fred Zollo's account of the historical impact of *Mississippi Burning* failed to add this critically successful performance to his chain of causation: no *Mississippi Burning,* he might have suggested, no *Ghosts of Mississippi,* no reinvention of Byron De La Beckwith.

For Hollywood's public relations purposes, of course, the impact of a movie generally regarded as historically distorted must by necessity stop at the imprisoning of Byron De La Beckwith, not with his compelling reincarnation. But the paternity of the resuscitated Beckwith can hardly be contested. With his scenery-chewing proclamations, flamboyant arrogance, and all-purpose "southern" accent, he is the geriatric descendant of a character type familiar to any moviegoer—the Hollywood cracker, the cinematic racist. As much a part of the iconography of southern films as cotton fields and magnolias, the cracker is the genre's dramatic centerpiece, its narrative *raison d'être.* It is he (and always a "he") who initiates and complicates the action, and it is he who is vanquished at movie's end by the only character capable of driving a stake through the heart of a Delta racist—his alter-ego, the man of law, the redeemed southern white man.

For the past decade, beginning with the release of *Mississippi Burning* in 1988, this has been America's most popular version of the civil rights story. During the year prior to the first stirrings of Hollywood's interest in retelling the story of southern crisis, American audiences saw the first broadcasts of Henry Hampton's multipart documentary *Eyes on the Prize.*

The new visibility of archival news footage of the era, along with increasing public interest in the Movement as reflected in the commercial and critical success of Taylor Branch's *Parting the Waters* in 1988 and the 1989 Hartford conference on the life and times of the Student Nonviolent Coordinating Committee, created a critical demand for greater historical authenticity in media re-creations of recent historical events. How Hollywood responded to this demand, however, says much about the power not only of stereotype in American culture, but of ingrained ways of imagining and representing the past.

Television drama had made several forays into civil rights history before movies entered the territory, most notably with *Attack on Terror* in 1975, the first retelling of the FBI's investigation of the Chaney, Schwerner, and Goodman murders; the four-hour biography of Martin Luther King in 1978; and *Crisis at Central High* in 1980, which depicted the Little Rock school desegregation crisis of 1957. Alan Parker's *Mississippi Burning*, however, was the first major cinematic re-creation of events in Movement history. Like *The Deer Hunter*, the 1978 film that triggered an avalanche of Vietnam films culminating in the 1989 *Born on the Fourth of July*, it appeared to mark a significant shift in public interest. The controversy surrounding its blatant disregard for historical accuracy only intensified its contemporary "importance"—and its commercial popularity. The way was opened for less sensationalized made-for-television movies that would focus on personalized, biographical tales of the era—the work of Mickey Schwerner (*Murder in Mississippi*); an aspiring black reporter's reminiscence of Watts (*Heat Wave*); the travails of Mississippi newspaperwoman Hazel Brannon Smith (*A Passion for Justice*); the pre-*Brown* legal maneuverings of Thurgood Marshall (*Simple Justice*); the life of Vernon Johns (*The Vernon Johns Story*); the rise and redemption of George Wallace (*Wallace*). Most ambitious of all was the short-lived, but critically acclaimed NBC series *I'll Fly Away*, with its evolving relationship between a white lawyer and his black housekeeper in small-town 1960s Georgia.

As a body, these works testify to the sustained popularity of stories related to the civil rights movement throughout the 1990s. In their studied adherence to biographical conventions, however, they reveal as well television's reverence for its own history. As a phenomenon experienced by millions as broadcast-quality images, as opposed to projection-quality images, the Movement was an inherently televisual spectacle. Increasingly lightweight handheld cameras with synchronized sound enhanced the ability of camera operators to capture spontaneous events, while the influence of cinema verité techniques prompted many of them to wade into the midst of dangerous confrontations. The privileged, engaged point of view came to dominate "crisis reporting," hence the reliance of tele-dramas on "eyewitness" accounts.

Narratives structured on journals and diaries abound in the genre, as does voice-over narration. The first "civil rights" docudrama, *Attack on Terror*, was adapted from Don Whitehead's nonfiction book on the FBI and was narrated by actor William Conrad in thunderous, Walter Cronkite fashion; excerpts from Little Rock teacher Elizabeth Huckaby's diary of 1957 are heard throughout *Crisis at Central High;* the memoirs of *Los Angeles Times* reporter Robert Richardson provide the narrative foundation of *Heat Wave;* and the soundtrack of *King* contains voice-over testimonies by many characters, including cameo narration by Ramsey Clark and Tony Bennett, both playing themselves.

The civil rights teledrama's investment in journalistic realism, however, is most clearly revealed in its extensive use of archival news footage. Documentary—or documentary-like—shots are often edited into the film, as if the fictionalized narrative were simply an extension of photographed history. Abby Mann, for example, in his 1978 *King,* reshot well-known news coverage of Birmingham, Selma, and Memphis using professional actors, and liberally spliced this black-and-white footage into archival footage hoping—one assumes—to create a seamless marriage of documented and restaged history. Major sequences in *Heat Wave* are introduced by news footage of Watts, and *Murder in Mississippi* contains clips from a 1964 NBC news special on the Freedom Summer. In docudramas like these, news footage often fills the screen and characters are embedded within it.

Most feature films that have attempted to re-create the civil rights era, however, have refused to yield ground to television's documentary capacity, insisting instead on what film has long claimed as its cultural prerogative to reshape and remystify the past. Like cinematic bookends, *Mississippi Burning* and *Ghosts of Mississippi* have spanned Hollywood's decade-long mission to "get the story right." Situated squarely within the decade, functioning as fulcrum to the project, has been the John Grisham phenomenon. As film adaptations of his best-selling novels have regularly sprung forth since the early 1990s, revisioning the civil rights era has taken on the appearance of a national obsession, with popular movies like *A Time to Kill* and *The Chamber* (both 1996) updating Deep South iconography for a contemporary audience.

But getting the postwar southern story "right" has meant different things to different people. To director Alan Parker, it was less a matter of history than of psychology: "If [*Mississippi Burning*] makes people feel something, viscerally and emotionally," he said in 1989, "if it makes them question the racism that exists in all of us now—and not just in 1964 among a bunch of Mississippi rednecks—only then will I have been true to the memory of James Chaney, Michael Schwerner, and Andrew Goodman."[5] To a great many historians and critics, Parker's "all of us" said it all. The film was a fable for, by, and *about* white characters (primarily FBI men), an irresponsible representation at best. Seven years later, Rob Reiner took a preemptive strike at charges of narrative racism when he defended his direction of *Ghosts of Mississippi:* "It's not just the Beckwith story or the Myrlie Evers or Medgar Evers story, it's also the DeLaughter story. Here was a white person who walked into this civil rights case and had to face his own feelings of racism. I can tell this story through this guy. I can start examining my own feelings through this character."[6] Straddling these positions, arguing for the primacy of *aesthetic* invention—as opposed to psychological or historical *truth*—has been Willie Morris, the man whose idea it was in the first place to rescript the third trial of Byron De La Beckwith. "Accuracy and truth are two different things," he writes. *Mississippi Burning,* he believes, is "metaphorically truthful" and *Ghosts of Mississippi* is "one hundred percent faithful to the spirit of the truth and eighty percent to the spirit of accuracy."[7]

In a sense, of course, Morris is right. *Metaphoric* truthfulness animates most culturally resonant popular art, especially film. Communicating social information through well-established generic codes, mainstream movies depend upon the audience's recognition of familiar narrative frameworks: the melodrama, the romance, the epic, and so on. Without this recognition, history is not a "story," and political strife has no identifiable purpose, individual struggle no empathic meaning. Within the world of film genre, however, society "makes sense"; traditional iconography and character types, in Hollywood's tautology, signify their own "significance." When Morris suggested to Fred Zollo in 1994 that a film be made of the last Beckwith trial, he shrewdly "pitched" the story as a number of possible generic formulas. "A stunning search," he offered. "A long quest for justice . . . maybe a modern-day *To Kill a Mockingbird* . . . maybe a love story?"[8] Regardless of structure, though, the film would make "a profoundly moving and dramatic story which I think envelopes [*sic*] what movie-goers like to see," not the least of which might be the recycled team of Gene Hackman and Willem Dafoe, updating their roles in *Mississippi Burning.* "A compelling thought," Morris asked Zollo, "Hackman as [Hinds County D.A. Ed] Peters, Dafoe as [Assistant D.A.] DeLaughter?"[9]

Despite the influence of *Mississippi Burning* on the next generation of civil rights-themed films, however, the movie itself was hardly the urtext of a new genre. The story of a lawman who rides into a dusty town to bring marauders to justice and rides out victorious with his sidekick is the most familiar American story of them all. Tipping his hand, perhaps, that the film was no more about historical reality than old westerns, director Alan Parker had the FBI set up local headquarters in an abandoned movie theater rather than a replica of the Delphia Courts Motel, where real agents worked in Philadelphia during the summer of 1964. Given this, the parameters of the fictional agents' investigation should hardly have been surprising. Launching their investigation from a rundown dream palace, they ultimately "discovered" well-worn characters in well-worn scenes— the shadows and ghosts of Hollywood Past.

It is perhaps fitting that filmmakers would turn to the conventions of the western film in their retelling of civil rights stories, for the genre has always been a major cultural arena in which Americans have dramatized issues of race. After World War II, westerns experienced a rebirth after ceding the field to war films, with nearly three hundred of them released between 1947 and 1956 and more than fifteen western television series between 1955 and 1967. The popularity of the genre is attributable in part, of course, to its blatantly overdetermined thematic concerns. The Indian-European conflict functioned largely as a displacement of postwar America's racial crisis, with countless films turning on the issue of miscegenation. The specter of mixed blood haunted these films, as countless white men embarked on missions to save their women from a fate worse than death. With his unbridled lust for white women and savage guerrilla warmongering, the Indian was himself a half-breed—half racial monster, half ideological phantom. A projection of the era's sexual and political obsessions, he was the worst nightmare of both the segregationist and the anti-Communist: the true Red Menace. The marriage of race and ideology was popularly acknowledged in the color-coded politics of the era: one's "red" background could land one on a "black" list, the no-man's land of economic and social exclusion.

In John Ford's 1956 film *The Searchers*, for example, the displacement is barely hidden as offscreen Cold Warrior John Wayne, playing unreconstructed Confederate soldier Ethan Edwards, takes every opportunity to express his genocidal rage. Believing it's better to be dead than Red, he is more than willing to kill his niece to prevent her becoming a "squaw." "He'll put a bullet in her brain," one character approvingly says. Like Ethan, Gene Hackman's Rupert Anderson in *Mississippi Burning* understands "the enemy" with a passion bordering on obsession. A former Mississippi sheriff wise to the ways of small-town southern bigots, Anderson functions as the FBI's—and the audience's—guide through the wilds of frontier barbarism. Just as Ethan "talks Comanche good," so does Anderson, an opponent of segregation, know how to "talk southern" to Klan members. He also, like Ethan, knows how to play as dirty as the enemy, with castration preferred over scalping as the method of vengeance

But a significant and disturbing difference marks the depictions of the two men's violence. By the mid-1950s, white vengeance could not be convincingly portrayed as unambiguous. With evidence of white brutality increasingly on display in newspapers and newscasts, the vigilante became a troubling figure in the media. In fact, John Ford took pains to imply that Ethan Edwards and his enemy, Chief Scar, were alter-egos. Scar had lost his family in a cavalry raid, just as Ethan had lost his to a Comanche raid; each spoke the other's language, and each committed similar acts of savagery. Ethan's violence, however, was often disturbingly unmotivated, his barbarism nothing short of pathological.

Paving the way for the liberal westerns of the late 1960s and early 1970s, in which Indians unsubtly stood in for victimized Vietnamese, postwar westerns like *The Searchers* began to betray a deep ambivalence about the imperatives of white America. Following the *Brown* decision, in fact, the genre increasingly questioned the "massive resistance" of frontier settlers and their army protectors, and made several attempts to portray Indians sympathetically. White thieves and poachers gradually supplanted Indians as acceptable villains, and even these characters were finally replaced in the late 1960s and early 1970s by corrupt institutions—banks, railroads, and cavalry itself—as the genre became a popular vehicle for social criticism.

This kind of evolving political complexity, however, has not been a characteristic of the civil rights film. Steadfastly refusing to call institutional racism into question, the new genre takes aim at character, and squares off the updated Indian fighter (now outfitted with suit, tie, and briefcase) against a suitably updated villain. But for liberal-minded Hollywood, the fashioning of an appropriate "them" to a new rainbow-coalitioned "us" has required a reorganization of the cinematic family tree. The new frontier savage no longer dwells in collectivist camps on the plains; his home is his castle and private property his creed. And his skin is no longer an emblem of otherness. All that remains of his "red" ancestry is the back of his neck: the raw mark of social exclusion, the stigmata of class. In Hollywood's revisit to the battlesites of freedom fighters, the new Red Menace is that most reviled of Palefaces: the cracker vigilante, the white-trash thug, the

Redneck. In his forceful removal of this diseased whiteness from his society, the southern man of law reclaims his homeland and redeems his race. The problem, it seems, has always been certain people.

The question of how the low-paid southern attorney or rural federal agent managed to metamorphose into a contemporary action-adventure hero raises a much more interesting question: when did such a metamorphosis occur? At what point after the *Brown* decision did the terms "southern lawman" and "hero" become culturally compatible, rather than oxymoronic? At what point could an *image* of southern law be created that didn't, to the nation at large and the rest of the world, connote *illegality*? In the summer of 1955, the obese, tobacco-chewing sheriff of Sumner County, Mississippi, Harold Strider, lumbered onto national television screens during the Emmett Till murder trial. As network news expanded into live coverage and longer nightly telecasts, Strider was replaced by a succession of near lookalikes—Bull Connor, Jim Clark, Lawrence Rainey, Cecil Price—all seemingly indistinguishable in manner and diction, and by innumerable men of law—governors, senators, mayors—who were visibly and vigorously resisting the law of the land. Pitting state and municipal law against national law, they lodged rhetorical appeals to the spirit of American independence and individualism, insisting that they and they alone were mustering resistance to a communist-inspired "invasion" and "takeover" of the country. Unfortunately for them, their "resistance" to northern aliens and black citizens looked like assault —not just on protesters, but on television viewers themselves. Not realizing the power of cinematic point of view (or simply not caring), lawmen like Jim Clark physically attacked cameramen.[10] No one at home saw the men behind the cameras; they only saw hands blocking their vision, images whirling in space, and blood and rain splattering their field of vision. When segregationist crowds spat on camera lenses, they spat—for all intents and purposes—on viewers.

Of course, many of the assailants were aware of this effect; they *intended* to attack all of those behind the camera who deigned to judge the white South; to their way of thinking, civil rights protests followed the press, rather than the other way around. Police chief Laurie Pritchett of Albany, Georgia, is perhaps the lone example of a southern lawman who understood on some level the nature of televisual journalism, and his counter-efforts to command the story helped undermine a powerful local movement. But this aberration only underscores the general rule that news cameras, whose operators were usually welcomed among civil rights groups, captured images of southern lawmen from the vantage point of those on the other side. Reversing the practice of narrative film, news footage objectified not African Americans but their opponents—it was they, in other words, who were made the "objects" of the camera's gaze. The practical and safe necessity of shooting at, rather than from among, the defenders of segregation inherently validated the subjectivity of civil rights protesters.

By the mid-1960s, the image of the southern lawman had become so estranged from national identification, so discredited as a point of view, that satire seemed the most appropriate mode for depicting the upholders of segregation. "During National Brotherhood Week," satirist Tom Lehrer sang, "Sheriff Clark and Lena Horne are dancing cheek-to-cheek." Lenny Bruce, Mort Sahl, and Woody Allen all took on redneck sheriffs in their skits. The American version of the British television series *That Was the Week That Was* featured tunes by the "Singing Segregationist Plumbers" (the class connotations of the occupation suggest the men's Strider/Connor/Clark overtones), while one of the show's lead performers, singer Nancy Ames, told *Life* magazine, "They ought to take a big scoop and just shove southerners into the Gulf of Mexico."[11]

In the midst of the media's sheriff-saturation, however, an odd phenomenon occurred: much of the nation fell in love with a southern sheriff. On October 3, 1960, *The Andy Griffith Show* premiered on CBS. From that year through 1967 it ranked in the top eight prime-time series on television, and was the top-ranked show in its final season, 1967 to 1968. Revolving around the domestic adventures of Andy Taylor, sheriff of tiny Mayberry, North Carolina, the show posed a strikingly odd contrast to the images filling the nightly news. Not only was Sheriff Taylor a normal-sized, non-tobacco-chewing nice guy, but he didn't even wear a gun. He was, in fact, almost a practicing pacifist who repeatedly taught others the lesson that calm common sense could solve most problems. The comic center of the show was his deputy, Barney Fife, an incompetent authority-monger who proudly toted a gun with its one bullet, on orders from Andy, kept buttoned in a shirt pocket. The idea for the show had evolved from a special episode of *The Danny Thomas Show*, which had aired earlier in 1960. In that episode, New York performer Danny Thomas was arrested by Andy for speeding through Mayberry on his way back from Florida. Throwing money at the hick sheriff and demanding to be recognized as a star landed the slick Yankee in Andy's jail, where he finally apologized for his arrogance. Learning that he should "slow down" and not expect "fast solutions" to problems, Danny came to appreciate the reasonableness of southern ways and the kind of sense a small-town sheriff could dispense.

As a weekly testament to the ideal of minimal social change, *The Andy Griffith Show* was ironically situated. Not only did it premiere the same year as the first student sit-ins in Greensboro, North Carolina, but its setting, the fictional Mayberry, was based on Griffith's own hometown of Mount Airy, North Carolina—sixty miles north of Greensboro. Although the show was set in contemporary times, the town of Mayberry seemed distinctly uncontemporary. Moreover, it was entirely white. Trouble occurred usually when outsiders—from the North or from California—came to town with nefarious schemes for bilking the citizens or introducing some kind of modernizing plan. Time and again, Mayberry, under the thoughtful leadership of Andy, resisted outside pressure to change. The static peacefulness of the setting was exaggerated by producer Sheldon Leonard's refusal to film the series before an audience. Using only one camera instead of the usual three, the show could move outside into "real" locations, where the silences of "real life" could punctuate the dialogue without the interruption of audience laughter. For a comedy series so intent on capturing an unusual level of emotional realism, the studied remoteness from the connotations of its setting was remarkable. But it was no accident. Describing his own work as writer on the show, Andy Griffith has claimed that both he and co-star Don Knotts had tried "to be true to our memories of the small-town South."[12] Both men came of age in the South of the 1920s and 1930s, and it is this sense of a *remembered* community that is most striking about the series. Mayberry, in fact, is nothing so much as a southern version of Andy Hardy's Carvel, the mythical white town of the most popular MGM series of the 1930s and early 1940s (the series that, it should be noted, was the archetype of future television situation comedies).

Clearly, any mainstream television program set in the contemporary South of the early 1960s faced immense staging problems. Although a number of social problem films that focused on race had been made in the immediate postwar years, the House Un-American Activities Committee investigations of the film and television industries that began in 1947, coupled with well-organized media surveillance by southern segregationists, made similar productions unthinkable for decades. In 1958, Rod Serling's teledrama based on the Emmett Till case was radically rewritten to omit any reference to the South, largely in response to Citizens' Councils' letters of protest. The broadcast version was set in New England, the victim was European, and even Coca-Colas—the ubiquitous southern drink—were banned from the set. Many southern stations refused to broadcast national programs featuring black performers throughout the

1950s and 1960s, aided by groups like the Louisiana-based Monitor South, which attempted to coordinate regional rejection of television shows with anti-South (i.e., anti-segregationist) bias. National sponsors repeatedly canceled support of programs which might offend the white South. On the Hollywood front, Mississippi Senator James Eastland called in 1959 for a constitutional amendment to give each state the authority to decide for itself what was censorable in the movies—states' rights, in other words, for movie-goers. Aware of the increasingly negative representation of their region in the national news, southern segregationists attacked what they called "the Paper Curtain," the barrier of "lies" constructed by the northern media which ran along the Mason-Dixon Line. The Mississippi State Sovereignty Commission even sent public relations emissaries north to lecture free to civic groups about the virtues of "the most lied-about state in the Union." In this climate, a prime-time series about a modern-day southern sheriff wouldn't have a chance.

The canniness of Griffith and producer Leonard, however, ensured the immense success of just such a show. As Ronald Reagan learned decades later, historical displacement is a powerful rhetorical tool. Reconstructing the Depression as a kinder, gentler time for white America, *The Andy Griffith Show* offered the tantalizing spectacle of a southern Shangri-la. Of its time, yet charmingly frozen on a studio back lot, Mayberry was CBS's prime-time challenge to its own evening newscasts. Coming into living rooms in the "family" hours following Walter Cronkite's stories from Birmingham and Selma, it suggested a different kind of realism—of selective memory, of silences and omissions.

If the temporal displacement of this program was purely suggestive and subliminal, though, that of another immensely popular southern story from 1960 was not. Like the Mayberry of *The Andy Griffith Show,* the Maycomb of Harper Lee's *To Kill a Mockingbird* was thinly based on its creator's hometown (this time, Monroeville, Alabama). But unlike Mayberry, Maycomb was a town divided by race and social class. By setting her story in the past, Lee was able to address mainstream television's taboo subject, yet here, too, the South took shape as a *memory,* a fantasy tempered by an acute awareness of its remoteness from present-day urgency. As Eric Sundquist has noted, "the novel harks back to the 1930s . . . to move the mounting fear and violence surrounding desegregation into an arena of safer contemplation."[13]

As remembered by the grown Scout Finch, her father Atticus was an early champion of tolerance, a small-town lawyer who dispensed legal assistance and common sense with enlightened equanimity. Like his prime-time brother Andy Taylor, he was a widower with children, an inherent pacifist, a fair-minded man of southern law. Around Atticus, however, revolved other men who would haunt his daughter's memory: Tom Robinson, a crippled black man wrongly accused of rape; Bob Ewell, Robinson's white accuser; and Boo Radley, Scout's reclusive neighbor. Robinson and Ewell are killed in the course of the novel, Robinson when he tries to escape from prison and Ewell when he attacks Scout and her brother Jem. It is Ewell's death at the hands of Boo Radley that ends the novel and brings to closure Scout's coming of age. Realizing that the "malevolent phantom" she thought had resided behind the rotten shutters of a once fine old house across the street has actually been her guardian angel, Scout must now recognize who the true ogre in her community has been all along: Robert E. Lee Ewell, the "bantam cock of a man" who bore "no resemblance to his namesake," the patriarch of a dump-dwelling brood of illiterates.[14] "People like the Ewells lived as guests of the county in prosperity as well as in the depths of a depression," Scout recalls. "No truant officers could keep their numerous offspring in school; no public health officer could free them from congenital defects, various worms, and the diseases indigenous to filthy surroundings."[15] Bob Ewell, the violent man whose "face was as red as his neck," is killed by Boo Radley, the gentleman with "sickly white" skin, "dead hair," and "gray eyes so colorless I thought he was blind." After saving Scout's life and escorting her down the sidewalk "as any gentleman would do," the valiant Boo disappears forever on Halloween night into his crumbling house.[16]

As Atticus reads aloud from *The Gray Ghost,* Scout falls asleep, secure in the knowledge that not only her father but her very own gray ghost stand vigilant in her protection—and guilt-free. Boo Radley, the fading specter of southern gentility, need never stand trial. "Taking the one man who's done you and this town a great service an' draggin' him with his shy ways into the limelight—to me, that's a sin," the local sheriff tells Atticus, interpreting the law for the community. "There's a black boy dead for no reason, and the man responsible for it's dead. Let the dead bury the dead this time, Mr. Finch."[17] With the sacrifice of the black man and the compensatory slaying of the redneck, the novel draws to a close. "Thank you for my children," Atticus tells Boo.[18] And, indeed, the chain of events that culminates in Bob Ewell's death awakens in Scout the social conscience that will produce, twenty years later, *To Kill a Mockingbird.*

The film of Harper Lee's novel appeared in 1962, winning an Oscar for Gregory Peck in the role of Atticus Finch. Oddly, Peck had just completed another film about southern justice when he began work on *To Kill a*

Mockingbird. The film, *Cape Fear,* was set in contemporary North Carolina and told the story of district attorney Sam Bowden (Peck), whose family is terrorized by a man Bowden once sent to jail. With its condemnation of laws that protect the rights of vagrants, outsiders, and "unwanted elements," *Cape Fear* seemed to turn the liberal politics of the moment on its head, for it argued that vigilante justice was not only the correct response of upstanding white men to those who threatened their security; it was the *only possible* response. With this premise, the film could easily have been the product of a state sovereignty commission, except for one point: the unwanted element in *Cape Fear* was not a black agitator, nor a white troublemaker from the North. It was a low-rent white man, a farm-boy rapist fresh from jail come to take revenge on the man who put him away.

As played by Robert Mitchum, Max Cady is the lewdest of crackers. With a straw hat pushed back on his head and shirt hanging outside his trousers, he strikes a discordant note the moment he appears in the film. In the first scene he strolls across the town square of a picturesque southern town and enters the courthouse. "Hey, daddy," he says to a black janitor, a crack that lets the audience know all they need to know about his social class and, implicitly, his racial attitudes. Cady's casual violation of propriety expands into savage explosions of violence as he circles his primary target: the moss-draped, white-pillared home of Sam Bowden. Bowden finds he can do nothing to stop Cady's stalking and imminent attack on his family. "I can't arrest a man for what might be in his mind," the police chief tells Bowden. "That's dictatorship." "A man like that doesn't deserve civil rights," Bowden's wife replies, and she is proved right in the film, for Cady is no man at all. He is in fact "an animal," "a beast," "a shocking degenerate." The fact that the score for the film was composed by Bernard Herrmann, best known for his Hitchcock and science fiction scores, only intensifies the horror of Max Cady's haunting of the Bowden family. When Bowden realizes that his daughter will most likely be raped by Cady, he is forced to abandon his dependence on the law and defend his family himself. With reassurances from his wife that their "pioneer stock" will ultimately triumph, Bowden plans and executes his own version of frontier warfare. Sequestering his women on a houseboat, he lures Cady into hand-to-hand combat in a primeval swamp, and reclaims the territory for white decency. Disappearing into mist and sludge at film's end, however, Max Cady, the cracker from hell, does not die. Like all mythic demons, he only takes a breather—this time for six months, after which he will reappear in Maycomb, Alabama, on Halloween night, in the guise of Bob Ewell.

If both *Cape Fear* and *To Kill a Mockingbird* constructed their respective villains as products of the South's underbelly, they could not agree on the causative factors. The conservative politics of *Cape Fear* pointed in the direction of inherent evil, yet hinted at a possibility that would have been unthinkable to Harper Lee: the intimate relationship between the redneck and the tolerant white man. Throughout the film Max Cady is positioned as Sam Bowden's alter-ego, his repressed double who voices that which Bowden cannot (in Martin Scorsese's 1990 remake, this subtext was brought to the surface). Cady knows the law as well as Bowden, and each man is able to think like the other and predict each other's moves. The central horror in the film is the lawman's recognition of this connection and his awareness that he must, by film's end, confront his despised kinsman.

No such recognition was required of Atticus Finch; in fact, the prospect of confrontation was so obscene that it could not even be visualized, only recollected by his child as the Halloween-eve sounds of a gray ghost vanquishing a drunken monster. *To Kill a Mockingbird* indicted systemic poverty to some degree for the Bob Ewells of the South, but held the moral center of the story, the white man of law, inviolate, unimplicated in the lawlessness which surrounded him. Both narratives, however, in their insistence upon the *inherent badness* of their arch-villains, shared a class-based view of sociopathology. By portraying Max Cady's violence as simultaneously *unconscious,* a function of animal-like cruelty, and *conscious,* a campaign of revenge, *Cape Fear* managed to encode its criminal as both Indian savage and lynch-mob racist. By doing so, the film was able, not only to disguise its concern for the threatened civil rights of *white* men as a concern for the rights of *good* men, but to cast its story as a conventional tale of frontier justice. To a lesser degree, Bob Ewell served a similar function in *To Kill a Mockingbird,* his violence, alcoholism, and racism fueling a mission of revenge against the family of a lawyer. In the fictional Deep South, the embattled men of law were the brave new cavalry scouts, all that stood between peaceful communities below the Mason-Dixon Line and the new rednecked hordes.

Clearly, this image could not withstand the reality principle. Atticus Finch and Andy Taylor resided in a fantasy of the past, and Sam Bowden's North Carolina town seemed to have just one black resident. By the mid-1960s the visual discrepancy between television news and narrative films and television shows like these approached surreality. Nervous networks continued to back away from realistic representations of the South, sending hillbillies to California (*The Real McCoys,* 1957–1962, was followed by

The Beverly Hillbillies, 1963–1971) and to the Marine Corps (Andy Taylor's friend Gomer Pyle was "spun off" in his own series from 1964 to 1969), while MGM created yearly cartoon-like settings for Elvis Presley. In fact, between 1963 and 1966, the number of feature films set even partially in the South dropped from an average of nine per year between 1956 and 1962 (with a high in 1958 of thirteen) to an average of four. The Tennessee Williams canon was exhausted by this time, and the few attempts to make "relevant" racial statements on film were commercial failures (*Black Like Me* and *Nothing But a Man* [both 1964] and *A Man Called Adam* [1966]). Television news filled the conspicuous void, with all three networks broadcasting more than eight major studies of civil rights issues between 1963 and 1966. The stylistic proficiency of many of these reality-based productions only exacerbated the tension between fiction and nonfiction on the nation's television and film screens; in fact, it seemed that an alternative South existed on the news, one far more compelling than the Technicolor, widescreen version.

With growing public absorption in live coverage of not only civil rights crises but the war in Vietnam, it stood to reason that any movie that attempted to deal with contemporary social problems would need to exhibit similar "signs" of reality. Borrowing techniques from documentary filmmakers, a number of mainstream directors and cinematographers began to craft a new style for American film. Hand-held camera shots, method-inspired improvisation, and relatively graphic violence, in fact, characterized a series of films released in 1967, all of which exploited "southernness" as a marker of daring "realism."

Chief among them was one film that finally broke Hollywood's silence about the contemporary South—and was richly rewarded for doing so. *In the Heat of the Night* was the first studio-produced feature film since 1949 that appeared to deal directly with what everyone had been seeing on the news for thirteen years: the racism of the southern legal system. With its ironic opening shot of a sign proclaiming, "You are now entering the town of Sparta, Mississippi. Welcome!" and its archetypal southern police chief Bill Gillespie (played by Rod Steiger as a composite of Harold Strider, Bull Connor, and Jim Clark), the film announced its liberation from the evasions and displacements of previous films and television shows. The mise-en-scène, filled with the props denied to Rod Serling nine years earlier in his doomed attempt to tell the Emmett Till story, impressed on viewers the "realism" of the location. Dr. Pepper bottles in the foreground, Coca-Cola machines in the background, malfunctioning air conditioning units, rifle racks, cotton fields, dingy jail cells, transistor radios squawking country music—the South that took shape onscreen was far removed from the familiar decadent plantation landscape of Tennessee Williams-inspired movies. The story that unfolded within this set also contained immediately resonant details: a black man wrongly accused and imprisoned by racist cops; a police chief hostile to outsiders (and who, in a fairly daring bit of scripting, confuses Philadelphia, Pennsylvania, with Philadelphia, Mississippi); and a non-southern character who gets to ask the questions raised by a decade of news footage: "My God, what kind of people are you? What kind of place is this?"

Giving indications that it might actually provide clues, if not answers, to the source of endemic racism, the film's plot revolves around a murder possibly committed by a wealthy plantation owner. Virgil Tibbs, the Philadelphia detective played by Sidney Poitier, tries his best to pin charges on the man; "I can pull that fat cat down! I can bring him right off this hill!" he says. The film, however, is not about to tread on that territory. All ends up right with the system: the fat cat is blameless, the racist deputy turns out to be a Barney Fife buffoon and the white rural police chief, himself a lonely outsider as it turns out, joins forces with the urban black man to unveil the real criminal in Sparta, Mississippi: white cracker Ralph Henshaw, night worker at the diner, the man whose intense, sweaty face is the first one seen in the film as he tries to shoot a fly with a rubber band.

In the Heat of the Night won Oscars for Best Picture and Best Actor (Steiger), but in the long run its most significant achievement may have been the impact of Stirling Silliphant's Oscar-winning script, which would become a blueprint for future films attempting to re-create the South of the 1960s. Although the plot of the film varied little from that of John Ball's 1965 novel of the same name, Silliphant moved the action from the North Carolina mountains to rural Mississippi, changed Tibbs's hometown from Pasadena to Philadelphia, and transformed Police Chief Gillespie from a tall young Texan to Steiger's familiar overweight, middle-aged quasi-redneck. In an apparent attempt to make a significant statement about contemporary Mississippi, however, he took his character cues from film history. By not implicating the white power structure in the major crimes of the story, by exonerating, in effect, the legal and economic institutions of the Deep South, Silliphant's screenplay managed to create a "social realism" that was both politically acceptable and commercially viable. Central to this strategy was the white working-class villain, the character whose inherent criminality would be the *sine qua non* of the new southern story.

While Andy Griffith, Atticus Finch, and Sam Bowden bore no resemblance to real southern lawmen (Atticus and Sam didn't even have regional accents), Steiger's Bill Gillespie accomplished a sleight of hand worthy of Houdini. Literally overnight, the enforcer of illegitimate law—states' rights and Jim Crow—metamorphosed into the protector and defender of legitimate law. The southern sheriff had now achieved his media clearance to become an American hero. By redeeming southern political authority, *In the Heat of the Night* resuscitated and refined a genre that had grown moribund. In the process, it redeemed whiteness itself by projecting the criminality of the race onto its lowest member. True to John Ball's novel, Stirling Silliphant's screenplay breathed life into a villain familiar to American audiences: the malingering redneck, "unschooled, prejudiced, and of a low level of intelligence," a man of "warped mind."[19]

We need only look at the success of the book and film versions of *Deliverance* three years later to verify the popularity of the theme of white redemption. Here, the crackers from hell are the most evil of guerrilla warriors, following up sexual assaults with bow-and-arrow warfare, and the southern sheriff—played by author James Dickey himself—is a shrewd voice of common sense. The residents of Rabun County, Georgia, were not happy when director John Boorman photographed mentally handicapped townspeople as evidence of the "horror" of the backwoods South. But the images proved compelling for the rest of the nation, and *Deliverance* entered popular consciousness as a cautionary tale of the unrepressed savagery awaiting civilized white men just off the road in the southern wilderness.

The iconography lives on, breathing life into otherwise stale narratives of the "nature versus civilization" variety. *The Prince of Tides*, for example, located a sensitive southern white man's neurosis in a childhood rape by rampaging redneck prison escapees in South Carolina, and a 1997 episode of *The X-Files* merged *The Andy Griffith Show* and *Deliverance* into a tale of repellent hillbillies who murder a black sheriff named Andy Taylor in a northern town called Mayberry. It has, moreover, proved easily adaptable to the series of civil rights-themed films inaugurated by *Mississippi Burning*. Like Bob Ewell, Max Cady, Ralph Henshaw, and the mountain mutants of *Deliverance*, the new enemies are rural rednecks all, their villainy emblazoned on their costumes: red, the color of the Grand Dragon's robes in *A Time to Kill*, the color of Klansman Sam Cayhall's death row jumpsuit in *The Chamber*, the color of Byron De La Beckwith's jacket that he wears shamelessly throughout his third trial in *Ghosts of Mississippi*. Just as evident is their ancestral link to the demons of earlier films. The spirit of Byron De La Beckwith seems to animate the bottle tree outside Bobby DeLaughter's daughter's room, frightening him into the decision to stop singing *Dixie* to her at night. "Maybe the ghosts are gone," Adam Hall says after Sam Cayhall is finally executed at the end of *The Chamber*, but the genre will insist otherwise.

Opposing and conquering the new savages are the rehabilitated southern white men of law: FBI agent and ex-sheriff Rupert Anderson, lawyer Jake Brigance in *A Time to Kill*, lawyer Adam Hall in *The Chamber*, and Assistant District Attorney Bobby DeLaughter in *Ghosts of Mississippi*. Like most western heroes, the new lawman fights practically alone—his victory demands a stripped-down, man-to-man battle against the Other, his repressed double, the unprogressive, ignorant cracker. In this battle, women can only look on, lending support but not sharing the knock-out punch. Rupert Anderson seduces a Klansman's wife into the betrayal of her husband; Jake Brigance's wife leaves him, to be supplanted by a friendly female attorney; and Adam Hall is assisted by a woman in the state government. Bobby DeLaughter's wife Dixie (the real name of De-Laughter's first wife) leaves him, allowing him to find a symbolically progressive second wife, and, oddest of all, Myrlie Evers sits at home or in the courthouse, waiting for DeLaughter's legal abilities to win or lose the day.

Attempts have been made to tell a different kind of civil rights story, one in which white men play consistently adversarial roles. *The Long Walk Home* (1990) and *Heart of Dixie* (1989) both focus on white women caught up in a southern crisis—in *Heart of Dixie* the integration of a fictional college in the 1950s, in *The Long Walk Home* (by far the more sophisticated of the two) the Montgomery bus boycott. While both films make their white heroines the centers of their narratives, they also attempt to link the civil rights struggle with a more general struggle against white male authority. In each case, the heroine leaves her husband or fiancé and visually bonds with a black woman. Neither film was commercially successful.

What *has* proved commercially successful is the spectacle of the redemption of white authority. If Gene Hackman's federal agent operated primarily as a bust-'em-up gunfighter with his heart in the right place, the lawyers of the 1990s have displayed the decade's fondness for public confession. By accepting his black client's description of him as "one of the bad guys," Jake Brigance plans a winning courtroom strategy in *A Time to Kill*: the raped black child could have been white, she could have been his own daughter. By extrapolation, then, Jake discovers that he is no different than his black client. Adam Hall must travel South to Parchman Prison and accept his heritage. He, unlike others in his family, will look the racism of his ancestors in the eye and defend his Klansman grandfather on death row, a grandfather who, it conveniently turns out, was not nearly as racist as others in his klavern. Bobby DeLaughter imagines himself as Medgar Evers, a leap that allows him to push onward in his case. In turn, director Rob Reiner imagines himself as DeLaughter, which allows him to push onward in his film.

Throughout the South of recent movies, it seems, white lawyers have been especially busy, cementing emotional bonds with criminals and victims, reaching out to take on the burden of racial guilt. As such, they have functioned as cinematic historians, researching the past, explaining it, and bringing it to closure. So convinced are the filmmakers of the social importance of their work that they have filled their works with centrally placed signifiers of "reality": in *The Chamber*, a famous photograph of a dual lynching in Marion, Indiana, in 1930 becomes "evidence" of Klansman Sam Cayhall's childhood experiences in the Mississippi Delta (the word "Daddy" is scrawled by the image of a child in the foreground of the photograph), and documents supposedly from the State Sovereignty Commission are formatted precisely like real documents from the Commission. In *Ghosts of Mississippi*, Reiner's crew went to inordinate expense to ensure the authenticity of props—even, for the final scene, flying trash barrels from the Hinds County Courthouse to Hollywood.

Nothing, however, signifies historical authenticity as strongly as videotaped images. As the medium of television news (although network-wide in the U.S. only since 1967), videotape connotes "reality" for film viewers in much the same way that black-and-white photography connotes "the past," and filmmakers intent on convincing viewers of the historical accuracy of their productions rarely hesitate to employ both conventions. When Willie Morris pitched his film idea for *Ghosts of Mississippi* to producer Fred Zollo, he suggested "going first and at considerable length with black-and-white, documentary-type footage of Mississippi in 1963 . . . then on in color to the new investigation and trial of the 1990s."[20] Rob Reiner used the convention in his opening credit sequence, a montage of sepia-toned black-and-white archival news footage that concluded with the title "This Story Is True." The appearance of documented truth, however, can create peculiar moments of postmodern irony, however unintentional. In *A Time to Kill*, Matthew McConaughey, as Jake Brigance, admires himself on simulated local news programs; in *The Chamber*, Chris O'Donnell, playing Adam Hall, watches and rewatches black-and-white video footage of Gene Hackman, playing his grandfather, supposedly from 1967; and in *Ghosts of Mississippi*, Alec Baldwin as Bobby DeLaughter studies James Woods as Byron De La Beckwith in meticulously re-created videotaped footage (in the same way Whoopi Goldberg, as Myrlie Evers, watches authentic archival film footage of John F. Kennedy in the early moments of the film).

Certainly, there is nothing new about fabricated news footage in the movies. *Citizen Kane*, *JFK*, and *Wag the Dog* may seem wildly dissimilar in their use of doctored or restaged footage, but each film is in its own way concerned with the power of media to shape, even invent, historical events. In their devotion to the "spirit of accuracy" touted by Willie Morris, however, the recent films about civil rights and the South seem odd throwbacks to an earlier cinematic era. Directors like Rob Reiner, in fact, resemble no one so much as D. W. Griffith, whose meticulously created "historical facsimiles" in *The Birth of a Nation* served a number of rhetorical purposes, not least of which was the construction of Griffith as popular historian. Like Griffith, the new tellers of the southern story set out to "heal" cultural wounds, to reunite the nation by reclaiming the alienated white southerner. In order to do this, however, someone else must fill the role of un-American Other. For Griffith it was the descendants of slaves, for the new storytellers it is the descendants of white tenant farmers and sharecroppers. Under the protective cover of the documentary conventions of their times, though, the master and the disciples of the historical facsimile school tell the old Halloween stories of demons and "malevolent phantoms" haunting the southern landscape.

Despite Willie Morris's surreal sense of the "uncanny blending of the 'real' and the re-created 'unreal'" in films like *Ghosts of Mississippi*, perhaps the only truly uncanny recent story of the contemporary South has not been one of burnings, killings, or ghosts, but of innocence rewarded. While not generally regarded as a "civil rights film," the immensely popular *Forrest Gump* (1994) is nothing if not a retelling of postwar southern history. The film signals its historical designs, in fact, in the first scene, in which a black woman waits for a southern city bus. Although the scene is set in present-day Savannah, the Rosa Parks connotations are unmistakable. As if taking his cues from the scenario, the dimwitted Forrest proceeds to offer up to the woman a virtual apologia for southern racism. Although many critics have trouble with the sheer *fact* of the apologia, it is the form of the defense that may well be the most problematic aspect of the film. Yes, the innocent Forrest is named after the founder of the Klan, and yes, his understanding of Klan terror amounts to "Sometimes we all do things that, well, just don't make no sense." But the footage that accompanies this narration isn't a historical facsimile in the tradition of Rob Reiner and company. It is, in fact, simulated footage from *Birth of a*

Nation, made parodic by Tom Hanks's cameo role as Nathan Bedford Forrest himself (we see Hanks as Forrest first in a sepia-toned freeze-frame, itself a simulated Matthew Brady photograph, which then becomes the animated opening shot of nightrider footage). Suggesting that the real Klan was somehow archived in *Birth of a Nation* may be morally reprehensible, but from a postmodern perspective, director Robert Zemeckis's instincts as a popular filmmaker are accurate: the culture *does* "know" history from Hollywood productions.

Further, by simulating *Griffith's* simulations, he implicitly validates the authenticity of the fiction film (after all, Reiner and others signify reality by similarly replicating older footage). By placing Hanks in the footage, though, Zemeckis collapses film history and American history into one seamless, thematically unified document. Fiction and nonfiction tell the same story throughout the film, teaching viewers to revisit historical images with a keener eye. Looking closely, we see that all along, obscured by the thunder and violence of race-related narratives, a kind and decent spirit haunted our screens—Forrest leading the Klan in silly bedsheets, Forrest following Vivian Malone through the schoolhouse door in Tuscaloosa like a guardian angel. Thanks to Zemeckis's industrial light and magic, we can now repixellate the gentle gray ghost in the machinery of southern racism: the good white man, the new Boo Radley. To prove his worthiness to the mantle, millionaire Forrest not only becomes landed gentry but bulldozes down the last vestige of crackerdom in the film: the shack of Jenny's white trash demon father.

If the film begins with a visual salute to the civil rights movement—the integration of public buses—it ends with the Movement's erasure. A rural Alabama schoolbus stops to pick up Forrest Jr., completely empty except for the white driver. In this final sequence, the issue of school integration effectively disappears as Forrest Sr. reigns over a nearly depopulated South—white, wealthy, decent. The fact that *Forrest Gump* was the most popular movie of 1994, the same year that Republicans swept national elections (led by a former history professor from Georgia named Newt Gingrich), says much about America's investment in the image of the law-abiding southern white man. In his vigorously asserted difference from his redneck and cracker cousins, Gump stands as an emblem of not only a reclaimed region, but a redeemed race. According to the movies, the southern problem has never been white people; it has, it seems, always been social class.

Notes

1. Willie Morris, *The Ghosts of Mississippi: A Tale of Race, Murder, Mississippi, and Hollywood* (New York: Random House, 1998), 83.

2. *Los Angeles Times*, February 22, 1989, A2.

3. Morris, *Ghosts of Mississippi*, 83.

4. Ibid., 31.

5. *Newsday*, December 8, 1988, II4.

6. Morris, *Ghosts of Mississippi*, 108.

7. Ibid., 232.

8. Ibid., 87.

9. Ibid.

10. For Jim Clark's assault on the cameraman, see the documentary *Eyes on the Prize*, series 1, part 6, produced by Henry Hampton (Blackside, 1987).

11. "That Was the Deb That Was," *Life*, June 26, 1964, 87.

12. Andy Griffith, interview by author, February 4, 1997.

13. Eric Sundquist, "Blues for Atticus Finch," in *The South as an American Problem*, ed. Larry J. Griffin and Don H. Doyle (Athens: University of Georgia Press, 1995), 186.

14. Harper Lee, *To Kill a Mockingbird* (1960; reprint, New York: Warner, 1982), 8, 170.

15. Ibid., 170.

16. Ibid., 170, 270, 278.

17. Ibid., 176.

18. Ibid., 276.

19. John Ball, *In the Heat of the Night* (New York: Harper and Row, 1965), 177, 183.

20. Morris, *Ghosts of Mississippi*, 86.

5

Hip Like Me

Racial Cross-Dressing in Pop Music Before Elvis

David L. Chappell

"In her, something miraculous burns . . ."
—Anna Akhmatova, "Music" (to Dimitri Shostakovich), 1958

In his biography of Charles Dickens, G. K. Chesterton says, "The true way to overcome the evil in class distinctions is not to denounce them as revolutionists denounce them, but to ignore them as children ignore them."[1] Feigning naiveté to offset the naiveté of revolutionists, Chesterton calls attention to one end of a spectrum of subversion, the end that is usually invisible to the scholarly eye. His insight, which applies to racial distinctions as well as to class distinctions, provides a key to the mysteries of the civil rights movement. Most historians of that Movement have focused on African American activists, who were revolutionists in the sense that they set out to destroy the political and social distinctions on which an entire region based its identity. Historians have all but ignored the other side, though it is just as important: the more playful, more childlike activity of black and white Americans who broke down racial distinctions without any political program, more or less accidentally, in the name of entertainment.[2] In the decade before mass protests broke out in 1955, black and white musicians bent and permeated racial barriers. They had irresistible fun doing so, and they appeared to be providing nothing but harmless diversion—or, rather, they made those who worried about the political implications of their fun appear to be tiresome fanatics. Building on a long history of cross-racial mimicry, they shaped Americans' conscious and subconscious attitudes about race and freedom, thus preparing the psychological and ideological ground for the changes that protests finally brought.[3]

Despite the general boom in the U.S. economy after World War II, the music industry was in crisis. There was a growing public aversion to jazz, to bebop in particular, and many blamed this aversion for the industry's failure to grow in the booming postwar consumer market. Louis Armstrong, still the most popular jazzman in America in the 1940s and 1950s, led what *Down Beat* magazine called an "anti-bop campaign,"[4] saying "bop will kill business unless it kills itself first."[5] Many of the leading jazz performers, including Ella Fitzgerald, Eartha Kitt, and Tommy Dorsey, joined Armstrong in his campaign.[6] Even "Mr. Bop," Dizzy Gillespie, distanced himself from Charlie Parker and blamed bop musicians' attitude for jazz's failure to hold the public's attention.[7] Band leaders shook off the bop label as fast as they could. Elliot Lawrence, for example, said, "ours is not a bop band and we don't like boplicity to that effect."[8] There was dissatisfaction among black as well as white audiences. The entertainment columnist for the *Baltimore Afro-American*, E. B. Rea, complimented rhythm and blues singer Ivory Joe Hunter for purging his band of a "bop cult." If Hunter's idea caught on, as Rea hoped, it would mean "better music and more patrons through the turnstiles." Too many music lovers were staying away from bands because of the "bop cult" and "the general . . . belief that most musicians are 'dope' addicts."[9]

The trouble for the major record companies was that they saw only one major alternative to bop. Though Armstrong and others were frustrated with bop's insistent obscurity, most of the other famous musicians from the period were bored with "popular" music. To them, the cause of the industry's woes was singers like Guy Lombardo and Perry Como, who sounded as though they were singing on Thorazine. Long before rock and roll, great performers like Frank Sinatra, who had to sing Tin Pan Alley's boilerplate, complained bitterly of how dull and unimaginative their material was. It all added up to what *Down Beat,* which monitored the habits of both highbrow and mass audiences, called the "succession of musical frustrations" America had gone through "since World War II." Reflecting the attitude of the industry, *Down Beat* remarked, "Something new in music is needed. Something akin to the excitement aroused by discovering an Armstrong, a Bix, the Ellington cohesion of sound, the electric shock of the rhythmic power of Basie, the poetic phrasing of Pres."[10] Britain's *New Musical Express* noted a desperate quest for novelty afoot in the American music industry: "The constant search for the new, the startling and the simple."[11]

An inkling of what the industry sensed it needed came from the most successful black musician in the postwar era, Nat "King" Cole, who said,

"I'm in the music business for one purpose—to make money." Cole cited the white singer Frankie Laine as his model—a case of a black singer copying a white singer who was himself copying black singers.[12] Laine had been struggling since the 1930s and broke through on the pop charts for the first time in May 1947 with "That's My Desire," in which he copied the black singer Hadda Brooks and sounded a bit like Billie Holiday.[13] Cole said, "Some people think [Laine is] a jazz singer, but he isn't. . . . He's a modern Al Jolson," and "Jazz is pretty dead commercially anyway." Cole was once a promising jazz pianist, but in response to the recession of 1937, he went on tour with a new repertoire. "We weren't trying to prove anything musically. All we wanted was work. . . . For seven years we knocked around. . . . I was lucky because I could sing a little. So I did, for variety." The vocals caught on, he said, and "expanded our audience." Cole became the greatest of the "Sepia Sinatras" who became popular after the war.[14]

Another inkling came from the most successful white singer of the 1940s. Frank Sinatra said his great vocal teacher "was Billie Holiday, whom I first heard in 52nd Street clubs in the early 1930s, who was and still remains the greatest single musical influence on me." Sinatra, by his promotion of and appearances with black musicians, conveyed the sense that racial barriers inhibited musical expression.[15] The music trade press was generally apolitical, only speaking out on issues that affected musicians directly, such as dope and union rights. Yet in the 1940s and early 1950s, the trade press voiced a militant opposition to Jim Crow, in the name of artistic freedom.

The biggest inkling of what was to come lay in the rise of a new genre, the so-called "Jump Blues." Jazz purists—not merely bop snobs but also many of the moldy figs—condemned this as a new form of commercialism.[16] But it saved the income of many jazz performers, the most important of whom was Louis Jordan.

Louis Jordan was the leader of the first all-black band to break the color bar in the Club Belvedere in Hot Springs, Arkansas, the famed resort where Al Capone and other gangsters went on the lam in the 1930s. The Belvedere's owners, trying to run a respectable joint, were having trouble with previous white musicians: they made passes at the "fashionable" lady customers. The color bar was so strict, the owners knew, that no black musician would do that. Maintaining class lines, in this case, required breaking a particular racial barrier, but that only worked because a more general racial barrier was assumed to be stronger than class.[17]

Jordan studied and was influenced by earlier black musicians who had broken color bars by selling their music to white audiences, especially Fats

Waller, Cab Calloway, Louis Armstrong, and Bessie Smith. But Jordan took a lot directly from white musicians, too. According to his biographer, John Chilton, Jordan's "taste was broad, and Duke Ellington took no more of his time than did the more commercial sounds of Fred Waring's Pennsylvanians." Jordan was also influenced by Paul Whiteman, the white bandleader of the 1920s whose millions of dollars' worth of "watered-down" jazz set the industry's standard of cultural theft. "It seems odd that a fine young black musician, raised with the sound of the blues and magnificent gospel music, should have been attracted to the output of one of the corniest bands in the world, but," as Chilton notes, "Louis appreciated diverse music, regarding every sound new to him as a possible ingredient to use in his performances." Illustrating how racial division often turned into a hall of mirrors, Jordan played for a long time with a black bandleader, LeRoy Smith, who copied Whiteman's arrangements, and even encouraged people to call him "the colored Paul Whiteman."[18]

In other words, a history of racial cross-dressing figured prominently in Jordan's career. Some literal cross-dressing may have given Jordan a special knack: he "was a little gay," according to the black singer Ida Fields, who ought to know since she married Jordan (or at least began living with him) in 1932. Jordan frequented Roscoe's, a transvestite bar in Philadelphia, where Fields once caught him in partial improvised drag "doing a striptease on top of a table." She dragged him home indulgently but gave the impression that this was not an isolated incident.[19]

In World War II, Jordan became phenomenally successful. He toured the country widely, playing to white, black, and mixed crowds.[20] By 1943, according to *Down Beat*, Jordan's band was "one of the highest-paid, if not *the* highest paid cocktail combo in the business." He repeatedly broke attendance records at clubs. His hits ranked high on the "race" chart that *Billboard* began in 1942, yet also "crossed over" onto the white or "pop" chart, where they were often big hits as well. He recorded with Ella Fitzgerald and Bing Crosby and made hit Hollywood movies, which featured his music.[21] James Brown, Chuck Berry, and Ray Charles, among many black musicians who later became huge stars, all named Jordan as a formative influence on their music.[22]

Some people criticized Jordan for being an "uncle tom"—Charlie Parker called him that as he refused an offer to play with him. And there is in many of his novelty tunes (i.e., most of his biggest "pop" hits) an aura of Stepin-Fetchit and blackface minstrelsy, an element of appealing to white caricatures of black life—as there is in much of Fats Waller, Cab Calloway, and sometimes Louis Armstrong. But Jordan's role in breaking down racial barriers was complex. As the jazz historian Ralph Gleason wrote, Jordan stood out among his contemporaries. "The Mills Bros. like the Ink Spots were really black men singing white songs. But Louis Jordan sang black and sang proud."[23] Jordan *did* make fun of black people by drawing on stereotypes, but his black audiences apparently appreciated these stereotypes—at least they bought his records and attended his shows in record numbers.[24]

There were plenty of other examples of black people mimicking black people, and it should not be assumed that all that mimicry was commercial exploitation for white consumption. The great historian of rhythm and blues music, Arnold Shaw, commented that, at a time when black people were becoming more assertive, more militant, and more successful in breaking down prejudice and discrimination, the "element of self-caricature . . . in Jordan's humor . . . might have accounted for his appeal to 'ofays' [pig latin for 'foes'—meaning white people]. There is also the possibility that middle-class blacks felt that they were laughing at things associated with rural and lower-class blacks. But there was also a measure of strength in the ability to laugh at oneself—and this is what, I think, Jordan may have communicated to black people."[25] Jordan's "Jump Blues" style soon evolved into rhythm and blues, the embryonic form of what later became rock and roll, doo wop, soul, blue beat, ska, Motown, rock, funk, disco, fusion, reggae, punk, new wave, rap, hip hop, and many lesser genres.

Jordan's background suggests that the usual story of rock and roll as a white commercial rip-off of genuine black culture is too simplistic. The usual story is illustrated by the famous line attributed to producer Sam Phillips of Sun Records in Memphis: "If I could find a white boy who could sing like a nigger, I could make a million dollars"—which Phillips did, of course, in Elvis Presley, though (perhaps through poetic justice) RCA ended up getting the millions.[26] That story is based on truth, and it *is* a big part the story of rock's origins. But there is much more to the story. For all Elvis's greatness, he was not the first to turn crossing racial lines into big business.

Not only had black performers like Louis Jordan and Nat Cole been copying white performers, but white copying of black styles was already a staple of mainstream pop—not just of jazz, and not just of Sinatra. *Ebony* magazine ran a feature in February 1951 titled "WHITES WHO SING LIKE NEGROES / Influence of Colored Singing Styles Heard in Voices of Top White Vocalists of Country." This discussed Sinatra and Frankie Laine, and others who are not surprising, such as Peggy Lee, Anita O'Day, Louis

Prima. But Doris Day is featured in the article as well.[27] That *Ebony* seemed eager to acknowledge, even exaggerate, this phenomenon is a testament to a kind of hopefulness afoot in those years, a feeling that black culture was being acknowledged by the stars of the white world—not simply that white folk were stealing black culture, but that they were also paying it homage. *Ebony* told the other side of the story of exploitation, encapsulated in Thelonious Monk's famous statement in the same era, "We're gonna make a music so hard they can't steal it from us," i.e., bebop. However admirable Monk's defiant possessiveness was, and whatever it may have done to motivate the unparalleled creative innovations of bop, it was commercially a dead end.[28] *Ebony*'s hopefulness about white imitation is related, it seems to me, to a hopefulness that integration, even interbreeding, would not result in the death of black culture through assimilation. Rather, integration would have closer to the opposite effect: it would allow white people greater freedom to emulate—and to support financially—black artists.

Even more obviously indebted to black performers than any singer *Ebony* mentioned was Johnnie Ray, whose smash hit "Cry," issued in November 1951 by OKeh records (a label aimed primarily at the "race" market), was the best selling record of the year. The trade press labeled Ray "the Next Sinatra." "Cry"'s sudden rise to number one on both the R&B *and* pop charts (it remained at number one for eleven weeks) raised the question whether radio listeners could place Ray racially. According to rock journalists Jim Dawson and Steve Propes, "Nobody listening to 'Whiskey and Gin,'" Ray's earlier recording (recorded in Detroit with Maurice King, the black bandleader who later became Motown's A&R man), "would have imagined Ray was white. They wouldn't even have been sure of his gender": after hearing Ray's voice, a Columbia executive reportedly said, "I don't think she's gonna make it." Yet the enthusiastic response of Ray's fans was likened to the "bobby sox riots" Sinatra had caused during the war, and even to the Great Awakening. Dawson and Propes find Ray's example prophetic: "When Sam Phillips at Sun Records reportedly made his famous remark about finding 'a white boy that sounds like a Negro,' he meant another Johnnie Ray."[29]

Was Ray "ripping off" black music? Perhaps. But after Ray became a popular sensation, according to an official history, he kept telling "anyone who'd listen" that Maurice King and the black singer Bea Baker "taught him everything he knew," and for that reason, OKeh soon hired King and Baker. Baker, who met Ray in a black-and-tan club in Detroit where, Ray said, "I was the only white entertainer on the bill" in 1951, went on to become known as LaVern Baker, one of the biggest R&B stars of the 1950s, with such big money makers for Atlantic as "I Cried a Tear," "Tweedlee-Dee," and "Jim Dandy."[30]

Marvin Gaye is one of many great black singers who made it clear that racial copying was a well traveled two-way street. Gaye identified black men among his four main influences, but he cautioned against simplifying his roots: "Don't make the mistake of thinking that my musical background was all black. I'm very sensitive to every sound around, and there was nothing I heard that didn't influence me." Gaye's childhood friend Reese Palmer told Gaye's biographer that one of his earliest memories was "Marvin in the projects recreation center [in southeast Washington, D.C.] singing 'Cry' and doing a near-perfect imitation of Johnnie Ray. First time me and Marvin started talking about singing he said he wanted to do pop, like Sinatra, and he never did change his mind." Gaye himself said, "My dream was to become Frank Sinatra. . . . Every woman in America wanted to go to bed with Frank Sinatra. He was the king I longed to be. My greatest dream was to satisfy as many women as Sinatra. He was the heavyweight champ, the absolute. Now this is going to surprise you, but I also dug Dean Martin and especially Perry Como."[31]

Berry Gordy, the legendary black entrepreneur-paternalist of Motown Records in the early 1960s, aimed directly for the white market. He was doing with Marvin Gaye what Sam Phillips did with Elvis, only in reverse. As Gaye's biographer put it, "Gordy wanted nothing more than a black Sinatra in his stable, with all the profits and prestige [that] would accompany such a coup." In the 1960s, Gaye finally covered a Sinatra hit, "Something Stupid."[32]

Chuck Berry is another example. Although as a child Berry listened to black blues artists, he said his favorite musical style, boogie woogie, came to him from a white performer: "Tommy Dorsey's 'Boogie Woogie' was the tune that launched my determination to produce such music. The music of Harry James, Glenn Miller and a lot of white bands [was] beginning to 'get down' then and show up on the jukeboxes and black radio programs." In Berry's first gigs before black audiences in East St. Louis, he said, "I would suddenly break out with a hillbilly selection that had no business in the repertoire of a soul-music-loving audience[,] and the simple audacity of playing such a foreign number was enough to trigger the program into becoming sensational entertainment." To Berry, hillbilly music was not foreign at all, and he put more and more of it into his act. "[S]ome of the clubgoers started whispering, 'Who is that black hillbilly at the Cosmo?'" Berry packaged country novelty tunes for black audiences in the same way that white and black artists packaged "race" novelty songs for white audiences. Berry's black audiences soon began to appreciate that there was more to country music than novelty. "After they laughed at me a few times, they began requesting the hillbilly stuff and enjoyed trying to dance to it. If you ever want to see something that is far out, watch a crowd of colored folk, half high, wholeheartedly trying to do the hoedown barefooted." Berry's first hit, "Maybellene," was, in his mind, a hillbilly song.[33]

"Maybellene," of course, became one of the best-selling rhythm and blues records of all time. Shortly after the song hit the charts in August 1955, Berry went on tour to cash in on it. When he showed up for a date in Knoxville, a burly stagehand came to the door and asked him what he wanted.

> I said, "I am playing here tonight and I came early so I could rehearse with the band." The guy broke into laughter and told me that Chuck Berry was playing there tonight and the show was sold out. I was sensing he had a little racial attitude about his air, so I cautiously proclaimed that I was Chuck and promptly produced the contract for the engagement that night. He observed it a couple of seconds and told me to wait a minute, closed the door in my face, and left me standing outside. About fifteen minutes passed and then another man opened the door and presented himself along with three other males and four females. The bossy looking guy spoke, telling me that he was sorry and that they had booked a hillbilly band for Chuck's backup. He went on, "It's a country dance and we had no idea that 'Maybellene' was recorded by a niggra man." They had sold out the place but couldn't permit a black person to perform, as it was against a city ordinance.

Berry spent the evening parked behind the stage door, and heard "my song played by the band they had hired to replace me." The Knoxville promoter demanded his money back from Berry's agent (the Gale Agency) in New York, arguing that the promotional photos sent with the contracts made Chuck Berry look white. The agency did not refund the deposit, and Berry learned that in such cases of default, he would be paid regardless, so he chalked the whole incident up to "fortune without fame."[34]

Ray Charles is another example from the two-way street. He was raised on black gospel and loved blues and jazz, but he also listened to the *Grand Ole Opry* on the radio every Saturday night. "I loved Grandpa Jones and those other characters . . . Jimmie Rodgers, Roy Acuff, Hank Snow, Hank Williams . . . Eddie Arnold—these were singers I listened to all the time."

Charles often played in white clubs when he started out in Orlando in 1946–47. He said his "strangest job" ever "was with an all-white country-and-western band. All-white, that is, except me." (The band was the Florida Playboys.) This was in "The Deep South, 1948, a black dude playing piano in a hillbilly band? Well, it happened." That was where he learned to yodel.[35]

Ray Charles always said he loved the blues, and he occasionally sang pure blues numbers. Ultimately he came home to a kind of hybrid of rhythm and blues and another African American form, gospel, the mixing together of which gave birth to the new genre called soul music.[36]

But the other early leader of the soul movement, James Brown, an uncompromisingly raw rhythm and blues singer in the early 1950s, had a very different experience with the blues: "I never liked them. This is going to surprise a lot of people: I still don't like the blues. Never have."[37]

James Brown, not surprisingly, named only black performers as influences.[38] Still, he was influenced by white musicians, including a mixed vocal band near his hometown in Macon, Georgia, and by frequent performances before white audiences, including fraternities at most of the major southern schools in the late 1940s and early 1950s.[39] Brown felt a powerful kinship with the greatest racial "rip-off" artist of the century. It was on a trip to L.A. in 1965 that Brown finally "got together" with Elvis Presley: "when it got late, we threw everybody out of the room, and Elvis and I sang gospel together. We sang, 'Old Jonah,' 'Old Blind Barnabas,' all the ones I'd been singing since I was little. He knew the harmonies, too. . . . That night . . . we were just two country boys singing the stuff we grew up on. . . . We sang together a long time."[40]

James Brown's affinity for Elvis went back to the beginning of his career. He emphasized that his first hit had made the charts the same week as Elvis's and that their careers followed similar trajectories. That is why Brown was haunted by Elvis's death.[41] Like the popular music he had done so much to create, Brown had gone through a period of malaise in the 1970s. He said he felt lost and did not know who he was or where he was going. Then, "When Elvis died in August 1977, I think I got a clue. For some reason his death hit me very hard. We were a lot alike in many ways—both poor boys from the country raised on gospel and R&B. . . . He had lived in Hollywood a long time and then, like me, had moved back home to try to preserve himself. Somehow or another he just didn't manage to do it. . . . When he died, I said, 'That's my friend, I have to go.'" Brown traveled to Graceland the night Elvis died. "I talked to Elvis's father, saying what I could to help console him. But when I walked over to the open casket, *I* needed consoling. I put my hand over his heart and said with tears in my eyes, 'You rat, why'd you leave me? How could you let it go? How could you let it go?' It was very strange; that was only the second time in my life I'd ever touched someone who was dead."[42] The first was his own father. None of Elvis's exploitation of black music seemed to bother James Brown, though by the time of Elvis's death Brown had long since become a political as well as cultural symbol of "soul," meaning, among other things, "blackness," in the era of "black consciousness" and "black is beautiful."[43]

Brown's 1968 anthem to black consciousness, "Say it Loud (I'm Black and I'm Proud)," may be the ultimate testimony to racial cross-dressing. The black kids who were originally chosen for the background chorus had to leave before they could be taped, so Brown ordered assistants to "just get kids off the street." They "got a bunch from a Denny's restaurant nearby" and others here and there. "After a while we had about a dozen. . . . Each time I sang 'Say it loud' all they had to do was answer with 'I'm black and I'm proud!' The funny thing about it is that most of 'em weren't black. Most of 'em were white or Asian."[44] Though Brown played "I'm Black and I'm Proud" at Richard Nixon's inaugural in 1969, he said the song caused him to lose a great deal of his white audience.[45]

What do all these stories tell us? There was a vast interracial world in the music industry after World War II, which means the whole racial "rip-off" experience has to be put in perspective. Like most great artists, Ray Charles copied the styles of others for many years before he found his own. "Funny thing, but during all these years I was imitating Nat Cole, I never thought twice about it, never felt bad about copying the cat's licks. To me it was practically a science. I worked at it, enjoyed it, I was proud of it, and I loved doing it." That throws the charged issue of racial exploitation into a more complicated light than it gets in most rock histories. "Today I hear some singers who I think sound like me. Joe Cocker, for instance. Man, I know that cat must sleep with my records. But I don't mind. I'm flattered; I understand. After all, I did the same thing."[46] Charles said he was not "angry at those white cats for taking from blacks. I've always said, just 'cause Bell invented the telephone doesn't mean Ray Charles can't use it. No, I gave those ofay boys some credit for having good ears."[47]

James Brown also was a kind of musical doppelgänger in his early professional life. Before he became a national star in his own right, Brown's biggest gigs consisted of imitating Little Richard, the black singer and transvestite who took his own musical and sartorial cues from Billy Wright and Esquerita, and who was wildly successful with white as well as black audiences. When Richard's first big hit, "Tutti Frutti," came in 1955, and he became too busy to fulfill his scheduled gigs in black clubs and joints around the South, his agent hired Brown to stand in. Brown recalled, "he sent me out as Little Richard," while Bobby Byrd fulfilled James Brown's own, lesser gigs. People had heard Little Richard on the radio but had never seen his picture. "I was getting paid as Richard while Bobby was getting paid as me. . . . I'd come out and do 'Tutti Frutti' and all those things, and then I'd do some Midnighters' stuff, some Roy Brown, and even [his own] 'Please, Please, Please.' . . . The audience thought I was really Richard." Brown did reveal to the audience, at the end of the show, that he was really impersonating the impersonator.[48]

At least one major black newspaper, the *Pittsburgh Courier,* understood the advent of rock and roll as legitimizing rather than expropriating black music—and as saving the music industry. In April 1955 the *Courier* reported on Moondog Alan Freed's "Rock and Roll" show, opening at Brooklyn's Paramount theater that month. "So great was the attraction of Rhythm and Blues" that Freed "asked patrons to please not come to the show as they could not get in. As a result of the great power of this type of show, theaters all over the country are striving to book it." This marked the end of the music industry's woes. According to the *Courier,* "The great surge [Freed] is causing looks like the answer to vaudeville or the live show return. Not since the late thirties and forties has there been so much interest in a musical mood. The huge lines around the Paramount . . . [are] the best answer to those who are daily attempting to down Rhythm and Blues and those who created it. From both an eye and an ear point of view it would seem that it is the thing with the new generation."[49]

Along with professional moralists of all stripes, segregationists opposed rock and roll music. They had good reason: it loosened up the practice of and attitudes toward racial separation. While most southern shows were still segregated and integrated bands still rare, racial purists were threatened by the increasing tendency of popular music to ignore or break down racial barriers. The new music increased the frequency of interracial concerts, dances, bands, and audiences and brought them into the public eye more than ever before.

Segregationists had to fight not only determined civil rights organizations, who were convinced that God was on their side, but also the entertainment industry, which owed its salvation to the new music that depended on racial mixing. The segregationists' position looked increasingly quixotic against such forces. Ultimately, the music industry created a

booming market and an irresistible force that spread around the globe—
and it showed how millions could be made from the new music (watered
down to varying degrees). In the process, the new lucrative business legitimized a basic form of African American culture to white people; it soon
became the "mainstream" by which America was defined. What is perhaps
more surprising, the growth of the industry made this kind of music respectable to the black middle class.[50]

Notes

1. G. K. Chesterton, *Charles Dickens* (London: Methuen, 1906), 142.

2. Cross-racial mimicry has a long history behind it. Examples of the literature
on black people "passing" include Frances Harper, *Iola Leroy* (1892; reprint, New
York: AMS, 1971); James Weldon Johnson, *Autobiography of an Ex-Colored Man*
(1912; reprint, New York: Vintage, 1989); and Nella Larsen, *Passing* (1929; reprint,
New York: Arno, 1969). On "blackface" minstrelsy, see Constance Rourke, *Ameri-
can Humor* (New York: Harcourt, Brace, 1931); Eileen Southern, *The Music of
Black America*, 2nd ed. (New York: Norton, 1983); Robert Toll, *Blacking Up: The
Minstrel Show in Nineteenth-Century America* (New York: Oxford, 1974); and Eric
Lott, *Love and Theft: Blackface Minstrelsy and the American Working Class* (New
York: Oxford, 1993). Michael Rogin, from whom I lovingly stole the phrase "racial
cross-dressing," carries the theatrical history of minstrelsy forward as it found
another home on the screen, especially in *Blackface, White Noise* (Berkeley: Uni-
versity of California Press, 1996).

3. Ann Douglas finds cross-racial mimicry to be the driving force of modern
culture in her brilliant *Terrible Honesty: Mongrel Manhattan in the 1920s* (New
York: Farrar, Straus, Giroux, 1995). Lewis Erenberg sees cross-racial mimicry as a
cause and an effect of the radical democratization of culture in the Swing Era
(mid-1930s to mid-1940s): *Swingin' the Dream: Big Band Jazz and the Rebirth of
American Culture* (Chicago: University of Chicago Press, 1998). In the post–World
War II era, cross-racial mimicry escalated. When white clarinetist Milton Mezzrow's autobiography was published in 1946, Mezzrow's effort to "become" black
could still seem outlandishly exotic and unconventional. By the time Norman
Mailer's famous essay "The White Negro" appeared in 1957, such imitation was
commonplace: a commercial fad in which every teenager in the country shared.
[Milton] Mezz Mezzrow, *Really the Blues* (New York: Random House, 1946). Norman Mailer, "The White Negro," in Mailer, *Advertisements of Myself* (New York:
Putnam, 1959).

4. *Down Beat*, December 30, 1949.

5. Debate among jazzmen at the Negresco Hotel in Nice, ibid., April 7,
1948, 2–3.

6. Ella Fitzgerald, ibid., September 22, 1948; Eartha Kitt, ibid., July 14, 1954;
Dorsey and others, ibid., December 30, 1949.

7. This was *Down Beat's* lead story: John S. Wilson, "Bop at the End of the Road, Says Diz," ibid., September 8, 1950, front page.

8. Ibid., May 19, 1950, 18.

9. "Ivory Joe Purges Band of Bop 'Cult,'" *Baltimore Afro-American*, December 1, 1951, 6, 8.

10. "Jazz Fare Is Awfully Thin These Days, Says Hoefer," *Down Beat*, January 12, 1951, 8. The musicians referred to here were Louis Armstrong, Bix Beiderbecke, Duke Ellington, Count Basie, and Lester Young.

11. In this case, the *New Musical Express* was commenting on a fad of folk music. *New Musical Express*, March 21, 1952, 5.

12. *Down Beat*, October 6, 1950.

13. Brooks first recorded "That's My Desire" on OKeh, but did not hit the charts with it. On Hadda Brooks, see James Marshall, notes to *The OKeh Rhythm and Blues Story*, 1949–1957 (New York: Sony Music, 1993), 13. Laine's "That's My Desire" went higher in the "race" chart (number three) than it did in the white chart (number four), and it stayed on the "race" chart longer (eleven weeks) than Ella Fitzgerald's rival version. Fitzgerald's version of "That's My Desire" hit the race chart on June 28, 1947, and made it to number three but stayed in the chart only one week. On Laine, see also Arnold Shaw, *Honkers and Shouters: The Golden Years of Rhythm and Blues* (New York: Macmillan, 1978), 49–57. Laine got in hot water for recording "Shine" in 1948. Deejays like Fred Robbins of WOV in New York deemed the song "offensive," though according to *Down Beat*, "the Laine version is far less so than those sung for years by many other vocalists, including many prominent Negro performers." Bing Crosby was among the earlier artists who recorded successful versions of the song. *Down Beat*, March 24, 1948, and April 21, 1948.

14. Mike Butcher, "The Story of America's Song-Plugger Supreme: Nat 'King' Cole," *New Musical Express*, May 2, 1952; *Down Beat*, October 6, 1950. Background information on Cole is from James Haskins and Kathleen Benson, *Nat King Cole: A Personal and Professional Biography*, rev. ed. (Chelsea, Mich.: Scarborough House, 1990). The Ink Spots did the same thing as Cole at the same time: they began as a hot jazz group in the 1930s, but made it big commercially by crooning for a broader commercial market.

15. Frank Sinatra, quoted in Arnold Shaw, "Billie Holiday and the Blues," in *The World of Soul*, Billboard Publication special pull-out feature, in *Billboard*, June 24, 1967, 12, 13. Benny Goodman, perhaps the most successful white musician of the 1930s, had exactly the same idea about racial mixing. Goodman was the first major white popular musician to perform regularly with black sidemen—including Teddy Wilson, Charlie Christian, and Lionel Hampton. See Erenberg, *Swingin' the Dream*. According to Whitney Balliett, Sinatra "has mentioned his admiration for Billie Holiday, and she seems at this late date [1982] to have subtly possessed him. He uses her exhilarating rhythmic devices and her sometimes staccato, rocking

diction. Occasionally, his voice resembles the heavy, robed one she developed in the 1940s." *New Yorker*, October 4, 1982, 142–43.

16. First associated with Count Basie, "jump" was a simpler style, with a harder and generally faster beat, than swing. Swing made dancers sway side to side as well as up and down; jump induced a simpler, pogo-like, up and down movement. Jump was confined to small combos, very often with vocals, rather than big bands. The size of the performing unit was important. Small combos were cheaper for recording companies and clubs; in many cases vocalists, who tended to be identified by name more readily than purely instrumental acts, could travel cheaply on their own and work with small combos as "house" bands, saving promoters a lot of expense and hassle. In 1950, *Down Beat* reported on an increasingly widespread formula for success that came from "a west coast promoter who bought two semi-name jump bands, Amos Milburn and Joe Liggins, for $1,000 against a fifty percent split" (i.e. guaranteed $1,000 or fifty percent of the total box office take—much cheaper than the "$2,500 a night guarantees" bands expected). Milburn and Liggins were not only cheap but wildly popular: "Just after the dance started, firemen closed the doors of the hall because it was filled to capacity with 6,000 eager patrons." Nothing had been so popular in years. *Down Beat*, October 20, 1950.

17. John Chilton, *Let the Good Times Roll: The Story of Louis Jordan and His Music* (1992; reprint, Ann Arbor: University of Michigan Press, 1994), 19, 24.

18. Jordan "also liked the shuffle rhythms created by another white band (popular in Philadelphia) led by Jan Savitt." The influence from Whiteman's band came particularly from the German-born trumpeter Henry Busse (1894–1955), who played a shuffle rhythm. Ibid., 31, 32.

19. Ibid., 37, 33. Louis Jordan's last wife, Martha Jordan, denies that Fields and Jordan were ever married. She thinks the transvestitism stories may be true, though she never saw her husband in drag or lent him clothes. Martha Jordan, interview by author, Little Rock, Ark., July 8, 1998. The entertainment pages of black newspapers in the late 1940s frequently refer to Ida Fields as Jordan's wife.

20. Chilton, *Let the Good Times Roll*, 107–8.

21. Ibid., 102, 106, 110–12.

22. See James Brown with Bruce Tucker, *The Godfather of Soul* (New York: Macmillan, 1986); Chuck Berry, *The Autobiography* (New York: Harmony, 1987); and Ray Charles with David Ritz, *Brother Ray: Ray Charles' Own Story* (New York: Dial, 1978).

23. Gleason quoted in Shaw, *Honkers and Shouters*, 63.

24. Jordan had more top-ten hits (54) on the black music charts from their beginning (1942) to the present than any other performer except James Brown (who had 58)—all the more remarkable considering that Jordan's active career (from 1942 through roughly 1952) was about one-fourth as long as Brown's. Jordan still holds the record for total number of weeks in the number one position on the

black chart, 113 weeks. See Joel Whitburn, ed., *Top R&B Singles*, 1942–1995 (Menomenee Falls, Wis.: Record Research, Inc., 1996).

A columnist for the *Baltimore Afro-American*, Ralph Matthews, suggested that some of his readers had become "hypersensitive" to mimicry. In a review of Japanese musical comedians who ably mimicked American Negro singers, Matthews noted that Japanese audiences appreciated the talents of the Japanese mimics without condescension, and also laughed uproariously at caricatures of Japanese visitors to the United States who were confused about how to operate elevators, pianos, telephones, and what not. "The manner in which the Japanese laugh at themselves" reminded Matthews of "the best comedy of Williams and Walker and our own early comedians before the colored public became too hypersensitive about our shortcomings." *Baltimore Afro-American*, August 18, 1951.

25. Shaw, *Honkers and Shouters*, 63.

26. Albert Goldman, *Elvis* (New York: McGraw-Hill, 1981), 110.

27. Doris Day "often follows style and even mannerisms of Ella Fitzgerald in her songs on the screen as well as on record performances." "Whites Who Sing Like Negroes," *Ebony*, February 1951, 49–54.

28. Scott DeVeaux struggles heroically to overturn the view that bebop is "anti-commercial" in his influential (and on the whole superb) *Birth of Bebop: A Social and Musical History* (Berkeley: University of California Press, 1997), 13–17, 170–71, 371–74, 439–44. Yet it seems to me that all he proves is that bop musicians, who obviously needed to survive, wanted to be paid for their work and longed to live in a better world where artists would not have to sell their souls and lose control over their work in order to know economic security and comfort. To see the matter as DeVeaux does is to equivocate on the usual meaning of anticommercial, and to ignore all the rhetoric of both pro- and anti-bop musicians at the time (see, for example, notes 4–9, above). The point is not that boppers were willing to live as mendicants on the street (though Parker sometimes came close), but that they saw the gross commercialization of swing and pop as artistically deadening, and that that attitude shaped their break from swing, their frequently noted aloofness from their audiences, and their lack of concern for "danceability." It probably also had something to do with their general commercial failure. With the notable exception of Gillespie, the famous boppers understood themselves and were understood by their contemporaries to be anticommercial in the only historically meaningful sense: they opposed commercialization as it worked in the real world in the time and place they happened to be. To require them to be emaciated ascetics is, in effect, to deprive the term anticommercial of any use at all.

DeVeaux's attempt to racialize the matter—to claim (206–7) that white musicians had a taste for "romanticizing poverty" and black musicians did not—appears (like many of DeVeaux's racializations) especially dubious. DeVeaux rightly notes elsewhere that many of the prominent black jazzmen had a middle-class upbringing, and that bop musicians were suspicious of attempts to racialize their creation, opening their sessions and bands up to white performers on the basis of merit.

29. Jim Dawson and Steve Propes, *What Was the First Rock 'n' Roll Record?* (Boston: Faber, 1992), 96–99. The roots of Ray in black music were well understood at the time: see "When You Hear 'Tweedle De Dee,' You Gotta Think of LaVern Baker," *Pittsburgh Courier*, April 2, 1955, 14, and Bill Coss, "CRY and the World Goes for You," *New Musical Express*, March 21, 1952. Ray told *Down Beat* that he was most influenced by Kay Starr and Billie Holiday, who "can make a bad song sound good. Incidentally, put in a plug for a gal who deserves more publicity, Little Miss Cornshucks. She had a strong influence on Kay Starr. And for God's sake, don't put in that comparison between me and Frankie Laine. There's not a living male singer who sends me. Perry Como is very pleasing, very relaxing—but I've never been genuinely inspired by any male singer." Born in Portland, Oregon, in 1927, Ray ran away to Los Angeles at age seventeen to begin in show biz, playing piano in a speakeasy there: "Speakeasy is a nice word for it," he said. "It was an upholstered sewer." *Down Beat*, December 28, 1951. Ray made the cover of *Down Beat* on April 18, 1952. By that date, "Cry" was the "second biggest selling pop record" in Columbia's history. On the OKeh label, see "Major Moves in R&B Field," *Billboard* May 19, 1951, in *First Pressings: The History of Rhythm and Blues*, vol. 1, ed. Galen Gart (Milford, N.H.: Big Nickel, 1991), 41, 44—in which it was stated Columbia "will designate OKeh as an exclusively rhythm and blues disk tag."

30. James Marshall, quoted in *The OKeh Rhythm and Blues Story, 1949–1957* (New York: Sony Music, 1993), 11, and Peter Grendysa, quoted in ibid., 6.

31. Gaye's major male influences were Rudy West of the Five Keys, Clyde McPhatter of the Dominoes and later the Drifters, Little Willie John (whose original of "Fever," made into a "pop" hit by Peggy Lee, is one of the great "rip-off" stories), and Ray Charles. Not surprisingly, Gaye's greatest female influence was the same as Sinatra's, Billie Holiday: "Her pain is what got to me. Billie turned herself inside out, all in the name of love. She was deeper than sex. The hurt she felt was the hurt of all humanity. Great artists suffer for the people. The greatest artist was Jesus, and the rest of us can only imitate his perfect suffering." Marvin Gaye, quoted in David Ritz, *Divided Soul: The Life of Marvin Gaye* (New York: McGraw-Hill, 1985), 29–30.

32. Gaye cut "Something Stupid" as a duet with Tammi Terrell. The urge to become a "black Sinatra" seems to run through Gaye's career like a theme, and is especially stressed by Gordy and Gaye's agent in his late years, Jeff Wald. Ibid., 75, 111.

33. "When I played hillbilly songs, I stressed my diction so that it was harder and whiter," than when he played bluesy numbers. "All in all it was my intention to hold both the black and the white clientele by voicing the different kinds of songs in their customary tongues." Berry, *The Autobiography*, 26, 86, 89, 90, and see 108.

34. Ibid., 136.

35. Charles with Ritz, *Brother Ray*, 42–43, 78, 87.

36. Even as he was giving birth to soul, the ever-resourceful, ever-popular

Charles, who had also studied classical piano in his youth, never lost touch with his jazz and country roots. He revisited and revitalized his jazz chops in his collaborations with Milt Jackson and Betty Carter in the 1950s, and of course became a leading figure in country with his 1962 hit, "I Can't Stop Loving You," and his album that year, *Modern Sounds in Country and Western*, ABC, 1962.

37. Brown with Tucker, *Godfather*, 6.

38. James Brown's first band, the Flames, formed shortly after he got out of prison in June 1952, "worked up a repertoire of about ten rhythm and blues songs, mostly things by the Dominoes, the Five Royales, the Orioles, a lot of stuff by the Five Keys, the Clovers, all those groups." Ibid., 54; names more influences, 62 (Jordan again the best of them all, though best *group* was Hank Ballard and the Midnighters). More than most, Brown emphasized his jazz roots as well as his rhythm and blues and gospel roots. Ibid., 82, 120.

39. Ibid., 60–61, 57–58, 66.

40. Ibid., 165, 166.

41. "Heartbreak Hotel" first hit the R&B chart on March 31, 1956, and "Please, Please, Please," first hit on April 7, but Elvis's record had hit the white charts almost a month earlier, on March 10.

42. Brown with Tucker, *Godfather*, 247–48.

43. Brown said, "Elvis was great. People still said he was copying, but he found his own style. . . . He was really a hillbilly who learned to play the blues." "Cats complain all the time about white people learning music from blacks. It's true we've kind of had a monopoly on certain kinds of music, but everybody's entitled to it. They shouldn't *steal* it, but they're entitled to learn it and play it. No sense in keeping all the drive on one side, because if you're teaching people, you're teaching people." Ibid., 165–66.

44. Ibid., 200.

45. Brown had originally supported Humphrey, but he did not want to turn down the honor. Duke Ellington and Lionel Hampton also played. Ibid., 200, 204.

46. Charles also "reclaimed" many black songs that had been covered by white artists, "and brought 'em back to where they started out." Those tunes "got dark all over again—in a hurry—when I got my hands on them." Charles with Ritz, *Brother Ray*, 86. Like Sinatra, Ray, Gaye, and others, Charles felt a special kinship to Billie Holiday; see ibid., 82.

47. Ibid., 87–88, 72, 126.

48. A few times, Richard's old bandleader, Fats Gonder, introduced Brown as "Little James." Brown with Tucker, *Godfather*, 72.

49. *Pittsburgh Courier*, April 23, 1955. The column listed the performers at Freed's show: LaVern Baker, the Penguins, Chuckles, Eddie Fontaine, Danny Overbea, Moonglows, Al Sears, Mickey Baker, Sam Taylor, the Moonlighters, and the Red Prysock Band; these had "established all kinds of attendance records at the Paramount here last week selling nothing but R&B."

50. Garry Wills notes, for example, that "Andrew Young's parents kept him apart from the lustier aspects of black culture." Young once told Wills that he, "a native of New Orleans, was not allowed to listen to jazz or the blues—he had to catch up with that side of culture later on, when he was in New York. For 'Negro music' he was taken to classical concerts sung by Roland Hayes or Marian Anderson." Garry Wills, "A Tale of Three Leaders," *New York Review of Books*, September 19, 1996, 61. Chuck Berry actually changed his name to "Berryn" for a time so that his fame would not taint his deeply religious father's reputation. At one point or another, most black musicians tell of pressure from their families and preachers to stop performing jazz, blues, or popular music.

6

"Climbing the Mountain Top"

African American Blues and Gospel Songs
from the Civil Rights Years

Guido van Rijn

In *Roosevelt's Blues: African-American Blues and Gospel Songs on FDR,*
the lyrics of blues and gospel songs were used to examine some of the
reasons why in the 1930s most African Americans abandoned their historic
allegiance to the Republicans, the party of Abraham Lincoln, and
switched to the Democrats, the party of Franklin Delano Roosevelt and
his New Deal.[1] Only one percent of the blues and gospel recordings made
at that time actually contained any overt political comment: then, as always, sex and personal relationships were the dominant themes of the
blues; God, sin, and salvation dominated gospel. Even those songs that did
embrace overtly political themes rarely gave formal expression to any particular ideology, and few advocated, or denounced, specific programs and
solutions associated with Roosevelt's New Deal.

Nevertheless, blues and gospel did deal with the effects of New Deal-
era events, policies, and personalities on the performers' own lives and
circumstances. Heavily dependent on metaphor and allusion, these songs
revealed the responses of the African American community to the material
and mental impact of the Depression, widespread reform, and finally war.
While hardly devoid of concrete details about African American poverty,
unemployment, abuse, and discrimination, or the effect of New Deal programs, blues and gospel also provided a valuable glimpse into an inner
world of changing African American consciousness at which stark statistics on economic conditions and voting patterns can only hint.

Many of the blues and gospel songs recorded between the end of World
War II and the murder of Dr. Martin Luther King Jr. in 1968 worked in
much the same allusive way with regard to the civil rights movement as

those of the 1930s had with regard to Roosevelt and the New Deal. While relatively few of the songs discussed the Movement directly, the Struggle provided an inescapable context for many of them. Their various moods and subject matters reflected the ebb and flow of rising expectation, frustration, celebration, and despair that accompanied the unfolding of the civil rights struggle.

Of course, regardless of any specific lyrical focus on civil rights issues, black popular music has always been deeply implicated in constructing the African American sense of self, community, heritage and destiny. Although there was something of a postwar flight away from blues and, to a lesser extent, gospel toward their rhythm and blues and soul progeny, these older styles continued to be enjoyed by many in the black community. Moreover, by the mid-1960s, heightened racial consciousness meant that these two protean musical forms were again widely appreciated as cornerstones, not just of black—and much white—popular music, but also of the entire African American experience.[2]

Having duly noted that the importance of blues and gospel in the African American community depended as much on their musical stylings, performance practices, and historic place within black culture as on their lyrical content, this essay nonetheless focuses on the handful of long-lost songs that did engage lyrically with the Movement. Fourteen blues and gospel recordings with overt civil rights themes were made between the death of Franklin Roosevelt in April 1945 and that of John F. Kennedy in November 1963, after which the numbers increased considerably. Yet if the corpus is small, at least one song was devoted to most of the major landmarks in the civil rights struggle up to Kennedy's death. As such they present a modest but impressive musical response to the struggle for African American freedom, a response that is undoubtedly representative of a much larger body of unrecorded protest songs in these styles.[3]

In addition to rescuing some of these civil rights blues and gospel songs from obscurity, this essay seeks to contextualize them within the racial politics of successive presidential administrations and the changing fortunes of the freedom struggle. A sub-theme here concerns the ways these songs illuminate how African Americans responded to various key public figures in the story of their struggle for civil rights, in particular Martin Luther King Jr. and the postwar U.S. presidents. It also considers why so few civil rights blues and gospel songs were recorded and released until the late 1960s, suggesting how the changing racial situation crucially affected the workings of the recording industry.

On April 12, 1945, Franklin Roosevelt suffered a fatal cerebral hemorrhage and Harry Truman became president of the United States. During Truman's two terms in office, civil rights came to occupy an increasingly important place in popular consciousness and national politics. In October 1947, the President's Committee on Civil Rights published its report on America's racial situation, *To Secure These Rights,* which proposed increased federal action to correct racial inequalities, and the creation of a permanent civil rights division within the Justice Department. Many of these ideas were eventually incorporated into the civil rights plank of Truman's 1948 presidential platform, causing dissent and defection among many southern white Democrats anxious to protect Jim Crow from any government meddling. In no small measure thanks to the support of northern black voters, Truman survived this Dixiecrat revolt and was returned for his first, and only, full term in the White House.[4]

It was partly in recognition of the growing importance of black northern voters that Truman agreed to address the annual convention of the National Association for the Advancement of Colored People (NAACP) at the Lincoln Memorial in Washington, D.C., on June 29, 1947. By contrast, Roosevelt had consistently refused to attend the NAACP Convention or to make any statement on race in his radio "fireside chats." Truman, too, had doubts about the wisdom of his decision to give a speech, writing to his sister, "I wish I didn't have to make it."[5] His declaration that "There is no justifiable reason for discrimination because of ancestry, or religion, or race, or color" gave an important fillip to hopes that African Americans were to be included in Truman's Fair Deal.[6] Again in contrast to Roosevelt, Truman openly advocated federal anti–poll tax and antilynching legislation. Further cause for guarded black optimism came as the NAACP won a series of landmark Supreme Court decisions against segregation in real estate practices and higher education, while in 1948 Truman (under pressure from the Association and labor leader A. Philip Randolph) issued Executive Order 9981 to desegregate the military. The president also favored the establishment of a permanent, if stripped down, Fair Employment Practices Commission—a temporary measure that Randolph's 1941 March on Washington Movement had extracted from the Roosevelt administration.

In sum, though Truman's tentative support for the civil rights measures he sent to Congress tended to lag some way behind his bold rhetoric, he could boast at least as strong a commitment to black civil rights as his predecessor—and could claim rather more in terms of concrete executive and legislative action in the field. Yet Truman was never celebrated in black song like Roosevelt; he never became a black hero. Maybe this was a consequence of raised African American expectations about their rights to equitable treatment in the wake of the War—expectations that remained largely unrealized during the Truman years. Indeed, despite all the activity in the civil rights arena, only five blues songs with explicit civil rights themes are known to have been recorded during Truman's first term. Just two more were cut during his second. None of them eulogized the president; most smacked of frustration and disgust at the postwar return to old patterns of racial oppression, especially in the South.

As journalist John Egerton has grimly chronicled, in the immediate aftermath of the War there was an "epidemic of violence" in the South.[7] Much of it took the form of brutal assaults by whites against returning black veterans. The War had stimulated a good deal of cautious black optimism that, with yet another patriotic sacrifice behind them, and racist ideologies thoroughly discredited as part of the wartime propaganda drive, they could look forward to full citizenship rights when peace returned. The murderous violence of the immediate postwar years represented a savage attempt to reassert white supremacy in the South, and to cement blacks back in their place at the bottom of the Jim Crow system.

Among southern states, only Alabama could compare with Georgia for the sheer ubiquity of murderous racial violence in 1946 and 1947; each claimed seven reported lynchings and numerous non-fatal incidents.[8] In the Folkways Records archives, there is a song from 1946 by "Champion" Jack Dupree called "I'm Gonna Write the Governor of Georgia" that refers to one of the worst of these incidents.[9] In the state's first multiple lynching since 1918, an African American veteran died when a group of hooded men pulled him, his wife, and another Negro couple out of a car at Moore's Ford, near Monroe, in Walton County. The mob lined the four of them up in front of a ditch and fired a barrage that left a reported 180 bullet holes in one of the corpses. Little wonder that Dupree was moved to complain, "I got people down in Georgia, that I'm afraid to see/Lord, I'm afraid that gang down there, Lord, they might lynch poor me."[10]

Ellis Arnall, the governor referred to in Dupree's song, was a model of racial progressivism compared to the demagogic Talmadges—Gene and Herman, the spiteful race-baiters who preceded and succeeded him respectively in the Georgia statehouse. It is a moot point whether Dupree would have considered a letter to either of the Talmadges worth the ink, let alone a recording. Arnall, however, was one of a handful of newly elected southern progressives who came to office with the aid of votes from returning GI's, women, and those African Americans able to take advantage of the 1944 *Smith v. Allwright* decision, which outlawed white primary elections. The moderation of men like Arnall represented some respite from the racist frenzy of the postwar years: a brief moment of equivocal southern racial liberalism amid the politics of racial reaction. Arnall boldly denounced the violence at Moore's Ford and dutifully ordered a full investigation.[11]

State investigators in Monroe complained, however, that in the face of a reign of terror against prospective witnesses and informers, "the best [sic] people in town won't talk about this." Nevertheless, they, the Federal Bureau of Investigation, and the NAACP eventually compiled enough evidence to take before a grand jury, but the jury declined to return an indictment and nobody was ever charged with the crime.

Revealingly, Jack Dupree's song remained unissued. Moses Asch, the owner of Folkways, was hardly a stranger to racial or political controversy. His influential label was home to many of the most important and forthright releases by Woody Guthrie, Paul Robeson, Pete Seeger, and Leadbelly. Nevertheless, at that moment of high, murderous racial tension, Asch may well have felt it was unwise to issue such potentially incendiary material.

Dupree himself may also have been reluctant to see the song released, fearing personal reprisals, or a loss of bookings if theater managers considered him too controversial and likely to attract trouble from white supremacists. This was a common pattern. Artists, their managers, and their labels, not to mention distributors, theater booking agencies, and radio station managers, were permanently concerned about the adverse effects overtly political songs might have on both their financial and physical well-being.

These understandable concerns, which continued well into the 1960s, were by no means restricted to the worlds of blues and gospel and undoubtedly help to account for the relative scarcity of songs explicitly about race relations and the Movement.[12] Similar fears of economic or physical reprisals probably explain why Memphis Slim, Big Bill Broonzy, and Sonny Boy Williamson requested that the pseudonyms "Leroy," "Natchez," and "Sib" were used to hide their identities when Alan Lomax recorded them talking candidly on racial oppression and the blues in 1947. Significantly, these unique recordings were first issued not in the United States, but in Great Britain a decade later.[13]

Also in 1947, Big Bill Broonzy's "Black Brown and White" was rejected by various record companies. "If you're white, you alright / If you're brown, stick around / If you're black, oh, brother: Get back, get back, get back!"

"I tried RCA Victor, Columbia, Decca and a lot of little companies, but none of them would record it. They wanted to hear it, and after I played and sung it they would refuse," Broonzy explained. When the singer asked for the reason he was told: "You see, Bill, when you write a song and want to record it with any company, it must keep the people guessing what the song means. Don't you say what the song means when you're singing. And that song comes right to the point and the public won't like that."[14] As a result Broonzy had to wait until 1951 before he could record "Black Brown and White" in Europe before a white audience.[15]

In fact, the first American recording of Broonzy's famous protest song was made, not by the composer himself, but by Brownie McGhee. McGhee cut it in 1947 for Encore, the small record company he briefly co-owned with Irwin Silber, the editor of the folk song magazine *Sing Out!*[16] Encore managed only two releases and with its slogan "People's Songs" was clearly aimed at the sort of leftist audiences associated with *Sing Out!* and the People's Songsters. At Encore, the combination of a black blues man and a white radical with progressive racial views as co-owners seems to have created a rare opportunity to record and release such forthright material.

Elsewhere in the blues of the Truman era, Jim Crow was attacked by Leadbelly in two versions of his "Jim Crow Blues," both probably recorded in 1947. Paralleling the conclusions of the President's Committee on Civil Rights in *To Secure These Rights,* Leadbelly reported that "Jim Crow" was not just a southern phenomenon but was to be found in examples of racial prejudice and discrimination all over the United States. His frustration over his abortive attempts to become a movie actor in Hollywood in 1944 and 1945 was clearly in evidence here: "Drop down in old California, you gonna find Jim Crow / that's the reason there ain't no more Negroes today, baby, in a movin' picture show."[17]

On August 21, 1947, Mississippi senator and former governor Theodore "The Man" Bilbo died in New Orleans. Bilbo had been an outspoken supporter of white supremacy and the Ku Klux Klan. In a speech in Greenville, Mississippi, delivered during his 1946 campaign, Bilbo had said, "I'm the best friend the nigger's got in the State of Mississippi. I'm trying to do something for 'em. I want to send 'em back to Africa where they belong."[18] In this context, the irony of the first verse of Andrew Tibbs's "Bilbo Is Dead" from December 1947 is obvious: "Well, I've been down to Dallas, Texas, even went to San Antone / But when I got to Mississippi, my best friend was dead and gone." Tibbs waited until his final verse to indicate his true feelings, concluding that the death of the vile Bilbo might make Mississippi a fit place to live again for the thousands of African Americans who had fled the Magnolia State for the cities of the North.

> Well, I feel like a lonesome stranger, yes, a stranger in my own
>   hometown.
> I was a playboy and a devil, I had times that was really wild,
> Since Mr. Bilbo is dead, it makes me feel like a fatherless child.
> Well, you've been livin' in the big city, broke and had to get along,
> But you can hurry back to Mississippi, 'cause Bilbo is dead and
>   gone.[19]

Released on Aristocrat, a precursor of the seminal Chess label in Chicago, Tibbs's song—and its deeper meanings—did not escape the notice of southern authorities: according to Muddy Waters, the record was widely banned in the region.[20]

Another remarkable protest song was recorded in 1948 by Tommie Jenkins for the tiny Olliet label. His "Freedom Choo Choo Blues" referred to the Freedom Train which visited various cities as a traveling exhibition of the history of freedom in America.[21] In late 1947 there had been controversies in the South over whether blacks and whites could view it together. Naturally, being condemned to watch this celebration of American freedom and democracy in a segregated setting deeply offended African Americans and "Freedom Choo Choo Blues" bristled with gathering impatience and militancy.

Jenkins's song derived additional resonance from the special place that images of travel, not least by train, occupied in both the blues and gospel lyrical traditions. For a people lacking true freedom, images of mobility were traditionally very important, with the Exodus story the most potent of all the tropes in African American culture. The blues and gospel were full of visions of escape, whether to the promised land of northern cities or to the afterlife. It was true that trains sometimes took loved ones away, but they just as often symbolized deliverance and release; the Freedom Train just brought further indignity.[22] "From 1776, down to this present day,/ Me and my baby've been waiting for this day," Jenkins sang, emphasizing that the promises of the Declaration of Independence had been a long time coming for African Americans. Only when they were needed to fight, Jenkins implied, were African Americans temporarily and half-heartedly included in the ranks of American democracy: "I've lived in a restricted district, mostly in a slum,/ Always kicked around, until my draft card has come."

The NAACP orchestrated the campaign against segregated arrangements for viewing the Freedom Train. In addition to its legal challenges to the operation of the Jim Crow system, encouragement of black voting, and investigation of lynchings, it also sought to protect African Americans from the abuses of southern courts and jails. This role was highlighted in a celebratory December 1950 recording by the Gospel Pilgrims called "I'm So Grateful to the NAACP."[23] Composer Otis Jackson cited the case of Samuel Shepherd, Walter Irvin, and Charles Greenlee, who were "saved from the electric chair" following their dubious conviction for the rape of a white woman in Groveland, Florida, the previous year.[24] The record was issued on Atlantic and, once more, the politics of the label owners were significant in providing the environment within which such a song could be recorded and released. Brothers Ahmet and Neshui Ertegun were among the few owners of a commercial record label to take a stand on racial issues at that time. Jazz- and blues-loving sons of a Turkish diplomat, the Erteguns had even made parties at the Turkish Embassy among the first integrated concert occasions in Washington, D.C.[25]

In 1952 Atlanta gospel group the Echoes of Zion recorded a song called "Keep Still (God Will Fight Your Battles)," which outlined African American presence in American history from the Boston Massacre to the Korean War.[26] With its stoical quietism and calls for faith in eventual divine deliverance, the song's message contrasted with the later militancy and activist appeals of some—if by no means all—African American preachers. Nevertheless, "Keep Still" pulled no punches in condemning America's failure to live up to the preamble to the Declaration of Independence, with its bold affirmation that all men are created equal. As in Tommy Jenkins's "Freedom Choo Choo Blues"—indeed, as in the freedom struggle more generally—such references to America's much-vaunted but unfulfilled democratic ideals, to the rhetorical and symbolic touchstones of American civic religion, were a crucial element in the quest for support for African American rights.[27]

Truman's successor, President Dwight Eisenhower, came in for some tough criticism by African Americans, and a number of blues singers joined this chorus of disapproval. With no particular personal interest in civil rights and a steady belief in states' rights and voluntarism, as opposed to federal compulsion, in most areas of social life, Eisenhower offered little encouragement to African Americans. Nevertheless, the freedom struggle gathered great momentum during his two terms in office. Eisenhower failed to publicly endorse the Supreme Court's historic *Brown* decision of May 1954, which had declared segregated schooling in the South—

and by implication segregation in general—unconstitutional. Indeed, he conspicuously failed to support genuine efforts to desegregate southern schools; his belated and reluctant intervention in the Little Rock School Crisis of 1957 came only when civic order broke down. True, the Civil Rights Acts of 1957 and 1960 carried great symbolic significance, being the first to pass for more than eighty years. But these were largely toothless gestures, for which Eisenhower had no enthusiasm and which remained largely unenforced.[28]

Five songs from Eisenhower's first term dealt directly with civil rights issues. In July 1955 female singer La Verne Holt signed a contract with record producer Joe Davis. Holt was to pay Davis $500, in return for which Davis would record two songs by her and distribute them throughout the South. A minimum of five hundred 78s and five hundred 45s were to be pressed. La Verne Holt, who was credited on disc as "Enyatta Holta," must have been desperate for a record release.[29] The vaguely Afrocentric lyrics of "Mr. Black Man" were ahead of their time for 1955, long predating the "Say It Loud, I'm Black And I'm Proud" vogue in the soul music of the late 1960s and early 1970s, and presaging some rappers' later concern with educating their audiences about African American history. "Oo-wee, Mr. Black Man, fine as you can be, but it's a real dirty shame you don't know your history," Holt sang.[30]

With the birth of the mass movement for civil rights, African American "manhood" was increasingly defined in terms of racial pride and political activism, rather than simply in terms of the fabled sexual potency that the blues had long celebrated. Big Bill Broonzy also played around with notions of black manhood. In October 1955, he recorded a song titled "When Do I Get to Be Called a Man," again originally outside the United States, while in London during a tour of Britain, although it was re-recorded for American Folkways the following year. Whites routinely used the term "boy" for all African American males, regardless of age, occupation or status, as a means of demeaning and belittling them. Broonzy sings that he was called a "soldier boy" in the army and a "plough boy" when he was working on a farm. Now he is old and gray and they call him "Uncle Bill." "They said I was uneducated, my clothes was worn and torn/Now I've got a little education, but I'm a boy right on."[31]

Nowhere were the twisted sexual and racial anxieties of the mid-1950s South more apparent than in the brutal murder in 1955 of Emmett Till, a fourteen-year-old African American boy who was slain because he had allegedly said "Bye, baby" to a white woman in a shop in Money, Mississippi. The photo of Emmett's cruelly mutilated body in *Jet* magazine did much to arouse African American anger and, as Julian Bond has written elsewhere in this volume, started many of his generation on the road to civil rights activism. As late as 1969 Brother Will Hairston recorded a two-part "The Death of Emmett Till," but there was also a contemporary recording with the same title.[32] The artists were a vocal group called the Ramparts and the song was composed by Madame A. C. Bilbrew, a Los Angeles community leader and musician. The facts of the case were related uncompromisingly and the two-part song was remarkable in its outspokenness:

Weights were placed upon his body, in the river they did fling,
Believin' that fiendish crime they'd hide,
But in time the body came afloat, still wearing daddy's ring,
Ring and feet Uncle Mose identified.[33]

Although the record was advertised in *Billboard* nothing more was heard of it. It was probably killed off by a lack of radio play in an era when even black-oriented stations were invariably white-owned and managed and did not want to offend sponsors, political bodies, or eavesdropping white listeners.

In 1955 Mrs. Mary McLeod Bethune, the great African American educator and civil rights activist, died. Otis Jackson and the Dixie Hummingbirds recited her praises in a two-part recording titled "The Life Story of Madame Bethune."[34] Bethune had been one of the foremost advisers on African American affairs to President Roosevelt. She had served as head of the Minority Affairs Office of the National Youth Administration, was a board member of both the NAACP and Urban League, and had been a founding member—and sometime president—of the National Council of Negro Women. "I think her race as a whole should mourn, to respect the battle she fought for us all, until Gabriel blows his horn," Jackson said. Although Madame Bethune was revered in the black community as a resolute champion of black rights, her emphasis on educational initiatives and her place in the company of presidents meant that she was not widely perceived as militant by whites. Consequently, African American businessman Don Robey of Peacock Records in Houston probably felt little risk in issuing this gospel eulogy.

Bethune died before she could witness another African American woman inaugurate an era of mass black activism in the South. Mrs. Rosa Parks's actions in refusing to surrender her bus seat to a white man in Montgomery sparked a year-long boycott movement and ushered in the direct action phase of the civil rights struggle. In 1956, Detroit gospel

singer Brother Will Hairston, "The Hurricane of the Motor City," sang
"The Alabama Bus—Parts 1 and 2" about the Montgomery protest, to the
clattering accompaniment of Washboard Willie's makeshift percussion.[35]
Rosa Parks was replaced by "a man," for the sake of either sexism—wasn't
such rebellion a man's job?—or scansion. Otherwise Hairston's account of
events was generally accurate, and his evocation of the emotions they
aroused, gripping. Moreover, his historical parallels with Moses, the hero
of the Exodus story, and (in Part 2) Lincoln, the Great Emancipator, are
telling. The song was released on Joseph Von Battle's JVB Records—another of the relatively few black-owned labels in operation at this time. It
was the first blues or gospel song to mention Dr. Martin Luther King. It is
worth reprinting Part 1 in full:

> Chorus: Stop that Alabama Bus, I don't wanna ride (3x),
> Lord, an Alabama boycott, I don't wanna ride.
> Lord, there come a bus, don't have no load,
> You know, they tell me that a human being stepped on board.
> You know, they tell me that the man sat on the bus,
> You know, they tell me that the driver began to fuss.
> He said: "Looka here, man, you're from the Negro race,
> And don't you know you're sitting in the wrong place?"
> The driver told the man: "I know you paid your dime,
> But if you don't move you gonna pay a fine."
> The man told the driver: "My feets are hurtin',"
> The driver told the man to move behind the curtain.
> I wanna tell you 'bout the Reverend Martin Luther King,
> You know, they tell me that the people began to sing.
> You know, the man God sent out in the world,
> You know, they tell me that the man had the mighty nerve.
> You know, the poor man didn't have a bus to rent,
> You know, they tell me, great God, he had the mighty strength.
> And he reminded me of Moses in Israel land,
> He said: "A man ain't nothing but a man."
> He said: "Looka here, Alabama, don't you see?"
> He says: "All of my people gonna follow me."
> You know, they tell me Reverend King was very hurt,
> He says: "All of my people gonna walk to work."[36]

Just as Eisenhower largely ignored the African American predicament
until compelled to act, so blues and gospel singers generally ignored him.

An exception was J. B. Lenoir's "Eisenhower Blues."[37] Although not specifically about civil rights issues, Lenoir squarely blamed the president for
the tax hikes and economic recession that hit African Americans particularly hard in the mid-1950s.

> Ain't got a dime, ain't even got a cent,
> I don't even have no money to pay my rent,
> My baby needs some clothes, my baby needs some shoes,
> Peoples, I don't know, what is I'm gon' do.
> I got them Eisenhower blues . . .

While there were no blues or gospel songs about civil rights affairs issued
during Eisenhower's second term, events in Little Rock were, however,
briefly mentioned in a 1962 track titled "Ride On Red, Ride On," recorded
by Louisiana Red for single release. Once more, the song described an
attempt to escape the racism of the South by constantly moving on, this
time against the backdrop of massive resistance to desegregation: "We
rolled into old Little Rock, had made another state, where it took the
whole US army to make one school integrate."[38]

While Truman and Eisenhower failed to excite the enthusiasm and
imagination of African American musicians in the same way as Roosevelt,
the 1960s saw the induction of two major and martyred figures into the
pantheon of black civil rights heroes. One, Dr. Martin Luther King, was an
obvious candidate. The other, John F. Kennedy, was in some ways a more
surprising addition. Although Kennedy owed his 1960 election victory in
part to black voters, African American rights had never been high on his
list of priorities. He spent much of his abbreviated term hoping that the
civil rights issue would go away, only responding when the southern
Movement, by this time in full tide, skillfully engineered a series of crises
that his administration could not ignore. Given a fillip by the sit-in movement, which spread across the South from Greensboro, North Carolina,
in 1960, the era was characterized by the Movement's bold use of direct
action tactics, designed to expose the iniquities of segregation and disenfranchisement, and the brutality with which southern whites sought to
preserve them.

Confronted by explosive events like the 1961 Freedom Rides and the
1962 Ole Miss crisis, when fatal rioting greeted James Meredith's admis-
sion to the University of Mississippi, the Kennedy administration initially
tried to deal with each civil rights conflagration on an individual basis and
prevaricated in introducing civil rights reform. But by 1963, it could delay

no longer. There were more civil rights demonstrations in the South that summer than in any other year, before or since. One hundred and fifteen of the region's cities saw formal protest activity of some kind, much of it met with savage repression. Piecemeal responses were no longer adequate to meet insurgency on this scale. Moreover, while too vigorous a civil rights program might once have alienated mainstream whites and thus jeopardized Kennedy's political ambitions, the Movement had succeeded so well in winning over substantial amounts of public sympathy that he could no longer afford to ignore the popular clamor for action.[39]

Amid the dramatic events of 1963, those in Birmingham, Alabama, during the spring, had been particularly significant in moving public, and eventually federal, opinion in favor of civil rights legislation. In Birmingham, a city with a terrible reputation for racial violence, Eugene "Bull" Connor, the quintessential southern racist lawman, roughly arrested protesters and used high-pressure water canons and police dogs against peaceful black marchers, including children. As blues guitarist John Lee Hooker appreciated, Birmingham had become a decidedly dangerous town.

Back in 1948, Hooker had coincidentally used "Birmingham Sam" as one of his many recording pseudonyms. In 1963's "Birmingham Blues" he sang that he dare not go down to the city alone. Unable to understand the motivations of the racists, he insisted, "A man is just a man," and affirmed the equality of all before God and Constitution.

I ain't goin' down, Birmingham by myself,
If I go, I gonna take someone with me.

Get me an airplane, fly over Birmingham,
Drop me a bomb, keep on flyin' on.

Feel so bad, I read about Birmingham,
Although I know one thing: a man is just a man.
God made this land, and this land,
Is no-one, no-one's land.
And God made everybody equal, equal, equal,
I don't know why Birmingham,
Treat, treat the people the way they do,
But I ain't goin' down, Birmingham by myself,
I 'clare I ain't. Yeah!

One thing I do know:
Our President, he is doing everything he can,

Make every man equal right,
It takes time, I do know,
But one day: Birmingham, Mississippi,
Georgia, Tennessee, Kentucky,
All them States,
Arkansas, gonna fall in line.[40]

"Birmingham Blues" was released as a single on Vee-Jay Records—yet again a black-owned company, this time based in Chicago. It seems likely that owners Vivian and James Bracken would have had some idealistic commitment to the song's message. But it is also true that the changed climate of the early 1960s may have made them believe it was now commercially safe, indeed lucrative, to issue such material. Certainly, the Brackens were capitalist eclectics, rather than racial purists, when it came to issuing recordings that might make them money. The same year that "Birmingham Blues" was released with its powerful civil rights message, Vee-Jay bought the first American option by an unknown English group called the Beatles, and had its biggest commercial success with the white vocal group the Four Seasons.

In "Birmingham Blues" Hooker's apparent willingness to drop a bomb on Birmingham rather put him outside the ranks of the nonviolent army that was forging a revolution in the South. Nevertheless, coupled with the song's aggressive delivery, such sentiments undoubtedly reflected the new militancy unleashed by the early Movement. Equally significant was Hooker's thoroughly favorable view of President Kennedy's handling of the civil rights issue. Hooker's conviction that Kennedy "is doing everything he can" to give a man equal rights may have raised a few eyebrows among Movement leaders in Birmingham and beyond. Nevertheless it was an opinion broadly shared by many in the African American community. And even those leaders frustrated by the slow and grudging rate of federal action rejoiced, when on June 11, 1963, Kennedy made a moving television address accepting the moral righteousness—as well as constitutional legitimacy—of African American demands for equality, and pledging his administration to comprehensive civil rights legislation.

Except for the John Lee Hooker song about Birmingham and the Louisiana Red song mentioned previously, the Kennedy years produced no other civil rights blues and gospel songs. B. B. King recorded "I'm Gonna Sit In Till You Give In," but that was basically a love song that employed a topical issue as a dubious metaphor.[41]

On August 28, 1963, the March on Washington marked the symbolic culmination of the early Movement. As the nation heard Martin Luther King's "I Have A Dream" speech, with its barely coded warnings that far more radical African American activists waited in the wings, should America continue to ignore the nonviolent Movement's demands for equality, public sentiment moved even more firmly to support Kennedy's proposed civil rights bill. On November 22, 1963, however, Kennedy was shot in Dallas.

Among many African Americans, Kennedy's assassination instantly turned him into a martyr for their cause. It was of little matter that his commitment to civil rights had been more pragmatic than heartfelt, that his actual record on racial issues was decidedly patchy, or that his successor, Lyndon Johnson, pushed through a far more sweeping and effective Civil Rights Act than Kennedy had ever contemplated. The sense of shock and grief, and of promise unfulfilled, quickly elevated Kennedy to a place alongside Lincoln and Roosevelt as heroes to many African Americans. Gospel legend Mahalia Jackson, for example, cut "In the Summer of His Years" for CBS, lamenting "A shot rang out like a sudden shout, and Heaven held its breath,/ For the dream of a multitude of men rode with him to his death."[42]

Other commemorative songs included "Big" Joe Williams's "A Man Amongst Men" and Mary Ross's "President Kennedy Gave His Life," which compared Kennedy's death with Christ's crucifixion: "Jesus died on Calvary Cross, with nails in the palms of his hands,/ The president died with a bullet in his head, that was made by man."[43] Eventually, at least forty-seven blues and gospel songs marking the death of President Kennedy were recorded in the period from 1963 to 1974, easily eclipsing the ten cut to commemorate the passing of Roosevelt.

After November 1963 both the frequency and the militancy of blues and gospel songs about civil rights began to increase steadily. Events in the parallel world of soul music may have partially inspired this trend. The success in 1964 of Sam Cooke's "A Change Is Gonna Come"—albeit with its most explicit verse about Jim Crow deleted from the released RCA single version— showed that songs that called explicitly for racial change could still be commercially successful.[44] Other soul artists, including Nina Simone, Curtis Mayfield, Joe Tex, and eventually, toward the end of the decade, James Brown, Marvin Gaye, and the Temptations proved that it was perfectly possible to sing of racial pride and denounce racial injustice, and preserve a lucrative career. Indeed, as the decade wore on, overt social comment and criticism become increasingly prevalent in most genres of American popular music.

Following the passage of the Civil Rights Act in 1964, the next major target for Movement activists was black disenfranchisement in the South. The 1964 Mississippi Freedom Summer helped to publicize this issue, culminating in a showdown with Lyndon Johnson when the multiracial Mississippi Freedom Democratic Party sought to unseat the regular all-white Mississippi delegation at the Democratic Party National Convention in Atlantic City.[45] The 1965 campaign in Selma, Alabama, was equally important in hastening the passage later that year of the Voting Rights Act. Reflecting the increased willingness of record companies to release topical material hot on the heels of major events, the Staple Singers cut "Freedom Highway" just a few days after protesters had marched from Selma to Montgomery in March 1965 to demand the right to vote.[46] When "Freedom Highway" was released on Epic, memories of the televised violence the marchers had suffered at the hands of Sheriff Jim Clark on Bloody Sunday, when they first attempted to cross Selma's Pettus Bridge, were still fresh in the public mind.

A similarly rapid response came when James Meredith was shot in June 1966 while marching through Mississippi. J. B. Lenoir called President Johnson to account in his "Shot on Meredith," in which he praised Meredith for "marchin' through Mississippi, leadin' my people to what he thought was right," until "some evil man tried to take his life."[47] This was a particularly difficult time for Johnson. Under increasing criticism for his Vietnam policy, which sucked huge amounts of cash from his "Great Society" programs, Johnson was deeply alarmed by the new cry of "Black Power" that rose up on the Meredith March.[48] Johnson was also disturbed by the wave of urban rioting that started in Watts in 1965 and spread to many American cities during the subsequent summers. The worst of these riots occurred in Detroit in 1967, and John Lee Hooker was again on hand to conjure up a powerful picture of Detroit in flames in "The Motor City Is Burning."[49]

At a time of growing personal paranoia, Lyndon Johnson felt personally betrayed by this new black militancy. He believed—with some justification—that he had done more than any president in history to secure at least equality in law for African Americans, yet he was never able to supplant the murdered Kennedy in their affections. What made this even more unbearable was that Johnson's nemesis, Robert Kennedy, appeared to command the black respect and devotion he felt should be rightly his.

Kennedy's assassination in June 1968 while campaigning for the Democratic Party's presidential nomination secured his own place alongside his brother in the small black pantheon of white heroes. By then, however, another political assassination, that of Martin Luther King Jr., had already marked the end of a distinct phase in the long battle for African American rights.

King's murder on April 4, 1968, also represented a watershed for blues and gospel songs about civil rights issues. His death itself was the subject of at least thirty-four such recordings between 1968 and 1974. Interestingly, while the ten songs about Roosevelt, who died naturally, tended to celebrate his achievements—mostly casting him, with a little historical license, as a racially blind friend of all the poor and oppressed—those about the murdered President Kennedy and Dr. King mainly mourned promise unfulfilled. Some even yoked together King and the Kennedy brothers as fighters for black freedom, as in Albertina Walker and the Caravans' "Three People": "Three people, three people, trying to make this country strong,/ Oh, oh, Lordy, John, Martin and Robert, oh, what did they do wrong?."[50] Others used the tragedy of King's death as an opportunity to contemplate the past and future of the African American struggle for freedom and equality. For example, in the aftermath of the nationwide riots that followed the assassination, producer Willie Dixon wrote a song for singer Koko Taylor titled "Separate or Integrate," a call for unity in a nation in danger of being torn apart.[51]

Another gripping tribute to King, "Hotel Lorraine," was recorded by Otis Spann, the most majestic of all postwar blues piano players. The recording location was a storefront church on 43rd Street in Chicago; the session took place just four days after King's death, as riots raged in the streets.[52] Spann's spontaneously improvised lyrics perfectly capture the grief caused by the irretrievable loss:

> They tell me, tell me he was talkin' to some of his friends at Hotel Lorraine,
> (spoken: It got to be in Memphis, Tennessee.)
> People that's where violence taken over, and the devil got into that evil man.
>
> While Dr. King was talkin,' you know he's in terrible pain,
> They tell me at eight o five, the world was all up in a flame.
>
> Dr. King was a man that could really understand,
> You know the last words he said: "God knows I'm goin' to the promised land."[53]

With its invocation of "the promised land," Spann's song exemplified another major theme in the recordings made to honor King. Amid the sense of sorrow and lost opportunity was a determination to celebrate King's unshakeable faith in the ultimate triumph of the African American freedom struggle. Several songs used King's final public speech—in which he had talked of how God had allowed him "to go up to the mountain. And I've looked over. And I've seen the promised land. I may not get there with you. But I want you to know tonight, that we, as a people will get to the promised land"—as a lyrical touchstone.[54] In "I've Seen the Promised Land," for example, the Swanee Quartet urged their listeners: "Ah, re-member the words, if you only please, that were spoken by this man:/'I've been to the mountain top, I looked over and I've seen the promised land.'"[55] Johnnie Lewis voiced similar sentiments in "I Got to Climb a High Mountain," tapping once more into venerable African American metaphors and images of struggle, deliverance and homecoming: "I got to climb a high mountain, trying to get home,/ I had to wade deep water, trying to get home."[56]

By the time Lyndon Johnson left the White House and Richard Nixon assumed the presidency in early 1969, African American musicians of all stripes—blues artists, gospel singers, the men and women of jazz, the stars of soul and funk—routinely addressed issues of racial injustice and civil rights protest in their work. Indeed, not to do so, at least occasionally, probably risked commercial ruin at a time of fierce black pride and height-ened racial consciousness.

This essay, however, has been concerned primarily with an earlier era, when songs about the Movement were much rarer and the risks involved in producing them much higher. It was on account of those risks that many of the blues and gospel recordings with an overt civil rights agenda were recorded in Europe, or for tiny labels with niche—usually black—audiences, or for labels with a left-wing philosophy and progressive racial politics.

Given the underrepresentation of African American label owners in the recording industry, a disproportionate number of these civil rights songs also appear to have been cut for black-owned labels. Maybe African American owners, as those within the industry with the greatest personal stake in the Movement's success, were sometimes more willing to go out on a limb to record potentially controversial material. Yet, in truth, there was hardly a stampede to cut such songs from anyone, black or white. And there was no guarantee of a public airing for those songs that were re-corded: fears of possible reprisals, doubts about their commercial appeal, and the certain knowledge that even if they avoided a formal ban, they would not get airplay on the radio, combined to ensure that many civil rights blues and gospel songs remained unissued.

All of this confirms how the racial situation provided a crucial context within which the artistry and commerce of African American popular music took place. By the same token, however, it also illustrates how much the story of the creation, distribution, and consumption of that music has to tell historians about the African American community during years of great social upheaval and change.

Notes

1. Guido van Rijn, *Roosevelt's Blues: African-American Blues and Gospel Songs on FDR* (Jackson: University Press of Mississippi, 1997).

2. The postwar decline in the popularity of the blues and, to a lesser extent, gospel is discussed in Brian Ward, *Just My Soul Responding: Rhythm and Blues, Black Consciousness and Race Relations* (Berkeley: University of California Press, 1998), 40, 187–90; William Barlow, *Looking Down at Up: The Emergence of Blues Culture* (Philadelphia: Temple University Press, 1989), 341; Giles Oakley, *The Devil's Music*, rev. ed. (London: Ariel, 1983), 216–33.

3. Some of the material in this essay is drawn from my research for a larger study, *Postwar Future: African-American Blues and Gospel Songs on Truman and Eisenhower* (forthcoming).

4. For good overviews of Truman's civil rights record, see Kenneth O'Reilly, *Nixon's Piano: Presidents and Racial Politics from Washington to Clinton* (New York: Free Press, 1995), 145–65; Steven F. Lawson, *Running For Freedom: Civil Rights and Black Politics in America Since 1941*, 2nd ed. (New York: McGraw-Hill, 1997), 30–37.

5. Harry Truman, quoted in Alonzo L. Hamby, *Man of the People: A Life of Harry S. Truman* (New York: Oxford University Press, 1995), 433.

6. Harry Truman, quoted in *Washington Evening Star*, June 30, 1947, A-5.

7. John Egerton, *Speak Now Against the Day: The Generation Before the Civil Rights Movement in the South* (Chapel Hill: University of North Carolina Press, 1994), 359–75.

8. Ibid., 366.

9. "Champion" Jack Dupree, "I'm Gonna Write the Governor of Georgia," c. August 1946; Folkways unissued.

10. For details of the Moore's Ford massacre see Taylor Branch, *Parting the Waters: America in the King Years, 1954–1963* (New York: Simon and Schuster, 1988), 63–64; Egerton, *Speak Now,* 366–69. In 1992, an eyewitness to the lynching, Clinton Adams, ten years old at the time, finally came forward to name the four

murderers, including Loy Harrison, the planter-employer of one of the slain couples.

11. For more on the growth and failures of southern racial liberalism at this time see Egerton, *Speak Now*, and Tony Badger, "Fatalism Not Gradualism: The Crisis of Southern Liberalism, 1945–1965," in *The Making of Martin Luther King and the Civil Rights Movement*, ed. Brian Ward and Tony Badger (New York: New York University Press, 1996), 67–95.

12. For Moses Asch and Folkways, see Robert Cantwell, *When We Were Good: The Folk Revival* (Cambridge: Harvard University Press, 1996) 81–83, 190; Peter D. Goldsmith, *Making People's Music: Moe Asch and Folkways Records* (Washington, D.C.: Smithsonian Institution Press, 1998). For the chilling effect of economic and personal considerations on rhythm and blues, which was similarly reluctant to embrace the Movement in song or deed until the late 1960s, see Ward, *Just My Soul Responding*, 289–303, 323–36.

13. Memphis Slim ("Leroy"), "Big" Bill Broonzy ("Natchez") and Sonny Boy Williamson ("Sib"), "Blues in the Mississippi Night," New York City, March 1 and 2, 1947; issued on Nixa NJLLP 8; reissued on Sequel NEXCD 121.

14. Yannick Bruynoghe, *Big Bill Blues: William Broonzy's Story as Told to Yannick Bruynoghe* (1955; reprint, New York: Oak, 1964), 58.

15. "Big" Bill Broonzy, "Black Brown and White," Paris, September 20, 1951; issued on Vogue 134; reissued on Vogue BLLP 512510.

16. Brownie McGhee, "Black Brown and White" (composer credit: "Big Bill Broonzy"), New York City, late 1947; issued on Encore 012; reissued on Bear Family 10CD 15720.

17. Huddie "Leadbelly" Ledbetter, "Jim Crow Blues," c. 1947; issued on Folkways LP 2034; reissued on Smithsonian CD 40.045 (with spoken introduction) and Document DOCD 5310 (without the introduction) and "Jim Crow Blues #2," c. 1946/7; Folkways unissued; issued on Smithsonian CD 40.045. The CD notes, which claim a recording date of February 1940, must certainly be in error as Leadbelly sings about his Hollywood experiences in 1944 and 1945.

18. For a full account, see Ray Astbury, "Bilbo Is Dead," *Juke Blues* 6 (Autumn 1986): 23.

19. Andrew Tibbs, "Bilbo Is Dead" (composer credit: "Chess-Aleta-Archia"), Chicago, December 1947; issued on Aristocrat 1101; reissued on Chess CD CHD4 9340.

20. Sandra B. Tooze, *Muddy Waters: The Mojo Man* (Toronto: ECW, 1997), 79.

21. Tommie Jenkins, "Freedom Choo Choo Blues" (composer credit: "Hunt"), Oakland, Calif., 1948; issued on Olliet OTH-1.

22. For the significance of the Exodus myth and images of mobility in African American culture, see Keith Miller, *Voice of Deliverance: The Language of Martin Luther King and Its Sources* (New York: Free Press, 1992), 13–28; Paul Oliver, *Blues Fell This Morning: Meaning in the Blues* (Cambridge: Cambridge University Press, 1990), 12–68; Ward, *Just My Soul Responding*, 211–14.

23. The Gospel Pilgrims (in the Atlantic files called "The Otis Jackson Quartet"), "I'm So Grateful to the NAACP," New York City, December 1950; issued on Atlantic 928.

24. Steven F. Lawson, David R. Colburn, and Darryl Paulson, "Groveland: Florida's Little Scottsboro," in *The African-American Heritage of Florida,* ed. David R. Colburn and Jane L. Landers (Gainesville: University Press of Florida, 1995), 298–325.

25. See Charlie Gillett, *Making Tracks: The Story of Atlantic Records,* 2nd ed. (London: W. H. Allen, 1988), 19–27; Ward, *Just My Soul Responding,* 21–22.

26. Echoes of Zion, "Keep Still (God Will Fight Your Battles)," Atlanta, c. 1952; issued on Gerald 105; reissued on Heritage LP 312.

27. For more on the Movement's manipulation of American civic religion, see Keith Miller and Emily Lewis, "Touchstones, Authorities and Marian Anderson: The Making of 'I Have A Dream,'" in *The Making of Martin Luther King,* ed. Ward and Badger, 147–61.

28. For Eisenhower's civil rights record, see O'Reilly, *Nixon's Piano,* 165–87; Lawson, *Running For Freedom,* 45–55; Robert F. Burk, *The Eisenhower Administration and Black Rights* (Knoxville: University of Tennessee Press, 1984).

29. Bruce Bastin, *Never Sell a Copyright: Joe Davis and His Role in the New York Music Scene,* 1916–1978 (Chigwell, England: Storyville, 1990), 238–40.

30. La Verne "Enyatta Holta" Holt, "Mr. Black Man," New York City, July 7, 1955; issued on Jay-Dee 123; reissued on Krazy Kat LP 796.

31. "Big" Bill Broonzy, "When Do I Get to Be Called a Man," London, England, October 27, 1955; issued on Nixa 2012; reissued on Sequel CD 119. "Big" Bill Broonzy, "I Wonder When I'll Get to Be Called a Man," New York City, c. 1956; issued on Folkways LP 2326. For more on the links between the changing sexual politics of African American music and the progress of the freedom struggle, see Ward, *Just My Soul Responding* 71–89, 150–59, 369–87.

32. "Brother" Will Hairston, "The Death of Emmett Till," (label reads "The Death of Emmett Teal"), Detroit, c. 1969; issued on Knowles LP 1,000,000.

33. The Ramparts, "The Death of Emmett Till," Los Angeles, c. November 1955; issued on DooTone 382.

34. Otis Jackson, "The Life Story of Madame Bethune," August 1955, issued on Peacock 1753.

35. Bob Laughton and Cedric Hayes, "Post War Gospel Recordings of the 40's & 50's," *Blues Unlimited* 139 (Autumn 1980): 37.

36. "Brother" Will Hairston, "The Alabama Bus—Parts 1 and 2," Detroit, 1956; issued on JVB 44; reissued on Blues Classics LP 12.

37. J. B. Lenoir, "Eisenhower Blues," Chicago, 1954; issued on Parrot 802; reissued on Chess LP 2AACMB 208.

38. Louisiana Red, "Ride on Red, Ride On" (composer credit: "Glover/Levy/Reig"), New York City, c. October 1962; issued on Roulette 4469; reissued on Polydor LP 2941002.

39. For the best account of the Kennedys' response to the Movement, see Mark Stern, *Calculating Visions: Kennedy, Johnson and Civil Rights* (New Brunswick, N.J.: Rutgers University Press, 1992). See also O'Reilly, *Nixon's Piano*, 189–237.

40. John Lee Hooker, "Birmingham Blues," Chicago, 1963; issued on Vee-Jay 538; reissued on Vee-Jay LP 1066 and Joy LP 1521.

41. B. B. King, "I'm Gonna Sit In Till You Give In," Los Angeles, Calif., March 1, 1962; issued on ABC 10316; reissued on ABC LP 456. Of course, the "sit-in" movement of the 1960s, like other protest campaigns, did produce a very large number of "freedom songs." Groups like the Carolina Freedom Fighters, the CORE Freedom Singers, and, most famously, the SNCC Freedom Singers from Albany, Georgia, were recorded by dedicated civil rights activists like Guy and Candy Carawan from Highlander Research and Education Center in Tennessee. Although many commercial albums with freedom songs were issued, the songs themselves have generally been neglected by blues and gospel experts. As a result they are not to be found in the standard blues and gospel discographies and we are at a loss about recording dates and locations and in many cases even the identities of the singers themselves. For more on the origins, recording, and significance of the freedom songs, see Bernice Johnson Reagon, "Songs of the Civil Rights Movement, 1955–1965: A Study in Culture History" (Ph.D. dissertation, Howard University, 1975); Bernice Johnson Reagon, "Voices of the Civil Rights Movement: Black American Freedom Songs, 1960–1966," booklet accompanying *Voices of the Civil Rights Movement: Black American Freedom Songs*, 1960–1966, Smithsonian Folkways Recordings, SF40084, 1997; Ward, *Just My Soul Responding*, 269–71, 293–96.

42. Mahalia Jackson, "In the Summer of His Years," November 29, 1963; issued on CBS EP 5694; reissued on Columbia 42946.

43. "Big" Joe Williams, "A Man Amongst Men" and Mary Ross, "President Kennedy Gave His Life," both Chicago, December 1963; issued on Testament LP 01; reissued on Testament TCD 5007.

44. Sam Cooke, "A Change Is Gonna Come" (composer credit: "Sam Cooke"), released on December 22, 1964; issued on RCA 8486; reissued on RCA FJL2LP 7194.

45. The Johnson administration's response to the civil rights movement and the emergence of black power are analyzed in Stern, *Calculating Visions*; O'Reilly, *Nixon's Piano*, 239–76.

46. The Staple Singers, "Freedom Highway," Chicago, early April 1965; issued on Epic 9825; reissued on Epic LP 24163. Three years later, this veteran Chicago gospel group would join Stax Records in Memphis and eventually release a string of powerful message songs to great commercial success.

47. J. B. Lenoir, "Shot on Meredith" (composer credit: "J. B. Lenoir"), Chicago, September 2, 1966; issued on Polydor LP 24820114; reissued on L+R LP 42012.

48. Perhaps surprisingly, Malcolm X, the posthumous inspiration for many of the diverse groups and individuals linked with the black power impulse, enjoyed no contemporary commemoration in blues or gospel, although Cooper Terry later

recorded a "Blues for Malcolm" in 1974. Cooper Terry, "Blues for Malcolm," probably Zürich, Switzerland, September 15, 1974; issued on Bellaphon BCHLP 33.002.

49. John Lee Hooker, "The Motor City Is Burning" (composer credit: "Al Smith"), Chicago, September 26, 1967; issued on BluesWay 61010; reissued on BluesWay BLSLP 6012.

50. Albertina and the Caravans, "Three People," New York, 1970; issued on Hob 1342; reissued on Hob LP 2124.

51. Koko Taylor, "Separate or Integrate" (composer credit: "Dixon"), Chicago, 1968; issued on Checker 1210; reissued on Chess CD 1007.

52. Otis Spann discography by Bill Rowe, in preparation.

53. Otis Spann, "Hotel Lorraine" (composer credit: "Otis Spann"), Chicago, April 8, 1968; issued on Roots TRLP 1005.

54. Martin Luther King, "I See The Promised Land," Speech, Memphis, April 3, 1968, in *A Testament of Hope: The Essential Writings and Speeches of Martin Luther King, Jr.,* ed. James M. Washington (New York: HarperCollins, 1991), 279–86.

55. Swanee Quartet, "I've Seen the Promised Land," 1968, issued on Creed 5188.

56. Johnnie Lewis, "I Got to Climb a High Mountain," Chicago, August 13, 1970; issued on Arhoolie LP 1055; reissued on Arhoolie CD 9007.

7

Free Jazz

Musical Style and Liberationist Ethic, 1956–1965

Peter Townsend

A propensity for continual change has come to be seen as one of the inherent properties of jazz. It is, as Ben Ratliff has recently written, a "stretchable" music.[1] Its definitions are frequently rewritten and widened, while still being incapable of predicting the adaptations that will be needed before its next redefinition. The rate of change in jazz has been high, and the impulse to change has seemed to be self-reinforcing. Only in recent times has thinking about jazz become conscious of this inherent changeableness, and only recently has jazz criticism begun to discontinue the habit of taking its energies from the conflict between those in favor of the current innovation and those against.

At no time in the history of jazz has the dynamic of change operated more explosively than in the years between 1960 and 1965. Change in jazz during those years seems to have been qualitatively different: it ceased to be gradual and incremental change and, for some artists, became a project of wholesale redefinition of their own activity or of the nature of jazz as an art form. New approaches to the playing of an instrument, or to the structure of the jazz ensemble, were in many cases driven by principles filtering into jazz from sources other than its own history.

The activity of improvising music took much of its inspiration from, and in some cases identified itself as a form of, the politics associated with the civil rights movement. Jazz became overtly sensitized to the political climate to a degree not evident at other stages of its history. The titles and dedications of some jazz compositions and recordings of the period refer to people and events in the conflict over civil rights, from the segregationist Governor Faubus of Arkansas to Malcolm X, to Martin Luther King Jr., to the Birmingham church bombings of 1963 for which John Coltrane's "Alabama" is titled.[2]

In the same way as the field of jazz has recently become conscious of its constant redefinition, so, even more recently, has it become aware of its history as a particular form of narrative. The work of writers such as Scott DeVeaux and John Gennari has raised awareness of the unexamined narrative "plots" that have underpinned conceptions of the music.[3] The evaluations of many critics, and the practices of many musicians, have been beholden to some idea of the direction in which, according to these narratives, the music is or should be heading. Anything stylistically new and different has to be accommodated into a new and modified narrative of history, just as it has to be fitted into an expanded definition of what jazz "essentially" is. Innovation sometimes challenges the prevailing narrative just as it challenges statements about essence.

By 1965, jazz was telling itself a story about its own history that was very different from the one that had seemed to be dominant a decade earlier. The recasting of history went deeper than a simple reimagining of the past and future of jazz itself. By 1965, it might have looked as though the narrative in which the new music situated itself was not that of "jazz" at all, but of a larger and wider African American musical tradition. The pressures exerted on the prevailing historical model were diverse and in some cases contradictory, but the process as a whole may be summed up as a reassertion of the continuity of a black musical culture that transcended or subsumed the confines of jazz, and, for that matter, those of any other particular musical idiom.

By the late 1950s, the established idea of the historical shape of jazz was of a developmental or an evolutionary process moving through gradual stages of musical complexity. The end that seemed to be posited for this process was for jazz to become a quasi-classical music, with a shift in its creative methods from improvisation to composition, and the growth of extended musical forms analogous to the symphony. This model both reflected and reinforced the practices of many contemporary jazz musicians, in whose work there were some of the textures and some of the cultural gestures of European art music. Some musicians, most notably Gunther Schuller and John Lewis, envisaged the music's destination in a "Third Stream" that would combine the techniques of jazz with those of western classical music.

A similar paradigm was applied to explain how jazz had developed up to its present level of accomplishment. Here, jazz was seen as recapitulating the same essential progression as European music.[4] This perspective necessarily focused attention on those elements of music that were definitive of European music and also demonstrable in jazz. The central thread of the narrative of change and development in jazz therefore became the increasing sophistication and complexity of its uses of harmony.

According to this model, jazz develops or advances or evolves from the simple triadic harmony of New Orleans music, through the four-note chords and the added ninths of swing music, to the full chromaticism of bebop. The history of jazz, in this version, becomes the story of gradually extending the range of permissible notes, or the story of the notes that can be added to the dominant chord. In the 1920s some dissonant notes began to appear, the 1930s released some more, and bebop in the 1940s rounded off this cycle by its discovery of the flattened fifth and sixth.

The musical innovations of bebop are for some historians virtually re-ducible to what the British writer Benny Green has called "the conquest of chromatic harmony."[5] The key text generally quoted in this connection is the statement frequently misattributed to Charlie Parker about his discov-ery, one night in 1939, in a chili house on New York's Seventh Avenue, of the "higher intervals of a chord."[6] Green has also written of Parker's use of a flattened fifth in his tune "Red Cross" as if the sounding of this note in itself marked the boundary of a new movement in art, a technical scandal like those that provoked riots at the premiere of *The Rite of Spring* or Victor Hugo's *Hernani*.[7]

According to this narrative, jazz had been recapitulating the harmonic trajectory of the European classical tradition. By the 1950s, it was up to speed and its next progression would be to explore the resources of com-position and extended musical form. From this thoroughly Europeanized perspective, there was nowhere else for jazz to go other than toward the familiar European classical configuration of composer, orchestra, and per-former.

Having become a complex music, with the dissonant notes of the oc-tave filled in like the periodic table of the elements, jazz would continue to progress toward some other level or dimension of complexity. This set of assumptions was in the early 1960s challenged by directions taken in the work of musicians like Charles Mingus, Ornette Coleman, and John Coltrane. The presumption that the music would pursue complexity was denied by some unforeseen kinds of simplicity, and the projected direction of the music was very quickly shown to have been based on a mistaken set of assumptions.

The "harmonic complexity" narrative is abstract. It has little reference to people, other than to the successive discoverers of lost chords, and, as

Ronald Radano has observed, it "remove[s] music from the social and ideological categories that had previously given it meaning."[8] According to Radano, these efforts to "reformulate jazz according to classicist precepts" project an image of "a classless and raceless society."[9] The categories of race and class, the contexts of particular cultural traditions, are cut across by a narrative of contributions to a music itself abstracted from its environments in American society.

In the late 1950s and early 1960s a number of musicians associated with the bebop style, among them Horace Silver, Charles Mingus, and the Adderley brothers, Julian ("Cannonball") and Nat, began to incorporate elements of gospel music into their material. The chord progressions of many of these pieces were relatively simple. The blues form, which in the bebop style had been augmented by complex chordal movements, was played with a renewed simplicity, in some cases with the harmonies cut back to the primitive three-chord progression. Charles Mingus's tune "Folk Forms," for example, recorded in 1960, is a simple blues in the key of F, "spontaneously organized," as Brian Priestley explains, "around a couple of simple rhythmic figures."[10]

John Coltrane seemed in some respects to be following a parallel course. In Lewis Porter's summary, "his blues pieces reflect a desire to get back to a primal mood, and away from the emotionally lighter, harmonically more complex blues of the boppers."[11] The expressive potential in these newer approaches is not located in harmonic elaboration but in other qualities: emotional intensity, responsiveness in a group situation, and what Priestley calls "soulfulness."[12] These are qualities that connect contemporary practice with older African American forms and with the wider African American vernacular. The artists' consciousness of this rediscovered connection is shown even in song titles of the period: from Charles Mingus, for example, there is "Wednesday Night Prayer Meeting" and "Better Git It in Your Soul." The word "soul" became for a time a marketable label for a kind of jazz that took its character from a thorough use of elements of black popular tradition, especially church music and the blues. Ben Sidran has linked this phase, which he calls "the 'soul' mystique of the late 1950s," with the changed social mood following the *Brown v. Board of Education* decision of May 1954, which declared segregated schooling unconstitutional and signaled the imminent end of Jim Crow in the South.[13]

In May 1960, four months after the southern-wide commencement of the lunch-counter sit-ins, Charles Mingus recorded "Prayer for Passive Resistance," a slow, incantatory blues.[14] A few months later, a second version was recorded of a tune titled "Fables of Faubus." In an earlier 1959 version, the bitterness of Mingus's attack on the leading actor in the Little Rock schools conflict had to be conveyed by the parodic simplicity of the opening phrases and the suggestion of menace in the changes of tempo, but in the 1960 version Mingus's group was allowed to deliver the very direct message of Mingus's text:

> Oh Lord, don't let them shoot us
> Oh Lord, don't let them stab us
> Oh Lord, don't let them tar and feather us
> Oh Lord, no more swastikas.

Even in a carefully planned piece like "Fables of Faubus," Mingus breaks up the routines that had come to characterize modern jazz. The swinging 4/4 rhythm is used only in four-bar sections that contrast with the constrained two-beat rhythm of the preceding eight bars, and Mingus, from the bass, directs further interruptions. The beat snaps into passages in double time or in a 12/8 pattern. The energy of the players is strongly held back and released according to the pattern of the unusual 71-bar framework or in response to the cues that come from Mingus himself.[15]

In Charles Mingus's music around this time, there were many other deviations from the established paradigm that over the next few years were to be carried to more radical ends by other players: a revaluation of some distinctively black musical traditions, a revival of collective rather than solo improvisation, and a gradual simplification of harmonic materials. What to do about harmony became one of the central issues for musical practice and theory during the phase of radical innovation of the early 1960s. Mingus's music, despite its numerous innovative features, remained on the whole based on the tonal system. But even before 1960 there was music already in the public domain that had abandoned tonality.

According to the Europeanized narrative of development, this change is not of itself surprising, because after tonality comes atonality, a negative or inverse of the old system, and there was the precedent of a similar change that had taken place in European music around 1900. But the historical parallel does not fit with the particular context in which the change was occurring in jazz. A preferred term for this step was "freedom," a word that by this time, as the jazz historian Ted Gioia puts it, already "stood out as a politically charged word in American public discourse."[16]

The saxophonist Ornette Coleman made a series of recordings between 1958 and 1961 in which he and his collaborators were already operating in the musical world of these new freedoms. Martin Williams's liner note to the 1961 album *Free Jazz* indicates that the liberties being taken concerned more than the absence of conventional tonality: "It is a continuous free improvisation with only a few brief pre-set sections. Not only is the improvisation almost total, it is frequently collective, involving all eight men inventing at once . . . . There were no preconceptions as to chord patterns or chorus lengths."[17]

Coleman himself distinguishes harmony (which he refers to as "background") from "the music," and urges his musicians "to try to play the music and not the background."[18] "The music," in this conception, is what emerges in the specific time frame of the performance, instead of being prompted by a pre-existing harmonic progression. The immediate musical context in which the individual player performs is not that of a given form or sequence, but is in effect the performance itself, consisting primarily of the texture created by the other players.

The improvisation is both collective and non-harmonic. Harmonic moments still occur in the music, but they arrive fortuitously and are handled intuitively by the musicians. The commingling of the notes that are played may create moments of harmonic tension and complexity, but in the contexts of the music it would make no sense to represent such occurrences as another level of complexity on the harmonic evolutionary scale. Coleman's music, by the totality of its freedoms, gives grounds for dispensing with this kind of explanation altogether.

The ideological implications of harmony were taken up in the early 1960s by Amiri Baraka (then known as LeRoi Jones) in a series of articles published during his tenure as jazz critic in the *Village Voice* and *Down Beat*. In a 1962 piece on John Coltrane, Baraka makes a reference to "the harmonic problem"; the nature of this problem for Baraka, and, by extension, for African American jazz musicians in general, becomes apparent in his writings over the next four years.[19] To some extent, the "harmonic problem" as Baraka sees it is a function of a problem of repertoire, of the materials that were available for improvising on. The harmonic progressions on which jazz musicians improvised were very largely derived from popular songs commercially published between 1920 and 1950. A musician like John Coltrane had already spent much of his earlier career improvising on the harmonies of show tunes and their jazz derivatives.

Even by the late 1950s, there could already be a certain cultural disjunction between the improvisational style Coltrane was developing and the standard material he was improvising on: the effect of hearing Coltrane state a melody such as "Bye Bye Blackbird" at the conclusion of one of his tumultuous solos can be close to bathos. A similar sense of cultural incongruity was apparent to other musicians too; the Chicago pianist Richard Muhal Abrams explains the motivation of his search for new material by the fact that "We could play a tune like 'Body and Soul' forever and not express what we feel."[20] The song "Body and Soul," written by Johnny Green in 1930, had been the basis of classic jazz improvisations for thirty years, and is still in everyday use, but it is not surprising in the context of the early 1960s to find its relevance to younger African American musicians being called into doubt.

Baraka credits the saxophonist Albert Ayler with "having done away with the popular song."[21] In an essay published in 1965 he reports that "Coltrane seeks with each onslaught to completely destroy the popular song," and again in the same year, in an essay titled "New Black Music," he uses a stronger formulation still: "Coltrane showed us how to murder the popular song. To do away with weak Western forms."[22] It is clear from these comments that a factor in Baraka's rejection of harmony is a rejection of the commercial song forms from which the harmonies come. Even Baraka's usage of the term "freedom" is closely linked with this attitude toward the values and the structures of popular song: "the new music . . . is 'radical' within the context of mainstream America. Just as the new music begins by being free. That is, freed of the popular song."[23]

But Baraka himself, and a number of other writers, indicate more fundamental reasons for the downgrading of harmony. Harmony is European, western, and an obstacle to the rediscovery of African musical values— just as, for some writers, its effect upon the preceding history of African American music has been repressive. A 1965 article by Baraka quotes the saxophonist Archie Shepp: "When black people came to these shores they didn't know much harmony . . . that's a Western musical phenomenon. But they had melodies and tremendous rhythm . . . 'Sometimes I Feel Like a Motherless Child' . . . I doubt that they were even thinking of harmony when they invented the melody, and the melody line is fantastic."[24]

As Ornette Coleman also argues, harmony can be seen as inimical to the free independent movement of melody and rhythm. The relegation of harmony to a minimal role is seen as both freeing up the individual improviser, in the playing situation, and, on a historical scale, as enabling African American music to liberate the repressed African values expressed in rhythm and in melody. Shepp explains this point in the same interview: "This new music is about a melodic and rhythmic approach to the music. In a way it's more of a throwback rather than a projection into some weird future. A throwback in the direction of the African influences on the music."

For some musicians, the long-term influence of tonal harmony is considered even more baneful. In Ronald Radano's words: "As the principal component of European-based music, [harmony] became a metaphor for white cultural dominance and oppression: harmony was a sonic reconstruction of the disciplinary practice that had objectified black difference, of the rationalism that had stifled African spiritualism. In rhythm and melody, on the other hand, the musicians identified formal attributes that stressed the communal, multilinear orientation of West African music and traditional African American styles."[25]

Among some of the musicians of the "freedom" movement, there was a deliberate effort to align their own musical practices with values and procedures they identified as African. Lewis Porter, in his biography of John Coltrane, is very specific in telling us that in May 1961 "Coltrane began consciously utilizing African elements in his recordings."[26] Coltrane's recordings for that year included "Liberia," "Dahomey Dance," and the extended piece arranged for a large ensemble, "Africa/Brass." At this stage of his career, Coltrane listened extensively to recordings of African music and went so far as to abandon the customary 4/4 jazz rhythms, favoring instead African rhythmic patterns as the organizing principle of some of his pieces.

For some musicians, the reclamation of Africa encompassed not only specific musical techniques, but also the recovery of a lost affinity with a wider musical and cultural tradition. A 1966 essay by Amiri Baraka speaks of the composer Sun Ra as "want[ing] a music that will reflect a life-sense lost in the West, a music full of Africa."[27] For the members of the Association for the Advancement of Creative Musicians (AACM), a collective inaugurated in Chicago in 1965, there was, as Radano puts it, the vision of "an immutable, pan-African musical legacy transcending cultural and historical categories."[28]

The changes that were taking place in jazz during this period were rapid and deep-seated. Harmony lost its primacy as the key to the evolution of jazz; jazz itself as an identifiably American idiom was seemingly in the process of being displaced by leanings toward Africa. One of the factors of musical performance frequently attributed to African sources was the new emphasis on collectivity. In this connection, too, the jazz narrative appeared to be going into reverse. Collective improvisation had ceased to be a common feature of jazz ensemble playing from the late 1920s, when, according to this view, the improvised group counterpoint of New Orleans was permanently transcended by the individual virtuosity of a stream of great soloists beginning with Louis Armstrong and Sidney Bechet. Yet the

1960s saw a return of collective improvisation, not only as a procedure but also as an ideal.

Ornette Coleman's *Free Jazz* carries the prominent subtitle "A Collective Improvisation." Here is another manifestation of Coleman's distinction between "the music" and "the background": the usual separation of roles within the jazz ensemble between soloists and accompaniment is overcome in an ensemble in which all the players are potentially equal contributors in the construction of a collective fabric. There is a lower differential between the volume levels of the various instruments in the recording mix of *Free Jazz* than in conventional jazz recordings. Soloists do not detach themselves so conspicuously from the ongoing improvisations of the other players.

The listener, like the player, is more conscious of interplay between the instruments, and of the need for responsiveness to this network of relationships within the group. This kind of collective work imposes its own etiquette, even its own ethics, which are different from those governing the prevailing norms of jazz musicianship. Appropriate conduct within the group is not so much a matter of good intonation, good timekeeping, and mastery of form but has much more of an interpersonal aspect. A recent study, Paul Berliner's *Thinking in Jazz*, has made clear the extent to which a form of collectivity has always been an important virtue in jazz playing, but the music of the early 1960s foregrounds this value and creates an environment in which the existence of the music is dependent on its functioning.[29] The musical self-assertion of the individual must be reconciled within the mutuality of the group.

In this form, the ideal of right behavior within the free jazz group is only a step away from being a political ideal. The negotiation between individual and group in freely improvised jazz was taken up by a number of writers as a metaphor for, or as an instance of, kinds of new political organization. A recent restatement of this view, by Charles Hersch, sets out the options with great clarity and places the argument squarely within the context of the later civil rights years. For Hersch, the difference between Coleman's "Free Jazz" of 1960 and John Coltrane's free improvisation "Ascension," recorded in June 1965, is the difference between the social ideals of Martin Luther King Jr., particularly his notion of the "redemptive community," and those of the emerging black power movement.[30]

"Free Jazz" and "Ascension" are similarly conceived: in both, there is an alternation between solo and ensemble passages, and both begin from a minimal initial phrase that the musicians are free to use or discard as they choose. Hersch sees the differing stylistic results of the two experiences as an analogue to a political shift between the earlier and the later stages of the civil rights movement. Coleman's music is genuinely "polyphonic"; it retains the capacity to reconcile the different voices within the ensemble, whereas "Ascension" is, as Hersch puts it, "textural": "Where 'Free Jazz' as the redemptive community overcomes the dichotomy between group and individual, 'Ascension' is unable to do so, alternating collective catharsis with individual soloing."[31] Hersch attributes some importance to the differences in group organization in the two recordings, pointing out that in "Ascension" the wind instruments keep silent when others are soloing, while in "Free Jazz" they continue to improvise collectively with the rest of the group.

Hersch's reading of "Ascension" is as a musical prefiguring of "the interest-oriented group called for by the emerging black power movement" and "the militaristic cadres like the Black Panthers,"[32] and this prefiguring works as a sign of failure in both the musical and the political domains. Amiri Baraka's writings in the 1960s, on the other hand, show no doubts either about "Ascension" or about the necessity for collective playing: "The return to collective improvisation, which the West-oriented, the whitened, say, is chaos, is the all-force put together, and is what is wanted."[33]

Recognizing the value of collectivity in the practice of improvised music transferred into a belief in the value of collective organization by musicians in the cultural market-place. From 1960 onwards a series of formalized groupings primarily of African American musicians were dedicated to the provision of better work opportunities, sympathetic recording and performing environments, and mutual support. The antifestival set up in 1960 in opposition to the Newport Festival by Charles Mingus and others established itself on a formal footing soon afterwards as the Jazz Artists Guild. Contemporary conditions imposed an increasing necessity for this kind of initiative. The evident radicalism of the music itself did not suggest great commercial potential, and after 1964 there was in any case a general collapse in the demand for jazz of any description. By the mid-1960s, cooperative musicians' organizations like the Jazz Composers Guild, set up in New York in 1964, had become economically essential. There were also cultural and political resonances to such groups, especially for African American musicians: the positive values associated with collectivity in the music itself, the analogy with nonwestern patterns of community organization, and, for some, a degree of cultural separatism.

The necessity for self-help was one of the arguments advanced with increasing emphasis through this period by Amiri Baraka. As well as helping to found an arts collective in his home town of Newark, Baraka used his dispatches to the jazz magazines to promote ideas for circumventing the lack of exposure free-jazz musicians were suffering: coffee shop gigs, cooperative jazz clubs, do-it-yourself record distribution. He commended Ornette Coleman's effort to open his own jazz club, and exhorted "do it yourself, brother. Not brother can you spare a ten per cent. Do it yourself, in nations, culture, products of the mind and soul."[34]

The AACM cooperative embodied an even fuller set of cultural ambitions. The weekly dues paid by members were used to support educational initiatives as well as to sponsor performances, and the organization's statements of intent included a commitment to the maintenance of high moral standards and "to promote Spiritual growth in Creative Artists." Radano attributes the AACM's long-term stability to the inspiration and example of the civil rights movement, and he sees the AACM's musical practices, which were founded on free collective improvisation, as a symbolic expression of its own, and the Movement's, social philosophy. The role of the pianist Richard Muhal Abrams, the first president of the AACM, indicates the breadth and depth of the aims that were being addressed. In Radano's words, "Abrams's guidance was a recipe for personal development, recalling similar messages being spoken by Rev. Martin Luther King Jr., and traditionally by Chicago's black religious leaders. In particular, his views resembled those of John Coltrane, who provided a new, priestly image for the nation's jazz youth."[35]

Jazz in America has not usually had to carry a sense of social mission, and even less so of spirituality, as part of its baggage. Residual elements of hymns and spirituals can be found in the repertoire, and many musicians have derived from a life in jazz a sense of personal fulfillment. Much is made of Charlie Parker's description of his religious affiliation as "devout musician" and many other players display an attitude of reverence toward the artifacts of jazz itself, but until this phase of the 1960s, jazz as a music was not thought of as a means of access to spirituality in the fully religious sense.

According to Radano, the members of the AACM referred to collective improvisation itself as "spiritualism" or "the spirit plane."[36] The notion of spirituality recurs more and more strongly toward the mid-1960s. John Coltrane's recordings from 1961 onwards include "Spiritual," "Ascension," and "A Love Supreme," the latter a four-part suite dedicated to the stages of his own spiritual rebirth. It was a considerable achievement on Coltrane's part to get the jazz audience to sit still for this kind of confession of religious feeling, and the fact that it was possible at all indicates how much the terms of the culture had been changed in the preceding years. Even before his death in 1967, Coltrane had become a figure accorded an unprecedented spiritual status. In the jazz literature he is frequently likened to Martin Luther King Jr., for whom he titled the 1966 recording "Reverend King," a piece that begins with the musicians performing a chant based on a Hindu scripture.[37]

Coltrane's spirituality takes on the character of a permanent personal commitment: "My goal" he is quoted as saying, "is to live the truly religious life and to express it in music."[38] For others, and often for Coltrane, the notion of spirituality has an African inflection. Baraka describes Sun Ra's Arkestra in the likeness of an African extended musical family: "fifteen or sixteen musicians . . . who are convinced that music is really a priestly concern and a vitally significant aspect of black culture."[39]

Within the timescale of the performance rather than of the lifetime, the spirit resides in the experience of the given occasion; when successful, free—especially collective—expression can lead, in the listener as well as the player, to an ascent into the spiritual realm. Here is Baraka's reaction to a free jazz performance by Burton Greene in Newark in 1966: "It was a mad body-dissolving music . . . rose and stayed there . . . ecstasy of understanding, then, evolution. The feeling such men make is of the consciousness of evolution the will of the universe. . . . Yes, it is music which, under the best fingers, is a consciously Spiritual Music."[40]

The politics present within and around free jazz manifested itself in a way without precedent in the history of jazz. It can be contrasted with whatever kind of politics was involved in the genesis of bebop. Bebop still seems to many commentators to have been about something, for or against something. As Scott DeVeaux puts it, it has "an unmistakable edge of resistance," but what it was a resistance to was not made explicit.[41] Bebop was cryptic and perverse, on the whole, in its namings and descriptions, and little is known about the actual political affiliations of the early bebop musicians. Bebop looked subcultural in a way that free jazz did not: free jazz did not generate any homologies of dress, language, or behavior, as bebop for a time had. The political meaning of bebop can only be inferred from the stance, the attitude sounded in the music itself, from what Eric Lott has called its "politics of style."[42] Amiri Baraka considers bebop as a precursor to the properly revolutionary phase that is reached in free jazz. Scott DeVeaux, on the other hand, argues that the radical ambitions of bebop begin and end in the domain of music; for him it is "an attempt to reconstitute jazz in such a way as to give its black creators the greatest professional autonomy within the market place."[43]

In any case, one distinction to be made between bebop and "free jazz" is that in bebop any interpretation requires an effort; meaning has to be read from the features of the music, whereas in the free jazz period of the early 1960s the politics becomes explicit. For the first time, the activity of jazz musicians in music communicated directly with a body of ideas. The relationship was reciprocal: it is not accurate to say that musical practice followed in the wake of ideas about social organization, or a reevaluation of spirituality. Part of the experience of having been a participator in the Movement was that sometimes, as Baraka says, "it was as if the music was leading us."[44] It was through this kind of unified process, with music never seen as uncoupled from the philosophy, that the free jazz movement of the early 1960s succeeded in making the inroads that it did.

One should be careful not to overstate the net effect of all this on the jazz scene as it then stood. In 1965 most of the celebrated players in earlier styles of jazz were still alive and professionally active, and most musicians were probably more shaken by the arrival of the Beatles than by small cadres of radicals. To imply that free jazz brought about a transformation would be to slide easily into another of the models that underpin the various narratives of jazz: that new musical styles supplant others, in the same way as theoretical frameworks in science—as if Louis Armstrong were Newtonian physics and Ornette Coleman Einsteinian physics. Old styles do not become disproved or discredited by new styles, though they usually have to forfeit some of their market share. In actuality, the majority of jazz players improvised in the same way in 1965 as they had done in 1955.

What the liberationist jazz of the 1960s did do, however, was to disturb the frame of reference, and this had longer-term effects on jazz culture as a whole. The unfamiliar, or at least undervalued, qualities of spirituality and collectivity were absorbed or reabsorbed into jazz discourse. Free jazz introduced a new seriousness, or at least a new kind of seriousness, into jazz. A considerable section of the record-buying public could, in the mid-1960s, treat John Coltrane's declaration of religious faith with respect. It became possible, if not always welcome, for jazz to wear its politics on its album sleeve.

Free jazz, except when it was regarded as lying outside of the territory of jazz altogether, made necessary a radical change in the way the history of jazz was conceptualized. It was not easy to assimilate it into the linear view of a music growing ever more complex and aspiring to the condition of European concert music. Free jazz was disruptive of historical continuity because it implied changes of value in too many areas all at the same time. It backed off from the accepted standards of musicianship. It revived musical procedures long presumed dead, and it emphasized spirituality and Africanness. It was more like a paradigm shift than another link in the historical chain.

In the late 1950s and the first half of the 1960s, the changes apparent in the playing styles of jazz reoriented the historical narrative along the lines of a different set of coordinates from what had usually been predicted. The soul jazz of the 1950s and the free jazz of the 1960s together amounted to a reassertion of a more distinctly African American narrative, one that saw a different network of links with a past, and one that attached its highest values to different potentialities of the music. Melody regained its significance relative to harmony, the collective relative to the individual.

There are some participants for whom the question of the history of jazz, whatever its orientation, is, in any case, of little consequence. In the end, for some musicians, it does not really matter whether one's output is properly positioned in terms of "jazz" at all. The scope of the term "jazz," which has often been considered a stereotyping label, has seemed unduly narrow for musicians engaged in what they see as a full-scale revision and revisiting of a broader and a more intimate history. Some members of the AACM substituted for "jazz" other terms that for them are more descriptive: "Creative Music," "Great Black Music." The writings of Amiri Baraka in the 1960s, with the broad sweep of his advocacy of Albert Ayler and Motown, reflect the same kind of perspective. Perhaps the history to be concerned about, to be writing again, is not that of something called "jazz" at all, but of something bigger, the history of black music, or of African American music, and this writing would discover its own parameters and select its own definition.

Notes

1. Ben Ratliff, *New York Times*, March 9, 1998, 21.

2. The relevant recordings are Charles Mingus's two versions of "Fables of Faubus," Archie Shepp's "Malcolm, Malcolm, semper Malcolm," and John Coltrane's "Dr. King" and "Alabama."

3. Scott DeVeaux, "Constructing the Jazz Tradition: Jazz Historiography," *Black American Literature Forum* 25, no. 3 (Fall 1991): 525–60; John Gennari, "Jazz Criti-

cism: Its Development and Ideologies," ibid., 449–523. See also the introduction to DeVeaux's *The Birth of Bebop: A Social and Musical History* (Berkeley: University of California Press, 1997), 1–17.

4. A good example of this is found in Andre Hodeir's *Jazz: Its Evolution and Essence* (New York: Grove, 1956), in which he proposes a historical model of this kind.

5. Benny Green, *Drums in My Ears* (London: Davis-Poynter, 1973), 129–30.

6. Quoted in N. Hentoff and N. Shapiro, *Hear Me Talkin' to Ya* (London: Penguin, 1962), 342–43. The full quotation attributed to Parker mistakenly includes explanatory comment by writers who had quoted Parker's words in an earlier publication.

7. Benny Green, *The Reluctant Art: Five Studies in the Growth of Jazz* (New York: Da Capo, 1991), 166–67.

8. Ronald Radano, *New Musical Figurations: Anthony Braxton's Cultural Critique* (Chicago: University of Chicago Press, 1993), 15.

9. Ibid.

10. B. Priestley, *Mingus: A Critical Biography* (London: Quartet, 1982), 113.

11. Lewis Porter, *John Coltrane: His Life and Music* (Ann Arbor: University of Michigan Press, 1998), 184.

12. Priestley, *Mingus*, 82.

13. B. Sidran, *Black Talk* (New York: Holt, Rinehart, and Winston, 1971), 125–26.

14. "Prayer for Passive Resistance" was recorded by Mingus in a big band format on May 25, 1960.

15. The first, instrumental, recording of the piece is "Fables of Faubus," May 5, 1959. The second version, with Mingus's text, is "Original Faubus Fables," recorded October 20, 1960. An analysis of the unusual formal structure of this piece is given in "Forms," in *The New Grove Dictionary of Jazz* (New York: St. Martin's Press, 1994), 399.

16. T. Gioia, *The History of Jazz* (New York: Oxford University Press, 1997), 337.

17. Martin Williams, liner notes (1960) to Ornette Coleman, "Free Jazz," recorded December 21, 1960.

18. Ornette Coleman, quoted in liner notes to "Free Jazz."

19. LeRoi Jones (Amiri Baraka), "A Jazz Great: John Coltrane," reprinted in Jones, *Black Music* (New York: Quill, 1967), 60.

20. Quoted in Radano, *New Musical Figurations*, 89n.

21. Jones, *Black Music*, 126.

22. Ibid., 105, 174.

23. Ibid., 209.

24. Ibid., 152.

25. Radano, *New Musical Figurations*, 105.

26. Porter, *John Coltrane*, 212.

27. Jones, *Black Music*, 128.

28. Radano, *New Musical Figurations,* 99.

29. Paul Berliner, *Thinking in Jazz: The Infinite Art of Improvisation* (Chicago: University of Chicago Press, 1994), especially Part III, 289–446.

30. Charles Hersch, "'Let Freedom Ring': Free Jazz and African-American Politics," *Cultural Critique* (Winter 1996): 97–123.

31. Ibid., 116–17.

32. Ibid., 116. For alternative readings of "Ascension," see Porter, *John Coltrane,* 262–264 and Barry Kernfeld, *What to Listen For in Jazz* (New Haven: Yale University Press, 1995), 34–38.

33. Jones, *Black Music,* 195.

34. Ibid., 140.

35. Radano, *New Musical Figurations,* 81. Frank Kofsky's history of the "free jazz" period comments that "No single figure in the history of jazz . . . ever possessed greater moral authority than John Coltrane." Frank Kofsky, *John Coltrane and the Jazz Revolution of the 1960s,* expanded and revised 2nd ed. (New York: Pathfinder, 1998), 323.

36. Radano, *New Musical Figurations,* 104.

37. Ibid.; page 81, for example, compares both Coltrane and Richard Muhal Abrams to Dr. King.

38. Porter, *John Coltrane,* 232.

39. Jones, *Black Music,* 129–30.

40. Ibid., 137.

41. DeVeaux, *The Birth of Bebop,* 27

42. Eric Lott, "Double V, Double-Time: Bebop's Politics of Style," in *Jazz Among the Discourses,* ed. Krin Gabbard (Durham, N.C.: Duke University Press, 1995), 243–55.

43. DeVeaux, *The Birth of Bebop,* 27

44. *The Autobiography of LeRoi Jones-Amiri Baraka* (New York: Freundlich, 1984), 177.

8

Jazz and Soul, Race and Class, Cultural Nationalists and Black Panthers

A Black Power Debate Revisited

Brian Ward

In the late 1960s and early 1970s, the correct role of black culture in the struggle for African American freedom became the subject of an intense debate between two broadly identifiable factions within the black power movement: cultural nationalists and revolutionary nationalists. Intensified by the covert promptings of the Federal Bureau of Investigation's (FBI) Counter-Intelligence Program to destroy organized black militancy, disagreements over tactics and goals between these groups sometimes escalated from angry verbal exchanges into actual violence. In the most dramatic of these confrontations, on America's west coast Maulana Ron Karenga's cultural nationalists, US, swapped bombs and bullets as well as insults with the most dynamic exponents of revolutionary nationalism, the Black Panther Party.[1]

For many years one historiographical legacy of this conflict was a tendency both to exaggerate and to simplify the genuine ideological and strategic differences between the two nominal camps. A complex, frequently ambiguous, and constantly evolving relationship was often reduced to a static, polar distinction between cultural nationalists who unreservedly celebrated and promoted a discrete black culture as both the means and the ends of black liberation, and revolutionary nationalists who dismissed cultural programs as an unnecessary diversion from organizing the black community's urgent pursuit of economic and political power.

More recent scholarship, most notably that of William Van Deburg and Komozi Woodard, has helped to finesse this crude picture. Refusing to draw overly rigid distinctions between cultural and revolutionary nationalists, Van Deburg sensibly concluded in *New Day In Babylon* that no black power group—indeed, no organization interested in the struggle for African American rights—was untouched by calls for a black cultural reawakening or indifferent to the potential of using black culture to advance its programs. "Ideological enemies may have been opposed to the cultural nationalists' ordering of priorities," he explained, "but they were not against incorporating cultural elements into their own definitions of black power." Conversely, as we shall see, few cultural nationalists were so obsessed with their naturals, dashikis, and bubbas as to be entirely indifferent to the need for practical political and economic organizing among the black masses.[2]

Yet if widespread agreement that black culture was an important element in the quest for black freedom might have provided a constructive link between disparate black power groups in the late 1960s and early 1970s, the fact remains that cultural politics often did become the terrain for bitter dispute and confrontation. This involved more than simply disagreements about "the ordering of priorities," of where cultural initiatives should fit into a grander strategy of organized struggle—although this contentious bone was much gnawed upon and merits close attention. It was also a question of precisely which sorts of black cultural production were deemed most appropriate in advancing the black cause. By comparing and contrasting the evolving cultural politics of the Black Panther Party—still a woefully under-explored topic amid the burgeoning literature on the Party—with those of leading cultural nationalists like Imamu Amiri Baraka and Maulana Ron Karenga, this essay suggests that it was here, in debates over the relative merits, utility, and "authenticity" of different strains of African American popular culture, that important ideological and tactical differences between cultural and revolutionary nationalists manifested themselves most clearly.[3]

More specifically, the essay focuses on black power attitudes toward the role of secular black popular music in the freedom struggle. Diverse and mutating responses to the unifying, liberating, and polemical potential of soul and jazz reflected many of the issues that most vexed and divided black power theorists in the late 1960s and early 1970s. In particular, attitudes toward popular music revealed much about the relative importance different groups assigned to race and class as coordinates of black oppression, and exposed some of the practical dilemmas faced by the broader Movement in trying to harness black creativity to effective racial protest and politics.

From its origins in the late 1950s, when artists like Ray Charles, James Brown, and Sam Cooke blended gospel with rhythm and blues to create a new soul idiom, to its commercial and artistic triumph in the mid-1960s, soul music had tended to avoid explicit lyrical discussion of the freedom struggle. There were some notable exceptions, like Cooke's "A Change Is Gonna Come," The Impressions' "People Get Ready," Nina Simone's "Mississippi Goddam," and Joe Tex's "The Love You Save May Be Your Own," but these were relatively rare. The conspicuous involvement in formal Movement activities of a handful of soul stars like Simone was similarly exceptional. Until the later 1960s, soul artists and their management largely eschewed public comment or agitation on the civil rights issue, fearing that such racial militancy might undermine their chances of reaching a lucrative mass white market. Indeed, at a time when integration was the watchword of the Movement, to compete successfully for the rewards of the mainstream with a music proudly bearing the stamp of African American culture seemed to symbolize what the Struggle was all about. Thus, soul's popularity with African Americans initially depended less on its occasional forays into social activism or commentary than on its distinctively black vernacular lyrics, its adoption of certain musical devices and performance practices drawn from a gospel tradition to which blacks had an intensely proprietorial relationship, and the conspicuous material success of its leading stars—not least among white fans.[4]

In 1966, however, Imamu Amiri Baraka predicted in an essay titled "The Changing Same" that the world of soul music was about to become more overtly engaged with the Movement and that "R&B songs will be more socially oriented."[5] At the time Baraka was intensifying a commitment to cultural nationalism that convinced him that "the solution of the Black Man's problems will come only through Black National Consciousness. . . . only a united Black Consciousness can save Black People from annihilation at the white man's hands."[6] Like other leading cultural nationalists, notably Maulana Ron Karenga, Haki Madhabuti (Don L. Lee), John O. Killens, Kasisis Jitu Weusi (Les Campbell), and John Henrik Clark, Baraka insisted that race, not class, was the fundamental determinant of black oppression. Paradoxically, however, these cultural nationalists also believed that race, or race-consciousness, could be transformed into the principal tool for black deliverance. "We must separate the mind, win the mind, wage the revolution to win the Black man's mind so we will begin to move together as a people conscious that we are a people, struggling for national liberation," Baraka argued. "Black power must be a program of Consciousness," he insisted.[7]

The cultural nationalists' desire to identify and encourage pride in a distinctively African American culture was broadly shared by all black power advocates. For some, however, that desire translated into an earnest but doomed quest to find a hermetically sealed "African" culture in America—a culture untainted by any white social, intellectual, economic, and artistic influences. When such an unimpeached black culture could not be found in real-life America, one was simply invented. This happened most dramatically with the promotion of an ersatz brand of Africanisms that tended both to misrepresent the genuine African component in the African American experience and to ignore the complex realities of black America's historic and reciprocal relationship with white, European-derived cultures. Maulana Ron Karenga was the most prominent of this generation of whimsical Afrocentrists. Karenga espoused his Seven Principles of Kawaida, purportedly a uniquely black philosophy distilled from timeless African wisdoms and practices, and encouraged all manner of Afrocentric cultural initiatives, like the wearing of Africanesque dress and the observation of invented "African" rituals like the holiday celebrations of Kwanzaa. This same impulse to isolate and celebrate a uniquely African component in African American life and culture would also shape the cultural nationalists' attitudes toward both jazz and soul musics.[8]

Contemporary critics like the Black Panthers were quick to point out that the precise mechanism by which the sort of cultural pride and racial solidarity promoted by Karenga were to be transformed into political and economic power usually remained obscure. Indeed, it is the image of cultural nationalists as dreamy, apolitical fantasists promoted by the Panthers and others that has dominated much of the historical literature on the black power era. Yet most were fully aware of the practical problems posed by black political powerlessness and economic dependency. Because they chose to prioritize race in their analysis of black oppression, they felt obliged to promote cultural regeneration and racial solidarity as the most important initial response to the black predicament, but this did not preclude engaging in other forms of activism. "We must free ourselves culturally before we succeed politically," explained Karenga, echoing Stokely Carmichael and Charles Hamilton's assertion in *Black Power*—a seminal text on both sides of the cultural-revolutionary nationalist divide—that "*before a group can enter the open society, it must first close ranks.* By that we mean that group solidarity is necessary before a group can operate successfully from a bargaining position of strength in a pluralistic society."[9]

Many cultural nationalists certainly recognized the limitations of a simple reliance on black cultural creativity for liberation and encouraged political mobilization, direct action protests, and economic activism in the black community. "We know that art alone will not liberate us. We know that culture as an abstract thing within itself will not give us Self-Determination and Nationhood," admitted writer-activist Larry Neal.[10] He insisted, however, that "a cultureless revolution is a bullcrap trip. It means that in the process of making the revolution, we lose our vision. We lose the soft, undulating side of ourselves—those unknown beauties lurking rhythmically below the level of material needs. In short, a revolution without culture would destroy the very thing that now unites us; the very thing we are trying to save along with our lives."[11]

This was close to Imamu Amiri Baraka's position on the relationship between cultural expression and political activism. At first deeply enamored of Karenga and his psychologically potent brand of Afromanticism, Baraka fully endorsed the principles of Kawaida as providing the basis for black nationhood in America. Indeed, according to Komozi Woodard, in the late 1960s and early 1970s, Baraka was "fanatical, almost religious in his faith in Karenga's leadership and doctrine."[12]

Yet Woodard also insists that Baraka demonstrated a consistent concern with challenging the reality of black economic, political, and social powerlessness, and diligently chronicles his many practical efforts to realize the black community's latent economic and political potential. These efforts often involved the sort of block-by-block, grassroots community organizing and political mobilization that are rarely associated with cultural nationalists. Indeed, there is ample evidence that Baraka was always wary of over-immersion in identity (or "expressive") politics at the expense of electoral (or "competitive") politics designed to wrest black power from a white-dominated political and economic system. For example, in Harlem during the mid-1960s Baraka's pioneering Black Arts Repertory Theater/School (BARTS) had helped to fan the flames of the national Black Arts Movement. Yet Baraka quickly abandoned the project when it fell under the sway of culturalist zealots who jealously guarded their own mystical vision of a discrete black genius, but had no interest in developing practical programs for the political, social, educational, and economic revitalization of the ghetto.[13]

Finding the right fit between "expressive" and "competitive" politics was a tricky matter, and Baraka often struggled to parlay cultural empowerment into an effective mass movement for reform. Nevertheless, even after the disappointments of the BARTS experiment, seeking an effective means to harness artistic and cultural energy to mass black activism remained central to his liberation politics. Newark, New Jersey, became the laboratory for his efforts. He was certainly the most politically savvy among the leaders of the Committee For Unified Newark (CFUN), a group dedicated to securing effective black representation in the city's municipal politics. It was Baraka who insisted on political education programs and hard-nosed precinct organizing in addition to the "Soul Sessions" that celebrated African American identity and encouraged cultural pride. CFUN's efforts culminated with the 1970 election of Kenneth Gibson as Newark's first black mayor. Ironically, this electoral success resulted from a pragmatic broad-front coalition between CFUN and a wide range of other black and Hispanic interest groups. Many of these groups were deeply suspicious of some of Baraka's more chauvinistic black nationalist outbursts, but nevertheless saw the value of his political coalition building.[14]

From his base in Newark, Baraka sought to organize blacks across the nation into a potent political as well as cultural force. This was the primary purpose of the Congress of African Peoples (CAP), founded to continue the work of the various national black power conferences and conventions that had been proliferating since 1966, many of them organized by Baraka. Even at the Congress's inaugural conference in Atlanta in 1970, some two years before Baraka assumed the chairmanship of the organization, he was stressing the need for more grassroots political and economic organizing amid all the identity therapy and pseudo-African mystification. Baraka joined Kenneth Gibson in proposing the creation of an independent black political party that would operate within the established framework of American politics, in "the four areas of political power. 1. Public Office (elected or appointed). 2. Community Organizations. 3. Alliances and Coalitions. 4. Disruption (actual or threatened)."[15]

As Baraka wrote in his carefully conciliatory introduction to the proceedings of the Atlanta meeting, he wished to keep open the lines of communication with all other factions in the black power movement. He even sought working coalitions with the more mainstream civil rights organizations who generally recoiled from the nationalistic and separatist overtones of much black power rhetoric. "Even though some of us might see the progress of the whole as being achieved in one way, and others of us might have more special views, it is still the duty of the body to be in constant intercommunication one part with the others, or there will be minimum movement all round," Baraka explained. Certainly, the presence of invited speakers from outside the strict culturalist cabal, like Gibson, Richard Hatcher (the black mayor of Gary, Indiana), Whitney Young of the National Urban League, Ralph Abernathy of the Southern Christian Leadership Conference, and Jesse Jackson of People United To Save Humanity, acted as an important counter-balance to the dedicated Africanists who dominated CAP. It also reflected Baraka's eagerness to construct a more flexible and inclusive sense of black nationhood that would embrace the widest possible range of black people, with their equally wide range of philosophical, economic, and political positions.[16]

Baraka's concern with converting this incipient sense of culturally rooted black nationhood into a genuine political movement for change was further evident in his role as one of the main architects of the 1972 National Black Political Convention in Gary, and its 1974 sequel in Little Rock. These meetings, part of a broader pattern of what Woodard dubs the Modern Black Convention Movement, established the National Black Political Assembly and nurtured the Congressional Black Caucus and the National Conference of Black Elected Officials. Thus, they effectively set the black political agenda for the next two decades with their attempts to reconcile key elements of black power, including its emphasis on cultural pride and psychological empowerment, with the practical demands of electoral politics and economic reform.[17]

This record of political activism suggests that Baraka generally avoided the withdrawal from the "social realities of the white power structure under the guise of separatist nationalist moods," which black social critic Harold Cruse cited as one of the chief dangers posed by an inward-looking brand of ego-gratifying cultural nationalism.[18]

Baraka clearly understood that the black economic, social, and political power and autonomy he sought in America were ultimately constrained by the operation of a hostile white-dominated socioeconomic and political system, and that real black power must necessarily be won within that context. Similarly, his most persuasive and illuminating writings on music were characterized and intellectually sharpened by his understanding of the ways in which black and white cultures had always interpenetrated each other in America. This insight had informed his best book, 1963's *Blues People,* which paid due homage to the African roots of black America's musical traditions, but rightly concluded that neither blues, nor jazz, nor gospel, nor any of their derivatives could possibly have emerged in Africa. These musical forms were the results of black innovation in America, where various European musical devices and techniques were absorbed and refashioned in a succession of overlapping musical syntheses, each designed to meet the changing social and psychological needs of peoples of African descent at particular historic moments.[19]

Similarly, in "The Changing Same," Baraka's recognition of the interdependency of black and white cultures and economies in America had informed his prediction of soul's imminent lyrical politicization. Grasping the fundamental power dynamic involved, Baraka appreciated that any major radicalization of soul's lyrics to address the contemporary black situation was contingent on the latest "cycle" in the white-dominated recording and broadcasting industries, which by the mid-1960s were successfully promoting political and social commentary in much white rock music. Baraka explained how, despite "integration (meaning the harnessing of Black energy for dollars by white folks, in this case in the music bizness) . . . that took the bite of specific protest out ('you know you can't sell that to white folks')," soul already carried certain latent social messages for African Americans: messages encoded in the music's gospel roots and occasional allusions to the Struggle, but made manifest in the act of shared consumption by the black masses: "The Impressions' 'Keep on Pushing' or Martha and the Vandellas' 'Dancing in the Street' (especially re: summer riots, i.e., 'Summer's here . . . ') provided a core of legitimate social feeling, though mainly metaphorical and allegorical for Black people. But it is my thought that soon, with the same cycle of the general 'integrated' music bizness, the R&B songs will be more socially oriented."[20]

Baraka did not dwell on the irony of his deepest insight here—that the emergence of the sort of truly relevant and politically engaged soul music needed to advance his black nation-building project required the economic and cultural sanction of white America. Nevertheless, his continued awareness of this dependency helps to explain why, despite his evident respect for, and personal delight in, much rhythm and blues, Baraka was never entirely comfortable about reifying soul as the manifestation of a discrete and uncompromised black genius or as the soundtrack to his attempts to construct a black nation within America. Moreover, having shrewdly identified and celebrated the hybrid nature of African American musical traditions in the early 1960s, under Karenga's influence he no longer saw this syncretic quality in terms of black creativity and adaptivity amid an ongoing process of cross-racial exchange (albeit much of it artistically unacknowledged and financially unrewarded when the flow of musical innovation was from black to white). Instead, Baraka increasingly saw this process in terms of the relentless dilution, compromise, and even betrayal of some putative black—African—essence.

Baraka was not the only cultural nationalist who felt obliged to look beyond soul for a "blacker," more "authentic" form of African American music to represent and raise "true" racial self-consciousness among the black masses. Most felt that at some level soul music was too bound up with the commercial paraphernalia of the white-controlled recording and broadcasting industries to serve as the music of the black psychological and political revolution. Ronald Snellings captured the conventional wisdom regarding the commercial and racial exploitation at the heart of the music:

> the recording companies are white-owned (the booking agencies are white-owned; the radio stations, the theaters, and the night clubs where the music is heard, are white [usually immigrant] owned). Broken down even further, this means, baby, that James Brown and the late Otis Redding, not to mention Aretha, are sending a lot of Jewish and Italian boys and girls to college and making their parents rich with the products of their Black souls. And further, none, or very little of this bread is going into the black communities that inspire the music.[21]

Equally troublesome was the fact that not only did whites occupy most of the key positions of power and influence within the business of soul music production and dissemination, but they constituted an important portion of the audience for the style. In addition, whites were heavily involved in the creative side of soul music. Much of the classic southern soul recorded at the Stax, American, and Fame studios by the likes of Otis Redding, Percy Sledge, Wilson Pickett, Aretha Franklin, and Joe Tex was penned and produced by whites, cut in studios using integrated groups of musicians, and then issued on white-owned labels like Atlantic and Stax. Even black-owned soul labels like Berry Gordy's Detroit-based Motown seemed far too covetous of—and successful in—the mass white market to fit the bill.[22]

Unsettled by soul's commercial and artistic relationship with white America, the cultural nationalists' pantheon of black musician-heroes tended to be dominated by modern black jazz artists: John Coltrane, Cecil Taylor, Archie Shepp, Albert Ayler, Pharoah Sanders, Ornette Coleman, Sun Ra, Eric Dolphy, and the ghost of bebopper Charlie Parker. Baraka, for example, admitted that the seemingly abstract expressiveness of James Brown's screams were "more 'radical' than most jazz musicians sound," and on one occasion commended the music of Motown's Jr. Walker as "superior to Ayler's or that [which] Ornette's making now." However, his preferred model for a genuinely responsive and responsible contemporary black music was ultimately the jazz avant-garde: the so-called New Jazz.[23]

Baraka did his best to increase the popularity of this music among the black masses, while the music itself literally underwrote many of his cultural endeavors. In March 1965, he partly funded his BARTS project by means of a live anthology of the "New Music" released on Bob Thiele's Impulse label, featuring Coltrane, Shepp, Sun Ra, Betty Carter, and many others. Similar musicians performed at the opening of the BARTS premises on Harlem's 130th Street, and were preeminent amid the street drama, poetry, painting, and dance being offered during the summer of 1965. Every night the Jazzmobile carried the sounds of the New Jazz to different locations around Harlem. Baraka's racial and cultural agenda here was obvious. "The only bad incident," he later recalled, "was when a white media famous tenor came up with an integrated group and someone threw an egg at him. We told the musicians we wanted black groups and boycotted them if they refused to make their groups all black."[24]

Baraka was hardly alone in championing the jazz avant-garde as a bastion of an uncompromised black identity, communal solidarity, and spiritual fulfillment. In 1967, black playwright Ronald Milner described how he had discovered a culturalist manifesto in the form of an advertisement for a New York poetry reading: "BLACK MAGIC, BLACK ART, WILL TOPPLE THE CITADEL OF RACIST AMERICA!" This advertisement prompted the skeptical Milner to reevaluate the political potential of black popular culture. His conclusion was that "Black art can do a lot to topple white, racist America, if it is black enough." For his definition of a "black enough" art, Milner also invoked the modern black jazz performer. Jazz, he contended, was "so far, the blackest of the arts," and the jazz musician "furthest along in self-assertion and unrestrained, unaccommodating self-expression." He celebrated John Coltrane as "a man who through his saxophone before your eyes and ears, completely annihilates every single western influence."[25]

Other cultural nationalists repeated this careful solipsism of Coltrane, his colleagues, and their unsullied black art. In *Black Fire,* an important culturalist anthology edited by Baraka and Larry Neal, James T. Stewart provides a theoretical justification for this attitude toward the New Jazz. Echoing Baraka's contention that "what's needed now for 'the arts' is to get them away from white people," Stewart called for a "Black Revolutionary Artist" who would construct an autonomous black aesthetic, which "means that he cannot be 'successful' in any sense that has meaning in white critical evaluations. Nor can his work ever be called 'good' in any context of meaning that could make sense to that traditional critique."[26]

For Stewart, as for Baraka and Milner, it was modern black jazz performers, with their willful flaunting of conventional western conceptions of rhythm, melody, tone, and above all harmony, who seemed to articulate the separatist ideals that were increasingly challenging the integrationist pieties of the early civil rights movement. Thus, as with Karenga-style Afrocentrism, the strength and political potency of the jazz avant-garde resided in its apparent racial exclusivity. Indeed, in a neat reflection of shared agendas, in 1968 jazzman Archie Shepp actually recorded an album titled *Kwanza*.[27] Meanwhile, Baraka, in particular, repeatedly stressed the New Jazz's connections to African rhythms, arguing that it was the drum that had preserved the essence of African culture and sensibilities in America throughout the ordeals of slavery, Reconstruction, Jim Crow, and into the tumultuous 1960s and 1970s.[28]

For the cultural nationalists, then, notions of musical excellence and racial rectitude had become almost synonymous; both were largely determined by the music's commercial and cultural independence from white influences and the conspicuous commitment of its artists, whether represented in musical terms, or by overtly political actions and gestures. Hence in 1971, Baraka criticized Ornette Coleman and the late Albert Ayler for the "world weariness and corny self-consciousness," of their recent releases, which was "white life hangaround total—i.e. what you get for being wit dem."[29] In other words, their artistic lapses were interpreted by Baraka in terms of their growing links to the white jazz fraternity. In Coleman's case especially, this was seen as tantamount to racial treason: "His tune was that hip . . . once!! It was his life, and his commitment, as path, that changed it."[30]

In fact, although the jazz avant-garde appealed to the cultural nationalists as a symbol of a much sought-after black cultural autonomy, and as more immune from the distorting effects of the white market and the white-controlled industry than soul, this cultural and economic independence was largely chimerical. White-owned companies—Blue Note, Prestige, Atlantic, Impulse, Fantasy—recorded much of the New Music. Whites owned many of the clubs and magazines that helped to create a radical hip mystique around the new black jazzmen, while modern Euro-classical experiments in atonality and serial composition had a considerable influence on modern jazz. Those who celebrated Coltrane's *Africa Brass* album for its proud return to African roots seldom commented on the fact that their hero was at least as interested in, and influenced by, Indian music and culture—especially the immense rhythmic wealth to be found in the talas at the heart of Indian classical music.

Still more disturbing for the claims of the cultural nationalists was the fact that whites constituted much the largest audience for the New Jazz. Notwithstanding Baraka's memory of "huge audiences" in the Harlem streets and his angry assertion that "the music critics that put down the new music as inaccessible were full of shit!" the fact is that the mass black public remained rather indifferent to the earnest, dazzling, but sometimes highly esoteric playing of these modern jazz giants.[31] Moreover, as sympathetic white commentator Frank Kofsky complained, "the music has been almost entirely created by blacks but almost entirely interpreted by whites."[32] Consequently, it was the often rarefied, rather precious world of white jazz criticism that provided some of the most fulsome praise and support for a music with limited mass appeal to either race.

Black jazz players themselves recognized and sometimes rebelled against these racialized commercial and critical realities. Long before Kofsky, Julian "Cannonball" Adderley, a saxophonist in the hardbop tradition, had complained in 1963 that, "our art and craft . . . has been championed, written about, almost totally by whites. . . . And we musicians have allowed white critics, writers and so forth to represent themselves as *the* authority on jazz."[33] Ornette Coleman, one of the most radical of the New Jazz players in his disregard for traditional western harmonic imperatives, withdrew from public performances for three years because no nightclub would pay him what he "knew" his music was worth. The fiery pianist Cecil Taylor also understood the basic racial configuration of power in the music business and called for "a boycott by Negro musicians of all jazz clubs in the United States. I also propose that there should be a boycott by Negro jazz musicians of all record companies. I also propose that all Negro musicians boycott all trade papers and journals dealing with music. . . . We're no longer reflecting or vibrating to the white-energy principle."[34]

Such protests were important in creating and sustaining the image of the new jazz performers as active participants in the liberation struggle. Archie Shepp's appearance alongside Baraka in the Newark streets, getting out the community vote, had a similar effect. So, too, did the repeated and explicit references to social and racial themes in the titles of innumerable jazz pieces like Shepp's own *All Things Must Change* with its hymn to "Martin Luther King, The Peaceful Warrior."[35] Equally important in establishing the connection between the New Music and the freedom struggle were politically engaged record liner notes, such as those supplied by Baraka for releases on Impulse. These followed saxophonist Sonny Rollins's lead in 1958, when he had affirmed his personal commitment to the civil rights struggle on the jacket of his *Freedom Suite* album.[36]

Despite the fact that some of these jazz performers were involved in conspicuous artistic and political commitments to the Movement long before the majority of their soul counterparts, even enthusiasts like Lawrence Nahs recognized the practical as well as theoretical problems in claiming revolutionary potential for a music that was not even reaching its intended audience.[37] In a review of A. B. Spellman's *Black Music: Four Lives in the Be-Bop Business,* Nahs accepted the New Music's prodigious artistry but questioned its ultimate claims to social relevance and a revolutionary message. "Currently, the only things revolutionary about the 'new music' are its technological innovations. And those are not enough." To be truly revolutionary, Nahs wrote, the music "must extend itself into the black community in a manner which, heretofore, it has failed to do. It must mean to the community what the Supremes, the Impressions, and James Brown now mean."[38] Spellman, himself, had to admit that the jazz avant-garde could not match the influence and prestige of soul music within the black community. "The reality is that it was Greenwich Village which heard the evolution of the New, not Harlem," he admitted. "The man standing in line for the Otis Redding show at the Apollo almost certainly never heard of tenor saxophonist Albert Ayler, and wouldn't have the fuzziest idea of what he was doing if he did hear him."[39]

Concentrating almost exclusively on the politics of the music's creation, cultural nationalists like Baraka had found black jazz artists tearing a fierce, angry, brutally beautiful music from the depths of their own experiences and fully expected the black masses to identify closely with it. Yet, as Lawrence Nahs realized, it was all very well championing an autonomous black aesthetic, but the black masses were not about to be badgered by well-intentioned black intellectuals into buying or listening to an ideologically correct music that did not actually entertain or inspire them in the same way as the soul styles dominating black charts, turntables, clubs, and radio playlists. The New Jazz never came remotely near to challenging the popularity of soul among the mass of black Americans and lagged some way behind in emotional resonance as well.[40]

The New Music's nationalist advocates thus faced a strategic dilemma that they never really resolved. In their opinion the jazz avant-garde embodied the correct political and racial messages, but it was soul that undoubtedly had the ear of the black masses, particularly at a time when black-oriented radio stations were playing little else. At some level, Baraka had always appreciated this disjuncture. It was fine to open up an experimental black arts project like BARTS with the sounds of the New Jazz, but when Baraka needed to get the mass black vote out in Newark, it was soul stars like James Brown, Stevie Wonder, Chuck Jackson, the Temptations, and the Supremes who drew black audiences to the CFUN rallies, and

Brown's anthemic "Say It Loud, I'm Black And I'm Proud," which blared from the sound cars patrolling the streets, that roused the black electorate.[41]

During the early 1970s, Imamu Amiri Baraka gradually distanced himself from Karenga-style cultural nationalism, tiring of its continued preference for easy "blacker-than-thou" posturing over the much harder work of political mobilization and organized agitation for black economic, educational, and social progress. Finally, in 1975, following a year-long debate among black intellectuals on the "class versus color" issue in the pages of Nathan Hare's *Black Scholar* journal, he abandoned black nationalism and switched to a broader, class-based, neo-Marxist analysis of the racial situation. Thus, he came to prioritize a view of the black predicament in America that had been subordinated, if never entirely absent, during his earlier culturalist phase.[42]

Revealingly, after his mid-1970s *volte face,* Baraka began to interpret the failures of cultural nationalism in terms of its parochial elitism. He dismissed Karenga's Afrocentrism as "a bible of petty bourgeois glosses on reality and artification of certain aspects of history to make a recipe for 'blackness.'" Although he maintained that the cultural nationalists had correctly identified the potential of culture and the arts to "help bring the people to revolutionary positions," they had failed to appreciate that "the culture of the black masses in the US is an African American working-class culture." Pseudo-African rituals had proved ineffectual in promoting revolutionary consciousness among African Americans because they were not grounded in the everyday social and historical realities of the mass black experience, which was delineated by race and class, not to mention gender and status, intersecting within a pervasive American context.[43]

Although Baraka himself failed to make the connection here, he had also identified the primary reason why the jazz avant-garde had generally failed to excite the black masses, let alone raise their revolutionary consciousness. The cultural nationalists' deification of Coltrane and the rest was at its core an elitist, intellectual project. It represented a variant on the sort of revised "talented-tenthism" promoted most forcibly by Harold Cruse, whereby a vanguard of self-appointed politically and racially "correct" artists and intellectuals were supposed to lead the black masses to true racial consciousness and cultural solidarity, and from there to political and economic power.[44]

Ironically, with its tendency toward exclusiveness, the cult of the New Jazz actually betrayed much more of the white western romantic ideal of the suffering, soul-searching artist, pitted permanently against an intoler-

ant and uncomprehending society, than most advocates of the "black aesthetic" were willing to acknowledge. Certainly the celebration of the modern jazz performer's self-conscious pursuit of a personally "meaningful
art," the studied embrace by many of social alienation as a musical and
political statement, had little to do with an African tradition, preserved
and endlessly extended in African American popular music, which invariably sought to collapse the distance between performer and audience, art
and social function. Instead, it merely helped render many modern jazz
musicians alien, occasionally incomprehensible, and largely irrelevant to
many ordinary blacks, for whom political messages and racial encomiums
were traditionally borne along on the compelling rhythms of dance music,
or atop an irresistible vocal wave.

The New Jazz was not too "difficult" for those masses, it was merely not
as relevant to the African American experience as soul, nor, ultimately, as
responsive to changes in black consciousness in a time of major social,
political, and psychological upheaval. Soul, because of—not in spite of—
its commercial orientation, depended for survival on its continued mass
appeal primarily, though not exclusively, to black Americans. The New
Jazz, meanwhile, flourished with the support of a much smaller, largely
white, elite audience and positively reveled in its professed indifference to
broader commercial considerations and mass taste.[45]

Around the time that Baraka shifted analytical positions, Ron Karenga
executed a somewhat similar ideological somersault. Karenga's contribution to the *Black Scholar* dialogue had served notice of his new stance.
"For Pan-Africanism to be real and of any historical importance, it must be
socialist in content," he explained. "In the final analysis, all struggles must
become one struggle, the struggle for socialist liberation."[46] Like Baraka,
who maintained his commitment to the political potential of African
American culture in fomenting black self-awareness, pride, and solidarity,
Karenga did not abandon the cultural front. Instead, he initially attempted
to synthesize his Kawaida principles with a political philosophy revoking
racial chauvinism and encouraging multi-racial alliances along socialist
lines.[47] The irony in all of this was that, following their respective left
turns, Baraka and Karenga had arrived at something very akin to the position on the relationship between black culture and politics adopted by
their much-vaunted adversaries, the Black Panther Party, during the late
1960s and early 1970s.

For the Black Panthers, cultural nationalism had always veered toward
a dangerous apoliticism. "Cultural nationalism," insisted East Oakland
Panther Linda Harrison, "can be summed up in James Brown's words—

'I'm Black and I'm Proud,'" but it ignored "the present political, social and economic realities. . . . it has no political doctrine."[48] Because of these deep misgivings, the Panthers have routinely been depicted as implacably—and sometimes violently—opposed to the sort of cultural initiatives promoted by Karenga and Baraka on the grounds that they were essentially racist, encouraged the commercial exploitation of ghetto culture by black as well as white capitalists, and diverted righteous African American anger and energies into harmless identity therapy. Cultural nationalism, the Panthers appeared to argue, was a reactionary social palliative, when what was needed was a catalyst for revolution. While there is much truth in this view, it presents too stark and static a picture of Panther attitudes toward black cultural politics. The Party consistently displayed a much greater interest in exploring the possibilities of art and culture as revolutionary tools than most commentators have allowed.[49]

There is certainly ample evidence of Panther tolerance of and cooperation with cultural nationalists, especially in the Party's early years. Indeed, cofounders Huey Newton and Bobby Seale had spent considerable time in the company of cultural nationalists prior to forming the Panthers in late 1966. While students at Merritt College, both had been members of the Afro-American Association founded by Donald Warden at Berkeley to promote racial consciousness and pride among young blacks. Warden was firmly committed to a program of psychological rejuvenation and empowerment through the study of black history and the embrace, rather than disavowal, of distinctively black lifestyles and cultural forms. Warden was especially keen to harness the elusive political potential of soul music to the struggle for black freedom. Contending that "the only thing that unites our race is music," it was Warden who finally persuaded a reticent James Brown to incorporate more explicit social messages into his songs and pledge more public support to the Movement.[50]

Although Newton quickly tired of Warden's relentless emphasis on the power of soul (not just the music, but the whole cultural phenomenon which by the mid-1960s was virtually a synonym for "negritude") to secure black freedom, he had at least glimpsed something of the potential of utilizing mass culture to engage black hearts and minds. Some of this understanding was incorporated into the Soul Students Advisory Council, of which Newton and Seale were founding members. This early interest in the political potential of African American culture did not simply vanish when Newton and Seale formed the Panthers in late 1966, picked up the gun, and began to advocate armed self-defense against white—mainly police—aggression, alongside various community welfare initiatives.

There was certainly an initial willingness to continue dialogue and share resources and expertise with those groups who favored another approach to black liberation. For example, the Panthers worked with Karenga in a series of "Free Huey" benefits designed to raise cash and community awareness for the Panthers' minister of defense, following Newton's arrest in October 1967 for the slaying of an Oakland policeman.[51] In March 1968, one such "Free Huey" rally at the Oakland Auditorium boasted appearances by the Party's "Assistant Revolutionary Artist" Matilaba, Stokely Carmichael, and the Impressions vocal group. Pictures of the event appeared in the *Black Panther* newspaper alongside the sort of "Black and Beautiful" and "We're a Winner" slogans more usually associated with the cultural nationalists.[52] Baraka himself had worked closely with the Panthers at the San Francisco Black House, a black arts and community center modeled on his own Spirit House in Newark. The Party shared Baraka's hopes that such cultural participation would forge the sort of pride and solidarity on which an effective political organization might be predicated.[53]

Beyond these examples of early cooperation with cultural nationalists, there were a number of important cultural initiatives that emerged from within the Panthers' own ranks. Taking a broad definition of cultural politics, the Panthers were always keen to promote a historical understanding of the black experience and the development of American race relations among the black masses. At a time when the struggle for black studies programs was being waged in schools and colleges throughout the nation, point five in the Panthers' "Ten Point Party Platform and Program" called for "education that teaches us our true history and our role in present day society. We believe in an educational system that will give to our people a knowledge of self."[54]

To this end, the Panther newspaper included a regular "This Week in Black History" column, which featured celebratory historical accounts of black resistance against racist oppression like Toussaint L'Ouverture's 1791 Haitian Revolution and Nat Turner's 1831 slave rebellion in Virginia.[55] Indeed, notwithstanding Molefi Kete Asante's misplaced criticism that the Panthers "failed to study David Walker, Henry Garnet, Marcus Garvey, and Malcolm X," the Party was desperate to legitimize its own efforts by placing itself within this long tradition of African American resistance and struggle.[56] "Denmark Vesey was a Panther. Marcus Garvey was a Panther. El Hajj Malik El-Shabazz, Brother Malcolm, was a Panther and in the end even Martin Luther King became an uptight black cat," insisted one Panther writer.[57]

African American history also provided the inspiration for some of the Panthers' own artistic endeavors. When Bobby Seale was bound and gagged by Judge Julius J. Hoffman during the trial for his role in the disturbances at the 1968 Chicago Democratic Party convention, cartoons by Minister of Culture and Revolutionary Artist Emory Douglas drew pointed comparisons with the 1857 *Dred Scott* decision, when Supreme Court Chief Justice Roger Taney had effectively declared that blacks in America had no civil rights that whites need respect. Panther poet J' Muff Kinard similarly linked the present African American predicament to the legacy of slavery: "A lot of years ago/ our people crossed the sea/ S-L-A-V-E-S in C-H-A-I-N-S/ And today . . . /Things is still the same."[58]

Kinard's mid-1970s verses reflected the revival of a Party commitment to poetry and black cultural activity in general—conspicuous elements in its early years. For example, the *Black Panther* regularly carried a page of "Black Revolutionary Poetry" contributed by readers. In the spring of 1968, when Baraka was himself in jail, the Panther leadership was happy to print "Free By Any Means Necessary" by Sarah Webster Fabio, in which the author pleaded, "Free Leroi/Free creativity & art."[59] The newspaper also featured a "Black Panther Book List" that, alongside a predictable catalogue of radical texts like Franz Fanon's *Wretched of the Earth* and *The Autobiography of Malcolm X,* also recommended Baraka's *Blues People* and Arna Bontemps's anthology *American Negro Poetry* as indispensable to the promotion of a revolutionary consciousness.[60]

There was, then, at first no blanket Panther condemnation of black cultural politics or its leading advocates and practitioners—just a concern about the misrepresentation and mystification of black history by Afrocentric zealots, and a wariness about the charlatanism and exploitation that the Panthers often saw masquerading as cultural nationalism. During late 1968 and early 1969, however, such concerns undoubtedly intensified. In December 1968, the *Black Panther* carried its first major attack on the cultural nationalists when Boston Fred Nolan argued that "While it is necessary to be aware of one's Black heritage, and to be proud, it doesn't do any good if we fall right back into the capitalistic trap. . . . Capitalists now make afro-wigs, african clothes, along with a horde of other so-called 'Black things,' not one stitch of false hair or manufactured thread will contribute anything to Black freedom."[61]

There were two main reasons for this increasingly hostile stance toward the cultural nationalists. The first was the mounting rivalry and, with the shootings of Alprentice "Bunchy" Carter and John Huggins on the UCLA campus in January 1969, murderous violence between Karenga's US and the Panthers as they jostled for power and prestige on the west coast. Actively encouraged by the FBI, this violence inevitably jaundiced Panther attitudes toward cultural nationalism more generally. As a result, the *Black Panther* began to carry ever more vitriolic denunciations, not just of Karenga—dubbed variously "King of the Bloodsuckers" or "Mama Llama Ron Karenga"—and his "pork-chop nationalists," but also of other alleged cultural nationalists. Subjects of Panther ridicule and scorn included the recently expelled Stokely Carmichael, "the uptight Prima-Donna of the 'I'm Black and Proud' set," who had been offered the post of honorary Panther Prime Minister just eighteen months earlier, and even "Uncle" Roy Wilkins of the National Association for the Advancement of Colored People, who was condemned as "the rankest of the foul black opportunists who function under the sham slogan of 'I'm Black and I'm Proud.'"[62]

The second important factor in the Panthers' growing contempt for cultural nationalism was the ascendancy of the Party's Minister of Information Eldridge Cleaver while Newton was incarcerated. As Baraka remembered, it was Cleaver who had the artists thrown out of the Black House, although informal cooperation between some Panthers and Baraka's Black House and Black Communications Projects continued around the Oakland area for some time afterward.[63] It was under Cleaver that the poetry page in the Panther newspaper was discontinued. It was also Cleaver who added a vicious polemical bite to Panther critiques of American capitalism and who increasingly identified the dispossessed of America, particularly the black lumpen-proletariat, as the proper focus of Panther attention. The lumpen, Cleaver insisted, would be the vanguard of the armed revolution he was doing his best to hasten, not least by temporarily swapping the Panthers' original doctrine of armed self-defense for a futile experiment in guerrilla warfare against the police.[64]

Although Cleaver spent seven years as a fugitive in Cuba and then Algeria following a shoot-out with police in April 1968, his rigidly class-based perspective and impatient demands for armed black insurrection crucially determined the Panthers' official attitude toward cultural nationalism prior to Newton's release from prison in August 1970. Armed with both the guns that guaranteed the Panthers' street-warrior credibility and a volatile, if not always fully digested, cocktail of Fanon, Malcolm, Mao, and Marx, Cleaver increasingly identified cultural nationalism with a reviled black intellectual and entrepreneurial elite who were too timid for revolution. "The basic problem of the type of nape we're discussing,"

Cleaver wrote, "is that he has Black bourgeois origins and has great difficulty relating to the brothers and sisters off the block, the Lumpen of which the Black Panther Party is composed."[65]

Years later, a somewhat more temperate Cleaver still emphasized this essential contrast between the revolutionary, gun-toting, streetwise, proletarian Panthers, and the rest of the black power movement: "Stokely and [H.] Rap [Brown] and James Forman . . . had grown up within the safety and protection of the black middle-class, the black bourgeoisie—and while they could use some daring language and point to threatening events, it was all played out on the secure carpet of a college dormitory, a student union ballroom or campus parking lot. . . . we were off the ghetto pavement and rather prepared for the sound of gunfire."[66]

Yet, despite Cleaver's hostility, even under his inflammatory influence the Panthers never entirely abandoned their own brand of cultural politics. During his exile, Cleaver himself had happily attended the July 1969 Pan African Cultural Festival in Algiers, using this meeting of "artists, musicians, dancers, writers, and political figures from twenty-four African countries" as an opportunity to rendezvous with various other members of the Panther leadership.[67] One of those present alongside Nina Simone, Archie Shepp, Haki Madhubuti, and playwright Ed Bullins was Emory Douglas. Douglas had once worked as a set designer and graphics specialist for Baraka's traveling Black Communications Project, which also included the Panthers' future minister of education, George Murray.[68]

Emory was a gifted artist, capable of blending strong-lined impressionism with stark social realism in his portraits of the black community. Yet it was his brutally explicit cartoons in the Panther newspaper that made the biggest impact, providing a powerful iconographical counterpart to the Party's violent rhetoric. Full of smoking guns, "offed" (righteously slain) pigs (police) and salivating rats (politicians), Emory's lapidary texts adorned the cover and filled several inside slots in each issue. Indeed, Emory's graphic representations of vengeance against white oppressors far exceeded any actual violence perpetrated by the Panthers. As Reginald Major put it, "Emory, as artist, is more of a vanguard than Panthers as politicians."[69] Emory could advocate, non-specifically, killing racist police and organizing for guerrilla warfare. Consequently, his art provided both catharsis and wish-fulfillment for a community that appreciated—even if Eldridge Cleaver sometimes could not—that any armed offensive against state power would have been suicidal, rather than revolutionary. When Newton emerged from jail and, following a final split with Cleaver, sought to steer his wing of the Party away from notions of armed revolution toward a more reform-oriented, mass-based organization with a renewed commitment to community survival programs and electoral politics, Douglas's art reflected the shift. He abandoned cartoonish violence in favor of powerful celebratory depictions of the black masses and their street culture.

Emory's secure place in the Panther hierarchy, even during the years of Cleaver's ascendancy, itself bespoke a continuing commitment to the political potential of black art. Similarly, a neglected series of letters, position papers, and manifestos revealed just how seriously the Panthers took the business of fashioning a revolutionary art from the everyday experiences of the black urban masses. John Ringgold's 1970 statement condemning Karenga, for example, revealed no simple rejection of a nationalistic cultural position; rather, it was a demand for a more honest one that dispensed with cosmetic Africanisms, focused on the historical tradition of black resistance to the trials of first enslavement and then a decidedly equivocal form of freedom in the New World. Ringgold embraced the soul phenomenon as the true expression of contemporary African American identity:

> Characterized by bubbas, ornaments and babbling Swahili, the US organization is composed of black provocateurs, the pork chop, cultural nationalists who speak of oppression abstractedly and solve the problem of this system by putting the evils of this society into a black context: i.e., Black Capitalism and Black Racism. . . . Our historical development from Africa in the slave ships and the conditions in which we were forced to live is all part of our culture. Bubbas and naturals cannot be used as a legitimate present-day culture. The culture of Black People here in America, includes our dancing, singing, shooting dice, eating chitterlings and black-eyed peas, and presently, in our attempt to gain our freedom, revolution and the gun.[70]

Other Panther polemicists echoed Ringgold's belief that what was needed was a black art rooted in the everyday street culture of black America. While Karenga contemptuously complained that "the 'Negro' has more records than books and is dancing his life away," George Murray insisted that the raw material for a revolutionary culture was "everything black people do, our food, songs, dances, music, art, literature, stories, poems, paintings, plays, speeches, talk, kisses, embraces, squeezes, and clothes."[71] Emory Douglas agreed with Murray that "Revolutionary art is an art that flows from the people"; it was not something that was imposed on the people by self-declared arbiters and guardians of black cultural authenticity.[72] Moreover, Emory argued that "revolutionary art" must be presented to the people in a form that they could instantly recognize, identify with, and learn from. It ought not to be obscure, or place its artistry ahead of its revolutionary message: "It must be a whole and living part of the people's lives, their daily struggle to survive."[73]

Emory sought, through drawings and paintings, to "enlighten the party to continue its vigorous attack against the enemy, as well as educate the masses of black people."[74] This was an obvious medium for a propagandist wishing to reach members of a social group with a powerful nonliterary tradition and a depressed literacy rate. Yet, Emory also had opinions on the revolutionary function and potential of black popular music, another non-literary form with which the black masses were familiar and in which they had traditionally found emotional solace, communal solidarity, and enormous pleasure, as well as political messages.

Like Baraka and the cultural nationalists, Emory expressed concern about the commercialization of soul music and the relative lack of conspicuous personal or lyrical commitment to the black struggle by its leading performers. Hence he denounced Aretha Franklin and B. B. King for "singing about cultural nationalism" and love, without advancing ideas or information that might concretely lead to revolution. The "Godfather of Soul" James Brown was even worse, using his unique popularity among African Americans and his appeals to black pride to make money for himself and perpetuate the capitalist exploitation of the ghetto. "You hear James Brown talking about Black and Proud, then you hear him on the radio saying, 'Why don't you buy this beer?'" Emory complained. This situation was unlikely to change, he suggested, while black artists were signing contracts with the "Mafia-controlled record industry."[75]

Baraka, of course, had earlier suggested in "The Changing Same" that as black pride and anger became marketable, a more politically engaged soul music might well emerge as a direct consequence of, rather than despite, the industry's profiteering agenda. This deeper insight aside, by 1969 there was really little substantive difference between Baraka and the Panthers in regard to the underrealized political potential and responsibilities of James Brown and soul more generally.

In an article titled "Nationalism Vs Pimp Art," Baraka denounced one of Brown's new message songs, the patriotic paean to the land of boundless opportunity "America Is My Home," as possessing only the surface texture of black culture and art, not its inner spirit of defiance.[76] The song, Baraka claimed, "was an example of Afro-American culture, an R&B song for sure, but it did not have the consciousness of Black, so it could not be called Black. To sing lies about America is not beneficial to the Black Nation, therefore, it's not conscious of Blackness. It is white manipulation, like the Cocacola commercial on a soul station."[77] Dave Hilliard of the Panthers shared Baraka's sentiments: "the only social relevance it [soul radio] has is that it has exploited us culturally. It has taken our music and given it to us with commercials every ten seconds."[78]

For Panthers and cultural nationalists alike, then, the politics and economics of soul music's production were the crucial determinants of its social meaning and political potential. Unlike the cultural nationalists, however, the Panthers never turned to the black jazz avant-garde as their model of a self-consciously committed, economically independent, and unimpeachably black art form. This reflected the Panthers' class-based critique of the black predicament and their powerful identification with the black masses and their cultural predilections. Jazz was never actually rejected, but soul's mass popularity made it the necessary, if by no means perfect or uncompromised, vehicle for most of the Panthers' flirtations with black musical politics.

Recognizing soul's currency in the community, rumor and reality collided as the Panthers attempted to enlist the support of leading African American performers in their revolution. Sly Stone, a hero of the Bay area and one of the biggest crossover stars of the era with ecumenical pop-funk anthems like "Dance to the Music" and "Everyday People," was allegedly pressured by the Panthers into firing his white manager David Kapralnick, who they felt had kept their singer dancing to the tune of the CBS corporation instead of singing songs of revolution.[79] The Panthers also courted Jimi Hendrix, but Hendrix tended to remain aloof from formal political allegiances and was in any case rather more interested in the struggle for Native American rights than the Panthers' program.[80]

Maybe, the Panthers reasoned, this frustrating mixture of temerity and indifference by black artists could be overcome by hard cash, and they sought to turn the commercialism they detected at the heart of the soul music industry to their own advantage. Thus in 1972 they hired the Ike and Tina Turner Revue to headline at an Oakland Auditorium fund-raiser, where former Sly and the Family Stone bassist Larry Graham and his new outfit Graham Central Station were to open. The Turners were promised $12,000 for a one hour performance. With $6,000 paid in advance, the Panthers produced another $5,500 in cash and a check for $500 when the soul stars arrived at the Auditorium. According to Elaine Brown, longtime deputy minister of information and subsequently chair of the Party, Ike Turner refused to accept the check and barricaded himself and his troupe in a dressing room insisting on cash. Only when a raging Huey Newton kicked in the door and threatened to destroy the band's instruments—and do worse to the musicians—did the Revue finally hit the stage. The performance ended after a single number as Ike explained to the incredulous audience that he was playing only under duress and ordered the band and dancers to pack up and leave. This was easier said than done, as several Panthers stormed the stage and proceeded to beat up the fleeing players.[81]

Given the difficulties that the Panthers, like earlier civil rights organizations before them, experienced in securing much in the way of personal support, artistic acknowledgment, or financial assistance from the world of commercial soul, it is perhaps not surprising that the Party eventually began to produce its own "revolutionary" music. The key artists here were Elaine Brown and the aptly named Lumpen. Brown was a sometime singer-songwriter, poetess, and exotic dancer when she first became involved in black radicalism in Los Angeles. Although not a student, she had joined the Black Student Alliance and represented it at meetings of the Black Congress, an umbrella organization for various west coast groups dominated by Ron Karenga and US. Brown recalled how, in the days before the Huggins-Carter murders, Aiuko Babu of the local Black Panther Political Party had regularly joined her, US member Clyde Halisi, and other young poets like Stanley Crouch and Quincy Troupe at the Black Congress's community poetry readings.[82]

When Brown joined the Panthers in the spring of 1968, she was not the first person to introduce music into the Party's world. Panthers had been singing "Free Huey" to the tune of the old spiritual "Wade in the Water" (recently popularized by soul-jazz pianist Ramsey Lewis) ever since their founder's imprisonment.[83] Newton, himself, had notably eclectic musical tastes. He was particularly fond of Bob Dylan, whose "Ballad of a Thin Man" he painstakingly interpreted for Bobby Seale and others as a song about self-respect and self-consciousness in the face of an ignorant and indifferent world. Dylan's song eventually became a Panther staple, "a big part of that whole publishing operation of the *Black Panther* paper," according to Seale.[84]

However, it was David Hilliard, the Party's chief of staff and himself a former vocal group member, who first fully appreciated how well Elaine Brown's musical and lyrical talents might serve the Party's propaganda and publicity needs. Songs like "Assassination" commemorated the Huggins-Carter murders, while "The Panther" was dedicated to Frank Diggs, ruthless head of the mysterious Panther underground responsible for enforcing internal Party discipline. Ironically, given the bitter feud that would later rage between Eldridge Cleaver on one hand and Newton-loyalists Hilliard and Brown on the other, the chief of staff particularly liked "The Meeting," a song about Cleaver that Hilliard imagined might become the Panther anthem.[85]

In the winter of 1969, Brown released *Seize The Time*, an album of her songs featuring lush-but-funky orchestrations by bandleader Horace Tapscott. Paradoxically, but not unusually, this slice of revolutionary black musical culture appeared on the white-owned Vault label, sporting a cover design by Emory Douglas. The original advertisement for the album reminded listeners of the limited role the Panthers believed music could play in the Struggle, even when it was produced by one of their own. "Songs, like all art forms, are an expression of the feelings and thoughts, the desires and hopes, and so forth, of a people. They are no more than that. A song cannot change a situation, because a song does not live and breathe. People do." The rest of Brown's statement and the album itself exhorted all the oppressed in America ("the working class" and "the non-working class [that is those who don't have jobs]") to join in the struggle to wrest power from the grasp of the racists and capitalists.[86]

Brown subsequently recorded one other album, and a single titled "No More," both for Motown's Black Forum subsidiary. Thanks largely to Motown executive Suzanne de Passe, with whom Brown forged a close professional and personal relationship, the Panthers received a much needed $10,000 advance for the album. It was not without its ironies that the Black Forum label should showcase both Brown's revolutionary Panther songs and poetry performances by leading cultural nationalists like Baraka and Larry Neal. The label was also significant in that it reflected Motown-founder Berry Gordy's belated public engagement in the Struggle. The most successful black capitalist entrepreneur of his generation, Gordy had conscientiously avoided letting his labels or artists become too closely linked to the early civil rights movement. In the late 1960s and early 1970s, however, the commercial success of more overtly politicized soul by Curtis Mayfield, Syl Johnson, the Staples Singers, and Donny Hathaway, as well as Motown's own Temptations ("Ball of Confusion") and Marvin Gaye (notably 1971's seminal *What's Going On* album), encouraged a somewhat bolder stance.[87]

Meanwhile, the Panthers, who had once vilified black entrepreneurs like Gordy as an intrinsic part of the problem afflicting African Americans, were happier to do business with him after Huey Newton's reassessment of black capitalism in the summer of 1971. Newton still argued that the Panthers were ultimately committed to "negate capitalism in our communities," but recognized that "people in the Black community have no dislike for the concept of Black Capitalism." En route to their socialist utopia, the Panthers therefore sought to distinguish between the black capitalist who simply pursued self-interest, and the more enlightened one who "has the interest of the community at heart" and "responds to the needs of the people." Gordy's advance and willingness to put out Brown's records were more than enough to see him placed in the latter category.[88]

Not long after the release of Brown's first album, one branch of the National Committee to Combat Fascism (NCCF) coalition offered its own evaluation of the revolutionary potential of black popular music. A report from New Jersey described how NCCF members Tony Horton, Ralph Portera, Cheryl Davila, Lois Newton, and Diane Thompson had been arrested for singing, "'There's a pig up on the hill, if the people don't get them the Panthers will,' while they walked through the black community selling papers."[89] This incident, the correspondent argued, symbolized the popularity of a new crop of revolutionary songs in the black community, songs that he believed could act as a spur to rebellion:

> The singing of revolutionary songs has spread throughout the Black Panther Party and NCCF's all across the country. Children have replaced their traditional meaningless songs with revolutionary songs that are full of the realities of the black community. . . . The singing of revolutionary songs is a very effective form of education for Black people, because they relate very heavily to music. Revolutionary songs not only tell the people that revolution has come and that it's time to pick up the gun but they also tell the people if they want things like, no more pigs in our community, they must seize the time and off the pig.[90]

Two weeks after this letter appeared in the *Black Panther*, the Party announced the release of a single by another of its own soul emissaries, the Lumpen, on the self-financed Seize The Time label.[91] Boasting music and lyrics by Bill Calhoun, this "Black Panther Party Production" featured "No More" and "Free Bobby Now"—a song dedicated to Chairman Bobby Seale, who was at the time awaiting trial for his part in the New Haven riots. The lyrics to "No More" were typically militant, describing black determination to rise up and seize power from the forces of oppression: "There were times, we stood by, like we could not see,/But there won't be no more, can't be no more./We'll get guns to defend our communities. . . . We'll control our destiny, no more murder of our people in their sleep."[92]

As the Lumpen joined Elaine Brown and white progressive rock bands like the Grateful Dead in a series of Oakland benefit concerts for the Party, the Panthers' Ministry of Information felt obliged to issue a statement to clarify its latest line on the group and soul more generally. "The Lumpen is a revolutionary singing group, that has taken the ideology of the Black Panther Party and put it into musical form. Singing the ideology does not discredit it in any way."[93] The Ministry then revealed its own misunderstanding of the way in which popular music works by again locating its message and political potential entirely in the intentions of its creators—the politics and economics of its production. The Panthers thus replicated the error many of the cultural nationalists had made when they assumed that the sincerity and commitment of the New Jazz ensured an ideologically and racially "correct" music with which the black masses must automatically identify.

"The Lumpen sing not to make profit or stimulate emotions, but to make revolution and stimulate action," the Ministry assured the Panther faithful, neglecting both the politics of pleasure—the sensual gratification that crucially shapes an audience's potential receptivity to any message in popular music—and the long history of awful music made with the best of intentions: music that invariably remains undigested or unheard by those for whose edification it was intended, because it fails so miserably to entertain.[94]

While proudly presenting the Lumpen's revolutionary credentials, the Ministry took the opportunity to warn against the perils of succumbing to the visceral and emotional pleasures provided by artists who did not share the Lumpen's selfless commitment to profitless, emotionless music:

Music today is tied up in stimulations, the blues makes you sad while rhythm makes you happy and you end up dancing to keep from crying, dancing while pigs are ripping off brothers and sisters in the streets of Babylon, and across the globe. We know music plays an important role in our culture, and we don't mean to stop singing or changing the sound at all. We dig singing and we dig the sound, but the words are what we're changing to fit our situation today.

We like the beat of James Brown, we say the Temptations sound great, but if we try to relate what they are saying to our conditions we'd end up in a ball of confusion. If we run around saying, "It's my thing and I can do what I want to do," we would never be free or singing "Cloud 9" to help the Mafia launch a new era of drugs, ain't no way. . . . So now when we hear the Temptations' song, "Old Man

River," tell them to keep the sound but to borrow the words from the Lumpen and sing "Old Pig Nixon."[95]

Somewhere in all of this was the beginning of a tentative acknowledgment that the actual sound of soul—even of the rock-influenced "psychedelic" Temptations—might constitute a legitimate and valuable, if commercially constrained, expression of contemporary African American identity. Again, this was much the same position that Imamu Amiri Baraka had advanced in "The Changing Same." Soul was the popular music of the black masses, not simply because James Brown sang "Say It Loud I'm Black and I'm Proud," or the Staples Singers "Respect Yourself," although such overt declarations of black pride were important; its appeal and significance depended more on its performance style and musical techniques, most of which were heavily dependent on "communalizing" gospel precedents with which the black community was intimately familiar and which it perceived as distinctively black. Soul's call and response patterns, its manipulation of musical repetition, the corporeality of its rhythms and the sheer, immanent physicality of its vocal style, created an inclusive music that drew audiences and performers together as they explored common black experiences in song. This communalizing quality was emphasized in lyrical terms by soul's preference for the stated or implied "we" of gospel over the "I" of the blues. As John Street has suggested, this powerful collective imperative in soul, its dependency on performer-audience interaction, provides an interesting analogue to the socialist vision of brotherhood and community. In this respect, the sound and style of soul performance fitted the Panther ideology rather well and they were willing to accept it, despite its unabashed commercialism.[96]

In the main, however, the Panthers continued to evaluate the revolutionary potential of black music almost exclusively in terms of crudely didactic, "right-on" lyrics and a conspicuous personal commitment to political struggle by its artists and entrepreneurs. This was a predictable perspective for an organization ideologically committed to wresting the means of black cultural production from exploitative capitalists of all races and treacherously apolitical artists. Ultimately, however, the Panthers, like the cultural nationalists, failed to appreciate that meaning and significance in popular music are not fixed, but contested and mutable, emerging from a complex matrix of often competing and contradictory influences. Lyrical and musical content, the political and racial agendas of the artists, and of those who owned the clubs, theaters, radio stations, and record companies responsible for the production and dissemination of the music, were important among those influences, but they were not absolutely decisive.

The politics of consumption, the ways in which different elements within the black community took meaning from their music, using it simultaneously as entertainment and as a way of dramatizing and celebrating their individual and collective experiences, were also vitally important in constructing its message and significance. It was beyond the scope of the cultural nationalists, or the Panthers, or for that matter the industry, to control that process of consumption and determine categorically the social or political meanings of the music. Consequently, attempts to utilize either soul or jazz for the promotion of specific political programs were inherently flawed. Soul and jazz might well encourage raised black consciousness, communal solidarity, and self-respect, but it was beyond the functional capacity of music to transform that psychological empowerment into a viable political strategy or revolutionary activism. That task lay elsewhere and ultimately neither the Panthers nor the cultural nationalists succeeded in fashioning an effective political program for African American advance that attracted mass black support.

In fact, perhaps the greatest indictment of the misplaced energies that were poured into the cultural-nationalist disputes of the black power era was that not only were the two camps often much closer to each other than they chose—or felt able—to acknowledge, but their feuding took place against a background of massive black indifference. The only people who really believed there were conceptual and strategic differences of such magnitude that they were worth literally fighting for, or that warranted the termination of meaningful dialogue with those of an alternative viewpoint, were those who were scrambling desperately for personal power and prestige within an unraveling Movement. With Martin Luther King dead, the black-white liberal consensus of the early 1960s shattered on the rocks of legitimate black aspiration and insurgent white conservatism, and the Nixon administration supporting police actions against black militancy and favoring a policy of "benign neglect" on civil rights issues, this was an inopportune moment for a bitter struggle for ideological ascendancy within the Movement. As the Student Nonviolent Coordinating Committee's Cleveland Sellers recognized, after 1968 the black masses became increasingly disillusioned with the course of the liberation struggle and deeply skeptical about its ultimate efficacy. "The black masses are no longer caught up in the drama and promise of the movement," Sellers noted. "They are passive; waiting on a viable vision, a new concept of success."[97] They wanted leadership, direction, a common purpose, and a renewal of faith. When they got a virtual civil war within the Movement instead, an already flagging interest in mass political activism waned still further.

Notes

1. See Kenneth O'Reilly, *Racial Matters: The F.B.I.'s Secret File on Black America, 1960–1972* (New York: Free Press, 1989), 293–324; Maulana Ron Karenga, *The Roots of the US/Panther Conflict* (San Diego: Kawaida, 1976).

2. See William L. Van Deburg, *New Day in Babylon: The Black Power Movement and American Culture, 1965–1975* (Chicago: University of Chicago Press, 1992), quote on 175; Komozi Woodard, *A Nation Within a Nation: Amiri Baraka (LeRoi Jones) & Black Power Politics* (Chapel Hill: University of North Carolina Press, 1999).

3. While there is still no authoritative history of the Black Panther Party, the following personal reminiscences and scholarly studies published during the 1990s are indicative of increasing interest in the Party and its legacy: Earl Anthony, *Spitting in the Wind: The True Story Behind the Violent Legacy of the Black Panther Party* (Santa Monica, Calif.: Roundtable, 1990); Elaine Brown, *A Taste of Power: A Black Woman's Story* (New York: Pantheon, 1992); David Hilliard and Lewis Cole, *This Side of Glory: The Autobiography of David Hilliard and the Story of the Black Panther Party* (Boston: Little, Brown, 1993); Charles Jones, ed., *The Black Panther Party Reconsidered* (Baltimore: Black Classic Press, 1998); Hugh Pearson, *The Shadow of the Panther: Huey P. Newton and the Price of Black Power in America* (Reading, Mass.: Addison-Wesley, 1994). While none of these works devote much attention to the Panthers' cultural politics they, and the following older works, offer useful insights into the organization: Earl Anthony, *Picking Up the Gun: A Report on the Black Panthers* (New York: Dial, 1970); Angela Davis, *If They Come in the Morning: Voices of Resistance* (San Francisco: NACFAD, 1971); Philip Foner, ed., *The Black Panthers Speak* (1970; reprint, New York: Da Capo, 1995); Reginald Major, *A Panther Is a Black Cat* (New York: William Morrow, 1971); Huey Newton, *To Die For the People: The Writings of Huey P. Newton* (New York: Random House, 1972); Huey P. Newton, *Revolutionary Suicide* (New York: Harcourt Brace Jovanovich, 1973); Bobby Seale, *Seize the Time* (London: Arrow, 1970).

4. The widespread caution among most soul performers when it came to overt support for the early Movement, either in song or by public activism, is discussed in Brian Ward, *Just My Soul Responding: Rhythm and Blues, Black Consciousness and Race Relations* (Berkeley: University of California Press, 1998), 289–93, 296–303, 323–36.

5. LeRoi Jones, "The Changing Same (R & B and New Black Music)," (1966) in Jones, *Black Music* (New York: William Morrow, 1967), 180–211. In the interests of consistency, I have used Baraka, rather than Jones, throughout the text.

6. LeRoi Jones, "The Legacy of Malcolm X," in Jones, *Home: Social Essays* (New York: William Morrow, 1966), 246, 250.

7. Imamu Amiri Baraka, quoted in Imamu Amiri Baraka, ed., *African Congress: A Documentary of the First Modern Pan-African Congress* (New York: William Morrow, 1972), 117–18; Imamu Amiri Baraka, "The Need for a Cultural Base to Civil Rites & Bpower Movements," (1967) in Baraka, *Raise, Race, Rays, Raze* (New York: Vintage, 1972), 47.

8. Karenga's Kawaida principles and other aspects of his cultural programs are described in Maulana Ron Karenga, *Kwanzaa: Origin, Concepts, Practice* (Los Angeles: Kawaida, 1977). See also Clyde Halisi, ed., *The Quotable Karenga* (Los Angeles: US Organization, 1967); Thomas Blair, *Retreat to the Ghetto* (New York: Hill and Wang, 1977), 149–54, 156–57; Van Deburg, *New Day in Babylon*, 172–73.

9. Karenga, quoted in Halisi, ed., *The Quotable Karenga*, 11; Stokely Carmichael and Charles V. Hamilton, *Black Power* (New York: Vintage, 1967), 44.

10. Larry Neal, "Black Art and Black Liberation," in *Black Revolution: An Ebony Special* (Chicago: Johnson, 1970), 40; see also Larry Neal, "The Black Arts Movement," *Drama Review* 12, no. 4 (Summer 1968): 32–37.

11. Neal, "Black Art and Black Liberation," 40.

12. Woodard, *A Nation Within a Nation*, 120.

13. For the distinction between "expressive" and "competitive" politics, see ibid., 143. For BARTS, see ibid., 63–68. Baraka's "mainstream" political activities are also discussed in Van Deburg, *New Day in Babylon*, 177–81; Blair, *Retreat to the Ghetto*, 205–10. See also *LeRoi Jones/Amiri Baraka: The Autobiography* (New York: Freundlich, 1984), esp. 202–313.

14. Woodard, *A Nation Within a Nation*, 115–55.

15. Baraka, *African Congress*, 115; also, ibid., 115–22. For Kenneth Gibson's comments, see ibid., 18–21. Woodard, *A Nation Within a Nation*, 160–64.

16. Baraka, *African Congress*, viii.

17. For accounts of the Gary and Little Rock conventions and their broader significance, see Woodard, *A Nation Within a Nation*, 159–218; Blair, *Retreat to the Ghetto*, 203–6; Manning Marable, *Race, Reform and Rebellion: The Second Reconstruction in America* (London: Macmillan, 1984), 137–38, 149–50; *Black Scholar* 4, no. 1 (September 1972), Special Issue.

18. Harold Cruse, *The Crisis of the Negro Intellectual* (New York: William Morrow, 1967), 439

19. LeRoi Jones (Imamu Amiri Baraka), *Blues People* (New York: William Morrow, 1963).

20. Baraka, "The Changing Same," 207–8.

21. Ronald Snellings, quoted in Blair, *Retreat to the Ghetto*, 141.

22. For the role of whites in southern soul, see Ward, *Just My Soul Responding*, 218–25.

23. Baraka, "The Changing Same," 210; Imamu Amiri Baraka, "The Fire Must Be Permitted to Burn Full Up: Black 'Aesthetic,'" in Baraka, *Raise, Race, Rays,*

Raze, 120. The history of the jazz avant-garde, also referred to as the New Jazz, Free Jazz, or the New Music, is best traced though partisan works like Baraka, *Black Music;* Frank Kofsky, *Black Nationalism and the Revolution in Music* (New York: Pathfinder, 1970); and A. B. Spellman, *Black Music: Four Lives in the Be-Bop Business* (1967; reprint, New York: Limelight, 1985); Valerie Wilmer, *As Serious As Your Life: The Story of the New Jazz* (London: Allison and Busby, 1977). These provide both narrative coverage and a powerful sense of the enormous social, racial, and spiritual importance attached to the music by its champions. See also Joachim Berendt, *The Jazz Book*, rev. ed. (London: Paladin, 1984), 26–38, 112–28, 413–16, 432–39; James Lincoln Collier, *The Making of Jazz* (New York: Macmillan, 1981), 454–93; J. C. Thomas, *Chasin' the 'Trane* (1975; reprint, London, Elm Tree: 1976); Ben Sidran, *Black Talk* (1971; reprint, New York: Da Capo, 1981), 135–60.

24. Baraka, *Autobiography*, 211–12; Woodard, *A Nation Within a Nation*, 64–66.

25. Ronald Milner, "Black Magic, Black Art," *Negro Digest*, March 1967, 9–12.

26. Imamu Amiri Baraka, "What the Arts Need Now," in Baraka, *Raise, Race, Rays, Raze*, 33; James T. Stewart, "The Development of the Revolutionary Black Artist," in *Black Fire: An Anthology of Afro-American Writing*, ed. LeRoi Jones and Larry Neal (New York: William Morrow, 1968), 3–9.

27. Archie Shepp, *Kwanza*, Impulse AS 9262, 1968.

28. For a fine discussion of Baraka's jazz writings see John Gennari, "Jazz Criticism: Its Development and Ideologies," *Black American Literature Forum* 25, no. 3 (Fall 1991): 449–523, esp. 485–96.

29. Baraka, "The Fire Must Be Permitted To Burn," 120.

30. Ibid., 122.

31. Baraka, *Autobiography*, 212.

32. Frank Kofsky, "The Jazz Tradition: Black Music and Its White Critics," *Journal of Black Studies* 1, no. 4 (June 1971): 403.

33. Julian "Cannonball" Adderley, on *Negro Artists and the Rising Tide of Black Anger*, (WNBC-TV: New York, June 9, 1963), Audio Tape P967 D2, Reigner Recording Library, Union Theological Seminary, Richmond.

34. Cecil Taylor, "Point of Contact," *Down Beat Yearbook—1966*, 19–31, quoted in Sidran, *Black Talk*, 143.

35. Archie Shepp, *All Things Must Change*, Impulse AS, 9212, 1971.

36. Sonny Rollins, *Freedom Suite*, Milestone 68104, 1958.

37. For jazz artists and the early Movement, see Ward, *Just My Soul Responding*, 302–6.

38. Lawrence P. Nahs, "Black Musician in White America," *Negro Digest*, March 1967, 56–57.

39. A. B. Spellman, "Not Just Whistling Dixie," in *Black Fire*, ed. Jones and Neal, 167.

40. David Rosenthal argues that jazz retained its audience in urban black America into the 1970s, but concedes that the most popular jazz form among the masses was the gospel-tinged soul-jazz of Julian and Nat Adderley, Jimmy McGriff,

and Horace Silver, rather than the more esoteric New Jazz. David Rosenthal, "Jazz in the Ghetto, 1950–1970," *Popular Music* 7 (January 1988): 51–56.

41. In the late 1960s, many black-oriented radio stations devoted as much as ninety percent of their airtime to soul music. See Michael Haralambos, *Right On: From Blues to Soul in Black America* (New York: Drake, 1975), 93. For more on black-oriented radio in the black power era, see Ward, *Just My Soul Responding*, 430–48; Woodard, *A Nation Within a Nation*, 148–49.

42. See Woodard, 253–54; Blair, *Retreat to the Ghetto*, 210.

43. Baraka, *Autobiography*, 254–55.

44. Cruse, *Crisis of the Negro Intellectual*; see also W.E.B. Du Bois, *Souls of Black Folk* (Chicago: A. C. McClurg, 1909), 74–87.

45. Significantly, even within the jazz field, the New Jazz was eclipsed in popularity in the late 1960s and early 1970s by the fusion style, pioneered by Herbie Hancock, Weather Report, Miles Davis, and Billy Cobham. Cultural nationalists might have noted that fusion's unusually wide commercial success for a postwar jazz idiom was built on a marriage of modern jazz and white rock influences. There was nothing pure about fusion, but it was genuinely, syncretically, African American. Fusion is discussed in Berendt, *The Jazz Book*, 38–47, 191–93, 441–46; Collier, *Making of Jazz*, 433–36.

46. Maulana Ron Karenga, "Which Road: Nationalism, Pan-Africanism, Socialism?" *Black Scholar* 6, no. 2 (1974): 27, 30.

47. Karenga has not always managed to maintain the openness to nonblack support and cooperation he proclaimed in the mid-1970s. Encouraged by the undoubted commercial and psychological success of his kwanzaa invention, and by the entrenchment of an academic brand of Afrocentrism—which has veered between excellent research on African retentions in African American culture and unsubstantiated nonsense—Karenga has sometimes succumbed to the temptations of racial chauvinism and Afrocentric myth-making. The most sophisticated analysis of the long popular tradition of Afrocentrism in African American history, of which Karenga is both heir and architect, is Wilson Jeremiah Moses, *Afrotopia: The Roots of African American Popular History* (Cambridge: Cambridge University Press, 1998).

48. *Black Panther*, February 2, 1969, 6.

49. Thomas Blair, in many respects an unusually sensitive early chronicler of the black power era, encapsulated this durable conventional wisdom in the late 1970s: "The definition of cultural nationalism as reactionary set the Black Panther Party well outside the popular emphasis on black studies and 'Black is Beautiful,' a tendency which (Huey) Newton and (Bobby) Seale denounced as a new 'trick bag' of racialist exploitation of black values. Referring with scorn to cultural nationalists like Ron Karenga and Imamu Amiri Baraka, the Panther leaders said that they had cloaked themselves in exotic Africanisms of dress, style, and language, which alienated them from the majority of blacks and whites, in the society. Cul-

tural 'blackism' is a retrograde concept, they said; it is more important to hold a correct race-class line." Blair, *Retreat to the Ghetto,* 94.

50. Donald Warden, interview by Robert Martin, July 25, 1969, Ralph J. Bunche Oral History Collection, Moorland-Spingarn Research Center, Howard University, Washington, D.C. For more on Warden's links with James Brown, see Ward, *Just My Soul Responding,* 389–90; for Brown's politics, see ibid., 388–92. For Newton and Seale's links with Warden, see Seale, *Seize the Time,* 34–46.

51. Clayborne Carson, *In Struggle: SNCC and the Black Awakening of the* 1960s (Cambridge, Mass.: Harvard University Press, 1981), 281.

52. *Black Panther,* March 16, 1968, 12.

53. Baraka, *Autobiography,* 250.

54. See Newton, *To Die For the People,* 4. The author wishes to acknowledge Dave Foster's contribution to this section on the Panthers' use of history. See David C. Foster, "'Let's Rewrite the Mutha': The Black Panther Party's Use and Abuse of History" (Undergraduate dissertation, University of Newcastle upon Tyne, 1998). Copy in possession of author.

55. See, for example, "This Week in Black History," *Black Panther,* June 1, 1974, 4; ibid., August 3, 1975, 4.

56. Molefi Asante, *Afrocentricity: The Theory of Social Change* (Buffalo: Amulefe, 1980), 36.

57. Mumia, "The Black Panther Party and History," *Black Panther,* May 31, 1970, 8.

58. J. Kinard, "Always Tomorrow," ibid., July 7, 1975, 21.

59. Ibid., May 18, 1968, 4.

60. See, for example, ibid., September 14, 1968, 6.

61. Boston Fred Nolan, "Letter," ibid., December 21, 1968, 4.

62. Eldridge Cleaver, "Stokely's Jive," ibid., May 31, 1970, 20; Randy Williams, "No. 1 Lackey of U.S.A. Fascism: Roy Wilkins," ibid., September 12, 1970, 16.

63. Baraka, *Autobiography,* 255–56; Anthony, *Picking Up the Gun,* 21.

64. Eldridge Cleaver, "Method, Time and Revolution," *Black Panther,* May 31, 1970, 18–19.

65. Cleaver, "Stokely's Jive," 20.

66. Eldridge Cleaver, *Soul on Fire* (New York: Dell, 1978), 89.

67. Kathleen Neal Cleaver, "Back To Africa: The Evolution of the International Section of the Black Panther Party (1969–1972)," in *The Black Panther Party Reconsidered,* ed. Jones, 212. See also ibid., 220–24.

68. Baraka, *Autobiography,* 248–49.

69. Major, *A Panther Is a Black Cat,* 142 (see also 139–43 on Emory Douglas).

70. John Ringgold, "Karenga—King of the Bloodsuckers," *Black Panther,* May 2, 1970, 12.

71. Karenga, quoted in Halisi, ed., *The Quotable Karenga,* 10. George Murray, quoted in *Black Panther,* September 7, 1968, 12.

72. *Black Panther*, October 20, 1968, 5.

73. Ibid.

74. Ibid., May 18, 1968, 20.

75. Emory Douglas, quoted in Phineas Israeli, "Emory Grinds Down the Pigs," ibid., November 22, 1969, 6.

76. Imamu Amiri Baraka, "Nationalism Vs Pimp Art," (1969) in, Baraka, *Raise, Race, Rays, Raze*, 125–32. Baraka also used this article to condemn the "misled" Panthers—and Cleaver in particular—for what he felt at the time was a treacherous fixation with white ideologies like Marxism. The outburst against Cleaver encompassed not only his Marxism, but also his affair with his white lawyer, Beverly Axelrod. "With the incarceration of Huey, and the move by Cleaver into the chief strategist's seat, the Panthers turned left on Nationalism, and turned left on Black people. And the love of Beverley Axelrod has left terrible Marx on the Dirty Lenin Black people have been given by some dudes with some dead 1930's white ideology as a freedom suit." Ibid., 130.

77. Ibid., 131. Despite his new lyrical engagement, Brown's basic conservatism and faith in the American system frustrated black power advocates of all kinds.

78. David Hilliard, quoted in Andrew Meyer, *Black Voices and Format Regulations: A Study in Black-Oriented Radio* (Stanford: ERIC Clearinghouse on Media and Technology, 1971), 72.

79. For Sly Stone's career and politics, see Ward, *Just My Soul Responding*, 358–60.

80. For Jimi Hendrix's career and politics, see ibid., 244–48.

81. Brown, *Taste of Power*, 336–41.

82. Ibid., 122–24.

83. Ibid., 126.

84. Seale, *Seize the Time*, 218.

85. Brown, *Taste of Power*, 185.

86. Ibid., 195–96. Elaine Brown, *Seize the Time*, Vault 131, 1969; Elaine Brown, quoted in *Black Panther*, November 22, 1969, 17.

87. See Brown, *Taste of Power*, 305–7, 311–12. For Gordy's attitude toward the civil rights and black power movements, see Ward, *Just My Soul Responding*, 268–75, 326–27, 393–400.

88. Huey Newton, "Black Capitalism Re-Analyzed," *Black Panther*, June 5, 1971, A–D.

89. Letter from "Tony," "People Arrested For Singing," ibid., September 12, 1970, 8.

90. Ibid.

91. The Lumpen, "No More"/"Free Bobby Now," (Seize the Time, 1970); *Black Panther*, September 26, 1970, 18.

92. Ibid.

93. "The Lumpen—Music as a Tool for Liberation," ibid., November 7, 1970, 12.

94. For the politics of pleasure in pop, see Simon Frith, *Sound Effects: Youth, Leisure and the Politics of Rock and Roll* (1978; reprint, London: Constable, 1983), 164–65.

95. "The Lumpen," 12.

96. John Street, *Rebel Rock: The Politics of Popular Music* (Oxford: Blackwell, 1986), 216–17.

97. Cleveland Sellers, *River of No Return: The Autobiography of a Black Militant and the Life and Death of SNCC* (Jackson: Universty of Mississippi Press, 1990), 253–54.

9

Villains, Demons, and Social Bandits

White Fear of the Black Cultural Revolution

William L. Van Deburg

The black power movement commanded considerable attention during the late 1960s and the early years of the following decade. Its supporters' impassioned rhetoric stirred emotions, inflamed tempers, and occasioned extended debate both within the academy and throughout society. In the context of the era, this militant thrust toward black liberation was an essential component in the larger societal movement toward realigning American realities with long misplaced priorities.

Despite an observable tendency for differing factions to claim the entire movement as their own, the multifaceted nature of black power was one of its most significant characteristics. One important mode of black power expression was cultural. Eager to formulate personalized visions of the militant protest sentiment, playwrights, novelists, songwriters, and artists used cultural forms as weapons in the struggle for liberation. By doing so, they provided a much-needed structural underpinning for the movement's political and economic tendencies. In this respect, black power can be conceptualized as a "revolt of culture"—a historically rooted, broad-based outpouring of African American cultural expression responding to the majoritarian culture's practice of ignoring, stereotyping, and degrading people of color.

Fueled by a soul-satisfying self-definition ethic, the black power movement provided a psychological antidote to despair and engendered a tangible sense of pride within African American communities. Commonly referred to as "black consciousness" or "the new blackness," this liberating spirit was both encapsulated in and expressed through soul music, natural hair styles, paintings and outdoor murals, Movement-inspired novels, poems, and plays. Over time, these culture-based instruments of dissemination served to spread the militants' philosophy much further than did mimeographed political broadsides. Ultimately, this revolt in and of culture proved to be more popular, longer-lasting, and at least as significant as the far more loudly proclaimed (and better reported) agendas of politically oriented nationalist groups.[1]

If this is true, one legitimately may ask, why did white people get so upset over the call for black power? Frightened and bewildered by the activists' rallying cry, many equated it with armed revolution and bloodletting. For example, a 1967 survey of more than 850 Detroit residents conducted by University of Michigan researchers showed that almost 60 percent of the whites interviewed believed the term was synonymous with violence and destruction, reverse racism, and black domination. "The Negro wants to enslave the white man like he was enslaved one hundred years ago. They want to take everything away from us—We'll all be poor," said one panic-stricken respondent. "Blacks won't be satisfied until they get complete control of our country by force if necessary," added another. "Black takeover—Take over the world because that is what they want to do and they will," noted a third. Only 9 percent of the blacks interviewed held similar views.[2] Unfortunately, such surveys did little to pinpoint the underlying causes of these dramatic differences in perception and opinion.

The polls were discouraging—and puzzling. Race relations had seemed to be improving. Whites were growing accustomed to and even becoming fairly comfortable with the "freedom now" message of the civil rights movement. Large numbers understood—or could rationalize—the need for the 1964 Civil Rights and 1965 Voting Rights Acts. Many were willing to pay good money to view—and admire—the dignified self-assertion of Hollywood's Sidney Poitier. And songs like the Impressions' "People Get Ready" and "Keep On Pushing" had reached the upper reaches of the national pop charts. What was so threatening about cultural renewal, about a little black freedom and pride?

To be sure, unsettling memories of Malcolm X proclaiming the need for a separatist revolution by any means necessary brought precious little comfort to anxious whites. Equally upsetting were news photos of black marchers carrying posters emblazoned with a snarling panther and the words, "MOVE ON OVER OR WE'LL MOVE ON OVER YOU." And then there was the new black music and poetry of Gil Scott-Heron, Nikki Giovanni, and LeRoi Jones. With barely contained rage, they would damn "a diseased species" to hell for "war, rape, . . . mass murder and inflicting pain."[3]

Were these vividly intemperate sentiments somehow to blame for fostering unease within the mainstream? Most certainly—especially when magnified in volume and importance by a sensation-seeking national press corps. But it should also be remembered that numerous nonblack ethnics and members of factionalized political constituencies had been calling each other names and fomenting social revolutions for generations. Few elicited the apocalyptic response occasioned by black power. Moreover, throughout this period, a variety of high-profile black activist spokespersons tried to calm the troubled waters by denying that they were about to initiate a violent antiwhite pogrom. The long-suffering masses might choose to engage in violent acts, they said, but only in self-defense. Couldn't frightened whites see that this retaliatory rhetoric actually might serve to promote racial peace by discouraging white-initiated terrorism and police brutality? Apparently not.

According to Julius Lester, writing in the seminal late 1960s text *Look Out, Whitey! Black Power's Gon' Get Your Mama!*, white America's conceptualization of blackness lay at the libidinal center of its unreasonable, but deep-seated fears: "Black! That word. BLACK! And the visions came of alligator-infested swamps arched by primordial trees with moss dripping from the limbs and out of the depths of the swamp, the mire oozing from his skin, came the black monster and fathers told their daughters to be in by nine instead of nine-thirty."[4]

Surely, the prescient Lester was sniffing around the right bog. It is both useful and appropriate to consider the psychological factors that help shape human belief and behavior—to ponder the notion that culturally transmitted understandings about skin color and moral character played key roles in helping whites (mis)interpret the African American liberation movement. In this model, it is the social construction of blackness (when considered in close proximity to power) that alienated and terrified whites, causing them to view all manner of black power activists as dangerous, threatening, even villainous and demonic. Here, the yin and yang of black empowerment can be traced to three closely related, culture-based tendencies: first, white Americans' long-term stereotyping of blacks as evildoers; second, blacks' spirited refusal to accept or validate these negative images; and, third, African Americans' equally determined efforts to transform literary, theatrical, and mental images of dark-skinned villains into totemic culture heroes supportive of group liberation.

Villains, by definition, are bad people. They are flawed or damaged beings whose negative moral attributes overshadow the positive. Lacking a well-developed social conscience, villains are prone to base behaviors and malevolent or criminal acts. Typically opportunistic and exploitative, they are habituated to greed, treachery, and the ignoble desire to expand their power over others. Whether termed a rogue or scoundrel, knave or blackguard, the villain is a mean-spirited individual who, to varying degrees, lacks the average mortal's requisite quotient of honesty, empathy, and compassion. Fully aware that evil lurks in the hearts of all manner of humankind, villains cherish this thought and seek to corner the market on immoral conduct. True villains enjoy the work and have made evil-doing a personal priority and lifestyle choice. In an existential sense, villains do not become real until they are causing someone, somewhere, considerable trouble or pain.

By functioning as a cultural yardstick with which to measure an individual's adherence to group mores, villains simplify moral choices and help shape the ritual drama of American social life. Moreover, villainy gives definition to heroism. While not exactly the relationship established by Robert Louis Stevenson's Dr. Jekyll and Mr. Hyde, heroes and villains maintain a complex interdependence. Through their bad behavior and nonconforming moral standards villains create a variety of crisis situations to which the hero must respond. Without the villain's challenge to the status quo, there would be far fewer occasions for heroic endeavor and a corresponding decline in socially beneficial results. No strangers to paradox and irony, villains often unwittingly promote and strengthen accepted community standards by inverting and deviating from them.[5]

A somewhat different moral universe is established when a villain defeats a hero. Even if only temporary, the hero's eclipse may prove to be more than a dramatic way of galvanizing the communal spirit in response to a threat posed by villainous outsiders. Such a precipitous event may signal a splintering of the assumed group consensus. Telling evidence that one person's hero can be someone else's villain, this disruptive turning of the tables often is the work of a disaffected societal subgroup questing for either physical or psychological freedom. Here, establishment pariahs become rebel heroes and reflect anti-institutional tendencies present within the oppressed population.

Perhaps better placed within the folk heroic tradition of social banditry, such individuals are the proper villain's first cousins. But they also display attributes—strength, courage, loyalty to cause—normally associated with fully accredited heroes. Social bandits like Robin Hood, for example, are highly selective in their villainy. Their cruelty is legitimized as vengeance. "Feared by the bad, loved by the good," as the theme song of the 1950s CBS television show would have it, Robin and his Merry Men were hunted as outlaws by representatives of a usurpative political elite. But to poor peasants long consigned to the lower depths of the social order, this troublesome band of scofflaws seemed an army of liberation—bold and selfless agents of justice whose moral compass pointed in the same direction as their own. In such cases, the social bandit/villain provides a useful counterpoint to skewed, imposed, or outmoded conceptualizations of morality and heroism.[6]

Like Ronald Reagan's description of the Soviet Union as an "evil empire," any abstract moral wrong becomes more immediate and tangible when personified. The pedagogical value of this technique is enhanced even further when the evil entity is given a virtuous and spirited adversary. Just as height is difficult to conceptualize if there is no depth, for its magnitude to be perceived correctly, great good must be viewed in the context of immense—not merely second-rate—evil.

Pitting God against Adam would be a colossal mismatch. As the traditional Judeo-Christian morality play would have it, Adam and Eve make convincing transgressors, but terrible villains. Seduced into facilitating the entrance of evil into human society by what Augustine termed "the misuse of free will," they are sinners, but not sin incarnate.[7] The creator God, it seems, could be blamed neither for intending evil nor for deigning to spar with midgets. Thus, humankind's Fall necessarily was accompanied by the rise of the Devil (a.k.a. Belial, Beelzebub, the Evil One, Lucifer, Old Nick, and Satan), a mighty fallen angel whose rebellion against God has caused trouble for Adam's descendants ever since they left the Garden.

Remarkably, this prideful deceiver makes relatively few appearances in scripture. Only sporadically identifiable as an objectified being, the Devil has made it hard for humans to agree on a standardized physical portrayal. As noted by nineteenth-century French poet Charles Baudelaire, perhaps this is due to the fact that "the finest ruse of the devil is to persuade you that he does not exist."[8] In any case, the Devil that we see in artist's renderings comes in a variety of guises.

Almost universally depicted as male, Satan is fearful to behold. Looking for all the world like prototypes of some of Hollywood's most imaginative nightmare fantasies, folkloric representations reveal him to be a monstrous, deformed being of mingled parts. Neither man nor beast, his tail and horns, cloven hooves or talons, large and enveloping bat-like wings, oversized nose and phallus, coarse body hair, and backward-facing knees (occasioned by the precipitous fall from heaven) provide graphic physical evidence of gross spiritual defect.[9]

Equally symbolic is the unambiguous color-coding of traditional European-American Devil lore. Only one of Satan's Old and New Testament incarnations is given explicit color. This was the "great red dragon" of Revelation 12. But before the end of the sixth century—and likely earlier—Christians who had no qualms about adding new mysteries to the sacred canon were writing about a Devil-like being described as "black, sharp-faced, with long beard, hair to the feet, fiery eyes, breathing flame, spiky wings like a hedgehog, bound with fiery chains."[10] Already, it seems, the die was cast. Estranged from goodness and light, the Evil One most often has been presented to us as having black skin or wearing dark-colored clothing. He rides a black horse, practices the black arts, commands the armies of darkness, and presides over the gloomy pit of Hell. Black cats and goats, shaggy black dogs, ravens, and bats are favored disguises.

One noteworthy consequence of our making the Devil black is that a disproportionate number of his helpers have become inextricably associated with darkness of one sort or another. Like Dracula (Rumanian for "devil"), prince of Transylvanian vampires, noteworthy evildoers favor black clothing and accessories. Certainly, no self-respecting, stereotypical Wild West outlaw or wicked witch would want to be seen doing dastardly deeds without a black chapeau. Frequently, this attire is complemented by the villain's "thick, heavy, languid, lustreless black hair," "bold, brilliant black eyes," and "beard of burnt-up black."[11]

Is there cultural significance in our blackening of prominent villains and in the manner in which they have been linked to the Great Deceiver, fount of natural evil? To be sure, not all "black hearted" souls have become feared enemies. With some, we tend to be charitable and overlook major flaws. Nevertheless, many who have been tarred with the dark pigment seem destined to remain in permanent moral exile.

Black is but one of many pigment shadings found in nature. Like all other colors, it is capable of eliciting emotions and setting moods. It can be used symbolically and interpreted as variously as any controversial news event. Cambridge University's John Harvey, a close observer of the emblematic and allegorical aspects of material culture, terms black a "paradox-color." Others categorize it as a non-color. According to the first chapter of Genesis, black is the most ancient of colors and was "upon the face of the deep" at the time of earth's creation. On the other hand, black also is the color of dirt, decay, and putrefaction. As an observed phenomenon, it is most like the dark of night even though it can be seen clearly in the light of day. But, when completely surrounded by it—as in a pitch-black cave—we say, "I can't see a thing!" At such times, black becomes invisible, a void of coloration.[12]

Throughout history, westerners have donned black clothing in order to reflect both formality and simplicity, professionalism and social position, asceticism, austerity, gravity, and penitence. The color has been a favorite of both ruling elites and countercultural nay-sayers. Badmen wear black, but so do clerics and many other good people. It is slimming on a size 3-X frame, but carries the weight of authority when seen on a Supreme Court justice.

Despite this impressive sartorial adaptability, the color black also has come to be associated with several of the most frightful and troubling aspects of the human experience. Mourners wear black and were doing so in ancient Greece and Rome. During the Middle Ages, lepers often were required to dress in black as were knights who had disgraced their Order. But, even earlier, people feared the darkness. Frightened by forest creatures that went "bump" in the night, as well as by those "ghoulies and ghosties and long-leggety beasties" that all suspected were lurking in the shadows, they linked evil with the absence of light. Through constant repetition of negative references, black devolved into a sinister color and has been made an accessory to crime.[13]

Whether drawn from primal instinct or learned response to real or imagined predators, this unfortunate relationship was confirmed by philosophers, theologians, and other writers. Many employed the color black in moral allegories about spiritual defect and societal decay. Here, black was a signifier for sin and served as a negative reference point for acceptable ethical behavior. It was the antithesis of white, symbol of purity, chastity, virtue, and innocence. Since God was spirit and light, the darkness and gloom associated with the color black could represent only those forces opposed to or alienated from God. If, as taught by both Plato and Augustine, physical light reflected "the pure fire within us," it was unlikely that "black sheep" would be allowed to enter the brightly lit heavenly homeland of the church triumphant. "Black," wrote Shakespeare, "is the badge of hell, the hue of dungeons, and the school of night."[14]

Thus, over time, villains, great moral evil, and the color black have been joined in unholy union. The resulting ebony-toned, Plutonic entity is a most impressive and useful cultural creation. The fear elicited by villains of this type has done much to steer us away from the pit. Their very presence makes virtue attractive. Without them, our stories would have fewer morals to teach. But the physical and spiritual darkness associated with such figures creates numerous problems as well. These affect real people in today's world, not just the stock characters of stage, screen, and fiction.

In effect, the villains' many evils have been imputed to African Americans irrespective of their individual character, deeds, or moral worth. This ongoing human and social tragedy is the result of thousands of interpretive acts over several centuries of European-American history.

The syllogistic notion that since villainy is closely related to blackness then those who are black by heredity are in some way villainous is both illogical and, seemingly, inescapable. Although seldom articulated, clearly, it informs and provides a historical subtext for the working out of all contemporary racial relationships.

Given this background, it should be somewhat easier to fathom the controversy over black power. During those tumultuous years of antiwar protest, urban rioting, and general societal upheaval, many white Americans selected black activists questing for empowerment as their villains of choice. Horrified at the prospect of becoming lost within a swamp of blackness, fearful whites circled their cultural wagons and broadcast a warning to those who would follow. Drawing upon ancient racial wisdom, they constructed pejorative portraits of power-hungry black power badmen who were prone to criminal behaviors and bereft of both compassion and social conscience. Whether subversively or openly evil, the stereotypical black power villain was excluded from whites' moral universe. To protect group distinctions from contamination, stalwart, law-abiding mainstream culture heroes patrolled the borders of this racial divide. Able promoters of majoritarian group unity, they stood with their supposed nobility, virtue, and high moral character in stark contrast to the death-dealing duplicity of black-hearted foes who, as Julius Lester noted, were thought to reek of sulfur and swamp ooze. In this manner, a black American cultural revolution was perceived as a white American Armageddon.

But most African Americans saw things quite differently. Increasingly, they celebrated rather than denied or excoriated their blackness. By the end of the 1960s, white America's once-potent power to define justice, morality, and heroism had been noticeably attenuated by a determined cohort of African American activists who would accept no shuffling minstrel Tom as their cultural standard-bearer. Instead, they transformed character-types that whites considered negative and dangerous into liberation-oriented heroes. Indeed, there came to be a special, even hallowed place within oppositional cultural expression for black social bandits. During the black power era, they starred in a latter-day episode of an ancient morality play in which key societal understandings and power relationships were contested within the sphere of popular culture.

That "outlaws" could be considered heroes should come as no surprise.

All who live in the complex, post–Ozzie-and-Harriet world have been introduced to such characters via newspapers and novels, teleplays and theatrical films. Our contemporary pop culture texts speak often of noble robbers, resistance fighters, insurrectionists, and avengers who break rank and risk all in order to rid their homeland of corrupt leaders and unresponsive governmental systems. Whether real or imagined, these tough, self-reliant figures partake fully of the warrior tradition. As agents of change, they may kill or maim, but do so in order to enhance the existence of those consigned to a state of living death. Their acts of terror inspire fear—proving that even societal underdogs are capable of exerting awesome, death-dealing power. If captured, social bandits are assured of their followers' active assistance in regaining precious freedom. Should they perish in the attempt, story and song immortalize—and often greatly enhance—their deeds. In such situations, memorials may come from: first, roguish compatriots who also find great virtue in badness; second, fellow idealists who, while deeming the outlaw's methods reprehensible, share a similar vision of the "good" society; and, third, students of the folk heroic who find themselves attracted to the bandit's audacious approach to surmounting life's adversities.[15]

During the black power years, African American novelists and filmmakers joined support groups such as these in record numbers. In doing so, they helped redefine villainy and heroism—melding the divergent concepts into a composite, potentially activist ideal. If frequently obscured by first-take cinematography and second-rate prose, many of their dynamic, larger-than-life creations were of page-turning, theater-filling caliber. As they prowled the shadowy recesses of the cultural landscape, this most arresting assortment of film and pulp fiction hustlers, dealers, pimps, gangsters, vigilantes, and rogue cops strived to set the record straight. Although their boldness sometimes shaded into excess, characters such as Iceberg Slim, Willie Dynamite, Mean Johnny Barrows, and *Super Fly's* lank-haired pusherman, Youngblood Priest, were shown to be bad in a good sense. As risk-taking agents of change, they strived mightily to "stick it to The Man"—to rid black communities of corrupt leaders and unresponsive governmental systems. Guided by countercultural codes of honor and unembarrassed to sing their own praise, these tough, self-reliant individuals confounded racist stereotypes, thereby altering the ground rules for racial representation and providing a rationale for modern-day social banditry.[16]

Nowhere were these tendencies more visible than in darkened Hollywood screening rooms and neighborhood movie palaces during what came to be known as American filmmakers' "blaxploitation" period.[17] And no black power era theatrical entertainment had a more profound impact on racial portraiture than *Sweet Sweetback's Baadasssss Song* (1971). Filmed in southern California in nineteen days by onetime kazoo-playing street busker, French language novelist, and expert media-tease Melvin Van Peebles, *Sweetback* told the story of a clever black picaroon on the lam.[18] After witnessing the savaging of a young brother on the block by two racist cops, Sweetback (played by Van Peebles) gets sweet revenge. Thereafter, he is transformed from a pleasure-seeking sexual athlete to a self-actualized Black Man on a quest for freedom South of the border. Van Peebles's protagonist doesn't actually do or say a great deal during the lengthy, often dreamlike and allegorical chase sequence. But here, style and vision—not the complexity of the plot—drive the filmmaker's message home. Indeed, the street smart, sartorially splendid hero conveys an aesthetique du cool that resonates with political wisdom. Relying on native wit, on an inexhaustible reservoir of sexual energy, and on his contacts within the black community, Sweetback eventually succeeds in out-distancing his adversaries.

Filmed in a grainy, sometimes jerky and disconnected cinema-verité approximation, Van Peebles's episodic "hymn from the mouth of reality" promoted a race-based ethic of survival by any means necessary. It encouraged the decolonization of minds and the growth of self-knowledge. Aglow with the first rays of Jubilee's dawn, the controversial film taught that "if you can get it together and stand up to the Man, you can win."[19]

Despite receiving its share of negative reviews from critics of all racial backgrounds and ideological stripes, *Sweetback* recouped its $500,000 production cost in record time.[20] Boosted by Van Peebles's voluble campaign to rid the film of its Motion Picture Association of America "X" rating and by aggressive marketing of movie-related paraphernalia, *Sweetback*'s first run gross of over $10 million astounded pundits.[21] This unanticipated box office bonanza provided Hollywood with a commercially viable model for the further development of the genre.

Not all black power era social bandits adopted Sweetback's monadic lifestyle. Nor were they all as uncommunicative, emotionless, and unattracted to prepackaged political ideologies. Nevertheless, most had a bit of Van Peebles's stolid, but quick-witted creation somewhere in their makeup. They both entertained and instructed. Whether male or female, heroic hustler or violence-prone vigilante, black champions relished the chance to join forces in support of a subversive psychological revolution.

Magically turning alleged racial debits into assets, they engaged their audience's most wistful retaliatory dreams. To be sure, their message was iconoclastic; their manner insistently in-your-face. But given the nation's history of turning a deaf ear to minority group claims and concerns, straight talk delivered at attention-getting volume was wholly warranted. Unintimidated by white power and blessed with oversized egos, they had little trouble conceptualizing themselves as superior to white culture champions on all counts. As Van Peebles noted, films featuring such proud, black stalwarts were, by definition, "victorious." Despite their shortcomings (and excesses) they allowed African American theatergoers to "walk out standing tall instead of avoiding each other's eyes." Here, courtesy of a newly invigorated black heroic, people of color finally were getting a chance to see "some of their own fantasies acted out"— technicolor visions of black folk "rising out of the mud and kicking ass."[22]

Influenced greatly by the style and message of contemporary political activists, pop culture social bandits were considered holy terrors by avowed enemies, but seen as sacred, soulful beings by confirmed admirers. Intimates believed that such figures could be regarded as true criminals only by those who feared a just social order. In this respect, they reflected the African American oral tradition that held dissembling proto-outlaws like the Signifying Monkey and Shine in high regard. Like these well-known folkloric precursors, black power badmen utilized both mental agility and physical prowess to triumph over great odds, took considerable pleasure in besting and humiliating societal elites, and—despite their proclivity to talk about other people's mothers "in a scandalous way"— typically "live[d] to signify another day."[23]

Although neither traditionally virtuous nor popular with everyone, the black badmen of film and fiction became major players in the cultural revolution of the 1960s and 1970s. Visionary vehicles of African American wish-fulfillment, they radiated the activist ethic that coursed throughout the land. Joining with real world counterparts to promote group unity and individual psychological well-being, most fought tenaciously—by any means necessary—to consign both black "invisibility" and all-too-recognizable stereotypes like Mammy and Little Black Sambo to oblivion. If black power was a revolt in and of culture that was fueled by major psychological revelations, white Americans' opposition to black empowerment was closely related both to inherited cultural beliefs and to the intimidating nature of this revisionist racial portraiture. During the black power years, ancient European-American fears were filtered through politically charged black cast entertainments. Together, they helped shape vivid mental images of African American activists-as-villains with designs on the nation's long-uncontested seat of power.

Notes

1. On black power as a "revolt of culture," see William L. Van Deburg, *New Day in Babylon: The Black Power Movement and American Culture, 1965–1975* (Chicago: University of Chicago Press, 1992).

2. Joel D. Aberbach and Jack L. Walker, "The Meanings of Black Power: A Comparison of White and Black Interpretations of a Political Slogan," *American Political Science Review* 64 (June 1970): 370–73, 387.

3. Gil Scott-Heron, "The ones who . . . ," in Scott-Heron, *Small Talk at 125th and Lenox* (New York: World, 1970), 10; LeRoi Jones, "I Am Speaking of Future Goodness and Social Philosophy," in Jones, *Black Magic: Collected Poetry, 1961–1967* (Indianapolis: Bobbs-Merrill, 1969), 99.

4. Julius Lester, *Look Out, Whitey! Black Power's Gon' Get Your Mama!* (New York: Grove, 1969), 97.

5. On this point, see Jean Starobinski, *Blessings in Disguise, or, The Morality of Evil* (1989; reprint, Cambridge: Harvard University Press, 1993), 8–9.

6. *The Adventures of Robin Hood*, CBS, 1955–58. On social banditry, see Eric Hobsbawm, *Bandits* (New York: Delacorte, 1969).

7. Augustine, *Concerning the City of God Against the Pagans* (1467), trans. Henry Bettenson (New York: Penguin, 1984), 523.

8. Charles Baudelaire, "The Generous Gamester," (1869) in *Twenty Prose Poems*, trans. Michael Hamburger (London: Jonathan Cape, 1968), 43.

9. See, for example, the illustrations collected in Genevieve Morgan and Tom Morgan, *The Devil: A Visual Guide to the Demonic, Evil, Scurrilous, and Bad* (San Francisco: Chronicle, 1996).

10. Montague Rhodes James, *The Apocryphal New Testament* (Oxford: Clarendon, 1960), 468.

11. *Dracula* (Universal, 1931); George Du Maurier, *Trilby* (1894) (New York: Oxford University Press, 1995), 11.

12. John Harvey, *Men in Black* (Chicago: University of Chicago Press, 1995), 13; Ad Reinhardt, "Black as Symbol and Concept," in *Art-as-Art: The Selected Writings of Ad Reinhardt*, ed. Barbara Rose, (1967; reprint, New York: Viking, 1975), 86; Linda Van Norden, *The Black Feet of the Peacock: The Color-Concept "Black" From the Greeks Through the Renaissance* (Lanham, Md.: University Press of America, 1985), 1–10.

13. Harvey, *Men in Black*, 42–43, 50, 52; John Bartlett, *Familiar Quotations* (1855), ed. Justin Kaplan (Boston: Little, Brown, 1992), 779.

14. John 1:4–9; Plato, *Plato's Cosmology: The Timaeus*, ed. Francis Macdonald Cornford (London: Routledge and Kegan Paul, 1966), 152–53; William Shake-

speare, *Love's Labour's Lost* (1598)(Oxford: Clarendon, 1990), 174. On the extramission theory of vision in which animal spirit or rays of light are held to be emitted from the eyes, see David C. Lindberg, *Theories of Vision from Al-Kindi to Kepler* (Chicago: University of Chicago Press, 1976), 1–146; Simon Kemp, *Medieval Psychology* (Westport, Conn.: Greenwood, 1990), 36–40. On negative connotations of the color black in various nonwestern traditions, see Kenneth J. Gergen, "The Significance of Skin Color in Human Relations," in *Color and Race*, ed. John Hope Franklin (Boston: Houghton Mifflin, 1968), 119–20.

15. The long-running (1952–1966) ABC-TV comedy *The Adventures of Ozzie and Harriet* schooled the baby boom generation in middle-class values. The show's wholesome nuclear family consisted of genial paterfamilias Ozzie Nelson, stay-at-home mom Harriet, and polite, well-adjusted sons David and Ricky. For a study that discusses the series in light of subsequent changes in both real-world and sitcom notions of domesticity, see Debra Baker, "Beyond Ozzie and Harriet," *ABA Journal* 84 (September 1998): 58–63. On the universality of the outlaw heroic tradition, see Hobsbawm, *Bandits*; Jack Katz, *Seductions of Crime: Moral and Sensual Attractions in Doing Evil* (New York: Basic, 1988), 227. On the outlaw-warrior connection, see Edward Tabor Linenthal, *Changing Images of the Warrior Hero in America: A History of Popular Symbolism* (New York: Edwin Mellen, 1982), xii, xvi–xvii.

16. For additional commentary on these characters, see William L. Van Deburg, *Black Camelot: African-American Culture Heroes in Their Times, 1960–1980* (Chicago: University of Chicago Press, 1997), 127–96.

17. On the blaxploitation films, see Ed Guerrero, *Framing Blackness: The African American Image in Film* (Philadelphia: Temple University Press, 1993), 69–111; Darius James, *That's Blaxploitation! Roots of the Baadasssss 'Tude* (New York: St. Martin's Griffin, 1995); Gerald Martinez, Diana Martinez, and Andres Chavez, *What It Is . . . What It Was! The Black Film Explosion of the '70s in Words and Pictures* (New York: Hyperion, 1998).

18. On Van Peebles's personal odyssey and autobiographical legend, see Thomas Cripps, "'Sweet Sweetback's Baadasssss Song' and the Changing Politics of Genre Film," in *Close Viewings: An Anthology of New Film Criticism*, ed. Peter Lehman (Tallahassee: Florida State University Press, 1990), 242–48; Karen Jaehne, "Melvin Van Peebles: The Baadasssss Gent," *Cineaste* 18, no. 1 (1990): 4–8.

19. "Power to the Peebles," *Time*, August 16, 1971, 47; Melvin Van Peebles, *The Making of Sweet Sweetback's Baadasssss Song* (New York: Lancer, 1972), 12; Horace W. Coleman, "Melvin Van Peebles," *Journal of Popular Culture* 5 (Fall 1971): 369, 371, 376.

20. For a sampling of black opinion on the film, see Lerone Bennett Jr., "The Emancipation Orgasm: Sweetback in Wonderland," *Ebony*, September 1971, 106–18; Huey P. Newton, "He Won't Bleed Me: A Revolutionary Analysis of 'Sweet Sweetback's Baadasssss Song,'" *Black Panther*, June 19, 1971, A–L; Clayton Riley, "What Makes Sweetback Run?" *New York Times*, May 9, 1971, 11; Don L. Lee, "The

Bittersweet of Sweetback/Or, Shake Yo Money Maker," *Black World* 21 (November 1971): 43–48.

21. On Van Peebles's commitment to creating a politicized yet commercial film rather than a "didactic discourse," see Melvin Van Peebles, "A Black Odyssey: 'Sweet Sweetback's Baadasssss Song'" in *Black Films and Film-Makers: A Comprehensive Anthology from Stereotype to Superhero*, ed. Lindsay Patterson (New York: Dodd, Mead, 1975), 227.

22. Van Peebles, *Making of Sweet Sweetback*, 13; "Sweet Song of Success," *Newsweek*, June 21, 1971, 89.

23. Oscar Brown Jr., "Signifyin' Monkey," in *Talk That Talk: An Anthology of African American Storytelling*, ed. Linda Goss and Marian E. Barnes (New York: Simon and Schuster, 1989), 456–57; Dennis Wepman, Ronald B. Newman, and Murray B. Binderman, *The Life: The Lore and Folk Poetry of the Black Hustler* (Philadelphia: University of Pennsylvania Press, 1976), 26. On the place of the Signifying Monkey in black folklore, see Henry Louis Gates Jr., *The Signifying Monkey: A Theory of African American Literary Criticism* (New York: Oxford University Press, 1988). On Shine, see Bruce Jackson, *"Get Your Ass in the Water and Swim Like Me": Narrative Poetry from Black Oral Tradition* (Cambridge: Harvard University Press, 1974), 35–38, 191–95.

10

"Pimpin' Ain't Easy"

Work, Play, and "Lifestylization" of the Black Pimp Figure
in Early 1970s America

Eithne Quinn

The pimp figure has long been a street cultural antihero in black America.
Stories about pimps (also known as "players" and "macks") circulated and
evolved chiefly through subcultural styles and pursuits and through vernacular lore and language. The subcultural pimp type became an emblem
of sartorial, gestural, and verbal exuberance in black male spheres, an
exuberance displayed and exchanged primarily in the urban street milieu.[1]
Toasts—such as "The Lame and the Whore" and "Pimping Sam"—celebrated the humorous and misogynist tall tales of pimping prowess in
extended narrative poems, recited primarily in the street, barbershop, and
prison.[2] Because of this stylized display and mythic lore, the pimp, though
a social malefactor, has for a long time been constructed and fetishized by
some as what William Van Deburg calls a "heroic hustler."[3] A prominent
figure in the pantheon of black American archetypes of the twentieth century, the pimp took on particularly striking shapes in the late 1960s and
early 1970s. For the first time, a cluster of mass-mediated and popular-
cultural representations emerged.[4] Fictional and putatively autobiographical pimp narratives, independent films, comedy routines, ethnographic studies, and the political rhetoric of black nationalist leaders were
some of the most notable forms, which deployed new modes of mediation
and technologies of transmission of this street type.[5] Transposed from an
oral, street, and subcultural base, new opportunities for self-recognition,
social group definition, and, above all, imaginary identification were
opened up. Through these divergent forms, the figure came to enjoy a high
profile and even an exalted status in the black male imagination, and

equally reached new socially and spatially removed audiences for the first time.

From the proliferation of pimp culture in the early 1970s, this essay focuses on three texts, which serve as exemplars of the repertoire. First, there is the autobiographic-fictional *Pimp: The Story of My Life* by Iceberg Slim (Robert Beck), set in 1930s and 1940s Chicago and first published by Holloway House. Undoubtedly the single most important and influential pimp text, its publication in 1969 fueled the explosion of pimp culture of the early 1970s.[6] *Pimp* became known simply as "The Book" in some black male circles, and the Holloway House edition alone has sold well over one million copies. The second exemplary text is the 1973 blaxploitation movie *The Mack,* directed by Michael Campus and starring Max Julien and Richard Pryor.[7] The pimp narrative's marketability was confirmed by the commercial success of *The Mack:* this independent movie grossed $3 million in domestic film rentals from a very low budget (a more than healthy return by blaxploitation standards, though only under half the gross of the Warner Brothers-distributed *Super Fly* a year earlier).[8] Black culture critic Darius James contends that these were the "two defining films of the 1970s blaxploitation cycle" and were "the two films mentioned most frequently" by African Americans during the research for his book *That's Blaxploitation!,* pointing to *The Mack's* high cultural profile in black America.[9] The final text under consideration is *Black Players: The Secret World of Black Pimps,* a study by white ethnographers Christina and Richard Milner about San Francisco pimps, first published in 1972.[10] The different formats of these texts—all of which romanticize the pimp—give some measure of the breadth and reach of pimp culture at that time. The sample includes ethnographic and autobiographical elements, most obviously in *Pimp* and *Black Players.* Also, real Oakland pimps, the Ward Brothers, appear in *The Mack,* in which there is a striking cinema verité scene shot at the actual Oakland Player's Ball.

In what follows, there are two interrelated lines of enquiry. One concern is how these texts construct the pimp as popular-cultural icon, and what modes of address they opened up for audiences. A second concern is the tensions between leisure and work mobilized by the pimp figure: between what might be called the pimp's "lifestylization" on the one hand, and his entrepreneurial imagination on the other. The axiom "pimpin' ain't easy" captures the tension between these dual imperatives. Ever the trickster, the pimp means it both literally (these texts are at pains to portray pimping as a difficult and dangerous occupation) and ironically (as Ice-

berg Slim puts it, "the popular belief that a pimp's life is dream stuff, like gangs of sexy girls and money and night-clubbing").[11]

The archetypal pimp tableau, which resides at the center of most pimp narratives, consists of an ostentatiously dressed player, his flashy car, and his scantily dressed prostitutes ("hos"). This pimp tableau was chosen for the publicity campaign of *The Mack*'s theatrical release, indicating its emblematic importance. The film poster captures the pimp pose: Goldie the Mack in the center, dressed in a white sable coat and big hat, holding a bankroll of money, surrounded by four glamorous "hos" (two black, two white), with a rather phallic convertible car in the background. Equally, the poster and title for another blaxploitative pimp film, *The Candy Tangerine Man,* foregrounds the "Black Baron's" spectacular red and yellow Rolls Royce. This preoccupation with the conspicuous and often customized signs of capital accumulation can be explained on both a functional and a marketing level. In terms of the pimp's occupation within the narrative, folklorist Bruce Jackson explains that "a doctor in jeans is still a doctor, but a pimp without flashy clothes and a sharp car is nobody at all."[12] The resplendent display then is an instrumental indicator of status. At the same time, on a marketing level, the focus on flashy display was motivated by its audience appeal. The pressbook for *The Mack* announces, "The illustration of Max Julien as the Mack with his coat, his car, and his girls, keys the campaign."[13] Promoters chose to present and sell these first pimp films to audiences through the deployment of spectacular images, establishing the extent to which pimp iconography accommodated itself to the pop-cultural representation.

The heightened investment in appearance is presented in several descriptive passages in Iceberg Slim's "autobiography" when, as a young wannabe pimp in the 1930s, he first catches sight of successful players. Passages begin with voyeuristic and desiring first-person sentences, communicating a kind of reaction shot to the splendor of the "pimpdafied" display: "A gleaming black custom Duesenberg eased into the curb in front of me. The top was down. My peepers did a triple take. A huge stud was sitting in the back seat. . . . He was sitting between two spectacular high-yellow whores. His diamonds were blazing under the street light." He goes on to attest, "I couldn't believe what I saw."[14] A series of eroticized glances and sensational sights are central to the pleasures of the pimp tableau. Emphasis rests on appearance, on a kind of "look," in two senses of the word; to appropriate historian Robin Kelley's pun, the pimp is "looking to get paid."[15] Iceberg Slim actually invokes a scopophilic metaphor when the passage continues: "My peepers jacked off just watching him and those high powered whores."[16] This graphically evokes the eroticized and even pornographic pleasures of the gaze. In *The Mack,* Goldie exclaims "I feel spectacular!" on the night of the Player's Ball. Goldie communicates his exuberance through the satisfaction furnished by a sense of his own image. Pimp texts are predicated quite literally on image: the pleasures derived from looking are reflexively written into the texts. Im-

portantly, the gaze is not primarily the male subject looking at the objectified female: instead the aspirational and identificatory gaze is exchanged between males or narcissistically directed at one's own masculine self-image. The modes of address opened up within the film self-consciously register the new pleasures offered to the male audience, so that a clear parallel can be established between the pleasures within the text and the pleasures of consuming the text.[17]

An interesting equivalence can be drawn between Iceberg Slim's titil-
lated viewpoint and the ethnographic gaze of the Milners in *Black Players*.
A revealing exchange of looks is signposted on the book-cover photograph:
on the right of the picture is a characteristic black pimp looking toward
the camera with his women, Rolls Royce, fur coat, and hat; on the left are
the white authors, looking over voyeuristically at the pimp tableau. Glamorous Christina, also wearing a lavish fur coat, faces her husband and
holds his arm as she looks over, open-mouthed. Interracial fascination is
powerfully displayed. There is a contemporary depiction of "colonial fantasy" captured in this charged image: it presents a striking evocation of the
uneven power relations in which white objectifies black in the fraught
realm of racialized sexuality. At the same time, the photo to some extent
intimates the productive pleasures of interracial exchange, and as such it
is importantly a complex multidirectional transmission.[18] The only characters entirely written out of the exchange are the white prostitutes in the
Rolls, who are rendered mere accessories. The Milners' gaze is more de-
sirous than disapproving, thereby endorsing the pimp's parade. The photo
frame incorporates the participants into a shared event. Participant observation, then, is curiously central to the enterprise of both ethnography and
pimp culture; however uneven the complex power relationship, ethnogra-
pher (and by extension reader) and pimp are working symbiotically.

Throughout this text, the authors seem to be "getting a bit of the other"
by appropriating some of the conventions of pimp culture at the same time
they register their difference (they take the ethical high ground with repeated assertions about the success of their own conventional and mo-
nogamous marriage). Much is made of Christina's good looks ("a lithe
young woman") and of the pimps' attempts to procure her, when, as participant observer, she becomes a dancing barmaid ("with very few clothes
on") to support herself and her husband through their graduate programs.[19] The pimping parallels are conspicuous. Alongside the interracial
exchange is an interesting intergender exchange insofar as this text provides a rare female perspective on pimp culture. Exploring the figure of
the prostitute is beyond the scope of this essay, but it is worth stressing the
powerful ways in which the book expresses the illicit (albeit problematic)
pleasures afforded women in texts customarily thought of in terms of male
pleasures, as an exclusively male exchange of looks, conducted in a male-
driven environment. In Christina, the "thrill-seeking white women" who
appear in *Pimp* are given a voice.[20] Moreover, there were surely great, if
under-acknowledged, pleasures for the black females viewing *The Mack*.
This R-rated film strategically avoided showing violence toward women,

much as the romanticizing posture of the Milners led them problemati-
cally to downplay the abusiveness of pimping. *The Mack* opened up considerable fantasized pleasures—particularly in the magnetic, smooth-talking figure of Max Julien—for black female as well as male viewers.

In their fascinating study of African American expressive culture,
Shane and Graham White are at pains to emphasize the "importance of
African American street life—of a space in which blacks could watch and
be watched," and particularly the site of "the Stroll" ("special thorough-
fares affording sites for aesthetic display").[21] The soundtrack for *The Mack*
includes a cut called "Mack's Stroll."[22] In pimp texts the Stroll is restaged,
transposing the street space into new contexts of mediated transmission.
The spectacle-driven form of film lent itself to transposing the street display, as any viewing of the burlesque scenes and flamboyant attire of the
blaxploitation cycle bears out. The press campaign for *The Mack* ("designed . . . mainly for the black audience") prefigured the pleasures afforded the movie audience, asserting that "it is highly recommended that
the disc jockeys, record dealers, key contacts be invited to the theater after
opening to see this picture with an audience. It's an experience!" There
was an interesting reconfiguring of community going on here. The campaign urged promoters to set up a highly mediated film-screening situation in which the black cultural gatekeepers watched the audience watch
the mack, who in turn registers on screen the pleasure of being watched
("I feel spectacular!"). When the cultural intermediaries were to review
the film they would be reporting not just on the text but on the event of the
screening. The site of the Stroll was in various ways transposed into the
movie theater or onto the page. Through these intermediaries and in the
social practices of consumption—particularly in the vocalized responses
of black working-class audiences—the viewer was given a participatory
role. The mediated enactment of the Stroll should not be understood as a
total break with the proximate street situation. The participatory street
exchange of styles, gestures, language, and lore was not simply replaced by
regulated passive pop-cultural consumption—say, the barbershop performance of a pimp toast replaced by *reading* Iceberg Slim's stylized words, or
a swaggering subcultural pimp type posing on the Stroll replaced by
watching Goldie strut on screen. Instead, in several ways, some of the
dynamics of the street exchange prevailed in the processes of consumption and circulation of these pimp texts.

The pimp tableau constitutes the heightened moment of success: long
striven for and difficult to maintain. The dandified display strikingly refuses dominant society's type-casting of African Americans as subordi-

nate. As such, the pimp shares some of the sophisticated and frequently resistive style politics that have long been identified in spectacular youth subcultures and in black diasporic cultural practices.[23] As Stuart Hall remarks, "within the black repertoire, *style*—which mainstream cultural critics often believe to be the mere husk, the wrapping, the sugar coating on the pill—has become *itself* the subject of what is going on." He goes on to characterize the signs of diasporic blackness as the "linguistic innovations in rhetorical stylization of the body, forms of occupying an alien social space, heightened expressions, hairstyles, ways of walking, standing, and talking."[24] The term "lifestylization" neatly articulates three elements of the pimp pose. First, it incorporates *the life* (or "the sporting life") from the hustling lexicon, grounding the term in a black subcultural and often illegal street milieu. Second, "lifestylization" calls up the leisured-class image and the aristocratic front of the parasitic pimp, whereby projecting an image of *lifestyle* becomes the pimp's very occupation. For instance, Goldie the Mack instructs his prostitutes to think of themselves as "ladies of leisure" and as "qualified stockholders," tapping into the "undesirable" aristocratic model of expenditure and public display. From this acute emphasis on the lifestyle pose, the pimp emerges as a key player in an alternative mythic hierarchy of black urban America, self-consciously constructed—at least on one level—in opposition to the Protestant work ethic.[25] That the pimp's very occupation is founded on the successful projection of lifestyle suggests a fusion of work and play that serves symbolically to disrupt the capitalist division between work and leisure.

Finally, "lifestylization" suggests a rearticulation of the style politics of the leisured class within the frame of heightened black *stylization*. It is above all in the heightened style—the gestures, clothes, language, and so forth—that the pimp announces racial distinctiveness and distinction. Through stylization the mack proclaims his ascendancy, which in turn extends to his core audience of lower-class black men.[26] The flashy, sometimes overblown spectacle asserts a powerful street identification. Thus, lifestylization is the fusion of upper- and lower-class identifications, a spectacular rejection of middle-American mores. Racially encoded dandyism presents a symbolic affront to a dominant social order founded on the tenets of the Protestant work ethic and classlessness, and it is from here that a good deal of the pleasure and power of the pimp pose is derived. Through outrageous style politics and occupational pursuits, the pimp type is seen to repudiate the "square world" where workers do "chump jobs" for "chump change." He serves as an icon for the rejection of not only unfulfilling, mechanized labor but also the very distinction between labor and leisure itself. In historical terms, this rejection of "square"-world tenets and embrace of an alternative world could probably have gained such popular cultural resonance only *after* the decline of the initial optimism and integrationist promise of the civil rights years. It reflected black disillusionment with the possibility or even desirability of being able to gain access to conventional society on equal terms.

The emphasis on lifestyle over occupation and style over substance positions the pimp within the black trickster repertory.[27] The Milners capture this equivalence: "the pimp hero is a trickster. By the use of wit and guile he earns a rich living and maintains aristocratic tastes without having to resort either to violence or to physical labor."[28] The image then is of spectacular ease (even if it "ain't easy"), of finesse and effrontery, and of a putative refusal of work and of violence. However, because the pimp is a trickster, these ostensible and ostentatious refusals cannot simply be taken at face value—though, for sure, it invites mainstream society to take it thus. In fact, the exhibitionist pose masks an equally important but introspective narrative of entrepreneurial endeavor and discipline. It comes as no surprise that Goldie's women are not "ladies of leisure"; equally, the mack is by no means simply an indolent dandy.

In tension with the mythic pimp's lifestylization is a lean and disciplined entrepreneurial imagination. One must not confuse his languid pose with complacency or lethargy. Instead, he presents a highly mannered leisured image, which fits well with the oxymoronic well-timed spontaneity, disciplined "cool pose," and practiced ease that have long been associated with the manners and practices of African Americans, perhaps most patently embodied by the figure of the jazz musician.[29] In pimp narratives, the hero stresses the hard work that goes into his lifestylization. The pimp needs to develop powerful rhetorical skills and street smartness, and he must adhere to a strict "race-specific code of conduct."[30] Iceberg Slim boasts more than once that his I.Q. is 175 and his advanced street psychology is intimated when he laconically invokes Freud.[31] In pimp texts, the code is developed through a kind of alternative schooling, which often takes place in the prison—a classic site of black male rites-of-passage and conversion narratives. An incarcerated Iceberg Slim ruminates: "I was fascinated by the yarns they spun about their pimping ability. They had a lot of bullshit, and I was stealing as much as I could from them to use when I got out."[32] The central relationship is between the established, paternalist player who teaches the "rules of the game" to the young aspirational hustler. In black idiomatic terms, he "pulls his coat." Narrative development often centers on this handing over of knowledge and power from father figure to young man. In *Pimp*, Sweet Jones schools Iceberg Slim; in *The Mack*, an Iceberg Slim-identified figure (recognizable because of his trademark raspy voice) teaches Goldie. The pedagogic impulse is underlined by the educational metaphors: the term "pimpology" has wide currency, and Iceberg Slim's autobiography has a chapter titled "A Degree in Pimping," indicating the difficulty, discipline, and time commitment associated with becoming a successful pimp.[33]

In terms of social consumption, anecdotal evidence points to interesting parallels between the transferals of knowledge in the narratives and the real-life exchange of pimp texts. Darius James recalls the memorable occasion when as an adolescent his father gave him *Pimp* ("I read it and shared it with my friends"). Hip-hop celebrity Fab Five Freddy remembers the great impact the book had on him, after it was recommended by "a brother who had a lot of knowledge of the streets." Gangsta rapper Tracey Marrow appropriated his stage name Ice-T from Iceberg Slim and in the liner notes to his first album acknowledges him as "my mentor." In "An Open Letter to Iceberg Slim," a distraught Vietnam War veteran seeks his counsel: "After having virtually memorized your three books, I decided I could come to you as you came to Sweet Jones in *Pimp* for advice."[34] An assertively black, male, lower-class mentoring process is intimated by this anecdotal evidence; an intergenerational street initiation is being negotiated in and through pimp narratives. The Book emerges as a kind of fusion of school textbook (for young men disaffected with, disappointed by, and economically excluded from institutionalized schooling), a sacred players' bible, and a self-help or etiquette manual on sexual relations and style practices, all of which involve very active reading practices. Crucially, this constituted a popular-cultural initiation into pimp culture and into careers in the entertainment world, and only very rarely an initiation into actual pimping. As James reflects: "We fantasized and talked about [the life]. We emulated the pimp in appearance. But most of us weren't cut out for it. *Especially me*."[35] Still, the fact that the pimp figure's influence operated largely on the level of fantasized identification is not to disclaim its powerful potential for masculinist and misogynist instruction. And these male-centered stories were echoed in and reinforced by other elements within African American popular culture at that time—perhaps most strikingly in the macho revival in post-1965 soul.

The pimp hero also practices impressive feats of sexual restraint. Though surrounded by attractive, submissive women, the pimp protagonist, following a strict code, abstains from sex unless it is economically motivated. The maxim "A pimp keeps his dick in his pocket" neatly conveys this enterprising sexual forbearance and control. The Milners explain that the saying is "a double entendre meaning (1) he controls his sexual desire, and (2) his dick is where the money is."[36] Tellingly, once Goldie becomes a pimp, the only woman we see him embrace in the rest of the film is his mother. In Donald Goines's *Street Players*, Earl-the-Pearl's macking empire starts to crumble as soon as he falls in love with Vickie and engages in sex for pleasure rather than power, thereby deviating from the code. The tension in these narratives is between the image of sexual prowess and the narrative of hard-won sexual discipline. Maintaining a strict business ethic in relations with women, the pimp is "a gutter god who has put his emotions and sex drive into a kind of commercial cold storage."[37] In sum, the mythic black pimp is heroic because he powerfully controverts the longstanding racist stereotypes (laziness, "brawn over brains," and sexual wantonness) while bolstering others (sexual prowess).

In light of these interior narratives of self-discipline, pedagogy, and enterprise, the pimp emerges in some ways as a consummate capitalist. From their interviews with pimps, the Milners learned that the "player conceives of himself as a small businessman within the capitalist tradition of free enterprise and considers himself to be no more corrupt in his methods than the legitimate businessman trying to get ahead in a ruthless, competitive, materialistic economy."[38] Hustling *mores* announce a leveling out of ethical distinction between legitimate and illegitimate business venture, long a mainstay of America's tradition of gangsterism. The Milners' volume came out in the same year that the blockbuster movie *The Godfather* powerfully glorified Italian American gangsterism, pointing to the popular fascination with these themes well beyond black America at that time. Equally, Iceberg Slim's hustling memoirs were doubtless informed by the ethnic gangsta chic of their 1930s Chicago setting. Thus for Van Deburg, black heroic hustlers "were aspiring magnates of materialism who needed no Wharton School credentialization to understand that organized crime occupied an unhallowed but secure place on the continuum of American business systems."[39] Yet as Robin Kelley importantly points out, black hustling ethics (certainly the pimp texts considered here) are often *anti*-accumulationist. "Possessing 'capital' was not the ultimate goal; rather, money was primarily a means by which hustlers could avoid wage work and negotiate status through the purchase of prestigious commodities."[40] This point is borne out by the pimp's fetishizing display, which could hardly be read as a simple ode to capitalism. Moreover, occupational security is never a feature of these narratives, which are predicated on the romantic notion of risk-taking, high-skill pursuits. Described disparagingly by the drug baron as a "penny-pushing pimp scheme" in *The Mack,* the role is constructed almost, ironically, as a "labor of love." This subcultural figure then is symbolically and substantively distinct from other black hustling enterprises (particularly from the figure of the drug dealer), yet further removed from the image of organized crime and assimilationist intent mobilized in other ethnic gangster narratives, and still further removed from the business ethics of mainstream enterprise culture.

Among the pantheon of heroic hustlers, the pimp's distinctiveness rests on an occupational practice that is predicated on the commodification of sexuality and the exploitation of women. The texts under consideration present very different takes on relations between pimp and ho—Iceberg Slim's extreme physical and psychical abuse of women is far removed from the hippie-inflected Bay-area macking of Goldie, which has more in common with the Milners, who emerge largely as pimp apologists. In all cases, male dominance and the commodification of sex in these accounts offer heightened versions of prevailing gender relations in America in ways that are at once productively unsettling and troublingly exploitative: they both demystify and remystify dominant codes. The pimping model, in which the patriarch owns a "stable" of women, certainly presents a more extreme, male-dominated alternative to the bourgeois patriarchal marriage. The subversive potential lies in the defamiliarizing effect that this alternative structure imposes on conventionally mythologized gender relations. Suggestive overlaps emerge between the two structures. Within the realm of American film, viewers have long been accustomed to texts that positioned women in passive and victimized roles, so the textual priorities of *The Mack* did not deviate far from the conventions of mainstream Hollywood of the early 1970s. Still, there can be little doubt that the overriding gender posture of these pimp narratives, with their pronounced controlling ethic (of self and of whore), worked to reinforce and romanticize masculine dominance.

All pimp heroes speak of "brainwashing," whereby the women are constructed as consummate occupational dupes who are tricked into a state of false consciousness by the smooth-talking player, then handing over their hard-earned cash. As Goldie sweet-talks his "hos" in the planetarium scene, we see their faces in close-up looking in awe at his light show in the darkened theater. The reflexivity is blatant: we too are beguiled in the movie theater, duped by the pleasures of this popular-cultural transmission.[41] The scene presents an ambivalent parable of the classic Marxist critique in which brainwashing mass entertainment bolsters capitalist relations. The self-consciously exploitative imperatives of these narratives are, of course, paralleled by the flagrantly capitalist terms and conditions of production and distribution in exploitation cinema and pulp fiction (which are only redoubled by racial and gender inequities in the production process). Exploitation films are motivated by the most crude desire to turn profit. Yet, as film scholars have argued, in their low-budget rendering of formulaic types, these films often productively expose the normative conventions that are naturalized in mainstream films. This process seems to hold especially true for *The Mack*.[42] The fact that its exploitative motivations are exposed and explained—that the pimp lets the audience in on his con game and that the formal operations of the film provide a heightened exposition of the "ground rules" on which mainstream movies are constituted—does have demystifying effects. It is important not to overstate the subversive potential of these textual strategies in the customary theoretical move of privileging formal meanings over content, but there can be little doubt that the film contains salient disruptive properties.

There are many reasons for the pimp figure's emergence and valence in the late 1960s and early 1970s—both in terms of why these narratives emerged at that time, and why they found such a receptive audience among working-class black men, and indeed among educated whites. American culture was undergoing dramatic structural changes in public attitudes toward sexuality, which fueled the relaxation of state regulations. There was a pronounced shift in ideas about what should and could be printed, filmed, and studied, opening up mass-mediated outlets to more alternative and explicit stories. At the same time there was a growing perception that, to use Daniel Leab's term, "Black is Box-office," so that African American markets were being both catered to and constituted in unprecedented ways.[43]

If new commercial conditions of supply were important then so too were new kinds of demand. The work, play, and lifestylization of pimp thematics may have negotiated particular predicaments and desires of working-class black men at the beginning of the 1970s. Many historians have suggested that a profound note of disappointment and disaffection was beginning to creep into black politics by the beginning of the 1970s. Critics point to the Nixon administration's shift to the right, marked by the cessation of the War on Poverty, which spoke to a posture of increasing white apathy toward black issues, and by the FBI's brutally repressive Counter-Intelligence Program, which worked to destroy the leadership of black activist organizations.[44] Historian Clayborne Carson dates the beginning of the "post-revolutionary era" to 1968, precipitating a simultaneous decline of black militant politics and an upsurge of conservative power in American politics during the 1970s.[45] In broad terms, then, the pimp's lack of faith in macrolevel change cohered with the changing black political complexion of the time. Political frustration and diminishing employment opportunities for blue-collar workers as the economy started to slump in the early 1970s may well have fostered a greater real and symbolic investment among lower-class men in underground and illegal activities. For young black men facing unemployment there were clear culture-building possibilities in exalting heroic hustlers—particularly the "lifestylized" pimp—who repudiated mainstream and menial jobs and joblessness in favor of antiassimilationist pursuits that at least promised a viable means of income. Importantly, this is not only a symbolic identification. Pimp narratives provided inspiration and guidance for young men aspiring to careers in entertainment and sport—the classic "legit" opportunities open to them that also constituted a rejection of menial and low-pay jobs. Moreover, as skilled and semiskilled manufacturing job opportunities started to diminish, the pimp figure's patriarchal authoritarianism, of all the black hustler types, may have offered young black men symbolic respite from perceived threats to traditional gender roles. Robin Kelley persuasively contends that the pimp's popularity among this group, in the late 1960s at least, was partially a backlash response to the image of black matriarchal dominance that had been promulgated by the 1965 Moynihan Report.[46] The exaltation of the pimp figure among black men may be understood as a hypermasculine rejoinder to the contents of the Report, and more generally, as Van Deburg puts it, as a "hostile counterproposal to the women's liberation movement."[47]

At the same time as socioeconomic conditions began to deteriorate for the majority of black people, new opportunities in black electoral politics and for black class advancement and social mobility were still emerging, in the wake of civil rights legislative gains. Income distribution among African Americans became more equal up until 1968, after which increasing black class polarization set in.[48] New economic and political divisions were opening up in black society after 1968, often negotiated in and around popular cultural sites. When the pressbook for *The Mack* prescribed posting in "mass transportation and outdoor advertising where it will reach the black audience" and advised television promoters to "buy black-oriented shows," it both described and perpetuated blaxploitation's primary audience demographic. The corporate and independent marketing strategies of these movies worked to cement new breaches in black class belonging. As Brian Ward has observed in the context of black recordings and radio, the "industry did begin to exploit, and thereby accentuate and help give musical expression to, the deepening fissures in black society in the post-revolutionary era."[49] While the black (male) urban moviegoers and readers emphatically returned the look of the mack, the largely disapproving black middle class absorbed the affront by rejecting this popular-cultural transmission.[50] The pimp figure's uncompromisingly ghetto-oriented posture, flamboyant attire, and lack of civic responsibility constituted a powerful repudiation of black middle-class assimilationist imperatives and, in turn, of that potential audience group. New processes of class and race identification emerged from the increasing purchase of mass-mediated culture in black (and white) life and especially from the new targeting of niche markets and the consequent recognition, perpetuation, and circumscription of working-class black leisure and pleasure. While identity and community have always been constituted through consumption and leisure practices, the evidence points to the suggestion that the social effects of cultural consumption were becoming more influential and far-reaching than they ever had been.

An examination of one emblematic relationship between two key archetypes of the era—the pimp and the figure of the black nationalist—sheds light on some of these shifting sensibilities. In *The Mack,* the political upheavals of young black men at the turn of the seventies are reflected in the parabolic relationship between Goldie and his brother Olinga (played by Roger E. Mosley). Set in Oakland, the birthplace of the Black Panther Party, the movie's central tension rests on the two brothers' opposing worldviews: Goldie's lumpen entrepreneurial imagination and Olinga's black revolutionary activism. The fraught fraternal relationship serves allegorically for the contested group affiliations of young black men, affiliations underscored by the classic Willie Hutch soundtrack single "Brother's Gonna Work It Out." Both brothers see the American system as racist and exploitative, but they differ in their responses to this situation. Goldie activates his cynicism better to exploit the system, whereas his brother tries to dispel the false consciousness of all oppressed people through community action. In a climactic scene, Goldie exclaims, "Being rich and black *means* something!"—expressing the purchase he places on his own affluent image and oppositional style politics. Then, addressing both his admirers within the film and his burgeoning blaxploitation audience in the movie theater, he announces, "there are all kinds of heroes now. There are kids out there that even look up to me!"

Carol Speed, the actor who plays Lulu (Goldie's "bottom woman" or chief prostitute), recalls the making of the movie: "There was a lot going on in Oakland. . . . During the time we were making *The Mack,* especially with Huey Newton (founder of the Black Panther Party) and the Panthers. That energy spilled over into the film. A lot of people used to come over to the movie set, which was in a nightclub, and hang out; people like Newton, Bobby Womack, and Sly Stone."[51] The sense of cultural innovation and political foment is remarkable: the expansive funk of the burgeoning and highly successful blaxploitation soundtrack form; vanguardist black musicians and actors; Richard Pryor's prodigious stand-up comedic aura; activist politics and the Black Panther Party—in short, the geographical and cultural site and moment of black stylized resistance and resistive style.

A year before the release of *The Mack,* the Milners prefigured the movie's central tension: "Today there are conflicting views of black manhood which imply two opposing strategies of getting Whitey. The black militant feels fulfilled in his manhood by confronting the Man and telling him where to get off. The pimp may agree with what the Black militant is saying, but he prefers the less visible strategy, one that has more cool, more game to it, and one which has immediate personal rewards."[52] Though affinities between the two figures had been explored in black nationalist literature—perhaps most fully in Eldridge Cleaver's grim notion of the "Supermasculine Menial"—they remained importantly distinct in pimp narratives.[53] Olinga operates in the realm of overt political mobilization and social politics where Goldie negotiates identity through lumpenproletarian style politics. Yet this is no dichotomy: Olinga's black nationalism is as assuredly stylized as Goldie's style is political. As Robin Kelley has persuasively argued in relation to Malcolm X, "his participation in the underground subculture of black working-class youth . . . was not a detour on the road to political consciousness but rather an essential element of his radicalization."[54] The black nationalist mission of politically mobilizing the hustler—transforming cynicism into militancy, individualism into insurgency—is written into the film. For Huey P. Newton, the Black Panther mandate was "to transform many of the so-called criminal activities going on in the street into something political."[55]

The Mack charts this narrative course of political awakening: at the end Goldie's mother has been murdered as a result of his pimping and he gives up "the life." Alone and stripped of his pimpsta garb in the closing scene, he takes the bus to Alabama. This marks a wholesale repudiation of the lifestylization of the pimp. Goldie counter-migrates to the South, a spiritual journey into heritage and past that inverts the black diasporic route from oppressive, old-world South to urban, sophisticated North. Goldie transforms twice, like Malcolm Little—who, after arriving in the North,

reinvented himself as Detroit Red the hipster and then, in a second political transformation, as Malcolm X.[56] After struggling to become a high-
profile pimp, Iceberg Slim, during a long prison term, experienced a spiritual and political conversion. Whether this was a real-life conversion is
the subject of critical contention, but either way it is importantly built into
the autobiographical narrative.[57] Like *The Autobiography of Malcolm X*,
Slim's hustling years are recounted retrospectively, from a privileged and
censuring position. This is the very moral and temporal distance that both
circumscribes and in some ways licenses the telling of the exciting,
lifestylized tales. It is the first spectacular transformation at least as much
as the second spiritual one that is carried away from these pop-cultural
documents. The seductive pleasures of pimp figuration encourage identification with Goldie's stylization, in much the same way that Detroit
Red's resplendent conk and zoot suit stay in our memories, however vehe-
mently he later denounced them. Certainly, these multifaceted narratives—particularly in the tensions between narrative and spectacle—open
up spaces for multiple audience identifications. Regrettably, the sense of
nascent insurgency captured in the style politics of these pimp texts and
realized in their narrative resolutions did not tally with the growing mood
of conservatism and disaffection as the 1970s progressed. This historical
context—the growing ascendance of style politics over conventional forms
of activism for working-class black youth—perhaps renders the spectacular pimp tableau more compelling than the conversion narrative, and may
start to explain the figure's continuing resonance in the post-revolutionary
era.[58]

The pimp culture of the 1970s presented a suggestive popular-cultural
take on what Robin Kelley has described as the "struggle to carve out a
kind of liminal space between work and play, labor and performance" in
lower-class black communities.[59] Complex negotiations of leisure as work
and work as leisure are played out within these texts. The culture-building
properties inherent in the interdependent dynamics of labor and
lifestylization speak to both the anxieties and aspirations of young black
men. At the same time, the "liminal space between work and play" extends
beyond narrative content; it also offers a suggestive description of the site
of popular-cultural engagement itself. In complex ways the audience,
reader, and participant observer are written into these texts. The formal
and narrative imperatives of pimp texts present spectacular attractions
and opportunities for active engagement. Competing reading strategies
can be seen to parallel the pimp's dual dynamics of work and play. Productive tensions emerge between, on the one hand, the sense of instant

gratification provided by the pimp's lifestylization that invites a passive, fantasized decoding posture and, on the other hand, the hard work impetus of disciplined enterprise that encourages a more active, realist mode of consumption. This formulation, though useful, does overschematize the divisions. In both pimp texts and consumption practices, the sense that work and play are feeding into each other, the sense of *liminality*, is crucial to their productive politics. The early 1970s was a moment of striking exuberance in lower-class black popular culture, arguably exemplified by pimp culture, at the same time as it was a time of increasing political-activist diffidence. Thus, it seems probable that mass-mediated popular culture was taking on a more important role in black lives as avenues for political action were foreclosed, or at least were channeled increasingly into the cultural field. This coheres with the wider forces of depoliticization and conservative retrenchment in 1970s America. In the responses of audiences, and even knowingly written into the pimp texts themselves, there is an acknowledgment of the great pleasures furnished by non-prescribed, stylized, and spectacular black popular culture. The articulations of racial and class identification in pimp texts were on the whole politically resistive. Pimp texts presented a symbolic fusing of upper and lower class, and of labor and leisure. The pimp became a totem of the antiaccommodationist, yet aspirational, desires of lower-class black men, negotiated through the complex depictions of working at leisure.

Notes

1. On the pimp's street style in the first part of the twentieth century, see Shane White and Graham White, *Stylin': African American Expressive Culture from Its Beginnings to the Zoot Suit* (Ithaca, N.Y.: Cornell University Press, 1998), 220–47.

2. For a transcription of pimp toasts, see Bruce Jackson, *"Get Your Ass in the Water and Swim Like Me": Narrative Poetry from Black Oral Tradition* (Cambridge: Harvard University Press, 1974).

3. William L. Van Deburg, *Black Camelot: African-American Culture Heroes in Their Times, 1960–1980* (Chicago: University of Chicago Press, 1997), 127–96.

4. For a survey of filmic portrayals of black heroic hustlers before this time, see Mark A. Reid, "The Black Gangster Film," in *The Film Genre Reader II*, ed. Barry Keith Grant (Austin: University of Texas Press, 1995), 456–73.

5. For blaxploitation films that center on pimps, see *The Mack*, Michael Campus, 1973; *Willie Dynamite*, Gilbert Moses III, 1973; *The Candy Tangerine Man*, Matt Cimber, 1975. For black lewd stand-up comedy routines, see the videos and sound recordings of Richard Pryor, Redd Foxx, and the eighteen albums of Rudy

Ray Moore, which have sold more than one million units. For black nationalist literature that draws on pimp themes, see Eldridge Cleaver, *Soul on Ice* (New York: McGraw-Hill, 1968); H. Rap Brown, *Die, Nigger, Die* (New York: Dial Press, 1969); Bobby Seale, *Seize the Time* (New York: Random House, 1970); Huey P. Newton, *Revolutionary Suicide* (New York: Ballantine, 1973). For pimp fiction, see Donald Goines, *Whoreson: The Story of a Ghetto Pimp* (Los Angeles: Holloway House, 1972); Donald Goines, *Street Players* (Los Angeles: Holloway House, 1973); Iceberg Slim, *Pimp: The Story of My Life* (1967; reprint, Edinburgh: Payback Press, 1996); and Iceberg Slim, *The Naked Soul of Iceberg Slim* (1971; reprint, Edinburgh: Payback Press, 1996). For 1970s pimp-themed music, see for instance Frank Zappa's "Willie the Pimp," *Hot Rats*, 1970, and the work of Johnny Guitar Watson.

6. There is some contention as to whether the date of first publication of *Pimp* was 1967 (as Peter A. Muckley contends in his account of the author's extraordinary life, "Iceberg Slim: Robert Beck—A True Essay at a BioCriticism of an Ex-Outlaw Artist," *Black Scholar* 26, no. 1 [1996]: 18–25) or 1969 (the more usually cited date).

7. The screenwriter of *The Mack*, Robert J. Poole, had served a five-year prison term for having pimped for twelve years, adding to the film's street credentials; the director and producer, as with so many blaxploitation films, were both white.

8. *Super Fly*, Gordon Parks Jr., 1972; sales figures from James Robert Parish and George H. Hill, *Black Action Films* (Jefferson, N.C.: McFarland, 1989), 210, 292.

9. Darius James, *That's Blaxploitation! Roots of the Baadasssss 'Tude* (New York: St. Martin's Griffin, 1995), 81.

10. Christina and Richard Milner, *Black Players: The Secret World of Black Pimps* (1972; reprint, London: Michael Joseph, 1973).

11. Slim, *Naked Soul*, 34.

12. Jackson, *"Get Your Ass in the Water,"* 106.

13. *The Mack* (Pressbook, Cinerama Releasing, 1973).

14. Slim, *Pimp*, 92.

15. Robin D. G. Kelley, "Looking To Get Paid: How Some Black Youth Put Culture to Work" in Kelley, *Yo' Mama's Disfunktional! Fighting the Culture Wars in Urban America* (Boston: Beacon, 1997), 43–77.

16. Slim, *Pimp*, 92.

17. My discussion of the reflexive pleasures of film draws on the work of Peter Krämer; see for instance, "Would You Take Your Child To See This Film? The Cultural and Social Work of the Family-Adventure Movie," in *Contemporary Hollywood Cinema*, ed. Steve Neale and Murray Smith (London: Routledge, 1998), 294–311.

18. Such depictions of interracial exchange were far from new. For a strikingly analogous exchange, see W. T. Lhamon Jr.'s discussion of folk drawings of the blackface lore cycle in *Raising Cain: Blackface Performance from Jim Crow to Hip Hop* (Cambridge: Harvard University Press, 1998), 1–55. At the same time, *Black Players* clearly tells a white middle-class story of its day: in the post-1960s "sexualized society," it enacts white fascination and desire at a time of increasing racial

interaction, and of course it expresses a blithe and problematic young white liberalism (exemplified by these Berkeley graduate students at the beginning of the 1970s).

19. Milner and Milner, *Black Players*, 15–27.

20. Slim, *Pimp*, 13.

21. White and White, *Stylin,'* 225, 220–47, 224.

22. Willie Hutch, *The Mack*, Motown, 1973.

23. For the classic Birmingham-school studies of youth subcultures see Stuart Hall and Tony Jefferson, eds., *Resistance Through Rituals: Youth Subcultures in Post-war Britain* (London: Hutchinson, 1976); Dick Hebdige, *Subculture: The Meaning of Style* (London: Methuen, 1979). For an influential discussion of black diasporic style practices, see Kobena Mercer, "Black Hair/Style Politics," *New Formations* 3 (1987): 33–54.

24. Stuart Hall, "What Is This 'Black' in Black Popular Culture?" in *Black Popular Culture*, ed. Gina Dent (Seattle: Bay, 1992), 27, 28.

25. On the hustler's rejection of the Protestant work ethic, see Robin D. G. Kelley, *Race Rebels: Culture, Politics and the Black Working Class* (New York: Free Press, 1994), 173–75; and Julius Hudson, "The Hustling Ethic," in *Rappin' and Stylin' Out: Communication in Urban Black America*, ed. Thomas Kochman (Urbana: University of Illinois Press, 1972), 414–15. Kelley explores subcultural style politics and the symbolic rejection of menial labor during the industrialization of World War II, when there was at least a relative availability of low-paid employment. It is interesting to pursue the idea that the real and ideological division between mechanized work and organized "free time" has increasingly decomposed for working-class people with the onset of deindustrialization in America's urban centers. The precipitous decline in even unfulfilling wage labor and the consequent new meanings of "free time" may have spurred a reconfiguring of the relationship between work and leisure, and between labor and entertainment, in lower-class spheres.

26. John W. Roberts sets out a useful "culture-building" model for the different but related context of black folklore in *From Trickster to Badman: The Black Folk Hero in Slavery and Freedom* (Philadelphia: University of Pennsylvania Press, 1989), 1–15.

27. On the affinities between trickster and pimp figures, see Lawrence W. Levine, *Black Culture and Black Consciousness: Afro-American Folk Thought from Slavery to Freedom* (New York: Oxford University Press, 1977), 382–86.

28. Milner and Milner, *Black Players*, 271.

29. Shane and Graham White draw out the real-life equivalence between pimp and jazz man, particularly in the person of Jelly Roll Morton. See *Stylin,'* 240–43.

30. Van Deburg sets out the "Rules" of the code in *Black Camelot*, 142–53.

31. Slim, *Pimp*, 38, 41.

32. Ibid., 35.

33. Ibid., 55–66.

34. James, *That's Blaxploitation!*, 91, 98; Ice-T, *Rhyme Pays*, Sire Records, 1987; Slim, *Naked Soul*, 128.

35. James, *That's Blaxploitation!*, 99.

36. Milner and Milner, *Black Players*, 63.

37. Slim, *Naked Soul*, 31–32.

38. Milner and Milner, *Black Players*, 244.

39. Van Deburg, *Black Camelot*, 140.

40. Kelley, *Race Rebels*, 174.

41. This forces an interesting audience identification with Goldie's women; at the same time it serves to reinforce the feminization of passive mass-cultural consumption.

42. See for instance Pam Cook, "Exploitation Films and Feminism," *Screen* 17, no. 2 (1976): 122–27.

43. Daniel J. Leab, *From Sambo to Superspade: The Black Experience in Motion Pictures* (London: Secker and Warburg, 1973), 235–63.

44. On the changing political complexion in recent black America, see Michael C. Dawson, *Behind the Mule: Race and Class in African-American Politics* (Princeton, N.J.: Princeton University Press, 1994), 1–44; on the changing socio-cultural climate of the black power era, see William L. Van Deburg, *New Day in Babylon: The Black Power Movement and American Culture, 1965–1975* (Chicago: University of Chicago Press, 1992).

45. Clayborne Carson, "Rethinking African-American Political Thought in the Post-Revolutionary Era," in *The Making of Martin Luther King and the Civil Rights Movement*, ed. Brian Ward and Tony Badger (London: Macmillan, 1996), 115–27.

46. Kelley, *Race Rebels*, 216.

47. Van Deburg, *Black Camelot*, 135.

48. Dawson, *Behind the Mule*, 36.

49. Brian Ward, *Just My Soul Responding: Rhythm and Blues, Black Consciousness and Race Relations* (London: UCL Press, 1998), 427.

50. *New York Times* critic Vincent Canby dismissed the film as "inept" at the time of its release. Canby, quoted in Parish and Hill, *Black Action Films*, 210; and, considering its high profile with black audiences, *The Mack* is surprisingly neglected in most critical accounts of the blaxploitation cycle. Equally, Iceberg Slim has been, as Muckley laments, "totally neglected by establishment critics," "Iceberg Slim," 22.

51. Gerald Martinez et al., eds., *What It Is . . . What It Was! The Black Film Explosion of the '70s in Words and Pictures* (New York: Hyperion, 1998), 168.

52. Milner and Milner, *Black Players*, 267.

53. Cleaver, *Soul on Ice*, 176–90.

54. Kelley, *Race Rebels*, 163.

55. Newton, *Revolutionary Suicide*, 141.

56. Malcolm X with Alex Haley, *The Autobiography of Malcolm X* (New York: Grove, 1964).

57. He dedicates the later postpimp *Naked Soul of Iceberg Slim* to Malcolm X, Angela Davis, and Huey P. Newton, among others. On the critical dispute over the sincerity of his spiritual transformation, see Muckley, "Iceberg Slim," 22.

58. To give an indication of the recent resurgence of interest in pimp culture, see Brent Owens's 1998 controversial HBO documentary "Pimps Up, Hos Down"; Allen and Albert Hughes's 1998 independent movie, *American Pimp*; a remake of *The Mack* is, at time of writing, in production at Twentieth Century Fox; the work of Iceberg Slim and other pulp-fictional authors have recently enjoyed high-gloss republication by, among others, Old School Books (U.S.) and Payback Press (U.K.). On the prevalence of pimp culture in gangsta rap, see my article "'Who's the Mack?': The Performativity and Politics of the Pimp Figure in Gangsta Rap," *Journal of American Studies* 34, no. 1 (April, 2000): 115–36.

59. Kelley, *Yo' Mama's Disfunktional!*, 57.

Acknowledgment

The cover of *Black Players: The Secret World of Black Pimps* is reprinted on page 215 by permission of Little, Brown and Company.

11

Mau-Mauing the Filmmakers

Should Black Power Take the Rap
for Killing *Nat Turner,* the Movie?[1]

Scot French

Nat Turner, sources said, was as good as dead.

The *Hollywood Reporter* broke the news on January 14, 1970: Twentieth
Century Fox was planning to announce a "feature film hiatus" that would
close the studio except for television production for at least six months.
"Immediately affected," the trade publication noted, "is *Nat Turner,* the
David Wolper production, which Sidney Lumet was to have directed." In
addition to *Nat Turner,* at least six other films slated for production had
been postponed or canceled, including *The Salzburg Connection, Port-
noy's Complaint,* and *Play It Again, Sam.* Heavy production costs on three
recently completed feature films, *Hello, Dolly!, Tora! Tora! Tora!,* and
Patton, were cited as one reason for the studio shutdown, high money
costs as another. Two days later, Twentieth Century Fox President Richard
D. Zanuck confirmed that the studio would not be shooting any feature
films for at least six months; *Nat Turner* was one of the casualties.[2]

The news out of Hollywood came as a shock to residents of Southampton County, Virginia, where the filming of *Nat Turner* was already in
preproduction. Not since August 1831, when Turner himself led a bloody
slave uprising that left fifty-seven white people dead and hundreds of
black people terrorized or killed in retaliation, had the sparsely populated
county been the locus of such frenzied activity. For nearly six months local
residents had been negotiating with the filmmakers over the historical
accuracy of the script, the rental of properties as staging areas, and the
hiring of extras to play masters and slaves. Deep-seated reservations about
the content of the film—based on the nationally acclaimed but locally
despised novel, *The Confessions of Nat Turner,* by Tidewater native Will-

iam Styron—were eased by promises of community involvement in vetting the script and economic benefits for black and white residents alike.[3]

Gilbert W. Francis, a white Southampton County lawyer hired by Twentieth Century Fox to serve as its community liaison, informed reporters that the film project had been temporarily delayed because of rising production costs. "Latest cost estimates have placed the budget figure as high as $6.5 million," he was quoted as saying. "By cutting out every possible nonessential, the company can get the budget down to about $5.5 million. But that is still $1 million more than the original estimate. They're now taking another look at things. They may try to include the movie in their next fiscal budget." Francis said he had spoken by telephone that day with Twentieth Century Fox unit production manager Francisco "Chico" Day. "From my discussion with him, I would say I don't think the project is permanently canceled."[4]

Reporters heard a more sensational explanation for the film's postponement when they asked Styron for his reaction to the news. "Black power protests," he declared, had forced the filmmakers to put the project on hold. "The protests were getting so loud I would say it was scaring them. I think they were worried." The film project, Styron recalled, had been "in trouble from the beginning." First, black activists, "led by a Negro story editor for one of the major studios," threatened a boycott unless the producer changed the title and credited sources other than Styron's novel. Then, when producer David L. Wolper capitulated to their demands, "the studio found itself in a position of trying to satisfy everyone." Styron said he started out as an adviser on the film but quit "because I became an embarrassment to them because of the black power protests." Styron acknowledged that "most Hollywood studios" were in financial trouble because of "a terrific clampdown from the banks," as widely reported in the trades. Nevertheless, he maintained that "the money situation was secondary" to "black power protests" as the cause of the film's delay.[5]

Styron had no firsthand knowledge or inside information from the studio that black power protests were responsible for the indefinite postponement of *Nat Turner*. Indeed, his comments suggest that he was simply grinding his own personal ax as he monitored events from his farmhouse in Roxbury, Connecticut. Styron knew full well that Wolper had reached a settlement with black protesters in Hollywood, and he told reporters he was unaware of "any dissension from the black people" in the Tidewater Virginia area, where the movie was scheduled to be filmed.[6] Yet his highly speculative comments and off-the-cuff remarks were widely reprinted, fueling white liberal paranoia about black power radicals extorting concessions and subverting civil rights. News reports, quoting Styron at length, went out over the Associated Press and United Press International wires; both the *New York Times* ("Styron Charges 'Black Pressure' on Turner Film") and the *New York Post* ("One Movie Styron Doesn't Want to See") ran feature articles of their own.[7]

The *Nat Turner* film project, as it turned out, was never revived, leaving historians to sort through conflicting accounts of its demise. Contemporary newspaper reporters, steeped in the professional ideal of objectivity, attempted to balance the "differing views" offered by Francis—the studio flack—and Styron—the embittered writer. Yet literary critics and historians, eager to illustrate the high-stakes cultural politics of the black power era, quickly adopted the Styron thesis as their own. Seymour L. Gross and Eileen Bender, coauthors of "History, Politics, and Literature: The Myth of Nat Turner," portrayed the shelving of the project as a capitulation to black power ideologues engaged in a "programmatic assault" on Styron and his book. More recently, Albert Stone asserted that "censorship became more than a vague threat" in the case of the "Nat Turner" film project. "The prospect of a black boycott with pickets and demonstrations became—at least in Styron's mind—prime reasons for the project's cancelation, although rising costs and persistent questions about historical inaccuracies in Styron's account were also mentioned." Neither Stone nor Gross and Bender made any attempt to verify Styron's widely reported claim—later retracted—that "black pressure groups" were responsible for the indefinite postponement of the movie. They accepted, without critical analysis, his caricature of militant black power advocates flexing their muscles, chanting their mau-mau, and scaring off the timid white filmmakers.[8]

In fact, "black power" had nothing to do with the decision by Twentieth Century Fox to shelve the *Nat Turner* film project in January 1970; the studio postponed or canceled at least a half-dozen other films at the same time. Moreover, the filmmakers were convinced that they had appeased black activists in Hollywood and Southside Virginia; they had no reason to believe that black power protests would disrupt the making or screening of the film.

This is not, by any means, to diminish the influence of black power as a social movement, a cultural phenomenon, or a lightning rod for public debate throughout the film controversy. Key principles of black power—self-definition and community control—shaped the demands of the black protesters who wrung concessions from the Hollywood filmmakers. Prominent advocates of black power, such as Stokely Carmichael and H.

Rap Brown, lent their names and prestige to the cause. Yet the organizers of the self-styled "antidefamation" campaign distanced themselves from the more militant, antiwhite utterances of black power advocates and self-consciously compared themselves to white ethnic groups with similar grievances. Moreover, the success of the grassroots movement rested on its ability to promote black unity across the ideological spectrum. The assassination of Martin Luther King Jr., in the midst of the campaign, provided an unprecedented vehicle for collaboration through the Black Congress, a short-lived coalition of black power advocates, mainstream civil rights activists, and conservative black church leaders. Finally, the strategy employed by the leaders of the Hollywood protest—the threat of a boycott, followed by a negotiated settlement—owed far more to the non-violent civil rights movement than it did to the incendiary street-level politics of black power.[9]

Bold in conception, pragmatic by design, black power commands public attention, like the enigmatic figure of Nat Turner himself. It is the task of historians, however, to look past the sensational headlines of the day and focus on the complex social, cultural, and political transactions that contributed to the making and unmaking of *Nat Turner* at the height of the black power era. Perhaps we will find that the color of power in Hollywood was not black, as Styron and others suggested at the time, but green.[10]

The Confessions of Nat Turner burst upon the American literary scene in 1967, at the end of a long, hot summer of rioting and rebellion in the nation's ghettos. Not surprisingly, many book reviewers drew historical parallels between the Southampton slave uprising of 1831—the subject of Styron's novel—and the recent "race riots" in Newark and Detroit. These reviewers, including some of the most distinguished literary critics and historians of the day, praised Styron for accurately depicting the horror and degradation of slavery and its legacy of racial violence in contemporary America. They admired the courage of a native white southerner who had transcended his racial and regional prejudices to explore the national trauma and human tragedy produced by slavery. Styron took particular pride in the endorsements of C. Vann Woodward, a white southerner, and John Hope Franklin, a black southerner, professional historians whose credentials as civil rights activists were beyond dispute.[11]

The backlash against the book set in slowly. It started with a few dissenting voices in left-wing journals and grew into a chorus that became loud enough to attract the attention of the *New York Times*.[12] Black writers, responding to the rave reviews and commercial success of the novel, drew their own parallels between the events of 1831 and 1967. They saw

Styron as one more southern white "liberal" who professed to be a friend of black people but who, in the end, sold them down the river. These writers did not share an ideology so much as a profound skepticism about the merits of a novel that had been widely hailed by white reviewers. Some expressed disappointment with Styron and his "failure of sensibility" as a writer. Others called him a racist who distorted black history and perpetuated degrading stereotypes about black men and women. Still others directed their anger at the "white-controlled" mass media for relying on a white man to interpret the experience of black people. The critical backlash culminated in a volume of essays titled *William Styron's Nat Turner: Ten Black Writers Respond,* a radical manifesto that warned white writers to keep their hands off black heroes.[13]

The Hollywood film project was announced in the midst of the national media hoopla surrounding the novel, before the critical backlash had fully set in. In November 1967, the *New York Times* reported that Styron had sold the motion picture rights to Wolper Pictures for $600,000, plus a percentage of the distributor's gross. Three months later, Twentieth Century Fox announced that it had completed negotiations with producer David L. Wolper and director Norman Jewison to finance and distribute the film worldwide. Styron used his enormous leverage as a best-selling author to ensure that he would retain some influence over the big-screen adaptation of his novel. He signed on as a paid adviser to the filmmakers and made at least one trip to Hollywood to confer on a "step outline." Yet the minute he sold the rights to the book he ceded artistic control to a producer and director who had their own set of prerogatives.[14]

Wolper and Jewison were both experienced filmmakers, highly regarded by black activists in the Los Angeles area. A native of New York City, Wolper had started his career as a traveling salesman, peddling motion pictures to independent television stations across the country. In the early 1960s, he produced an award-winning series on black athletes; while the films "were sensitively made and well-received," according to his biographer, "most Southern television stations refused to show them." He followed with a series of compilation films on Hollywood and its stars, then turned to historical biographies. He began to see himself as a "cinematic historian," purchasing nonfiction books for television documentaries. In 1965, Wolper sold his production company to Metromedia, Inc., and, with the financial backing of the giant media conglomerate, began to branch out into feature filmmaking.[15]

Jewison, a Canadian with an outsider's perspective on American culture, began his career as a producer and director of television variety shows, then expanded into motion pictures. His 1966 Cold War satire *The Russians are Coming! The Russians are Coming!* was a huge commercial success. In 1967, he produced and directed the civil rights–inspired drama *In the Heat of the Night,* which explored racial and class tensions in a small southern town. The story focused on the relationship between a black Philadelphia detective, played by Sidney Poitier, and a white southern sheriff, played by Rod Steiger. "It was the first film I can think of in which the black man hit the white man," Steiger later recalled. The film won five Oscars, including best picture and best screenplay.[16]

Wolper and Jewison could not have foreseen the uproar that would ensue over their plans to make a film adaptation of *The Confessions of Nat Turner.* Black actors and writers with connections to the Hollywood film industry seethed over the announcement that Styron's book would be made into a movie. They began to talk among themselves about the possibility of organizing a campaign against the movie project. The driving force behind the movement was Louise Meriwether, a forty-three-year-old fiction writer who had recently quit her job as a story analyst at Universal Studios so that she could work full time on her first novel. The campaign began, she recalled, with a few casual conversations among friends in the Los Angeles area. When Vantile Whitfield, a black actor and set designer, mentioned that he had been asked to read for a part in the movie, Meriwether "cursed him out like a dog." A similar exchange took place between Fritzie White, a staffer at the Watts Writers Workshop, and Godfrey Cambridge, a black actor and comedian who had also been invited to read for a part. Whitfield suggested that they "collect signatures and endorsements from other outraged citizens" and "put them together in an imaginative brochure and bombard Hollywood with them."[17]

The organizers decided to call their ad-hoc group the Association to End the Defamation of Black People, later shortened to Black Anti-Defamation Association, or BADA. Meriwether insisted that the name bore only coincidental resemblance to the Anti-Defamation League of B'Nai Brith, the well-known Jewish advocacy group. Nevertheless, it is significant that the founders of the Black Anti-Defamation Association (BADA)—all of whom worked closely with Jews in their professional lives—chose a name associated with ethnic pride and cultural pluralism, not racial separatism. On several occasions group spokesmen drew pointed analogies between their campaign against racism and Jewish campaigns against anti-Semitism, a rhetorical strategy that could suggest either a historical partnership or a bitter rivalry.[18]

Meriwether and her fellow organizers began their campaign by solicit-

ing the endorsements of black celebrities from the world of arts and entertainment. The first two endorsements came from LeRoi Jones (later
Imamu Amiri Baraka), the playwright and poet, and Godfrey Cambridge,
the actor and comedian. Both men were militant advocates of black power
who eschewed the philosophy of nonviolence; both described the making
of a movie based on Styron's book as an act of cultural aggression against
black people. BADA also secured the endorsements of several prominent
political figures whose names were synonymous with black power. Stokely
Carmichael and H. Rap Brown issued a joint statement from the Student
Nonviolent Coordinating Committee (SNCC) headquarters in Atlanta.
"Nat Turner is a black hero who belongs to our people," they wrote, "and
hunkies [sic] such as William Styron do not have the right or authority
from black people to speak for us or interpret our heroes."[19]

The Hollywood protesters found their most eloquent—and media
savvy—spokesman in Ossie Davis, the veteran actor and playwright. In a
letter to Meriwether, subsequently edited and published as a broadside,
Davis wrote that Styron's novel fed white racist fantasies and promoted a
reactionary social agenda. "Certainly the implications about black men—
and black rebellion—in Mr. Styron's book . . . [are] magnified as only the
motion picture can magnify, and thrown into the anger and frustrations
white Americans are already feeling about the black revolution . . . . Certainly, to feed this inflammatory lie to angered white racism on a mass
scale is the height of social irresponsibility." Davis urged black actors and
writers to boycott the film. "I am not against Hollywood making the book
into a movie—provided they take one of their greatest box office giants—
and put blacking on his face! That way we will all know what the industry
really thinks about black sensibilities in our country . . . that way Hollywood would confess its own racism."[20]

With celebrity endorsements in hand, BADA officially announced its
objections to the film in a five-page letter to Wolper and Jewison. The
letter, dated March 28, 1968, began: "Gentlemen: You are murdering the
spirit of Nat Turner, one of the great ethnic heroes of black Americans. You
are distorting and falsifying the history of black people in this country, and
by extension, defaming the entire black race. You are pandering to white
racism and deepening the gulf of alienation between the races. These are
the crimes you are committing and will continue to commit if you persist
in producing a motion picture based on The Confessions of Nat Turner by
William Styron." The group proceeded to cite numerous scenes from the
book that they considered both historically inaccurate and defamatory.
Most of the objectionable scenes involved the portrayal of black charac-

ters engaged in—or fantasizing about—sexual activities with whites. Such scenes, the protesters charged, perpetuated harmful and degrading stereotypes of black men and women as hypersexual; they also gave the false impression that black men and women viewed white men and women as more desirable than members of their own race.[21]

The protesters also objected to some of the larger historical claims embedded in the book. Styron claimed that Turner's rebellion was "the only sustained effective revolt"; in fact, "there were at least two hundred reported revolts and conspiracies in United States history." Styron claimed that the uprising took place in "an otherwise peaceful era"; in fact, federal troops had been sent to Virginia months before the uprising "to aid in the suppression of slave rebellions." Styron claimed that "gleeful armed slaves" helped to put down the rebellion; in fact, Turner's rebellion demonstrated the willingness of slaves to fight and die for their freedom.[22]

The letter concluded with two demands: first, "that a motion picture be made based on the historical facts of Nat Turner, or no picture be made at all"; second, "that no picture bear the title of William Styron's book lest it lend validity to his falsification of history." The protesters did not say what action they would take if their demands were not met. They simply noted that BADA represented a broad cross-section of the "black community"— a pointed reminder of the economic and political pressure that could be brought to bear on the filmmakers.[23]

The protest made headline news in the Los Angeles area. "Negroes Protest Turner Bio" read the headline in the *Hollywood Reporter*: "Cambridge, Davis, Jones Urge Wolper-Jewison Drop Filming Styron Best-Seller." Director Norman Jewison told the trade publication that he had no intention of capitulating to the demands of the protesters. He, too, saw Turner as "a heroic, revolutionary figure, a man who was a black Gideon influenced tremendously by the Old Testament. But who are they to tell me what's going to be in a screenplay when it's not even written? I think *In The Heat of the Night* speaks for itself as far as my feeling toward social problems in this country." Producer David Wolper was quoted as saying that Styron's novel "stands on its record and reputation," and that he did not see "anything in the novel that is racist." Wolper noted that James Baldwin, the literary voice of black militancy, had publicly praised the book; he also cited the popularity of the book among historians and literary critics, including several "Negroes."[24]

A subsequent meeting between representatives of BADA and the filmmakers "came to an impasse." After that, most of the negotiations took place in the press. The *Los Angeles Times* ran a feature story, "Civil Rights and a Producer's Dilemma," on the front page of its Sunday "Calendar" section. The story portrayed Jewison as a friend of the civil rights movement who suddenly found himself under attack from a small but vocal group of black militants. Jewison dismissed the claims of the protesters as unfounded and somewhat hysterical; he insisted that he would not cave in to the pressure. "I'll make the film my way," he said, "and nobody is going to tell me how to do it." The black protesters, he suggested, were guilty of racial chauvinism. "They claim that a white man like Styron shouldn't write a novel about a black slave," he said. "Well I'm not concerned about the color of Mr. Styron's skin. I am, however, impressed that he spent six years on his book and that his knowledge of slavery is better than almost anyone else's, black or white." Incensed by Jewison's comments, Meriwether fired off a letter of rebuttal to the editor of the *Times* on behalf of BADA. "The most serious misstatement," she wrote, "is that we claim a white man like Styron shouldn't write a novel about a black slave. We never made such a statement." Meriwether also took issue with Jewison's assertion that BADA was "in the minority" within the black community. "How does he know?" she asked. "We represent organizations that cut across every economic and political line, ranging from the grass roots level to college professors, from black nationalists to the churches."[25]

Meriwether had the signatures to prove it. The assassination of Rev. Martin Luther King Jr. in April 1968 generated an unprecedented show of unity among black groups in the Los Angeles area. Representatives of some forty organizations from across the political spectrum formed an umbrella group called the Black Congress to coordinate memorial activities and channel anger into activism. BADA took advantage of the institutional framework provided by the Black Congress to solicit endorsements from local leaders of the National Association for the Advancement of Colored People, the Southern Christian Leadership Conference, SNCC, Ron Karenga's US, the Black Panther Party, the Malcolm X Foundation, and various churches, student unions, newspapers, and political groups in the Los Angeles area. Dozens of black men and women signed petitions; others wrote letters of support. Just how many of these signatories actually read the novel and how many simply responded to the call for black unity is an open question.[26]

In mid-April, BADA took out a full-page ad in the *Hollywood Reporter*, urging black actors to boycott the film. The ad, Meriwether recalled, "blew Hollywood away." Meriwether sent press releases to black newspapers across the country—some two hundred media outlets in all—describing the escalating protest campaign and soliciting letters of support. Her quotes appeared in the New York *Amsterdam News,* the largest black newspaper on the East Coast: "We are ignoring director Norman Jewison's newspaper statement that we can't tell him what to do. We don't have to depend upon the whim of producers. If the black actors refuse to accept roles in this picture Hollywood will have to abandon it or play it in blackface. Several black actors have already indicated they will not play in the picture unless it conforms to the historical trust, and we hope other actors will hold to this line."[27] Just how many black actors observed the boycott is impossible to gauge. Sidney Poitier, the leading black actor of the day, refused to take sides in the public debate. He bristled when reporters asked his opinion of the *Nat Turner* film project. "I prefer not to comment," he responded curtly. "In any case I'm not interested in doing a period piece." Jewison told the Newspaper Enterprise Association that he had not given much thought to the casting of the film but was leaning toward the idea of an unknown actor playing the role of Nat Turner.[28]

As a public relations gambit, Wolper and Jewison moved quickly to hire a black screenwriter. Less than two weeks after receiving the letter from BADA, Jewison told the *Los Angeles Times* that he hoped—"rather remotely because he's very busy"—that James Baldwin would write the screenplay for Styron's book. When Baldwin declined, the filmmakers secured the services of Louis Peterson, a black screenwriter with numerous Hollywood and television credits to his name. Peterson was best known for his autobiographical play, *Take a Giant Step,* which had a brief run on Broadway in 1953; an off-Broadway revival led to a film adaptation starring Johnny Nash and Ruby Dee. Perhaps more significantly, Peterson had written a screen adaptation of Styron's previous novel, *Set This House on Fire,* and the two men enjoyed a good rapport. Peterson did not feel that the filmmakers were trying to forestall black protest when they first approached him around Christmas 1967. "I don't think they thought there was going to be that much trouble at the time," he recalled. Still, by the time Wolper and Jewison announced Peterson's hiring in May 1968, they surely realized that having a black screenwriter would shield them against charges of racial insensitivity. Moreover, at a time when civil rights organizations were pushing for more blacks in the Hollywood film industry, the hiring of a black screenwriter was good publicity. "Negro Will Screenplay 'Turner,' Slave Revolt," read the headline in *Variety.* The article went on to note that Peterson attended Morehouse College in Atlanta, "the alma mater of the late Dr. Martin Luther King Jr."[29]

The film controversy simmered throughout the summer of 1968. BADA announced in May that "the black intellectual community" had joined the Hollywood protest. Beacon Press of Boston was about to release an edited volume, *William Styron's Nat Turner: Ten Black Writers Respond,* containing "ten brilliant essays attacking Styron's falsification of history and racist dogma." *Ten Black Writers Respond* became the political and cultural manifesto for the united front that the leaders of the Hollywood protest had been building at the grassroots level. Ossie Davis, writing in *Freedomways,* praised the volume as a "devastating" scholarly critique of Styron's book and a militant expression of black manhood in the face of "cultural aggression against black people." The publication of the book offered "absolute proof" that black people were no longer weak or helpless in the face of aggression, "cultural or otherwise." They would stand up to the white man and challenge his racist assumptions, no matter how widely shared or richly rewarded. Davis struck a tone of defiance in the first line: "Ten writers, black and angry, flying into the face of the American Literary Establishment, have written a book with which to attack a book: a bestseller, winner of the highly coveted Pulitzer Prize; soon to be made into a super-colossal technicolored motion picture." The writers were engaged in scholarship, not polemics, yet their "retaliatory essays" placed them in the vanguard of the black revolution. "These essays are just the beginning," he wrote. "Tomorrow a whole new world is coming right this way." If white liberals insisted on standing in the way, they "might just get run over!"[30]

In December 1968, nine months after the protest officially began, Wolper and Jewison offered to meet with representatives of BADA to discuss a settlement. Wolper recalled the meeting years later.

> It got to be a lot of screaming and yelling, with Lou Peterson, Norman Jewison, and myself [on] one side of the room facing 15 to 20 shouting angry black people. At one point, someone said you guys over there just don't know what it is to be black and Lou Peterson stood up, walked over to the person who said that, and said, "Hey, brother, don't you ever fuckin' say that to me again. Take a good look at my black skin and don't you ever say 'you guys' to me again." That was the kind of tenseness that went on during those meetings, but things cooled down, as we were trying to solve a problem, not to create one.

Wolper described the confrontation as if it were the climactic scene from a Hollywood movie in which the ideal of interracial cooperation ultimately triumphed over the rhetoric of black separatism. The hero of his story was Lou Peterson, who showed his black brothers and sisters that racial pride need not lead to racial chauvinism.[31]

BADA kept its own records of the meeting, documenting each concession made by Wolper and Jewison. When BADA representatives demanded that Wolper and Jewison substitute "historical facts" for the "distortions" in Styron's book, the filmmakers assured the group "that such things as lusting after white women, rape, black slaves putting down the rebellion, homosexuality, were not included in Lew Peterson's screenplay." When BADA insisted that Wolper and Jewison present a "positive image" of Nat Turner "on the screen," Jewison responded that "he envisioned Nat Turner as a black revolutionary fighting for his freedom." When BADA demanded that the filmmakers base the movie on sources other than Styron's book, Wolper responded that "they had found nine books containing material about Nat and they wanted to use all of this source material to create a positive and heroic Nat Turner."[32]

The final point of contention concerned the name of the film. BADA insisted that "no picture bear the title of William Styron's book lest it lend validity to his falsification of history." The filmmakers apparently balked at this demand; Wolper had paid for the rights to the book and the publicity that went with the name. The protesters argued that the use of Styron's title would "stimulate sales of the book and lend it credence." In the end, the filmmakers agreed to shorten the title to *Nat Turner*. Meriwether typed up an agreement and sent it to Wolper and Jewison for their signatures. As a bargaining chip, Meriwether promised that BADA would "call off the troops" as soon as Wolper signed the agreement. Six months later, after a series of minor disputes over the wording, Wolper signed.[33]

Wolper was satisfied that he had appeased the black protesters, thus allowing production of the film to begin. "When all of the meetings were finished, and the changes that those black people wanted to see in the film script were agreed upon," he recalled, "everyone came out of the last meeting backing the film." Wolper insisted that he had conceded little in agreeing to delete "certain passages in which Styron wrote about what was going on in Turner's mind . . . because as a filmmaker you don't do the mind part of the story, what a person is privately thinking, but you only do the physical part of the story that can be shown." In other words, the concessions were largely symbolic gestures, with little if any impact on the still-unwritten script.[34]

A skeptical press portrayed the Hollywood filmmakers as yielding to "black pressure" and demanded an explanation. Wolper told the *Los Ange-*

les Times that he acted out of deference to black sensibilities: "The story being as important as it is to the blacks, we don't want it to be harmful to that community." Wolper confessed that he felt "uneasy" about yielding to outside pressure. "But I tried to understand the pressure," he said. "I was making not only a work of art but also a social work. Once I understood the pressures, I did what I felt was necessary to continue with the film the way I liked it and at the same time satisfy the problems that cropped up in the black community." Wolper made no mention of threatened boycotts or demonstrations; he described the changes as a gesture of goodwill toward an ethnic minority. "You don't go forward and make a film about a black hero if the entire black community feels it is wrong," he explained, "any more than you'd make a film of 'Exodus' if the Jewish community felt it was wrong."[35]

New York Times columnist Tom Wicker, a white liberal who covered the civil rights movement as a journalist, took Wolper to task for yielding to the demands of the black protesters. He argued that the integrity of a work of art rested in the creative vision of its author, not the "social acceptance" of a particular community or group.

> This is quite different from student demands for black study programs, more black faculty, a greater black voice in university affairs; all these may well be justified, depending somewhat on the place and the circumstance. But no one ought to support, say, a demand for rewriting or not teaching Conrad's "Nigger of [the] Narcissus" or Melville's "Benito Cereno"—both of which use black men as symbols of evil. These are great works of literature, part of the heritage of blacks and whites together, and like all such works, they are essentially about the human condition. They defame no one who does not want to be defamed.

By focusing on the creative process rather than the historical content of the film, Wicker managed to avoid taking sides in the controversy over the characterization of Turner. The point was not "whether Nat Turner was depicted by Styron as being moved by sexual desires, or by Wolper as a 'hero,'" Wicker argued, but whether Styron and Wolper had the freedom to express themselves as artists.[36]

Conspicuously absent from press coverage of the negotiated settlement was any comment from William Styron. The *Times* reported that Styron, "who has frequently defended his book against attacks by Negroes," was in Africa on safari and unavailable for comment. Wolper spoke for him, saying that Styron was "completely aware of what's going on and has no objections." The *Times* added that Styron had "no official role in preparing the film"; the screenplay was "being finished by Lew Peterson, a Negro writer." In an interview with the *Boston Globe,* published several weeks after the settlement was announced, Styron spoke sympathetically of Wolper. "He's been forced to compromise." Styron gave no indication that he felt betrayed by the filmmakers. Apparently he had resigned himself to the necessity of such a compromise and, in effect, signed off on it.[37]

With the threat of a boycott removed, Twentieth Century Fox announced the signing of James Earl Jones to play the title role in *Nat Turner.* Jones was then starring in the production of *The Great White Hope* and could not get free of his Broadway commitment until the following spring. That created a scheduling conflict for director Norman Jewison, who was subsequently replaced by Sidney Lumet.[38]

In the summer of 1969, Wolper and Lumet began scouting locations for *Nat Turner.* They considered various sites in Maryland and West Virginia before settling on Southampton County—the original scene of the rebellion—as the ideal locale. To secure the support of local residents, they hired local attorney Gilbert Francis as their liaison. Francis prided himself on his ability to communicate with people of widely divergent social backgrounds and political views. "Practically speaking," he boasted, "I believe I have the best relations with the Negro community of any other white person in the area, and, ironically, I am also tied by heritage to the old Southern families and to the political and governmental Establishment." Francis persuaded the filmmakers that he could get the entire community behind the project so long as they made the movie "in accordance with the true history—and not like Styron said it."[39]

Francis aimed his diplomatic initiatives at three groups—the "political-business community," the "White Community," and the "Black Community." The "political-business community," as he defined it, consisted of town and county officials and representatives of local businesses and industries. The "White Community" was somewhat more diffuse. "This group," he told a *Richmond Times-Dispatch* reporter in 1970, "was fearful that the filming of the movie here in this area would trigger new racial unrest and that each Negro would try to be a 1970 Nat Turner. Such a fear was even voiced in our local historical society (of which I happen to be president), when some of the 'little old ladies with umbrellas' bitterly protested the proposed local filming. Ultimately, however, and without my request or urging, the society passed a resolution approving the filming in Southampton County."[40]

Francis reached out to the "Black Community" through its established community leaders. He kept the filmmakers apprised of his progress. On November 22, he reported, "we had a very successful meeting with the Negro community and we had a wide spectrum of representation." Three days later, he reported, "we had a luncheon meeting with a group of Emporia Negroes which not only elicited favorable response but which called our attention to an Emporia recreational facility which might be ideal for your needs." In early December, Francis proposed "a further meeting with the black community which will embrace the Emporia area as well as Southampton County and include Charles B. Higgins, leader of the Assembly of Southampton, our most radical group." Francis respected the power wielded by Higgins and made every effort to include the "radical" black leader in the decision-making process.[41]

While carefully avoiding any specific promises of preferential treatment, Francis assured black leaders that the "Black Community" would profit from the making of the movie. He asked the Emporia group to submit a proposal for the use of its recreational facilities. He asked for a list of black people who owned area construction and renovation businesses so that the filmmakers could consult with them before signing any contracts. He asked direct descendants of Nat Turner to submit a resume of their abilities, along with a Turner genealogy "to distinguish them from other applicants," so that they could be considered for employment "consistent with their abilities."[42]

Black residents of the area responded enthusiastically to such invitations. On January 8, the Nat Turner Foundation Association sent Francis a list of "materials and people" that might be used in the making of the movie. Mr. Claudie Grant Jr., the president of the group, was "a very good organizer and leader." Mrs. E. M. Cooper, the secretary of the group, was an "amateur singer" and "amateur actress." Mr. W. A. Joyner Jr. had farm materials to offer: a two-wheel cart, a steer yoke, a four-wheel wagon, two mules, a water pit, all kinds of horse-drawn equipment and cooking utensils, a log barn, and a cabin on a lake. Others offered to lend their authenticity to the film by virtue of their bloodlines. Mr. Hugh Whitehead noted that his "wife and children are direct descendants." The names of twenty-six black people, each with something special to offer the filmmakers, appeared on the list. The president and secretary of the group asked Francis to give the list his "greatest consideration."[43]

In his dealings with black residents, Francis deployed what historian Richard H. King, quoting philosopher Laurence Thomas, calls "moral deference." The term, as used by King, suggests a sort of racial etiquette in which white Americans recognize the "unique traumatic experience" of African Americans and, thus, strive to understand history from that perspective. It was Styron's "failure of 'moral deference,' or, perhaps tact," King writes, that led to his bitter falling-out with black critics over his novel. Francis, by contrast, had years of experience as an "interracial" diplomat in the Jim Crow South. Though he did not share the same reading of "Nat Turner's Rebellion" as black residents of the area, he treated their views with respect, knowing that their memory of past events had been colored by their unique traumatic experience. Francis was no egalitarian; he believed white people were superior to black people and carried himself accordingly. Yet, as a self-proclaimed "liberal" in a conservative, white-dominated county, he prided himself on soliciting the input of black people and protecting what he saw as their best interests.[44]

Just when Francis appeared to have everyone on the bandwagon, the wheels fell off. On January 12, Francis learned from unit production manager Francisco "Chico" Day that the movie had been postponed. Day asked Francis to keep the news a secret until he received the "full information and details" from David Wolper. On January 14, *Variety* reported the "Possible Delay of *Nat Turner* Start." Wolper refused to comment. News of the delay spread from the West Coast to the East, from Hollywood to Richmond to Southampton County. When a reporter for the *Richmond Times-Dispatch* called Francis to ask about the *Variety* article, Francis— who was still waiting to hear from Wolper—declined to comment.[45]

Francis became increasingly frustrated at being kept in the dark about the status of the film. The Hollywood-based filmmakers did not seem to appreciate the impact of their action—or inaction—on the local community. Worse, they did not seem to understand the pressures on him as a member of that community. On January 20, Francis wrote a plaintive letter to Wolper, saying he needed to know more about what was happening in order to cope with "developing situations." For example, the production manager had "told the community that he would start procuring horses, mules, wagons, etc. in early January. Since he has not returned, I have almost become a horse trader or buggy dealer in his absence. I have not known how to proceed or how to deal with constant inquiries. The owners of properties involved in the sets are also asking questions. I have been trying to put them off. The motel operators need to know how to schedule their reservations. The builders and suppliers are impatient." And then there were the inquiries from the press. "I doubt that my 'no comment' will continue to be acceptable."[46]

Francis feared that the cavalier attitude of the filmmakers, who were delaying the film without a word of explanation, might sour the community on the project and spoil both the short-term and long-term prospects of making a movie in the area. He reminded Wolper of "the difficulties we encountered in getting the community to accept the filming in this area. Now that we have gotten their approbation, a delay could further complicate matters." As the local liaison for the filmmakers, Francis also feared that his own credibility would be irreparably harmed by their mishandling of the situation. Francis knew that, sooner or later, he would have to answer to the people. "They are expecting me to level with them," he wrote, "and already they are wondering why procurement and construction have not begun. We cannot afford a credibility gap if we are going to take advantage of the progress already made. Furthermore, I feel that my reputation is at stake because of their reliance upon my judgment and assurances of your good faith."[47]

Francis was stunned by news reports suggesting that "black power" was responsible for the delay. Had he been misinformed? On January 28, he dashed off a note to Day, asking for clarification. "You telephoned me on January 13th that the movie had been postponed, and that Dave would call me and give me the specifics of the situation. *Dave has not called.* To prevent erroneous rumors from spreading, I released the information you had given me. Apparently, the paper called Mr. Styron and he gives a somewhat different version. I am enclosing copy of it for your file. What are the complete facts?"[48]

Day assured Francis that Styron was just plain wrong. "In my heart I can truthfully say that it was not the 'Black Power,' but the money that caused this postponement. 20th Century spent about fifty thousand dollars to send me to Virginia to get the facts about costs and costs only. You were the one that we were all being guided by to tell us how the communities felt about doing the film—and your word was good enough for me. Also you know that I was present in several of the meetings you arranged with Whites as well as Blacks and I was satisfied that all was well." In the end, Francis concurred with Day "that 'Black Power' had nothing to do with canceling the movie. In fact, we could not have asked for any more support and cooperation with them."[49]

Francis held out hope that Hollywood would revive the project one day. "If the movie is ever to be made," he told a reporter for the *Richmond Times-Dispatch,* "I want it to be made in Southampton County. I have gone to great lengths in unwinding the commitments between Twentieth Century and members of the community in an effort to maintain confidence in the project so that we can more easily start where we left off if and when the time comes." But the project was never revived. Day broke the bad news to Francis in October 1970: "*Nat Turner* as far as I know is dead—that is with 20th Century Fox. I do not know if Dave Wolper is negotiating with any other company. He and his office stopped calling from the moment I was off their payroll."[50]

In 1975, long after the press had lost interest in *Nat Turner*, Styron qualified his earlier remarks about the collapse of the film project. "It was partly the Black protest that buggered the works badly," he told an interviewer for the *Mississippi Quarterly*, "but they were going to go ahead and do it anyway." Styron no longer blamed Louise Meriwether or Ossie Davis for the demise of *Nat Turner*. The more likely culprits, he maintained, were *Dr. Dolittle* and *Hello, Dolly!* In 1969, just as Twentieth Century Fox was putting *Nat Turner* into production, the studio was losing millions on those other big-budget films. "Both of them flopped," Styron explained, "and *Nat Turner* was the casualty. They simply didn't have the money at the moment, so it was shelved and they never made it."[51]

As Styron spoke those words, he sensed that the more militant phase of black power had run its course. Perhaps the time was ripe, he suggested, for Twentieth Century Fox to revive the *Nat Turner* project. "There's a much better chance now that the movie will be a good one than there was at the time," he mused, "because they were going to turn it into some terrible piece of propaganda, you know, a lot of heroic blather." Still, Styron was not about to invest any emotional capital in the project. "I don't honestly care," he said. "I've seen so many bad movies made of people's works that I am just as happy if it is forgotten."[52] A 1999 article in the *New Yorker*, written by Tony Horwitz, reported renewed interest in the *Nat Turner* film project. African American filmmaker Spike Lee met with Styron, at the urging of Henry Louis Gates Jr., head of the Afro-American Studies Department at Harvard University, to discuss the possibility of a film adaptation that would not shy away from the novel's depiction of violence and interracial sex. Gates reflected on the sea-change in the attitudes of black intellectuals toward the book. "Back then, there was a tiny representation of blacks in academia and the media—the whole thing was a blanket of whiteness—and all black people could do was raise hell and throw stones. Now we have much more input and control of the image of black people."[53] *Nat Turner*, it seems, may yet live again.

Notes

1. The title is a variation on "Mau-Mauing the Flak Catchers," a phrase coined by journalist Tom Wolfe to describe the ritualized intimidation of bureaucrats by black militants seeking poverty grants and community organizing jobs in the late 1960s and early 1970s. I have used the phrase here to satirize the way in which the contemporary news media, followed closely by historians, caricatured black protests against the making of *Nat Turner*, the movie, in the same historical period. Tom Wolfe, *Radical Chic & Mau-Mauing the Flak Catchers* (New York: Bantam, 1971).

2. "20th Fox Plans Feature Hiatus," *Hollywood Reporter*, January 14, 1970; "Richard Zanuck Reports No Pics Until June, Says Fall Sked To Be Heavy," *Hollywood Reporter*, January 16, 1970.

3. "Southampton County Most Likely Location for $4 Million Movie on Nat Turner Rebellion," *Tidewater News*, September 25, 1969.

4. "Nat Turner Movie Plans Halted By Fox Studio," *Tidewater News*, January 26, 1970.

5. "'Nat Turner' Postponed," *Virginian-Pilot*, January 27, 1970.

6. Ibid.

7. Associated Press, "'Nat Turner' Film Stalled, Views Differ," undated news clipping, unidentified source; United Press International, "'Revolt' Stops Nat Turner," published in the *Washington Daily News*, January 28, 1970; "One Movie Styron Doesn't Want to See," *New York Post*, January 27, 1970; "Styron Charges Black Pressure on Turner Film," *New York Times*, January 28, 1970.

8. Seymour L. Gross and Eileen Bender, "History, Politics, and Literature: The Myth of Nat Turner," *American Quarterly* 23 (1971): 180; Albert E. Stone, *The Return of Nat Turner: History, Literature, and Cultural Politics in Sixties America* (Athens: University of Georgia Press, 1992), 14.

9. Civil rights groups have long struggled to influence the depiction of African Americans in Hollywood films. See Thomas Cripps, *Slow Fade to Black: The Negro in American Film, 1900–1940* (New York: Oxford University Press, 1977); Thomas Cripps, *Making Movies Black: The Hollywood Message Movie from World War II to the Civil Rights Era* (New York: Oxford University Press, 1993).

10. For an illuminating study of black power as a social movement and cultural phenomenon, see William L. Van Deburg, *New Day in Babylon: The Black Power Movement and American Culture, 1965–1975* (Chicago: University of Chicago Press, 1992).

11. Prominent literary critics who praised the book included: Philip Rahv; Clifton Fadiman; Louis D. Rubin Jr.; C. Vann Woodward, "Confessions of a Rebel: 1831," *New Republic*, October 7, 1967, 27; John Hope Franklin, *Chicago Sunday Sun-Times Book Week*, October 8, 1967. Most of these early reviewers agreed that the book had something important to say about race relations in 1967. See, for example, Geoffrey A. Wolff, *Washington Post*, October 24, 1967: "The book is more

a psychological narrative for 1967 than it is a social narrative of 1831, and will undoubtedly be read by many people in the interest of 'Negro-White Understanding.'"

12. "Some Negroes Accuse Styron of Distorting Nat Turner's Life," *New York Times,* February 1, 1968.

13. June Meyer, "Spokesman for the Blacks," *Nation,* December 4, 1967, 597; Albert Murray, "A Troublesome Property," *New Leader,* December 4, 1967, 18; Cecil M. Brown, "Books Noted," *Negro Digest,* February 1968, 51–52, 89–91; Loyle Hairston, "William Styron in the Rogues' Gallery," *Freedomways* (Winter 1968): 7–11; John Henrik Clarke, ed., *William Styron's Nat Turner: Ten Black Writers Respond* (Boston: Beacon, 1968).

14. "Wolper Projects UA Slave Revolt Pic," *Variety,* October 18, 1967, 2; "'Nat Turner' Brings $600,000 as a Movie," *New York Times,* October 19, 1967; "Nat Turner Saga to Be Filmed," *Cleveland Plain Dealer,* February 18, 1968, G-5.

15. David L. Wolper with Quincy Troupe, *The Inside Story of TV's "Roots"* (New York: Warner, 1978), 1–26.

16. "A Master's Indelible Gifts to the Screen," *Maclean's,* December 26, 1988, 30; "The Movie Magician," *Maclean's,* April 4, 1988, 36.

17. Louise M. Meriwether to Kenny [last name omitted], January 15, 1965 [1969], records of Association to End the Defamation of Black People/Black Anti-Defamation Association, in possession of Meriwether, used by permission (hereafter cited as BADA records); Louise Meriwether, interview by author, April 1995, New York. Actor Godfrey Cambridge, a BADA supporter, drew a black-Jewish analogy in his letter of endorsement: "Personally I would have felt less upset about this book and its scheduled film production if Hollywood had shown the same kind of sensitivity and honesty in depicting heroes by, say, having hired a repentant Adolf Eichmann to write the story of the Bible or *King of Kings* for world-wide distribution." Cambridge statement, undated [February 1969], BADA records.

18. Meriwether interview.

19. Stokely Carmichael and H. Rap Brown, prepared statement to Louise Meriwether, February 20, 1968, BADA records.

20. Ossie Davis to Louise Meriwether, March 4, 1968, BADA records.

21. Association to End Defamation of Black People to Wolper and Jewison, March 26, 1968, BADA records.

22. Ibid.

23. Ibid.

24. "Negroes Protest Turner Bio; Cambridge, Davis, Jones Urge Wolper-Jewison Drop Filming Styron Best-Seller," *Hollywood Reporter,* March 29, 1968, 1; "Negro Group Sees 'Nat Turner' NSG For Race; Wolper, Jewison: Bum Rap," *Variety,* April 3, 1968, 2.

25. "Civil Rights and a Producer's Dilemma," *Los Angeles Times,* April 14, 1968, Calendar Section, 1; Meriwether to the editor of the *Los Angeles Times,* April 16,

1968, BADA records. An edited version of Meriwether's letter to the editor was published on April 21, 1968, Calendar Section, 4.

26. The Black Congress became a symbol of black unity and a vehicle for social organizing in the Los Angeles area. As riots raged in the black sections of Washington, D.C., and other cities, Los Angeles remained "tense but relatively calm," thanks in large part to the Black Congress and its "Operational Unity" campaign. For references to the Black Congress, see "Dr. King's Murder Spurs Unity Display by L.A. Groups," *Los Angeles Times*, April 7, 1968, B-1, and "L.A. Negro Leaders Call for Tribute to Dr. King," ibid.

27. "Re: 'The Confessions of Nat Turner,'" full-page advertisement in the *Hollywood Reporter*, April 18, 1968, 13; "Protests Mount On Filming of Nat Turner," *Amsterdam News*, May 4, 1968, 19.

28. "'Lone Black Star' Poitier Rejects 'Good Guy' Role as Race Spokesman," *Variety*, June 12, 1968, 2; "Filming of 'Nat Turner' Opposed by Negroes," Newspaper Enterprise Association, June 10, 1968.

29. For Jewison's reference to Baldwin, see "Civil Rights and a Producer's Dilemma," *Los Angeles Times*, April 14, 1968, Calendar Section, 1. Louis Peterson, interview by author, August 1995. "Negro Will Screenplay 'Turner,' Slave Revolt," *Variety*, May 29, 1968, 2.

30. "Protests Mount On Filming of Nat Turner," *Amsterdam News*, May 4, 1968, 19; Ossie Davis, "Nat Turner: Hero Reclaimed," *Freedomways* (Summer 1968): 230–32.

31. Wolper with Troupe, *The Inside Story*, 59.

32. Minutes of "Nat Turner Meeting," December 13, 1968, BADA records.

33. Ibid.

34. Wolper with Troupe, *The Inside Story*, 28.

35. "Over the 'Nat Turner' Screenplay Subsides," *New York Times*, March 31, 1969. (The first word of the headline was apparently omitted.)

36. Tom Wicker, "In The Nation: What Sense in Censorship?" *New York Times*, April 3, 1969.

37. "The Contentions of William Styron," *Boston Sunday Globe Magazine*, April 20, 1969, 11.

38. "Norman Jewison Off 'Nat Turner'; Other Changes," *Variety*, February 6, 1969; "James Jones to Play 'Nat Turner' For 20th Fox," *Hollywood Reporter*, February 3, 1969, 1; "J. E. Jones as Turner," *Variety*, February 5, 1969, 22.

39. Gilbert W. Francis to Francisco "Chico" Day, December 17, 1969, papers of the late Gilbert W. Francis, Boykins, Va., used by permission (hereafter cited as Francis papers); Gilbert Francis, interview by author, Boykins, Va., April 1996.

40. Gilbert W. Francis to Sidney Lumet, December 4, 1969, Francis papers.

41. Ibid.

42. Gilbert W. Francis to Francisco Day, January 5, 1970, Francis papers.

43. The Nat Turner Foundation Association (signed by Claudie Grant Jr., Presi-

dent, and Mrs. E. M. Cooper, Secretary) to Gilbert W. Francis, January 8, 1970, Francis papers.

44. Richard H. King, "Politics and Fictional Representation: The Case for the Civil Rights Movement," in *The Making of Martin Luther King and the Civil Rights Movement*, ed. Brian Ward and Tony Badger (New York: New York University Press, 1996), 166–67.

45. Francisco "Chico" Day to Gilbert W. Francis, January 12, 1970, Francis papers; "Possible Delay of 'Nat Turner' Start," *Variety*, January 14, 1970; Gilbert W. Francis to David L. Wolper, January 20, 1970, Francis papers.

46. Gilbert W. Francis to David L. Wolper, January 20, 1970, Francis papers.

47. Ibid.

48. Gilbert W. Francis to Francisco Day, January 28, 1970, Francis papers.

49. Francisco Day to Gilbert W. Francis, February 2, 1970, Francis papers; Gilbert W. Francis to Francisco Day, February 24, 1970, Francis papers.

50. Gilbert W. Francis to Carole Kass, February 20, 1970, Francis papers; Francisco Day to Gilbert W. Francis, October 21, 1970, Francis papers.

51. Ray Ownbey, "Discussions with William Styron," *Mississippi Quarterly* (Spring 1977): 294–95. The interview took place in April 1975.

52. Ibid.

53. Tony Horwitz, "Untrue Confessions," *New Yorker*, December 13, 1999, 86. Horwitz read an earlier draft of this article, with the author's permission, and incorporated information on the *Nat Turner* film controversy into his essay.

12

The 1960s Echo On

Images of Martin Luther King Jr. as Deployed
by White Writers of Contemporary Fiction

Sharon Monteith

At the close of Mary Ward Brown's story "Beyond New Forks," two elderly women, black and white, are sitting in the home of the black woman, Queen. Queen has worked for the white woman and for her family for decades. They have grown accustomed to each other's company—they may even be friends—but they are still unwilling or unable to communicate about their cross-racial connection and the color-line which has divided their southern experience. The white woman is about to leave, her deepest concerns for the other woman left unsaid as usual, when her eye is drawn to the fireplace and the reader is directed to the pictures on Queen's mantel, silent symbols whose presence echoes through the women's paralyzing silence on the subject of race and racism in the South: "We were all still there, crowded together. Jesus and Martin Luther King were in gold frames and in color, one on each side for balance. Everyone else was propped against the wall or each other, in curling snapshots cracked with age, recent Polaroids, glossy school prints, and posed studio portraits in cardboard folders: black people and white people in her family and mine."[1]

In novels by contemporary white writers, images of King proliferate in photographs, on television screens, in the minds of black and white characters. Mary Ward Brown saves the image of King for the final paragraphs of the final story in her collection *Tongues of Flame.* But across her stories his public crusade for justice touches the private, parochial world she creates. It is a world populated by the old and fragile; black and white live in close proximity in one of the poorest counties in Alabama, Perry County. Their children have moved away from the South to find good jobs but the old remain and remember. The whites live in old plantation homes, built by slaves, that may have to be opened to the public if they are to endure, and some of the blacks still exist in run-down cabins on the edges of the town. An elderly judge and his servant, Pot, went "through civil rights, together, with him on the bench and Pot's people in the streets."[2] Mary Ward Brown tries to open up what she calls "the whole Pandora's box of race." For the white characters it is to finally address "all the unconscious, unintended, even unrecognized withholdings of respect, status, privilege, even rights we never thought about, much less understood at the time."[3] The fear one of her narrators voices is that opening the box may lead initially to uncomfortable, debilitating silence since the radical democracy King envisioned is still to be realized. The road home in the final story seems to be "leading back to the past instead of on to the future."[4]

The texts discussed in this essay are not "Movement fictions" in the way of Rosellen Brown's *Civil Wars* or Meredith Sue Willis's *Only Great Changes*. They are not even political fictions in the keenest sense of apprehending the complexities of the politics of the day. But they quietly renew the focus on racial equality that remains one legacy of the civil rights movement. Ellen Douglas's *Can't Quit You Baby*, Connie May Fowler's *Sugar Cage* and Nanci Kincaid's *Crossing Blood* focus on white women characters who respond specifically to the image and philosophy of Martin Luther King Jr. in novels that negotiate cross-racial friendships and relationships in the 1960s. As Mary Ward Brown shows, the relationship between black and white women in the South is historically contingent and one of the concerns here will be to discuss the extent to which the fictions may also be utopian, even nostalgic and backward-looking, or whether they actually "look forward into the past," to reconfigure Brown's phrase.

The image of Martin Luther King Jr. endures as a symbol of hopes and dreams deferred and unfulfilled. He is also the charismatic symbol of the apogee of the civil rights movement. According to Walter Benjamin, images are a means by which we might connect momentarily with the past: "The past can be seized only as an image which flashes up at an instant when it can be recognized." But, he warns, "every image of the past which is not recognized by the present as one of its own concerns threatens to disappear irretrievably."[5] In the fictions under discussion, the image of King functions metonymically for the civil rights struggles of the 1950s and 1960s. Martin Luther King Jr. has not disappeared, despite worries that heroes turn to dust, in the thirty years since his death.[6] His deep-rooted relevance to millenarian concerns about community, nationhood, and social justice is often made manifest in the words of white writers and politicians—for example, in President William Clinton's calls for civil involvement and his statements on affirmative action.

Clinton, influenced by King and more recently by Amitai Etzioni's reinterpretation of communitarianism in *The Spirit of Community*, said in 1995, "In our national community we're all different, we're all the same. We want liberty and freedom. We want the embrace of family and community. . . . Remember we're still closing the gap between our founders' ideals and our reality."[7] Two years earlier, Clinton had visited one of the churches in Memphis where Martin Luther King Jr. spoke in the days before his death and there the President spoke of social changes still to be achieved "from the inside out," changes involving "values, the spirit, the soul."[8] This moral and religious civic discourse is the discourse of mutuality and mutual social obligation of King's vision of *agape:* "We are caught in an inescapable network of mutuality, tied in a single garment of destiny. Whatever affects one directly, affects all indirectly." The motif of the "garment of destiny" is one to which King returned on a number of occasions, but in the "Letter from Birmingham Jail," he continued, "Never again can we afford to live with the narrow, provincial 'outside agitator' idea. Anyone who lives inside the United States can never be considered an outsider anywhere within its bounds."[9]

In recent years, writers and politicians alike have appropriated King and his magisterial rhetoric, but they often edit out what King actually said along with the specifics of his political agenda. Most particularly, his radical stance against Vietnam and his socialist war on domestic poverty in the last two years of his life are frequently swept aside when his image is deployed as a kind of moral and ethical shorthand for hope, sacrifice, and civic virtue. African American writers and critics have been quick to point this out. Julian Bond, following the first celebration of Martin Luther King Jr. Day in 1986, noted that the focus was on "the dreamer" and not "the anti-war activist . . . the challenger of the economic order . . . not on the complete Martin Luther King."[10] June Jordan in "The Mountain and the Man Who Was Not God" provides a complex reading of a man who suffered anger and despair but whose power in suffering transcends his death and outlasts his life. More recently, journalist Patricia Raybon worries that "heroes too quickly become caricatures or symbols. And King, more so perhaps than other contemporary American heroes, has been rendered sanitized and sacred—too pure now for hard analysis or tough debate. Too holy in our memories for the piercing scrutiny that he, ironically, conducted so well on other issues himself."[11] Instead, images of King—of his life's work and of his death—have been deployed as *leitmotifs* in the iconography of civil rights in fictions in which cross-racial cooperation as a politics of citizenship is a key concern. For many white writers the urge to include King is the urge to dream, to create utopian possibilities in texts that engage with continued struggles to build coalitions and communities at the dawn of the twenty-first century. Some writers are seduced by the possibility of beginning to resolve in fiction what cannot be resolved in life, in the way that Frederic Jameson has described a "symbolic act" that enables "real social contradictions, insurmountable in their own terms, [to] find a purely formal resolution in the aesthetic realm."[12]

The portraits and televisual representations of King that are described in fictions remind us, as John Berger has, that photographic images "confirm, prophetically, the later discontinuity created by absence or death."[13] In my analysis, images of King as reworked in contemporary fictions of the 1980s and 1990s also reflect this discontinuity; the sense of loss and the disappointment that, as Todd Gitlin states, "whether more could have been done to overcome the unequal conditions of blacks and whites if the civil rights coalition had been sustained against all odds cannot be known."[14] There is no trenchant critique or sustained evocation of King or his philosophy in any of the texts discussed here. But his legacy as the spiritual standard bearer of the Movement lies at the heart of novels that serve as models for the present even as they are set in the past. Recently, white critics like T. V. Reed and Jay Clayton have discussed the importance of what have come to be called the "new social movements"— antiracist struggles, postcolonial struggles, environmentalist movements —and their relation to political change. King figures in these discussions, as activists and creative writers alike attempt to recapture the moral high ground he held.

Many contemporary white writers of fiction specify King as a major influence. North Carolinian Kaye Gibbons speaks assuredly of King and adds: "I think that conquering prejudice is a spiritual and an emotional exercise, and the only way it can be done is by seeing and being with people of color."[15] Eugenia Price, another southern writer, follows through: "To me, Martin Luther King was right. Integration is the answer."[16]

Consequently, novels by contemporary white writers often focus on cementing cross-racial friendships and on friendship as a protocol for more transformative social change. They also screen out the complexities of King in order to refine their focus. Analysis of texts by white writers in which King and his civil rights philosophy is evoked can tell us much about white fantasies of racial difference, and of white responses to the post-civil rights era. Fictions may help to facilitate a thinking through of those social and economic factors that continue to polarize blacks and whites in America. But setting novels about race relations in the era of civil rights reforms leaves the pitfall of romanticizing black lives in lyrical and sentimental oversimplicity, in fables and parables that mine the already highly mythologised drama of the 1960s. This is difficult literary and cultural terrain to navigate.[17]

The "Martin Luther King" created by Douglas, Fowler, and Kincaid is a signifier embedded in texts and encoded in a symbolic language. He exists between the plot lines, in dialogue, and in a dialectical relationship to what is quotidian for the characters. He remains behind the ideology through which segregated relationships are anatomized. His meaning is transparently decoded by some white characters while it remains unmined and only half-acknowledged by others whose white solipsism continues to efface the realities of the black women with whom they spend much of their time.[18]

In *Sugar Cage*, Rose Looney is assured by the timbre of King's voice that he cannot be the devil incarnate as her racist husband impugns. Connie May Fowler sets *Sugar Cage* in Tiama, a small town just outside of St. Augustine, Florida, the site of Martin Luther King Jr. and the Southern Christian Leadership Conference's campaign in the "long hot summer" of 1964. The white backlash that is Fowler's focus was particularized in the case of St. Augustine: the oldest city in the United States was about to celebrate its quadricentennial in 1965 and the unwillingness to integrate this historically segregated city was seen as something of a test case for King and his supporters in the fight against token integration. The history underpinning the novel is implicit, but Rose finds herself part of a white protest against "De Lawd" and his marchers, at which her racist husband elicits her presence. However, listening to King's words assures her of his moral surety in the face of her husband's blind hatred, as does her alliance with her black cleaner and babysitter, Inez, who follows "the Good Doctor" in agitating for voter registration as a grassroots participant.

King is never referred to by name in the text. "De Lawd" was first coined in Albany by members of the Student Nonviolent Coordinating Committee (SNCC) in opposition to what they perceived as King's gradualism and in reference to his "preacherly" style and his appeals to Christian values. In *Sugar Cage* it is taken up by hard-line segregationists and offset by Inez's repeated references to "The Good Doctor," her "hope in a bleak,

bleak sea."[19] In this sense, King is differently appropriated—bifurcated—and his presence in the novel straddles the opposing camps. To each, his presence in St. Augustine is dangerous; as Inez fears for his safety, the segregationists fear that he alone is capable of breaking apart their status quo. Rose waves a flag along with the rest of the white counterdemonstrators, who are singing "Dixie" and speaking of preserving "a beautiful way of life" as they festoon the Old Slave Market with symbols of the Confederacy, until she is suddenly overcome by this drama of human error and what her presence alongside them denotes. At this moment she thinks of Inez, her only black friend and her touchstone in times of trouble, and challenges her white friend Eudora with her newfound egalitarianism: "Listen to me, Eudora. You mean to say that Inez Temple is not as smart as the two of us put together? And if she's so dumb, why do you let her babysit Louella for hours on end? Maybe the coloreds are even smarter than us. That's what I think. Maybe they will take over the world, and maybe they should."[20] For Rose, in the middle of a violent demonstration it can never be other than one of two "nations" dominating the other, but later she begins to replay King's words. She has gone on from the protest to listen to his sermon through an open window at New St. Paul's church and she quickly becomes convinced that he is a healer ("those words that poured from his sweet face were healing words"), drawing on King's own metaphor of racism as a disease at the core of society.

King's visit to St. Augustine is the centerpiece of *Sugar Cage* and draws all the characters together: inside or outside the church they listen to his words and enter public history. King becomes a character in Fowler's novel; when he moves into 63 Orange Drive in St. Augustine, Rose's husband drives over and parks to watch the place, "as though I might discover something important." He does. He sees what he recognizes as King's face behind the curtains watching him, "calm, unafraid": "There was no hate there—not any—I swear to God. Just mild curiosity. For a split second our eyes met. And I thought, Jesus Christ, Charlie Looney, who in the blue blazes cares where the man lives—he's not hurting you. I jerked my gaze away. I pressed the gas. As I headed back toward the A1A, I felt just slightly like a fool."[21]

In Kincaid's *Crossing Blood,* Sarah Sheppard responds much more openly to King's calls for responsible social reform but she is presented as exceptional. She lives in the last house occupied by a white family on the edge of the black community in Tallahassee. She is enthralled by Martin Luther King Jr.'s televised speeches and writes to her local paper with homespun wisdom: "A neighbor is not just the person next door but all the people who share the world with you."[22] To many of her white neighbors she is a "nigger lover" and her husband fears she will get the family killed. But she is no more clearly understood by her black neighbors who perceive her as incredibly eccentric. Sarah writes the letter "so I can live with myself" but she is also captivated by a romantic ideal she perceives in King.[23] Convinced that men are generally insensitive creatures, she decides that King is a man who "could speak the things right out of her heart."[24] Her cherished and intensely personal belief in his success in moving other people's hearts and minds is made to contrast starkly with her black neighbor Melvina's cautious pragmatism: "As crazy as he's talking, he's going to get hisself killed."[25] Sarah's daughter, whose first person narration encodes the views of both women, is secretly proud of her mother: "Everybody else's mother was in love with Frank Sinatra—but Mother gave him up completely when she saw Martin Luther King."[26] This representation of a white woman's response to the image of King she sees and augments for her own needs is unusual in its fervor, and Sarah's home becomes the site of an ideological struggle when her husband continues to support George Wallace in the face of her appeal.

For Sarah, the man who is the public voice of the Movement is "straight from heaven" but, unlike Gwendolyn Savage in Joyce Carol Oates's *Because It Is Bitter and Because It Is My Heart*, she does not fall into easy, glib conclusions about his role. Oates's Gwendolyn is a staunch and narrow Presbyterian who is so comfortably cocooned in her domestic world that she shows scant awareness of wider political issues or the changes sweeping the nation. Watching the television coverage of the civil rights rally that began the March on Washington in August 1963, she simply coos: "I do admire Reverend King, it's a blessing from God that the Negroes have such a saintly leader. If it weren't for him there'd be such *anger* everywhere."[27] Mrs. Savage is one of those self-deluding whites King described as aspiring toward a "middle-class Utopia embodying racial harmony" that he feared was merely a "fantasy of self-deception and comfortable vanity."[28] Her fears of black anger and of the potential violence she assumes lurks beneath its surface belie her admiration of King. With tremendous economy, Oates captures the woman's narrow-mindedness in two sentences. On the surface, equally naive though purer in heart, Sarah Sheppard in *Crossing Blood* incorporates a critique of the white southern Church and its propensity to undermine civil rights progress and optimism into her response to King's clarion call for unity: "It is sad to realize that the church is perpetuating segregation and racism. Is the southern church really the hotbed of ignorance and hatred that the editorial page would lead us to believe? The only thing that redeems the word 'Christian' in recent months is Martin Luther King. He brings it dignity."[29]

Characters like Sarah Sheppard are set against the propensity of whites to close their eyes to the realities King talked about all the time in his speeches. *Southern Living* magazine, that bastion of white southern etiquette and fashion published in Birmingham since 1966, never mentioned Martin Luther King Jr. or the civil rights movement for the remainder of the 1960s and 1970s. It certainly never mentioned the violence perpetrated by Eugene "Bull" Connor on black men, women, and children in Birmingham in 1963.[30] Television coverage of Connor's officers setting dogs on small children is described in Jayne Anne Phillips's *Machine Dreams*, but, tellingly, the young white protagonist, Danner, also notes with regret that civil rights struggles are never openly discussed in her experience: "No one spoke of it in social studies class at the junior high. They were supposed to discuss current events every Thursday when the *Scholastic Readers* were handed out; once the front of the six-page paper was a big murky photo of the marchers. Further on was a photo of President Kennedy in the new Rose Garden, and the teacher discussed the history of the White House."[31]

Contemporary white writers endeavor to invoke and interrogate what King called the "appalling silence of the good people," the silence of those who lived through the struggles but who were impeded by parents or schools from comprehending their full significance, or who chose to remain aloof. The writers do so through post-civil rights revisions of what Ellen Douglas has called the "confusions of history and personal life."[32]

White characters are sometimes versions of Betty Friedan's protagonists in *The Feminine Mystique,* middle- and upper-class housewives troubled by the "sickness without a name" who seek personal and social fulfillment. In *The Long Walk Home,* the Hollywood film of the Montgomery bus boycott, Miriam, played by Sissy Spacek, is stirred to political action precisely because her safe but limited life is turned about when her maid Odessa, Whoopi Goldberg, joins in the boycott.[33]

Cornelia in Ellen Douglas's *Can't Quit You Baby* is another "sheltered woman" who attended a finishing school and whose kitchen is her "throne room" where she "holds court."[34] Douglas sets herself the dilemma of representing an insular white woman who has never asked a question of life but "has only said occasionally, reading the morning paper, of some new catastrophe: My God we're fortunate." Douglas addresses the problem via a narrator who is constantly trying to "resist the need to keep herself comfortable" but instead opens up what lies beneath Cornelia's general apathy and atrophy.[35] In this novel, race sounds "the endlessly repeated ground bass" and so Cornelia's refusal to deal with life is juxtaposed with her maid's engagement with the problems that beset her. Tweet, the maid, really has no choice but to deal with racist assaults on her personhood and to struggle against what King called a "degenerating sense of 'nobodiness.'"[36] Where their coming together is concerned the narrator is, however, left only with "surfaces" and "scenes" and it is one such scene in which Martin Luther King Jr. is the focus.

The characters are specifically represented in relation to the historical event of King's death as it struck at the core of America and precipitated fires and demonstrations across a divided nation. In *Can't Quit You Baby*, Cornelia pays a bereavement call to her black housekeeper on the day following King's assassination and, on this rare visit to a black neighborhood, discovers that she is unable to cross the cultural space that divides the two women, the one in grief, the other in sympathy.[37] The effects of losing him are felt all over the town: industries—especially the service industry—have come to a standstill and Tweet has not arrived for work in Cornelia's home. In an uncharacteristically decisive mood, Cornelia sets out to make the journey across town that Tweet makes in the opposite direction every day. It is as much as she can muster but she has failed to consider the full or intended purpose of her journey. She is ill at ease; she has forgotten her handbag and has, for once, stepped outside of the territory she and Tweet ostensibly share but which she controls. Tweet is sluggish and deadened from grief, much like Inez in *Sugar Cage* who shuts the curtains as if to shut out the violence, disconnects the telephone, and cancels the newspapers. Tweet is uninterested in polite social formalities and the two women "face each other in a half-open doorway" under the gaze of King, whose portrait presides over this scene as it did over Queen and her employer in "Beyond the Forks." Silently above the mantel King is backgrounded in a scene that again fails to fulfill its promise of coalition: "Tweet cannot nod. She turns away and shakes her head, as if to say, What do *you* know about it? 'I'm sorry,' Cornelia says again. But she dares not reach out, dares not cross the two paces that separate them."[38]

Much later Cornelia revisits the scene and reprises it in her mind, more comfortably to counter the impasse it suggested. She remembers another time she visited Tweet's home and privileges this occasion in 1967, misremembering it as the same year as the bereavement call. In this scene, reworked entirely outside of Tweet's possible interpretation or intervention, Cornelia is helping Tweet and her mother as they care for Tweet's stepfather, who is dying of cancer: "It seems to Cornelia that they act as one, their intimacy and mutual understanding is perfect."[39] Much of what Cornelia remembers or believes is a fantasy of cross-racial cooperation. The extent to which she relies on Tweet is submerged beneath more comfortably appropriate images of their coordination as nurses, turning a bedridden old man. The fact that Tweet was the person she instinctively chose to call to support her when her husband died never merits consideration. Even when she confuses Tweet's telephone number with her own, she remains oblivious to the fact that Tweet is the nearest she has to a friend. Nor is the fact that Tweet mourns Cornelia's husband for her, when the white woman crumbles into silent repose, a circumstance she can deal with. Points at which the women converge are always those in which Cornelia needs strength; in more poised moments when southern etiquette intervenes, Cornelia politely derides the very resilience in Tweet that she relies on to maintain her own lifestyle.

Can't Quit You Baby is an especially metafictional self-conscious working-through of issues of individual responsibility within the crucible of race relations in Mississippi in the 1960s. The narrator returns to the scene in which Cornelia pays a bereavement call on Tweet twice more in the novel. On each occasion, King's meaning is redoubled, in the way that Wayne Booth has talked of the individual as a "field of selves," and he is drawn into wider discussions. One critic, Charles Fister, reads Douglas's narrator as questioning the motives behind translating "large issues like the history of race relations or Dr. King's death downward into domestic situations like the personal histories of two Mississippi women. When an author does this, is it merely to celebrate her own powers as a creative artist?"[40] Implicit in the question is a judgment that risks deeming "race" —and Martin Luther King Jr.—special territory that cannot or should not be examined at the "micro-level" of personal relationships in contemporary (and especially popular?) fiction. But Douglas, having herself raised the question, also confronts it in *Can't Quit You Baby* via her narrator: "I wrote nothing, for example, of Martin Luther King's death, except that Tweet turned away from Cornelia's gesture of sympathy. What tangle of snakes have I been skiing over?"[41] This problem of skirting issues is especially pertinent in relation to the fictions where white women writers also risk appropriating the black women characters they create as secondary or auxiliary to their white protagonists.

Ideas of friendship and community as the basis of an interracial America underpin white writers' images of King as they key into a literary tradition that invokes Emerson's "nation of friends," King's "beloved community," and SNCC's "redemptive community" of black and white Americans in the organization's pre-1965 phase; James Baldwin's assertion that "we, the black and the white, deeply need each other . . . if we are really to become a nation" and Ralph Ellison's avowal that "I will not Jim Crow my imagination"; Jesse Jackson's "Rainbow Coalition," his Democratic "quilt of unity"; and continued efforts to build multiracial coalitions in the United States. These contemporary fictions, written by white southern women, pursue communitarian ideals and utopian projections, pushing these concerns further, toward ideals of national redemption as a direct consequence of racial justice in the future.[42] Helen Taylor reminds us, via *Uncle Tom's Cabin* and *Gone with the Wind,* of the "political significance of fictional texts in the ideological construction of the South and its racial history."[43] Popular fiction has a cognitive value when it helps to raise social and ethical questions. Fictions may illuminate historical moments like King's assassination but may also work to reflect current dilemmas and debates, like those about race relations in the present, in a period that has witnessed the Howard Beach murder, the beating of Rodney King and the angry response of black people in Los Angeles that followed the acquittal of the white police officers, and the horrific and racist murder of James Byrd in Jasper, Texas.

King's appeals to white moderates were consistent in their citations of Lincoln, Jefferson, and the Declaration of Independence and the Constitution. He utilized the American Dream, the pilgrim fathers, the entire rhetorical fabric of American mythology.[44] King reconstituted the most powerful American myths that had heretofore excluded blacks and reworked them in speeches and essays addressed to blacks and whites. When writers rework King's image and ideas, it seems inevitable that moral and ethical considerations will arise in the reading and critiquing of contemporary fictions that set out to imagine connections across racial lines when these remain so tense and problematic.[45] If the political backlash against affirmative action as "racial preferences" and what has come to be oversimplified as "political correctness," together with legislation aimed at "Black Welfare Mothers" and talk of "Angry White Male" and "white flight" from inner cities, would seem to confirm Jesse Jackson's idea of a "whitelash," then much contemporary fiction by white women writers would seem to challenge it.[46] However, the effectiveness of this challenge is limited by its location within popular fiction. Ellen Douglas has talked about the "pervasive self-deception among white people about what their own behavior was" and what its significance might have been in the civil rights decades. It is this problem that white writers are beginning to address in small but significant ways in their fictions.[47]

Frederic Jameson defines "nostalgia film" in a way that aids critical examination of fictions as well as films in which "usable pasts" are imagined:

> Nostalgia film, consistent with postmodernist tendencies generally, seeks to generate images and simulacra of the past, thereby—in a social situation in which genuine historicity or class traditions have become enfeebled—producing something like a pseudo-past for consumption as a compensation and a substitute for, but also a displacement of, that different kind of past which has (along with active visions of the future) been a necessary component for groups of people of their praxis and the energizing of their collective project.[48]

At first glance it might appear that white writers and filmmakers risk demonstrating a nostalgia for the period of segregation in the South when the social spaces blacks occupied were clearer because of their direct antithesis to those assumed by whites. Manning Marable has argued that "no black American could ever be 'nostalgic' for Jim Crow." And he goes further, asserting that it is impossible to forget that "the demise of the rigid racial segregation laws throughout the United States during the first six decades of the twentieth century was not the result of a moral metamorphosis by white politicians, corporate executives, and philanthropists."[49]

The white writers discussed here seem unable to entirely shake off the idea of a moral metamorphosis on the part of the individual white characters they create, whom they locate in historical contexts where segregation still applies. Some sense of coming to consciousness about their own whiteness in direct relation to another's blackness, and a consequent social and ideological sea change, occurs in each of the novels. The writers experiment with the idea of interracial cooperation as a basis for, or an impulse toward, a plural and more just community. The "ordinary" white girls and women they imagine do not represent those like Mary King or Casey Hayden, who were active in promoting change through movements like SNCC or related activism, but they alter their perceptions of race and racism in accordance with a developing personal relationship with a single black character. This is not simply a liberal humanist but a liberal reformist vision and, as King himself opined, liberalism can be "all too sentimental concerning human nature," leaning toward "a false idealism."[50]

There is no comparable paradigm in which black characters created by black writers achieve a politicized sense of self and become aware of the nexus of race and power as the result of a single intimate engagement with a white counterpart; in texts, as in life, black children apprehend a sense of the significance of their racial identity in America far earlier than most white children.[51] Consequently, the white protagonist's coming to consciousness via a black friend is a disturbing trope worthy of note, and consequently of investigation, although only Ellen Douglas of the authors discussed here interrogates this paradigmatic relationship to any significant extent.

As Ella Shohat and Robert Stam have observed, noting the tendency in popular culture to represent what Leslie Fiedler has referred to as epiphanies of racial harmony and Henry Louis Gates a "nostalgic return to some monochrome homogeneity": "The challenge . . . is to translate the utopian energies behind these consolatory representations of ethnic harmony with the necessary mobilization for structural change that alone can make racial equality a quotidian reality."[52] It is well known that in *Personal Politics* Sara Evans discusses the basis of the civil rights movement as a "move from individual discontents to a social movement." She traces the ramifications of such a shift as it precipitated collaborative action on the part of some whites with blacks in SNCC, and empowered those white women whose feminist consciousnesses were raised first through their apprehension of black civil rights struggles.[53] These novels respond to civil rights imperatives as they engage with ideas of what may be socially and politically desirable in women's friendships and coalitions. They strain toward democratic dialogues, or a "dialogic communitarianism."[54] They begin to overcome what is mendacious and inequitable at the level of personal friendship and look forward to such friendships translating into social reform according to more egalitarian ideals. They imagine national and personal recovery through coalitions built with reference to the past and to the civil rights reforms of 1964 and 1965, but with faith in the future.

King's moral authority and the moral imperative of the civil rights movement motivates white women characters, whose conscious or unconsciously "liberal" sentiments underpin their relationships with black maids, housekeepers, and "friends." In these texts, liberalism is firmly based in the appeal of King to white moderates, those "people of good will" who might not openly oppose segregation but who could not sanction violence in its support. King's ideas of *agape* and of a "beloved community" in a participatory democracy, together with the shocking violence of his death, embolden the principles of white women characters whose quotidian experience is to rely almost exclusively on black women. They become participants in King's idea of self-transformation as integral to the rhetoric of national freedom. King said on a number of occasions that it was never easy to accept the "role of symbolism" he was expected to uphold.[55] In many senses in contemporary novels by white writers he is a spiritual progenitor but is also encoded as a romantic hero, his philosophy turned into catechism for the white women characters. Much of King's power lay in his appeal to the consciences of individuals, shaping views of a participatory democracy through the philosophy of politicized personalism and it is this feature of his philosophy that is the moral impetus in novels by white women writers.[56]

This essay has sought to determine whether contemporary fictions provide a space in which a certain nostalgic hope for the kinds of moral and social certainties that characterized civil rights struggles may be reasserted, or a space within which the social and moral dilemmas the struggles began to articulate continue to be critically and creatively explored. David L. Chappell begins his history of blacks and whites in the civil rights movement with a statement about the relationship between morality and politics and goes on to explore how "[t]he moral and political are in constant tension, and can probably coincide only temporarily, but their temporary coincidence is what makes the civil rights movement momentous and interesting."[57] The novels discussed may not take the Movement as their specific backdrop but they respond to its imperative and, therefore, cannot be considered other than political, even as they so often vacillate between the idealistic and utopian and the self-consciously socially reflective. These sorts of novels may have more to tell us about the impact and legacies of the civil rights movement for "ordinary" people than expressly self-conscious "Movement fictions." The white protagonists function as synecdoches for the times as well as the settings of the novels in which they appear, drawing out, via a complex cooperation with their black counterparts, the threads of ideological debate in and following the civil rights era. These fictions, in which images of Martin Luther King Jr. invigorate the protagonists' civic personhood, articulate a specific association with King's hopes and achievements, his reforms and promises, including those that remain unfulfilled. White writers are often seduced by a "figure of hope," to borrow Ernst Bloch's term for utopian expression, that is King's assault on the specter of segregation. This idea continues to beguile, finding its way into even the most recent of novels. King's name sets off a litany of positive and noble associations and "King" becomes himself a text functioning on a synchronic and diachronic level. The symbolic consciousness of King becomes part of the narrative consciousness of the novels. They help to create a kind of post-civil rights pedagogy that attempts to re-create some of the drama of the civil rights movement in the imaginative space that fiction affords.

Notes

1. Mary Ward Brown, "Beyond New Forks," in Brown, *Tongues of Flame* (Tuscaloosa: University of Alabama Press, 1986), 161–62.

2. Ibid., 100.

3. Ibid., 152.

4. Ibid., 160.

5. Walter Benjamin, "Theses on the Philosophy of History," in Benjamin, *Illuminations* (London: Fontana, 1992), 247.

6. Images of King are (re)created in a number of recent fictions by African American writers: Julius Lester, *And All Our Wounds Forgiven* (New York: Harcourt Brace, 1994) and Charles Johnson, *Dreamer* (New York: Scribner, 1998), for example. See Trudier Harris in this volume and my "Revisiting the 1960s in Contemporary Fiction: 'Where Do We Go From Here?'" in *Gender in the Civil Rights Movement*, ed. Peter J. Ling and Sharon Monteith (New York: Garland Press, 1999).

7. President Clinton "Remarks By The President on Affirmative Action," July 19, 1995, 10, Press Release, The Rotunds, National Archives. One critic has described the phrase "civil society" as the "motherhood-and-apple pie of the 1990s." See Anne McElvoy, "A Time To Choose, Again," *Times Literary Supplement*, December 5, 1997.

8. President Clinton, "Remarks to the Convocation of the Church of God in Christ in Memphis," November 13, 1993, as quoted by Michael J. Sandel in *Democracy's Discontent: America in Search of a Public Philosophy* (Cambridge: Harvard University Press, 1996), 327–28. Sandel believes that Clinton has "ventured onto moral and spiritual terrain that liberals of recent times have sought to avoid."

9. Martin Luther King Jr., "Letter from Birmingham Jail," in *The Norton Anthology of African American Literature*, ed. Henry Louis Gates and Nellie McKay (New York: Norton, 1997), 1854.

10. Julian Bond, "Saving Dissenter from His Legend," *New York Times*, January 20, 1986, 5.

11. June Jordan, "The Mountain and the Man Who Was Not God: An Essay on the Life and Ideas of Dr. Martin Luther King Jr.," in Jordan, *Moving Towards Home: Political Essays* (London: Virago, 1989), 192–202. Patricia Raybon, *My First White Friend* (New York: Penguin, 1996), 139–42.

12. Frederic Jameson, *The Political Unconscious: Narrative as a Socially Symbolic Act* (London: Methuen, 1983), 79.

13. John Berger, *Ways of Telling* (New York: Pantheon, 1982), 87.

14. Todd Gitlin, *Twilight of Common Dreams: Why America Is Wracked by the Culture Wars* (New York: Henry Holt, 1995), 134.

15. Kaye Gibbons in *Broken Silences: Interviews with Black and White Women Novelists*, ed. Shirley M. Jordan (New Brunswick, N.J.: Rutgers University Press, 1993), 67.

16. Jordan, "The Mountain and the Man Who Was Not God," 209.

17. It is, of course, possible to write about a subject without ever making direct mention of it in a novel. Certainly, Eric J. Sundquist has argued that the best books about the Scottsboro case are Arna Bontemps's *Black Thunder* (New York: Macmillan, 1936), a historical novel set in 1800 in which Gabriel Prosser's slave rebellion is the overt concern, and Harper Lee's *To Kill a Mockingbird* (Philadelphia: Lippincott, 1960). See Eric J. Sundquist, "Blues for Atticus Finch: Scottsboro, Brown and Harper Lee," in *The South as an American Problem,* ed. Larry J. Griffin and Don H. Hoyle (Athens: University of Georgia Press, 1995), 181–209.

18. Adrienne Rich has written in many essays about the problem of white solipsism, or what she calls "the vast encircling presumption of whiteness," and has been followed by Minrose C. Gwin in "A Theory of Black Women's Texts and White Women's Readings, or . . . The Necessity of Being Other," *NWSA Journal* 1, no. 1 (1988): 21–31.

19. Connie May Fowler, *Sugar Cage* (London: Bantam, 1992), 222.

20. Ibid., 132–33.

21. Ibid., 179.

22. Nanci Kincaid, *Crossing Blood* (New York: Avon, 1992), 102.

23. Ibid.

24. Ibid., 96.

25. Ibid.

26. Ibid.

27. Joyce Carol Oates, *Because It Is Bitter and Because It Is My Heart* (London: Picador, 1992), 311.

28. Martin Luther King Jr., "Where Are We?" in King, *Where Do We Go From Here: Chaos or Community?* (Boston: Beacon, 1968), 5.

29. Kincaid, *Crossing Blood,* 103.

30. See Diane Roberts, "Living Southern in Southern Living," in *Dixie Debates: Perspectives on Southern Cultures,* ed. Richard H. King and Helen Taylor (London: Pluto Press, 1996), 85–86.

31. Jayne Anne Phillips, *Machine Dreams* (London: Faber and Faber, 1985), 170–71

32. King, "Letter," 1860, and Ellen Douglas, "I Have Found It," *Southern Quarterly* 33, no. 4 (1995): 8, 12.

33. Richard Pearce, *The Long Walk Home,* directed by Richard Pearce (Miramax Films, 1990).

34. Ellen Douglas, *Can't Quit You Baby* (London: Virago, 1991), 6.

35. Ibid., 11.

36. Ibid., 5; King, "Letter," 1857.

37. For a more detailed reading of the novel, see my "Across the Kitchen Table: Establishing the Dynamics of an Interracial Friendship," in *overHERE: European Journal of American Studies* Southern Studies Issue 14, no. 2 (Winter 1994): 19–35.

38. Douglas, *Can't Quit You Baby,* 99.

39. Ibid., 201.

40. Charles Fister, "Not Just Whistlin' Dixie: Music, Functional Silence and the Arbitrary Semiotics of Oppression in Ellen Douglas's *Can't Quit You Baby,*" *Southern Quarterly* 33, no. 4 (Summer 1995): 116.

41. Douglas, *Can't Quit You Baby,* 240.

42. See my *Advancing Sisterhood? Interracial Friendships in Contemporary Southern Fiction* (Athens: University of Georgia Press, 2000).

43. Helen Taylor, *Scarlett's Women: Gone With The Wind and Its Female Fans* (London: Virago, 1989), 121.

44. For the ways in which King utilized the ideological/historical and emotional touchstones of civil religion see Keith D. Miller, "Voice Merging and Self-Making: The Epistemology of 'I Have A Dream,'" *Rhetoric Society Quarterly* 19, no. 1 (Winter 1989): 23–31 and *Voice of Deliverance: The Language of Martin Luther King Jr. and Its Sources* (Athens: University of Georgia Press, 1998).

45. For a moral and ethical critical reading of King's public discourse, see Frederick J. Antczak, "Learning to Read Martin Luther King's 'Pilgrimage to Nonviolence': Wayne Booth, Character, and the Ethical Criticism of Public Address," in *Rhetoric and Pluralism: Legacies of Wayne Booth,* ed. Frederick J. Antczak (Columbus: Ohio State Press, 1995), 153–63.

46. See, for example, Todd Gitlin for a history of the term "affirmative action," its application in recent years in the press and on American campuses, and the media-panic that has been created around its use; in Gitlin, "The Recoil," in Gitlin, *Twilight of Common Dreams,* especially 169–77. Zillah R. Eisenstein discusses contemporary debilitating images of black women, like the "Welfare Mother," and argues that the "silent subtext" behind all such negative portrayals is the middle-class white woman as "decent" wife and "good" mother. See Eisenstein, *The Color of Gender: Reimaging Democracy* (Berkeley: University of California Press, 1994), 217.

47. Ellen Douglas in interview, quoted by Susan V. Donaldson, *Southern Quarterly* 33, no. 4 (1995): 57.

48. Frederic Jameson, *Signatures of the Visible* (New York: Routledge, 1990), 137.

49. Manning Marable, *Race, Reform and Rebellion: The Second Reconstruction in Black America 1945–1990* (Jackson: University Press of Mississippi, 1991), 191, 213. This is part of an ongoing discussion. See, for example, Onita Estes-Hicks, "The Way We Were: Precious Memories of the Black Segregated South," *African American Review* 27, no. 1 (Spring 1993): 9–18. bell hooks explores this idea a number of times across her books, as does Henry Louis Gates in *Colored People: A Memoir* (New York: Viking, 1995).

50. Martin Luther King Jr., "Pilgrimage to Nonviolence," in *A Testament of Hope: The Essential Writings and Speeches of Martin Luther King, Jr.,* ed. James M. Washington (New York: Harper, 1986), 36.

51. Various writers and critics make this point, among them Judith Porter in *Black Child, White Child: The Development of Racial Attitudes* (Cambridge:

Harvard University Press, 1971); Midge Wilson and Kathy Russell, *Divided Sisters: Bridging the Gap Between Black and White Women* (New York: Anchor, 1996), 39.

52. Henry Louis Gates, *Loose Canons: Notes on the Culture Wars* (New York: Oxford University Press, 1992), xix. Ella Shohat and Robert Stam issue the challenge in *Unthinking Eurocentrism: Multiculturalism and the Media* (New York: Routledge, 1994), 236.

53. Sara Evans, *Personal Politics: The Roots of Women's Liberation in the Civil Rights Movement and the New Left* (New York: Vintage, 1980), 24.

54. Elizabeth Frazer and Nicola Lacey, *The Politics of Community: A Feminist Critique of the Liberal-Communitarian Debate* (Hemel Hempstead, England: Harvester Wheatsheaf, 1993).

55. See, for example, the "Face to Face" interview with John Freeman (BBC television, 1964).

56. James J. Farrell discusses "civil rights personalism" as King's social gospel in the chapter "Civil Rights Personalism," in Farrell, *The Spirit of the Sixties: The Making of Postwar Radicalism* (New York: Routledge, 1997).

57. David L. Chappell, *Inside Agitators: White Southerners in the Civil Rights Movement* (Baltimore: Johns Hopkins University Press, 1994), xxi.

13

The Power of Martyrdom

The Incorporation of Martin Luther King Jr.
and His Philosophy into African American Literature

Trudier Harris

Preachers convert. That axiom holds true for the majority of religious
practitioners in African American communities. It is especially true when
the preacher has national and international stature as a result of commun-
ing with presidents and kings. Black American folk communities are willing to grant to their preachers power and influence unmatched by any
other figures. Historically, even persons not in the church recognize the
hold that preachers have on their churches. Such skeptics may wash their
cars or cut their grass on Sunday morning instead of attending church,
and they may tell the jokes about preachers that saturate the African
American oral tradition, but they are nonetheless respectful of the unique
position that preachers have in their communities.

When the preacher takes up a political agenda, however, his ability to
convert may clash with those who have opposing political views, whether
those persons are of his own ethnic/racial group or not. Dr. Martin Luther
King Jr. was undoubtedly one of the greatest—if not *the* greatest—of African American preachers. However, his philosophical clashes with militant
young black activists of the 1960s, whose nationalistic views and strategies
of self-defense were in opposition to his advocacy of nonviolence, sorely
tested his ability to convert. The famed oratorical skills for which he was
noted did not convince Stokely Carmichael to renounce self-defense. Nor
did they convince LeRoi Jones to give up his desire for poems that could
kill. And they certainly did not convince Don L. Lee to stop talking about
George Wallace's momma. The philosophical differences between King
and these young poets manifested themselves in a generational division in

which it became necessary for the sons and daughters to at least disagree with the father if not slay him altogether.

Perhaps their differences would have been unreconcilable if King had not been killed. Ironically—but perhaps not unexpectedly—his death heightened and transformed his potential to convert. Through death, he became the quintessential preacher who, in black communities at least, probably did not have a single detractor who would make himself or herself known as such. Everybody fell into the acceptable grief party line, and that was no less true for the young black writers and activists who had disagreed with King while he lived. They were all converted to true believers, but not exactly in King's God or his belief in the political power of nonviolence. They uniformly expressed their belief that white Americans should die for the crime of King's death and that America itself should be destroyed. In the ultimate paradox, King's death converted these young writers into a violent wish for the destruction of their own country.

The period following King's death in 1968 may well be termed the Martin Luther King Jr. Retaliatory Literary Movement. The movement coalesced all the dissident forces among writers of the Black Arts Movement. Don L. Lee and Nikki Giovanni, between whom there was no love lost, as the folk expression goes, were uniform in their expressions of outrage toward those they felt responsible for King's death. In death, the symbolic site of King's body became a rallying cry for justice and for retaliatory violence. As one of the young poet trumpeteers usually identified with the Black Arts Movement, Giovanni was in the forefront of articulating the retaliation. In "Reflections on April 4 1968," she writes in the first verse paragraph:

> What can I, a poor Black woman, do to destroy america? This is a question, with appropriate variations, being asked in every Black heart. There is one answer—I can kill. There is one compromise—I can protect those who kill. There is one cop-out—I can encourage others to kill. There are no other ways.[1]

The second verse paragraph reveals the source of Giovanni's calmly controlled anger: "The assassination of Martin Luther King is an act of war," for which she blames Lyndon Johnson and others.[2] She eulogizes King by violating the expected in such forms:

> May he rest in peace. May his blood choke the life from ten hundred million whites. May the warriors in the streets go ever forth into the stores for guns and tv's, for whatever makes them happy (for only a

happy people make successful Revolution) and this day begin the
Black Revolution.[3]

The paragraph verse structure of the poem and its methodically controlled
tone indicate clearly the weight of emotion Giovanni attempts to contain.
The boxiness of the verses is a visual representation of the effort to contain. In her choice of interrogative and imperative approaches to the issue,
Giovanni assumes the mantle of attempting in turn to incite in others a
violent reaction to King's death.

In a fascinating appropriation of the biblical rhetoric that informed
King's own speeches, Giovanni concludes: "God will not love us unless we
share with others our suffering. Precious Lord—Take Our Hands—Lead
Us On."[4] For Giovanni, as for many African Americans who found their
biblical models in the Old Testament rather than in the New Testament,
vengeance for King's death is justified by appropriating the violent intentions inherent in the very biblical base King used to articulate his stance of
nonviolence. Through the emotional impact of using one of the songs
King loved ("Precious Lord"), Giovanni intertwines his death, biblical history, and the need to transform nonviolence into violence. God will lead
those who retaliate for King's murder, Giovanni asserts, just as surely as
He led King through his own difficult times.

By asking questions and offering a blueprint for action in the quiet and
calm way she does, Giovanni manages to move beyond the heated rhetoric
of the Black Arts Movement and into a realm where words are inadequate
to measure anger. The rather quiet words she chooses simultaneously
make clear the inadequacy of the language and the great gap between
what can be expressed and what the poet actually feels. By containing her
desire for the beginning of Black Revolution and the destruction of
America in this very didactic way—reminiscent of litanies or prayers and
other recitations that become innocuous through repetition—Giovanni
succeeds in soothing her readers through tone and diction into accepting
what otherwise might appear impossible to them.

The extent to which Giovanni was affected by King's death can be measured in part by her return to the subject in several poems. Indeed, scholars have argued that most of the political poems in Giovanni's *Black Judgment* were inspired by King's philosophy or by his death. In "Poem for
Black Boys (*With Special Love to James*)," Giovanni advocates a more direct approach to change than the one King espoused: "DO NOT SIT IN DO
NOT FOLLOW KING/ GO DIRECTLY TO STREETS," a philosophy that other poets
would stress upon King's death.[5] "His headstone said/ FREE AT LAST, FREE

AT LAST," Giovanni writes in "The Funeral of Martin Luther King Jr.," "But death is a slave's freedom/ We seek the freedom of free men/ And the construction of a world/ Where Martin Luther King could have lived/ and preached nonviolence."[6]

While Giovanni articulated the grief and quietly called for Black Revolution, other poets marked King's death as the end of nonviolence in America or questioned—as Giovanni did—how King could have been shot with so many policemen around. "[N]on-violence is dead/ it died last night," Donald L. Graham (Dante) writes in a poem titled "April 5th."[7] And when the speaker and his sister listen to a white man reading King's "I Have a Dream" speech on television, the sister "moaned/ Lord strike their ass/ for they know what/ they do."[8] The sister's desire for retaliation echoes Giovanni's in that those who now report the news are implicated in King's death. Graham, as does Giovanni, connects Old Testament biblical tenets to the current situation and transforms them into a recognition that the whites who now ostensibly lament King's death were also the ones who *knew* that they were killing him.

Don L. Lee expands Graham's assertion that whites knew what they were doing to King to explore what exactly that knowledge meant. Consider Lee's short poem titled "Assassination":

> it was wild.
> the
> bullet hit high.
>   (the throat-neck)
>
> & from everywhere:
>   the motel, from under bushes and cars,
>   from around corners and across streets,
>   out of the garbage cans and from rat holes
>   in the earth
>
> they came running.
> with
> guns
> drawn
> they came running
> toward the King—
>   all of them
>   fast and sure—
>
>   as if

the King
was going to fire back.
They came running,
fast and sure,
in the wrong
direction.[9]

For Lee, absence signifies guilt and complicity. If the policemen had truly been concerned about King, they would have been on the scene from the beginning, and they would have performed the investigative actions usually attributed to policemen. The fact that they turned *toward* King suggests that they were more interested in verifying his death than in looking for those who killed him. Lee's implication of guilt connects to Giovanni's desire to destroy America by implicitly asserting that policemen who fail so miserably in their duties should not simply be fired, but destroyed. Just as their badges have not converted them from racism, the badges have similarly not inspired them to attempt to locate the assassins.

Running toward King, Lee suggests, replicates the act of blaming the victim that characterized white reaction to black people's fights for civil rights throughout the King era. Problems were inherently thought to be *within* black communities instead of within the larger society. Even King's death, Lee asserts, could not change this erroneous perception. It only had the effect of solidifying the stereotypical gaze upon black people and upon black communities. Perhaps somewhat surprisingly, Lee selects irony as his mode of commenting on King's death instead of blasting away in the tone that so characterized the Black Arts Movement as well as his own poetry. This change of tactic could be another measure of the tremendous impact King's death had on these young writers. Certainly they could cry out in rage, but would that have been the most effective response? Would it perhaps not have been better to urge rethinking of the circumstances surrounding the death, loudly suggest conspiracy, and perhaps reap some justice from events that may have followed that suggestion/accusation?[10]

For Lee and young—as well as older—poets of the 1960s and early 1970s, King's death was tantamount to an enemy attack on a homeland. All factions within that homeland immediately rallied to the cause of the fight for the larger good. For black people in America, that larger good was specific justice for King's death and generalized justice for all black people. As perhaps the most prominent of the voices of the Black Arts Movement, the poets, appropriately, would be heard the loudest in the literature. Still, voices in drama and fiction have also registered their reaction to King's death as well as incorporated his philosophy—or what they consider its ragged edges—into their works. Yet, whereas voices of the poets are frequently more supportive than detracting, able to embrace posthumously a black man slain by racist America, playwrights who incorporate King's philosophy into their works remain more skeptical about preachers in general and King's message of redemptive love and nonviolence in particular.

Two plays that illustrate rather negative reactions to the *atmosphere* that King's philosophy created are Joseph White's *The Leader* and Ed Bullins's *The Gentleman Caller: A Parable in One Act*. "Atmosphere" is emphasized here because neither play mentions directly the name of Martin Luther King Jr. Clearly, both were inspired by preachers and issues of leadership in the 1960s. Both were similarly inspired by a criticism of the philosophy of nonviolence. Indeed, in White's case, not only is nonviolence the problem, but so is the implied Uncle Tomism that accompanies it. Bullins rejects nonviolence altogether and uses the implication of King's work as a forum for transforming a docile maid into a violent revolutionary.

It is unclear if White's play was ever performed, or if he simply wrote it for publication in LeRoi Jones and Larry Neal's *Black Fire*. What is clear is that he wrote the play prior to King's death and that it served as a treatise criticizing current tactics to advance black equality in America. What is equally clear is that White has little respect for black preachers in prominent leadership roles and takes as part of his purpose to unmask their hypocrisy. Rev. Abraham Lincoln Brown, the antihero of White's dramatic representation, is a pompous, proud, self-congratulatory charlatan who has a white mistress and who constantly schemes to increase his media exposure. His faithful attendant, Johnson P. Johnson, is a sycophantic mirror to Rev. Brown's aspirations. Together, they orchestrate and execute a philosophy in which they pretend concern for the black masses but are interested only in their own leadership and popularity gains.

Dramatic action revolves around Johnson's efforts to rid Rev. Brown of the white Cora, whom he believes to be bad for public relations; Johnson and Rev. Brown's attempts to pacify a couple of black church ladies who want them to come South to help with a voter registration drive; and Rev. Brown's efforts to increase his media coverage through an interview and a scheme in which he will set himself on fire in front of the White House. Johnson is assigned responsibility for calling the crowds to the burning preacher and for dousing the fire; if the plan works, it will lead to newspaper and television coverage across the nation. As might be anticipated, Rev. Brown's burning scheme backfires when Johnson seemingly loses his ability to toss water; he also miraculously seems to lose his voice. Instead, he watches Rev. Brown burn to death and assumes the mantle of leadership.

White raises several issues in the play. Questioning the motives of preachers involved in the civil rights movement is a primary one. Such leadership roles, White implies, were ripe for exploitation and hypocrisy, and Rev. Brown exhibits both traits. His authority and the power that has accrued to him through trust bestowed upon him become his own personal playing ground. He acts selfishly, only for his own rather small-minded reasons. His constituency, *if* he has one, is not immediately apparent in the play. Certainly Mrs. Harris and Mrs. Scott, the two visiting church ladies, revere Rev. Brown, but there is no indication that he has a church and parishioners whom he attends on a regular basis. This implied detachment from a base of support is certainly not something for which King was known, but it was nonetheless a potential problem with any and all preachers involved in the civil rights movement.

Another problem with such leaders, sacred and secular, was the potential to mix, as one critic put it, "the ass struggle with the class struggle." Rev. Brown is clearly pursuing the former. Cora, a *"sophisticated, witty, intelligent"* thirty-five-year-old white woman, is nonetheless *white*.[11] For Joseph White, that designation alone should have exempted her from the intricacies of Rev. Brown's operation, and it should certainly have exempted her from his bed. Yet it is clear that Rev. Brown has a comfortable, familiar relationship with Cora and that she has had a hand and a voice in the strategies he has adopted to ensure his leadership. The play opens with her coaching him on the delivery of his next speech. *"Vocal inflections"* receive more attention than substance, and the self-satisfaction that attends Rev. Brown's practice delivery bodes ill for any real cause.

The practice session ends with Cora "nestling" against Rev. Brown and declaring: "My beautiful, beautiful black leader. My white womanhood is yooooours *forever*."[12] A few speeches later, she asserts to the skeptical Johnson: "All I know is that Reverend Abraham Lincoln Brown is a man among men, a human pillar of strength. And I love him with every fiber of my soul."[13] Her emphasis on Rev. Brown's name highlights White's ironic use of the name Abraham Lincoln. Lincoln may have symbolically freed enslaved black people, but Rev. Brown has voluntarily re-enslaved himself to Cora. He is therefore the ultimate Uncle Tom.

The fantasy world that Rev. Brown has created around himself leads him to believe that he can do anything he wants, including publicly flaunting a white mistress. In a parody of a fairy tale trope, White has Rev. Brown look into a mirror at strategic points in the play and, in the tradition of Snow White's evil stepmother, declare his beauty and power. "Mirror, mirror, on the wall, am I not the most powerful black man of them all?" he asks in the first adoption of this trope. "There are other leaders," he continues, "whose names we know, but when Negroes want action (*brief laugh*), they know where to go (*points to himself*)."[14] The dual implication of "action" applying to politics as well as to sexuality serves to undercut, again, any true potential leadership Rev. Brown may have. He is as fanciful in believing that he is a leader as he is in thinking that his sexual prowess can be touted so publicly.

White finally questions the potential for altruism in such leaders and their assistants. No one, he suggests, is immune from the disease of self-interest that accompanies power and leadership. Underlings ever desire to supplant the current leader and, given the opportunity, will do so. That is precisely what Johnson does to Rev. Brown. The immediate impetus to the event is an incident in which Rev. Brown refuses to hear what Johnson has to say about Cora. As a result of Cora's having made a disruptive, drunken entrance while the two church ladies are visiting, Johnson changes his insulting tactics with her and briefly compliments her; in response, Cora makes sexual advances to Johnson. When Johnson informs Rev. Brown that Cora is undiscriminating in her preference for black men, Rev. Brown refuses to believe him. It is that rejection that leads in part to Johnson's refusal to play his role in the burning scheme. How could Rev. Brown, Johnson seems to ask, believe in a white woman so much that he would refuse to take the word of a black man with whom he has worked for years? This little scenario mirrors in microcosm the splintering that was often characteristic of the Movement in debates over the extent to which whites should or should not be involved. By reducing the friction to the level of the sexual, playwright White satirizes even more these so-called leaders.

As Rev. Brown's helper, Johnson has been learning the tactics of leadership by observing him over the years. It is Johnson who controls access to Rev. Brown by setting up interviews and visits. He is therefore thoroughly aware of the public and media dynamic that surrounds Brown, and he knows the potential impact that a fake burning will have on Rev. Brown's ever increasing popularity. Although Johnson is initially skeptical about the burning scheme, he nonetheless acquiesces, and the implication is that a part of the acquiescence is inspired by the conversation about Cora.

Johnson's refusal to scream as Rev. Brown is burning indicates the dangerous consequences of factionalism in the civil rights movement, especially factionalism that is brought on by such a frivolous cause as a disagreement over a white woman. The progress of an entire people is thus reduced to this minuscule level of pettiness. On the other hand, the burning episode succeeds admirably well in making White's point about the will to power. The incident with Cora finally becomes a minor point on Johnson's way to emerging as the next leader. He proves as willing to sacrifice Rev. Brown as he has been to sacrifice Cora. His loyalties—as it becomes apparent that Rev. Brown's are—are only to himself. The combination of jealousy and anger that catapults him to power makes the civil rights movement look like a children's game out of a George Orwell novel.

The depth of Johnson's motives and his desire to become the one and only leader are evident at the end of the play. As the new head of the National Freedom Association, he completes an interview with a reporter and, upon the man's departure, looks into the same mirror that once so attracted Rev. Brown's attention. It is now his turn to address the mirror: "Mirror, mirror, on the wall, *noooooow* who's the most powerful black man of them all?"[15] Jealousy and petty squabbling have deprived the Movement of one charlatan leader only to replace him with his mirror image, so to speak.

White succeeds well in his criticism of leadership during the civil rights movement. By mocking the motives and presumed altruism of unscrupulous and superficial leaders, White suggests that they have no constituency other than themselves. They have no loyalties other than to their own self-serving motives. And there is no way they can be viewed as benefiting black communities. White's ridiculing of such men and their motives is one of the ugliest literary representations of African American ministers and the people who work for them.

Implicit in White's portrayal is the need for change in tactics and leadership during the civil rights movement. By mocking the idea of nonviolence with a self-inflicted burning that goes out of control, White implicitly suggests that all ideas of nonviolence should be burned up, tossed out, because they have not served the masses of blacks effectively or efficiently. By allowing a leader of the Movement to accidentally burn himself to death, White urges a reconsideration of what violence can accomplish. It can get rid of the outmoded methods—represented by Rev. Brown—of dealing with social issues. Just as Langston Hughes suggested in 1926 that the little magazine *Fire!!* would burn up some old ideas about how Negroes should exist in America, so White burns up one of the old Negroes who holds such ideas. His recognition of the split between more militant blacks and more conservative Negroes is a split that several young writers of the 1960s chose as subject matter for their works. The Negroes had to go, and what better way to get rid of them than to symbolically burn them up—that is, reject their outmoded ideas?

While White's demand for change is implicit in *The Leader*, Ed Bullins's is violently explicit in *The Gentleman Caller: A Parable in One Act*. An expressionistic work, *The Gentleman Caller* presents the symbolic house of America, ruled over by a white mistress and an invisible white Mr. Mann and in which a stereotypical black maid rules with the proverbial mammyish iron hand. All the characters are in their place—psychologically, socially, financially, racially—until a mysterious young black man appears; he is a stereotypically aspiring, upwardly mobile Negro who clearly wants a piece of the house of America.[16] His presence and the insistent ringing of a telephone throughout the short drama bring to a climax the undoing of traditional roles.

Symbolism carries the drama, as Bullins describes the back wall of the comfortably furnished living room as containing "*a gun rack with rifles and shotguns in it. Upon the wall are mounted and stuffed heads of a Blackman, an American Indian, a Vietnamese and a Chinese.*"[17] As Clinton F. Oliver and Stephanie Sills point out, these are the "trophies of rich white America," tangible signs that they control all black people.[18] The fact that the gentleman caller wants to become a part of this world by claiming the beard of the invisible Mr. Mann illustrates the wrong-headedness of some of those blacks who pursue upward mobility through education, those who are whitewashed by the gleam of the American dream. Such persons, Bullins asserts, are dispensable to the struggle for black civil rights. A necessary part of the change he calls for, therefore, is the elimination of such Negroes from the Struggle.

His instrument of elimination is a transformed domestic worker. The maid who has served faithfully in the Mann house, the house of America, is finally pushed to change when she sees the young man so shamelessly desiring entrance to what the white world has to offer, which means he is desiring his own subjugation and exploitation. In the role of mother turned militant, she eliminates not only the white threat to black progress, but the black threat as well. After a series of twisted emotional interactions in which the white mistress fires the maid, then begs her not to go, and after the mistress reminisces about suckling at the maid's breast, the maid announces that she is quitting. She cements her quitting by going offstage, shooting Mr. Mann with a shotgun, and dragging his dead body onto the stage.

As she re-enters the stage, she transforms the meaning of several stereotypical stage lines and roles associated with African Americans. "Now hare come de judge," she announces in a substantive transformation of a line used in a comic routine.[19] In the routine, the black person announced the coming of someone else; here, the maid informs the mistress and the gentleman caller (who has not said a word in the play but has listened to the mistress articulate her historical role and sexual frustrations to him) that she is the ultimate judge, the ultimate determiner of how race relations in America should be set right. She also invokes a Stepin Fetchit line—"Feets . . . do yo duty"—as she wrestles with dragging the dead Mr. Mann onto stage.[20] The feet doing their duty here are not taking the scary black man away from a haunted house or some other uncomfortable scene, they are taking the maid to freedom.

Mamie Lee King's conversion to violence here carried a special resonance, given that ever since Rosa Parks had initiated the Montgomery bus boycott, black domestics were perceived as the quintessential supporters of Martin Luther King Jr.'s brand of church-based, nonviolent direct action. Bullins suggests that if the state of racial affairs in America has deteriorated to the point that even a domestic worker can embrace violence, then there is something seriously wrong with King's philosophy. By locating his call for change through violence among the sort of women who were seen to be in the vanguard of King's nonviolent campaign, Bullins sharply undermines the preacher's credibility and casts doubt on the efficacy of his tactics. Instead of relying on King, Bullins suggests, these women need to rely on themselves.

The onstage scene with Mrs. Mann, the dead body of Mr. Mann, the silent gentleman caller, and the maid is one in which Mrs. Mann refuses to recognize what most of white America refused to recognize during the 1960s: that black people would no longer be content with their social and political circumstances. To admit that the maid has killed Mr. Mann would be to admit that the sun comes up in the west, so Mrs. Mann effects self-delusion even in the fact of the bloody evidence before her.

Madame: [to maid] . . . you him found dead . . . dead in the john?
Maid: Yas'sum.
Madame: . . . dead from a self-inflicted wound in the throat . . .

Maid: If you say so . . . ma'am.
Madame: . . . from a straight razor!
Maid: Yas'sum. From a straight razor.[21]

The maid's seeming acquiescence in Mrs. Mann's need for illusions is just that—seeming acquiescence, for her agenda includes shooting Mrs. Mann in the head with the shotgun, which she proceeds to do.

The suggestion that white America, in the form of Mr. and Mrs. Mann, could only be destroyed, gets reinforcement from Mrs. Mann's final speech in the play. She refuses to acknowledge the maid's role in Mr. Mann's death, and she stubbornly, deliberately clings to her ideas of the "proper" relationships between blacks and whites. The maid, she says, "was like the mountains . . . unchanging. Like time . . . limitless. Always faithful . . . always the source of inspiration . . . the very blood and marrow of the universe . . . ."[22] White America, Bullins asserts, can only be shocked out of its somnambulence through violence. And black people who adhere to the roles in which whites would like to have them remain must similarly be dispatched violently.

Mrs. Mann emphasizes an "unchanging" quality in the maid. But change is precisely what Bullins advocates—a change from preacherly tactics of nonviolence. When the gentleman caller evinces no desire to change (indeed, he still reaches for Mr. Mann's white beard), only one option remains: he, too, must be dispatched. The maid insists that he help her carry Mr. Mann's body offstage, and he does so, but he stuffs the beard in his pocket. The audience hears a final gunshot offstage and it becomes clear that the maid has also killed the gentleman caller. Allowing his execution offstage might have been a bow to persons who would have complained about violence against white people leading to violence against black people. Whatever the rationale, it was obvious to the maid that the gentleman caller, the Negro, was incapable of change, or he desired whatever change would be granted by the ruling whites. The maid brings about change in her own decisive way.

One of the fascinating things about the maid is her name: Mamie Lee King. Her connection to Martin Luther King Jr., combined with her strategies for achieving liberation for her people, showcase Bullins's harsh criticism of the civil rights movement as led by King. What King needed most, Bullins offers, was a transformation in belief in the violent possibilities of the Movement. Only by actively seeking to destroy white America would true change come about. As soon as the bodies are offstage, Mamie Lee King returns "*wearing an exotic gown of her own design. Her bandana has been taken off; her au naturel hair style complements her strong Black features,"* and she answers the telephone that has been ringing throughout the play in her new role as the "Queen Mother" of black liberation.[23] She speaks to a "father" and informs him that "it is time for Black people to come together."[24] Notice that Negroes—in the figure of the gentleman caller and Martin Luther King Jr.—are eliminated. The play ends with the Queen Mother calling for "DEATH TO THE ENEMIES OF THE BLACK PEOPLE!" and intoning "All praises is due to the Blackman."[25]

For Bullins, as for White, Negroes are expendable, so both playwrights get around the issue of blacks committing violence against other black people. As one scholar observes:

> The black revolution of the 1960s had no place for "gentleman" call-
> ers, who, because they identified themselves as gentlemen, would
> not sever connections with the white world. Anyone who, though
> black in skin color, did not recognize his spiritual blackness, could,
> like any white, be sacrificed in the interests of unity and nation-
> building; the black revolutionary, Mamie, kills the "Negro" hanger-
> on, whose attitudes are, in fact, barely a step removed from the "col-
> ored" attitudes of a couple of decades before.[26]

If killing Negroes (and the Negro in herself) is the price that Mamie Lee King and Ed Bullins must pay to ensure violence directed toward its proper targets, that is, toward white people, then so be it.

The blatant allusion to Martin Luther King Jr. and the transformation of the maid from mammy to militant serves further to illustrate Bullins's perception of King and the value of his leadership. To Bullins, King was just as shuffling as Mamie Lee King in her role as mammy. There is also the suggestion that Bullins identifies King in part with the gentleman caller; in this case, King is pictured sitting and begging for entrance into the white house of America. Both roles are expendable. In addition, the fact that Bullins applies King's namesake to a woman shows further his sense of King's neutralized ability to achieve anything significant. By femi-nizing King, and then making King's feminine namesake ultimately more militant than King could ever be, Bullins succeeds in a provocative name-calling that he could never have effected outside the safety of literary portrayal.

Contemporary with King, and comfortable in their criticism of his poli-tics, Joseph White and Ed Bullins execute thorough examinations of the effect of his Movement on African American society as well as American society. Once King died, literary criticism seemed to have diminished, as the poets rallied to the political site of his dead body. In the interval since the 1960s and early 1970s, few writers have considered the fact of King's death or his philosophy literary enough to keep in constant view. However, one writer to whom the subject matter has remained dear is Charles Johnson. His 1998 novel, *Dreamer,* which began as a short story "in the early 1980s," will surely revitalize discussions about King, his place in African American history, and his evolving place in African American literature.[27]

Johnson's project in *Dreamer* is basically sympathetic to King's memory as he follows King from 1966 through his death in 1968. By allowing the dramatic incidents surrounding Chicago and Memphis to guide his novel, Johnson focuses his narrative more in the direction of historical novel than fiction cut from whole cloth.[28] Still, he separates history and literature by not professing to provide a complete story of King. Yet, the very fact that the novel uses King as its subject matter could have made it almost impossible to draw the line between fact and creation. In order to draw that line sharply, Johnson creates a character who is the stranger/twin of King and allows dramatic tension to develop from contemplation of the possibilities that result from that double's standing in for King, accepting awards for him, and being available to make speeches for him.[29]

Dreamer is narrated in part by Matthew Bishop, an idealistic college student who is between financial stints in school in Chicago. He works as King's assistant during the Chicago campaign. Matthew and Amy, a student who will become Matthew's lover, are assigned to transform the look-alike into a passable King once King has met him and approved of having a double. Matthew's first person narration alternates with an omniscient voice that follows King, his interactions with his family, and his emotional responses to his campaigns between 1966 and 1968. Johnson creates dialogue between King and Ralph Abernathy during the Memphis campaign, and he relies upon news reports and historical records to provide the texturing for this portion of the narration. There is no ploy to change names to hide the innocent: King, Abernathy, Jessie Jackson, and others who shared the spotlight with King all retain their names.

The King double, a man named Chaym Smith, has a checkered and fascinating background. He has been a military man, a student of eastern philosophies, and a sometimes husband who may have killed and mutilated his wife, Juanita Lomax, in addition to strangling her three children. Chaym's name, Matthew informs us, could easily have derived from the biblical Cain, with all its connotations of brothers killing brothers. As a man of mystery and an independent thinker, Chaym does not make it clear what motivates him, when he will be able to absorb the King role or when something in him, including his use of heroin, will cause him to blow his cover.

Given Johnson's background in philosophy, his selection of Chaym as King's double is a natural choice. Johnson comments on this philosophical incorporation into the novel: "No one talks about Dr. King in terms other than his being an important civil rights leader. They don't talk about him in terms of his importance as a moral philosopher and as a trained philosopher . . . I always felt that Black American literature could be more philosophically vigorous."[30] Chaym has studied with eastern priests in addition to having considered becoming a minister. He has absorbed intensely all of his experiences and serves to allow Johnson to interject various philosophies, similar to the process through which he saturates his other texts. Selection of such a character enables Johnson to showcase Chaym as a kindred philosophical spirit to King who is therefore doubly able to sympathize with and effect the role of King.

Chaym's last name, Smith, highlights the invisibility attendant upon mystery men, but it also intensifies the possibility for identification with King. In addition to being a legitimate surname, Smith is also a universal common name that covers other identities of the persons who select it. Chaym Smith is a vacuum of sorts, then, into which he can pour traits of King or effect any other transformation he desires. During Chaym's interview with Matthew and Amy, Matthew observes that he "could have sworn Smith was playing her masterfully like a finely tuned lyre, one keyed to her (all of our) affection for King, fluidly shifting from one mask to another as the occasion demanded, as if maybe the self was a fiction—or, if not that, a multiplicity of often conflicting profiles."[31] A short while later, Matthew is "startled by Smith's talent, his shape-shifting ability to change styles as rapidly as others changed their garments."[32] Presumably, with his philosophical, ministerial, and metaphysical potential to understand King, combined with these shape-shifting components, Chaym can succeed whenever and wherever he is selected to stand in for or impersonate King.

What makes the choice of Chaym even more fascinating is that readers learn, almost in an aside, that Chaym is perhaps the last of the famed Allmuseri tribe of Africans to whom Johnson gives special powers in his early works.[33] In *Oxherding Tale*, for example, Reb the coffin maker, who is of the Allmuseri tribe, is the only man who escapes from Leviathan, an infamous plantation, and whom the Soulcatcher (the ultimate manhunter) cannot retrieve. In *Middle Passage*, slavers make the mistake of capturing the Allmuseri and their god on a trip to Africa; their end can only be misfortune. The Allmuseri are capable of incredible powers of manipulation of mind and matter, both theirs and their adversaries. By assigning Chaym to that group, Johnson also assigns King to the realm of the mystical and the magical.

Consider the implications of this assignment for the novel as well as for King's reputation and work. In the role of King, Chaym is mistakenly shot as Matthew and Amy are driving him from a church. Although the gunman empties the gun into the backseat where Chaym is sitting, miraculously only one bullet enters his body. Matthew recounts:

> From inside his coat the old man withdrew a nickel-plated, Colt semiautomatic, pointing the ancient pistol straight-armed at Smith, who instinctively threw up his left hand and tried to turn away. The old man pulled the trigger over and over, pumping five rounds into the backseat. The muzzle flash blinded me; then I saw Smith dancing like a marionette on the cushion as the old man emptied his gun, firing, spiderwebbing the windows, frosting them with bullets that ricocheted crazily around the car like bees.[34]

Chaym suffers a difficult wound, but he does recover. At a glance, there is no way that Chaym should have survived the incident, except that he is of the Allmuseri. Yet he does, and he recovers—only to have two government types who have been watching his transformation into King claim that they need him to do important work for the country; that work would presumably involve compromising King to the point that he would commit suicide. Although Chaym is blackmailed (he does not want to have the issue of how Juanita Lomax and her sons died brought up again) into *seeming* to go along with the scheme, he simply disappears from the novel when he disappears with the two government types (Reb effects a similar disappearance in *Oxherding Tale*). In the few months between his disappearance and King's death, readers are unaware of any activity in which he is involved.

It might be argued that Chaym, drawing upon the power of the Allmuseri, simply overpowers his ostensible psychological enslavers and goes about his business. To where, or why, there is no certainty. What is certain is that by assigning Chaym these characteristics and aligning him with King, Johnson also consigns King's work to the realm of the mystical and the magical. Was King merely, as the title suggests, a dreamer? By highlighting two campaigns in his civil rights leadership during which King made gross miscalculations about strategies—when he underestimated the viciousness of racism in Chicago, and when he could not prevent militants from taking over the march in Memphis—Johnson shows him to fall far short of his reach. That falling short simultaneously humanizes King even as it makes him more than human: in fact, the ultimate dreamer. At one point, as King is shuttling between Memphis and Atlanta, the omniscient narrator comments about King: *"for the first time he felt like a dreamer gently roused from sleep and forgetfulness."*[35]

Nonetheless, Johnson, a King convert and true believer, retains a certain sympathy for and engagement with King and his legacy. His, after all, is the most sustained literary work to date to focus on King, his philosophy of nonviolence, and the Movement he led. There is clearly a love for King that comes through in Johnson's portrayal of his family relationships, in his reflective moments, and at the pausing times during which his very flawed humanity is obvious. Yet to pursue King this long after his death and this close to the actual incidents of his life is to make Johnson himself a dreamer, one who tries to re-write history in spite of the fictional mode in which it is created, one who desires to change the ending of the tale, and one whose urge to resurrect King has led him to spend this many pages and words with him. And these pages and words are mere condensations of the research, energy, and creative imagination that went into the production of the novel.

Why, ultimately, in the 1990s, would an American Book Award-winning novelist turn his attention to writing about a fallen African American martyr? Perhaps the answer is in the question. Martyrdom is its own special attraction. There is obviously nothing new that Johnson can add to the story of King's death, little that he can say to ease the pain of loss that Nikki Giovanni felt so keenly, absolutely nothing he can do to change history. However, for more than two hundred pages of *Dreamer*, he succeeds in engaging his readers so thoroughly that they perhaps join him in wishing that the story could have a different ending, or at least in believing that Martin Luther King Jr. may have worked magic on all those who sought to harm him by rejoining the Allmuseri tribe of which he himself, along with Chaym Smith, were the last two descendants.

Notes

1. Nikki Giovanni, *Black Feeling/ Black Talk/ Black Judgement* (New York: William Morrow, 1970), 54.

2. Ibid.

3. Ibid.

4. Ibid., 55.

5. Ibid., 50.

6. Ibid., 56. Giovanni also refers directly to King's death in "A Litany for Peppe," a poem addressed to her nephew: "They had a rebellion in Washington this year/ because white people killed Martin Luther King/ Even the cherry blossoms wouldn't appear." She asserts throughout that only "Black Power" can achieve "a sweet Black Peace," and she ends the poem by continuing to urge for retaliation: "Blessed is he who kills/ For he shall control his own death." Ibid., 57.

7. Donald L. Graham, "April 5th," in Stephen Henderson, *Understanding the New Black Poetry: Black Speech and Black Music as Poetic References* (New York: William Morrow, 1973), 320.

8. Ibid.

9. Don L. Lee, "Assassination," in Lee, *Don't Cry, Scream* (Chicago: Broadside Press, 1969), 32.

10. Giovanni perhaps penned most poems on King, but several other poets in addition to those treated here also wrote poems about King's death. These include Hart Leroi Bibb, "Six Sunday," in *The New Black Poetry*, ed. Clarence Major (New York: International, 1969), 28; Edwin Brooks, "Tulips from Their Blood," in *The New Black Poetry*, ed. Major, 30–31; Margaret Danner, "Passive Resistance," in Henderson, *Understanding the New Black Poetry*, 231; Clarence Franklin, "Two Dreams (for mlk's one)," in *Black Fire: An Anthology of Afro-American Writing*, ed. LeRoi Jones and Larry Neal (New York: William Morrow, 1968), 364; Michael Goode "April 4 1968," in *Soulscript*, ed. June Jordan (Garden City, N.Y.: Doubleday/ Zenith, 1970), 6; Robert Hayden, "Words in the Mourning Time," in *Collected Poems*, ed. Frederick Glaysher (New York: Liveright, 1985), 90–100; June Jordan, "In Memoriam: Rev. Martin Luther King, Jr.," in *Soulscript*, ed. Jordan, 115; Audre Lorde "Rites of Passage To MLK Jr.," in Lorde, *Undersong: Chosen Poems Old and New* (New York: Norton, 1992), 44; Dudley Randall "Ballad of Birmingham," in Henderson, *Understanding the New Black Poetry*, 233–34; and Quincy Troupe, "A Day in the Life of a Poet," in *New Black Voices*, ed. Abraham Chapman (New York: Mentor, 1972), 347–48. In his poem, Troupe asserts that he "wrote three poems to the peace/full lamb/ from Atlanta," thus joining Giovanni in incorporating the tragedy of King's death into multiple poems.

11. Joseph White, "The Leader," in *Black Fire*, ed. Jones and Neal, 605.

12. Ibid., 607.

13. Ibid., 608.

14. Ibid., 606–7.

15. Ibid., 630.

16. For a discussion of the various roles drawn in the play and their historical interactive dynamics, see Trudier Harris, *From Mammies to Militants: Domestics in Black American Literature* (Philadelphia: Temple University Press, 1982), 168–79.

17. Ed Bullins, "The Gentleman Caller: A Parable in One Act," in *Contemporary Black Drama: From A Raisin in the Sun to No Place to Be Somebody*, ed. Clinton F. Oliver and Stephanie Sills (New York: Charles Scribner's Sons, 1971), 371.

18. Ibid., 368.

19. Ibid., 379.

20. Ibid.

21. Ibid.

22. Ibid., 380.

23. Ibid.

24. Ibid.

25. Ibid.

26. Harris, *From Mammies to Militants*, 177.

27. Victoria Valentine, "A Philosopher's Novel View of King," *Emerge: Black America's Newsmagazine*, June 1998, 67.

28. Working in "the land of Lincoln" has its ironic implications here just as Joseph White's Rev. Abraham Lincoln Brown has ironic implications in "The Leader." See Charles Johnson, *Dreamer* (New York: Scribner, 1998), 63.

29. Many fiction writers have made references to Martin Luther King Jr. or incorporated his philosophy into their works. While I have limited my discussion here to Johnson's *Dreamer*, other works include James Baldwin's title story in *Going to Meet the Man* (New York: Dial, 1965); Linda Beatrice Brown, *Crossing Over Jordan* (New York: Ballantine, 1995); Leon Forrest, *There Is a Tree More Ancient than Eden* (New York: Random House, 1973); Ernest J. Gaines, *The Autobiography of Miss Jane Pittman* (New York: Dial, 1971); Gaines, *In My Father's House* (New York: Knopf, 1978); Lance Jeffers, *Witherspoon* (Atlanta, Ga.: G. A. Flippin Press, 1983); John Oliver Killens, *'Sippi* (New York: Trident, 1967); C. Eric Lincoln, *The Avenue, Clayton City* (New York: Morrow, 1988); John McCluskey, *Look What They Done to My Song* (New York: Random House, 1974); and Alice Walker, *Meridian* (New York: Harcourt Brace Jovanovich, 1976).

30. Valentine, "A Philosopher's Novel View of King," 67.

31. Johnson, *Dreamer*, 56.

32. Ibid., 58. This motif of mask-wearing and the inability to know the true self surfaces again and again in the text. Chaym asserts at one point that "everybody's playing a role anyway, trying to act like what they're supposed to be, wearing at least one mask, probably more, and there's nothing underneath" (ibid., 86). Matthew recounts King wondering about his public self, if it is a "mask" (ibid., 137), and he is unable to determine if he is listening to Chaym or King during one speech (ibid., 140). When Chaym takes his final leave, Matthew comments that it is "as if a djinn had passed into our lives and just as miraculously disappeared" (ibid., 214).

33. Ibid., 205.

34. Ibid., 146.

35. Ibid., 82.

Contributors

Julian Bond teaches in the Department of History at the University of Virginia and is Distinguished Professor in Residence at the American University. He was a founder of the Atlanta student antisegregation movement in 1960 and of the Student Nonviolent Coordinating Committee that same year. He served for twenty years in the Georgia General Assembly and is presently the chairman of the board of the National Association for the Advancement of Colored People.

David Chappell teaches at the University of Arkansas at Fayetteville. He is the author of *Inside Agitators: White Southerners in the Civil Rights Movement* (1994) and has published articles and reviews in the *Journal of American Studies, World Policy Journal, Georgia Historical Quarterly, In These Times, Newsday,* and the *Raleigh News and Observer.* He is currently doing research on segregationist propaganda.

Scot A. French is associate director of the Carter G. Woodson Institute for Afro-American and African Studies at the University of Virginia. He is the coauthor, with Edward L. Ayers, of "The Strange Career of Thomas Jefferson: Race and Slavery in American Memory, 1943–1993," in *Jeffersonian Legacies,* ed. Peter S. Onuf (1993). His *Remembering Nat Turner: The Rebellious Slave in American Thought* will be published in 2002.

Allison Graham is professor of communication studies at the University of Memphis. She is the author of *Lindsay Anderson* (1981) and numerous other works on American film and popular culture, and the coproducer of *At The River I Stand* (1993), an award-winning documentary on the Memphis Sanitation Workers' strike and the last crusade of Martin Luther King Jr. She has recently completed *Framing the South: Hollywood, Television, and Race During the Civil Rights Struggle* (2001).

Trudier Harris is J. Carlyle Sitterson Professor of English at the University of North Carolina at Chapel Hill. Her books include *From Mammies to Militants: Domestics in Black American Literature* (1982); *Exorcising Blackness: Historical and Literary Lynching and Burning Rituals* (1984);

Black Women in the Fiction of James Baldwin (1985); *Fiction and Folklore: The Novels of Toni Morrison* (1991); and *The Power of the Porch: The Storyteller's Craft in Zora Neale Hurston, Gloria Naylor, and Randall Kenan* (1996). She coedited *The Oxford Companion to African American Literature* (1997); *Call and Response: The Riverside Anthology of the African American Literary Tradition* (1998); and *The Literature of the American South: A Norton Anthology* (1998). Her latest book is titled *Saints, Sinners, Saviors: Strong Black Women in African American Literature.*

Sharon Monteith is senior lecturer in the School of American and Canadian Studies at the University of Nottingham. With Peter Ling, she coedited *Gender in the Civil Rights Movement* (1999), and her latest work is *Advancing Sisterhood? Interracial Friendships in Contemporary Southern Fiction* (2000). She is currently working on a book exploring film and fiction and the civil rights movement.

Eithne Quinn is lecturer in American studies at the University of Central Lancashire. She is currently preparing a book on gangsta rap music and has had related articles published in *Borderlines: Studies in American Culture* and *The Journal of American Studies,* as well as chapters in several edited collections.

Guido van Rijn is a teacher of English at Kennemer Lyceum in Overveen, the Netherlands. In 1970, he cofounded the Netherlands Blues and Boogie Organization, whose work culminated in the annual Utrecht Blues Estafette. He has published many articles in specialist magazines like *Blues Unlimited* and *Blues and Rhythm,* and has produced seventeen LPs and CDs for his own Agram label. His Ph.D. dissertation from Leiden University was revised as the award-winning *Roosevelt's Blues: African-American Blues and Gospel Songs on FDR* (1997). He is at present working on a sequel about blues and gospel songs dealing with presidents Truman and Eisenhower.

Peter Townsend teaches American literature, film, and creative writing in the Department of English, University of Huddersfield. He has published work on discourse analysis, Theodore Adorno, and jazz, and is the author of *Jazz in American Culture* (2000). He addressed the Duke Ellington centenary conference, "Ellington 99," in Washington, D.C., and is continuing research on Ellington and other aspects of the history and cultural setting of jazz.

William L. Van Deburg is professor of Afro-American studies at the University of Wisconsin-Madison. He has contributed to a number of anthologies and reference works, and is the author of *The Slave Drivers: Black Agricultural Labor Supervisors in the Antebellum South* (1979); *Slavery and Race in American Culture* (1984); *New Day in Babylon: The Black Power Movement and American Popular Culture, 1965–1975* (1992); *Black Camelot: African-American Culture Heroes in Their Times, 1960–1980* (1997); and *Modern Black Nationalism: From Marcus Garvey to Louis Farrakhan* (1997).

Jenny Walker is a former Ph.D. student at the University of Newcastle upon Tyne, where she researched black violence and nonviolence in the civil rights and black power eras. She is the coauthor (with Brian Ward) of "'Bringing the Races Closer?' Black-Oriented Radio and the Southern Civil Rights Movement," in *Dixie Debates: Perspectives on Southern Culture,* ed. Richard King and Helen Taylor (1995), and author of "The 'Gun-Toting' Gloria Richardson? Black Violence in Cambridge, Maryland," in *Gender in the Civil Rights Movement,* ed. Peter Ling and Sharon Monteith (1999).

Stephen Walsh is a former graduate student at the University of Newcastle upon Tyne, where in 1997 he completed a Ph.D. on postwar black-oriented radio and the civil rights movement. He is currently collaborating with Brian Ward on a book-length study of radio and the African American freedom struggle.

Brian Ward is associate professor of American history at the University of Florida. During the 1990s he taught at the University of Newcastle upon Tyne, where he served as director of the 1993 and 1998 Martin Luther King Jr. Conference on Civil Rights and Race Relations. His publications include *The Making of Martin Luther King and the Civil Rights Movement* (co-edited with Tony Badger, 1996) and the award-winning *Just My Soul Responding: Rhythm and Blues, Black Consciousness and Race Relations* (1998).

p. 296 is blank

Index